C000152518

Motherhood

from 1920 to the present day

Living Memory

Living Memory is a series of oral history books giving voice to experiences from the recent past. Other titles include:

Footsteps and Witnesses: Lesbian and Gay Lifestories
Edited by Bob Cant

The People's Past
Edited by Edward Cowan

Kings, Queens and People's Palaces
Vivien Devlin

The Sang's the Thing
Sheila Douglas

The Springburn Experience
G. Hutchison and M. O'Neill

Odyssey: Voices from Scotland's Recent Past
Edited by Billy Kay

Voices from the Spanish Civil War
Ian MacDougall

Voices from the Hunger Marches (Vols 1 and 2)
Ian MacDougall

Miners 1984–1994
Edited by Joe Owens

Motherhood

from 1920 to the present day

Edited by
Vivien Devlin

Polygon
Edinburgh

© Polygon 1995

Reprinted 1997
Published by Polygon
22 George Square
Edinburgh

Set in Meridien by WestKey Ltd, Falmouth, Cornwall
Printed and bound in Great Britain

A CIP record is available

ISBN 0 7486 6163 8

The Publisher acknowledges subsidy from

THE SCOTTISH ARTS COUNCIL

towards the publication of this volume.

CONTENTS

Acknowledgments vii

PREFACE
The Experience of Motherhood 1

The Literature of Motherhood 12
Lynn Knight

CHAPTER 1
Family Histories: Childhood Expectations and Aspirations 14

CHAPTER 2
Relationships, Marriage and Family Planning 38

CHAPTER 3
Pregnancy 65

CHAPTER 4
Labour and Childbirth 91

CHAPTER 5
Trauma and Tragedy 151

CHAPTER 6
Nourishing and Nurturing 179

CHAPTER 7
Commitment to Motherhood 228

CHAPTER 8
Social change and family life in the modern state 268

CHAPTER 9
Having it all: Fighting for Equality 315

CHAPTER 10
Women's Destiny; The Changing Experience of Motherhood 341

Contributor List 382

Permissions 393

'And, they tell us, we at home
Live free from danger, they go out to battle fools!
I'd rather stand three times in the front line than bear
One child.'

Medea, Euripides: [431 BC]

'Throughout pregnancy and nursing, women are urged to relax, to mime the serenity of madonnas. No-one mentions the psychic crisis of bearing a first child, of a heightened sensibility which can be exhilarating, bewildering and exhausting. To have borne and reared a child is to have done that thing which patriarchy joins with physiology to render into the definition of femaleness. But also, it can mean the experiencing of one's own body and emotions in a powerful way.'

Of Woman Born, Adrienne Rich: [1977]

'We married when I was twenty-seven and we had our first child the following year. I considered a family as the natural and desirable result of married life.'

Patricia Rogers [born 1909]

'At eighteen and single, having a baby was what I wanted. I was idealistic and very much into being a woman and I saw it as a very feminine thing I wanted to experience.'

Rachel Lockey [born 1967]

'I would go to the clinic to collect a supply of free orange juice and cod liver oil. Our children had a spoonful of cod liver oil after dinner every day. It probably makes some mothers today curl up with disgust, but I do think it gave them a very good start. Everyone was doing it.'

Mary McKerrow [born 1915]

'I started them on solids with cereals, rice, carrots – mainly home cooked food. I then blended our meals for them, so that there was an incongruous smell of garlic from the mouths of young babies. They both like roast dinners and fruit, but the elder child also likes novelties – dinosaur-shaped food and I indulge him.'

Diane Connolly [born 1961]

ACKNOWLEDGEMENTS

In the writing of any book, an author is more often than not dependent on help from their friends and all sorts of people and organisations. I would first of all like to thank Lynn Knight, the former director of Virago Modern Classics, for her inspirational and professional advice in the selection of extracts from novels, poetry, biography and journalism written by women over the past seventy years; her specialist knowledge of women's fiction was invaluable. I thank her too for contributing her fascinating introduction, 'The Literature of Motherhood'. I am also indebted to Maeve Haran for her time and interest.

I have been fortunate in having the services of four extremely reliable assistants who have shared the research involved in compiling an oral history. I would very much like to thank Kirsteen Cameron, Johanna Hall, Morag Malloy, and Isobel Rae for their meticulous work in researching fictional and factual extracts, and recording interviews with mothers and other contributors all over the country. I appreciate their dedicated interest in the project; it has been such a pleasure to collaborate with them.

I am also grateful to Sister Norma Aikman of the Simpson Memorial Maternity Hospital, Hamish Leal of Lothian Health Board, Barbara Littlewood of Glasgow University, Dr Bernard Lunan of Glasgow Royal Infirmary, and Kathy McGlew of the National Childbirth Trust, for information and advice. For the loan of out-of-print childcare books I would like to thank Joyce McPherson, Sue Rook and Carol Walton. I am grateful to my family and friends – Geoffrey Baskerville, Anna Bennett, Barbara Bryan, Joan Brydon, Jan Fairley, Corinne Harris, Peter Whitebrook and June Williams, amongst many others, for their inspiring support and willingness to indulge in long conversations on women, work and motherhood.

I would like to take this opportunity to thank with great affection, Michael Ridings, Lecturer in English at Edinburgh University, for his enthusiasm and encouragement throughout my university course, which stimulated and nurtured my serious interest in drama, world literature and, especially, women writers.

Finally, I thank Marion Sinclair, Editorial Director of Polygon, who has always expressed great commitment to this project from my first proposal. I am extremely grateful for her professional guidance, patience and understanding – especially in giving me a few extra months of writing time – which enabled me to complete this book.

Cow & Gate have been identified with mothers and babies since 1904. In that year, Dr. Killick Millard, the Medical Officer of Health for Leicester, asked the company to produce a large quantity of powdered milk to supplement the diets of infants in the poorer areas of the country.

The experiences recorded in this book cover the period from 1920. By coincidence, in that year Cow & Gate published a book entitled "Motherhood", which was widely used and recommended by doctors and midwives as a guide to pregnancy and infant care. It was updated and reprinted for over thirty years.

Today, the Cow & Gate Babyfeeding Information Helpline answers over 35,000 queries each year from parents on infant feeding, and sends out, on request, a wide range of leaflets and booklets. The company also receives many spontaneous letters and photographs from generations of Cow & Gate babies now with families of their own.

Cow & Gate, White Horse Business Park, Trowbridge, Wilts. BA14 0XQ.

22 October 1997

PREFACE

The Experience of Motherhood

The American writer Erica Jong has always been a feisty, exuberant commentator on women's lives, from her outrageously sexy novel, *Fear of Flying* twenty years ago, to her recent fragment of autobiography, *Fear of Fifty*. Interspersed throughout her memoirs are reflections on feminism, love affairs and the powerful ties of motherhood. She describes her first experience of pregnancy and childbirth at the age of thirty-eight, in her essay 'Baby, Baby, Baby' which begins with this personal and resolute observation:

'Motherhood is supposed to be a part of Nature: timeless, immutable, a kind of female Rock of Ages. In truth, nothing is more mutable than motherhood – ringed round with its conventions and pretensions of the society in which it appears. Everything about motherhood changes with our ideologies: breast feeding and swaddling, mother-infant bonding or separation, anaesthesia or natural birth, giving birth standing, sitting or lying down, alone or with kin, midwife or obstetrician. Even the feelings the mother supposes she is supposed to have can be changed.'

After having corresponded, conversed, debated and discussed the subject with a couple of hundred of women during the course of compiling this book, I feel I can challenge, to a certain extent, Erica Jong's statement that 'nothing is more mutable than motherhood'. I consider that she is basing her views on a very limited perspective. My aim in writing this book was to observe motherhood – what the state of being a mother means – in Britain over the past seventy years, as a broad social and historical overview.

I have talked at length to mothers, from the age of fifteen to ninety-three, about their desires and dreams as young girls, why and when they planned to have a child, their concerns and qualms during pregnancy and childbirth, and their views and beliefs on feeding, nurturing and childcare. Moreover I concentrated on assessing the level of commitment to mothering and family life in order to compare and contrast how women have approached the role of motherhood across the generations.

I would surmise that, while medical developments in childbirth and child care routines have been made over time, it is not 'motherhood' itself as a social and cultural role which has changed, but rather the status of women and their place in contemporary society. Women, and women as mothers, now seek to improve their position in terms of education, marriage and employment, which in turn has offered the possibility of financial independence, equality and freedom of choice.

Until very recently, marriage and having a family were seen as traditional duties and an inescapable destiny; the motherhood mandate defined the stereotypical female role and a woman's identity in society. For all women, whether or not they do eventually have children of their own, the expectation of becoming a mother has often been the central focus of their socialisation process and upbringing. Little girls are given, and enjoy playing with, dolls and toy teasets; they are encouraged to help around the house and have usually been guided away from academic achievement at school, towards an adult life as housewives and mothers.

As the writer Eva Figes recalls in her memoir, *Coming to Terms*, 'My prime destiny was to look after a husband and children, and knowing how to cook and wash up was far more important than anything I might learn at school.'

During the 1920s and 1930s, women made up only twenty-nine per cent of the workforce and only ten per cent of married women worked outside the home. During the Second World War women were needed in the labour market, as teachers, shipyard welders, drivers and factory workers, but in 1945 the housewife was expected to down tools and return to her home, husband and children.

By the 1950s and 1960s, employers welcomed a new source of cheap, flexible labour with a growing number of women now keen to take on part-time work. Yet the notion that a working mother was a neglectful mother prevailed. Rising juvenile delinquency was blamed on mothers leaving their 'latchkey' children to roam wild after school. It was seen as far more respectable and natural for mothers to stay at home.

Since the late 1960s, the madonna image of woman as mother, which was reinforced by various biological and cultural ideologies, has been the subject of critical debate by many feminist writers. Women began to re-evaluate their 'natural' role and come to terms with their reproductive capabilities which, with the development of the contraceptive pill, they were now able to control. They began to decide when to start a family and indeed question whether to have children or not.

The feminist debate centred on whether having children affected their identity and situation as independent women, and to what extent the social institution of motherhood restricted women's potential both in the workplace and in terms of personal fulfillment. Women now realised that they wanted the same rights and choices as men in employment, in relationships, marriage and family life. The American poet and writer, Adrienne Rich recognises how the patriarchal society is an ideal system for men:

'Power is both a primal word and a primal relationship under patriarchy. Through control of the mother, the man assures himself of possession of his children; it would seem therefore that from very ancient times, the identity, the very personality of the man depends on power over others, beginning with a woman and her children.'

The power struggles for equality of the 1960s and 1970s resulted in the Sex Discrimination Act and equal pay legislation, and within the last ten to fifteen years there have been some advances in terms of equal opportunities in virtually every job or profession. A recent survey showed that over 70 per cent of all women with very young children expect to continue working; the working mother is becoming an accepted fact of life, where only one in five British men and women believe that a woman's place is in the home. It seems that a quiet social revolution has taken place.

There is another aspect to this social revolution. A growing number of women today are beginning to reject the basic view of gender which assumes feminine and masculine identities are biologically determined. While the majority of women still have an innate desire to bear children, many are delaying the decision to start a family until their mid to late thirties. The average age of a woman having her first baby today is 29 and rising. Single women are also choosing to have babies, a scenario which has evoked very serious and complex political and social concerns, ranging from the plight of the teenage mother in need of housing and income benefits, to the decline of the nuclear family. The increases in the number of single mothers, and the cohabitation and divorce rates, also clearly illustrate how women have changed their attitude towards patriarchal dependence and the expectation that a mother has full-time responsibility for child care. In her inspiring critique, *Sex and Destiny*, Germaine Greer has a cogent view on the role of a mother:

'The management of pregnancy, childbed and childraising was the principal expression of the familial and societal network of women, itself one of the essential cohesive elements in any society and a necessary leaven to the competitive hierarchies of men. It is largely as an unconscious reaction to this diminution of women's role that women are now exerting such pressure to be allowed into the competitive male hierarchy.

The closer women draw in social and economic status to the male level, the more disruptive childbirth becomes. The acknowledgement of her pregnancy means that she must step down from all that and enter the psychological equivalent of the birth hut; a mother is no longer self-sufficient but at the mercy of the child's indomitable love and egotism. From henceforth her attention will be divided.'

Mothers today, especially if they have enjoyed a stimulating, fulfilling job for several years before deciding to have a baby, often feel exhausted, isolated at home and socially ostracised. If they have to give up full-time work, they are likely to suffer a crushing loss of status as they begin to come to terms with the realities of daily child care, domestic chores and family life. As Greer observes, 'the best mother in the world cannot continue for long on a diet of dreary routine chores and insatiable infant demand; she must have stimulation and communication from supportive peers as well as rest.' And she sounds a warning note: 'In our immediate past mothering was negatively reinforced by the severe limitations on women's options; women who plan their babies and therefore believe sincerely that they wanted them, find themselves driven to desperation. They did not know that motherhood was like this; how could they have known? If mothering is not positively reinforced, women will cease to do it.'

Penelope Leach, the child care expert is also critical of the way society today has become insensitive to the needs of mothers and children. Bringing up a family, she argues, is at least as creative and professional as any high-status job. Yet in the current economic era a dual income family is almost essential and women are therefore encouraged to work.

'Children are our future, and we *can* afford the resources for people who wish to give two or three years to each child out of a forty year working life.'

I see this as very much a late twentieth-century predicament. From my researches, the vast majority of women bringing up their children between the wars and well into the 1950s and 1960s accepted their role as wife and mother intuitively, and dedicated their lives to their husbands and families, with pride and contentment.

One mother who had her children in the 1940s, believes 'You can't really expect to have everything in this life. I still consider that a mother should be at home. Not for anything would I have turned over the care of my young children to someone else and have deprived myself of the daily shout, "Mummy!" when they came tearing in from school'. One woman recalls the pleasure of daily chores: 'What is nicer than a nice line of clean nappies'; another believes their commitment to family life was because 'we had lived through a war; we valued our husbands and family life because we had been separated for so long.' Many of the women I spoke to suffered financial hardship: 'My husband's wage of £9 a week to feed nine people was far from sufficient. As a family we would go berry picking so that we could afford new school uniforms. It was a continual struggle but we have been married for forty-five years and have thirteen grandchildren.'

And this mother's remark sums up, I think, the common view of the older generation: 'I never went back to work after I married and devoted myself to my family. I had a very strict routine with an afternoon walk every day. I was always there for my children.'

So who are the women in this book and how did I find and select them?

Having planned to compile an oral history of motherhood – that is, the personal testimonies, experience and stories of mothers – I began by particularly seeking out women who are now in their eighties and nineties who would have had their babies between the wars. The Daily Telegraph published a 'Call to Mothers', a short note requesting women, especially inter-war mothers, to contact me.

Within the next few days, I must have received fifty or more letters and cards, the majority from older women. I was astounded at the immediate and eager response, from Somerset to the north of Scotland. From Argyll I received a three page essay on the subject: 'I married in

1924 and had three children within five years. I hope my account of child rearing is of use to you. Good luck with your project. It is certainly time some comparisons were made about the changes in family life over the past seventy years.'

From Sheffield, one lady wrote: 'I am eighty-seven and have three daughters, born in 1938, 1942, and 1948. I have ten grandchildren. I shall be pleased to give you any assistance I can.' And from Sussex: 'I saw the little note in the *Telegraph*. I was born in 1915, the second in a family of six children. I married in 1939, and had eight children. . . . I would very much like to be involved in your oral history.'

Somewhat encouraged by this early crop of interested contributors, I then advertised in numerous newspapers and women's magazines, including *The Guardian, The Scotsman*, local papers, *Nursery World, The Midwives Chronicle*, as well as community centres and family planning clinics. The letters and cards continued to pour in, this time from women of all ages, social classes and regions of the United Kingdom, from Cumbria to the Channel Islands and beyond: 'I am a young[ish] mother living in France since 1992, but receive the *Aberdeen Press and Journal* by post once a week to keep in touch . . .'. Several women wrote to say that they and their mother or daughter would both like to contribute so that I could compare mothers' lives within one family. 'I happened to see your letter in the *Dundee Courier* and was intrigued with the idea of your history. I am a mother and a grandmother to twelve grandchildren. If you want a younger mum who tries everything and is sometimes quite scatterbrained, my eldest daughter would I'm sure enjoy joining in.' And from Whitley Bay: 'I am fifty-eight, but my own mother is eighty-nine with all her faculties and a wealth of memories . . .'

The Guardian prompted many younger women to contact me. 'I am a twenty-six year old mother with one daughter, Bella. I was a single teenage mother and remain a single parent today very much through choice.'

There were also several women who were keen to relate their personal stories of sadness and tragedy. A letter from Wales: 'My youngest daughter was brain damaged at birth.' One from Edinburgh: 'I have three children. My eldest child, Julia, is five and is profoundly handicapped by cerebral palsy.' On a postcard from London, a woman told me of her extremely traumatic labour of fifty-five hours: 'I've been very ill for the past nine months.'

I would especially like to express my gratitude to a courageous woman from Aberdeenshire who wrote to tell me of the birth of her baby last year. 'I am writing to you only five weeks after the death of my first and very much wanted baby. My waters broke prematurely when I was twenty-six weeks pregnant and my son Martin lived for just one hour. His wee lungs could not sustain his life. I was a mummy for such a short time . . . but for me to help with your book will be a small memorial to Martin and the many babies like him each year who die soon after being born.'

I also received many letters from midwives of all ages, who were eager to describe their experiences of hospital and home births from the 1930s to the present day. I also was put in touch with a General Practitioner, now in her eighties, who delivered babies at home in rural East Anglia during the Second World War with no medical backup within fifty miles. And one retired midwife kindly lent me not only her own, but her mother's case study diaries which she had kept when she was training as a midwife in Glasgow in 1902.

My oral history was beginning to take shape. I was delighted and inspired by the rich diversity of women who had written to me, all so willing to be interviewed, including the mother of six children whose postscript was 'By the way what *is* a written oral history – and I wonder if I might be able to contribute usefully?'

I was therefore feeling rather more confident that I had a sufficiently broad body of women as my primary sources for a comparative social history. I could now set about contacting these women to arrange to interview them either face to face or by questionnaire. From the two hundred plus letters I had received, I selected around one hundred and fifty women as my representative sample of mothers who would contribute their views on the changing experience of motherhood and family life over the past three or four generations. I compiled a detailed eight page questionnaire and posted copies out with a sudden sense of apprehension. Suppose the initial spark of interest in my book had fizzled out and that only a handful of women would find the time or inclination to complete it? My fears were groundless. Within a month to six weeks, back came around eighty-five per cent of the forms, neatly filled in by hand or in many cases, beautifully typed. An additional five or ten pages were often attached as I had asked women to elaborate as much as possible with anecdotes and personal views on every aspect of being a mother.

Each generation has its own child care fads and fashions, from Truby

Motherhood

King's pre-war strict routine of four-hourly feeds to the baby-led demand feeding of today. The approach is now very much more relaxed compared to the days when mothers were guided by a universal code of conduct, recalls Carol Walton, midwife and mother:

'Since I trained as a nurse in 1962, what I notice in particular is how the rigid regimes for bathtime and bedtime have changed. There were rules for everything. Babies went outside in the pram every day, unless snowing or foggy. They always wore bonnets in winter and sunhats in summer. Bedtime was six o'clock. Bathing babies followed a strict pattern and we were taught to do everything with the baby on our lap, not in the cot or on a changing mat on the floor. As most mothers stayed at home, fathers took very little responsibility, or even interest, in baby care. Baby clothes have changed enormously. Nighties were worn by boys and girls for the first few weeks and most mothers knitted baby jackets, bootees and mittens. Nappies were made of cotton towelling and washed daily.

'My mother always said bringing up babies was common sense. She felt it was quite unnecessary to read Dr Spock. She now says, "I told you so", as he has reversed some of his opinions.'

I needn't have worried about shortage of material or indeed lack of candour. Many women were happy to confide every detail of their relationships and marriage. 'I married in 1941 knowing very little about sexual matters or birth control. I had never seen an undressed man.' They revealed their innermost feelings of the pain or euphoria of childbirth, their sense of joy and of failure as mothers. I have encountered the most remarkable, stimulating, resolute and perceptive women. Every mother's story is personal and unique, from the war-time mothers coping alone, with food rationing and no electricity, to mothers with sick and handicapped children. One woman expressed her feelings over many years, while suffering great emotional distress from post-natal depression; and there are the stories of unhappy marriages, the sadness and strain of divorce and single parenthood. At times I felt like an agony aunt, as they shared their most intimate thoughts and memories, woman talking to woman. It was as if they had been waiting for this opportunity to write their memoirs and to confide hidden emotions with an openness and honesty that I had not anticipated.

The Canadian poet and novelist, Margaret Atwood, evokes a similar sense of this 'Woman's Hour' approach to private female conversation in her book, *Significant Moments in the Life of my Mother*.

The Experience of Motherhood

'There are stories which my mother does not tell when there are men present; never at dinner, never at parties. She tells them to women only, usually in the kitchen, when they or we are helping with the dishes or shelling peas, or taking the tops and tails off the string beans, or husking corn. She tells them in a lowered voice, without moving her hands around in the air, and they contain no sound effects. These are stories of romantic betrayals, unwanted pregnancies, illnesses of various horrible kinds, marital infidelities, mental breakdowns, tragic suicides, unpleasant lingering deaths. They are not rich in detail, or embroidered with incident. They are stark and factual. The women, their own hands moving among the dirty dishes or husks of vegetables, nod solemnly.'

But, equally, there are many happy moments and memories recalled as well. The woman with five daughters who eventually had a son at forty-six. The midwife who shares the elation of a home birth. The mother, moved to tears with love at the sight of her three year old son playing in the garden in the rain, looking so adorable in his wellingtons and sou'wester. Many of the younger mothers, while they talk of the wonder in watching their babies grow, also stress their need to work and fulfil themselves intellectually; how they strive to have-it-all, juggling domestic duties, family life and a career. Their views are succinctly given in a recent article by journalist Justine Picardie:

'Fifteen years ago when I had just arrived at university, I had a room of my own and I read *A Room of One's Own* and I sat in my room and talked to my friends about Feminism and the Meaning of Life and our Brilliant Careers.

'I now live with three men, – well, two small boys and a husband and I fear that I have become that most pathetic of species, the failed feminist. I can't concentrate on writing because of the sea of Lego and broken toys that surrounded me and that anyway, my brain had turned into porridge after several years of sleep deprivation.

'According to my friend Antonia, I'm not really a failed feminist, just a part of a new kind of sisterhood. I think she's right. It's called motherhood.'

Family values, personal goals and social morality have reformed and shifted over the past seventy years. The older generations in this book describe how their marriage was the start of a sexual relationship and family life – they married with a view to being a wife and mother, with their husband as breadwinner. 'I saw myself as a Mum and a wife. I accepted that as my role. I was not a person in my own right in those days', admitted one woman who brought up five children in the 1950s and 1960s. Many are now very concerned at the rising numbers of cohabiting couples and single mothers, and at the devaluing of the institution of marriage.

These concerns are the main focus of a recent book on marriage by Dr Jack Dominian, which argues that marriage is in a state of evolutionary transition and that the divorce epidemic is evidence of this. The marriage partnership worked successfully in the past primarily because it was a collusion of social roles. It has gone for good, he believes (with a rather negative conviction), because of what he outmodedly calls women's emancipation.

However Rosalind Coward, in her book, *Our Treacherous Hearts*, reminds us that marriage [and second marriages] is still extremely popular, with over seventy-five per cent of us carrying on the tradition. She refers to the continuing complicity of women in thus acknowledging the female role as wife and mother. She talks about how women must free themselves from the myths of femininity and womanhood which are at the heart of women's collusion with men.

The British sociologist Ann Oakley, in her book, *Housewife*, fervently echoes Coward's view:

'Of all the rationales offered for woman's presence in the home, the myth of motherhood seems the most persuasive for even if the housewife role is capable of change, the maternal role is not. Women's position in the family is founded in their maternity, now and for all time. As with other myths, the function of the myth of motherhood is a validation of the status quo.'

With combative talk like this no wonder there is cynical talk of a feminist conspiracy that has begun to destroy the family as we know it. The nuclear family may be less stable, and women's status within the family and in society has certainly changed, but perhaps something equally rewarding has replaced traditional family structures and social roles. While feminism has been central to the notion of self-centred individualism, that personal liberation is the most important criterion for social success; it is true that women, if they wish to pursue wider horizons, can achieve new intellectual opportunities and freedom of choice. Women can enjoy their lives as equal partners, independent women and mothers who are as devoted to their children as their great-grandmothers were in their day.

Motherhood was the only career for past generations of women;

today, for some women, it is seen as a career break. 'After my second baby, I went back to work part-time to fulfil my needs as an individual. I wanted to work and have not felt guilty.'

'I have never been one to say I want to get married, have children, and do nothing else with my life. I need to work as well for my own sanity.'

'In a previous existence, I was a history graduate – I am now committed full-time to motherhood, but I wish I wasn't!'

These responses are typical of the feelings of the thirty-something career mother. A comparison in attitude between the generations might imply that the role of motherhood *has* radically changed, as Erica Jong proposes, but again it is the perspective with which it is viewed that has altered. I would argue that today's mothers' feelings are part and parcel of the personal and social expectations of women today. The madonna image has been replaced in the media by that of Shirley Conran's Superwoman, expertly coping with the home, family and work. But when it comes down to the day-to-day caring and protective nurturing of their children, the maternal instinct is, I believe, as natural, 'timeless and immutable' as ever. Perhaps this is best illustrated by the wise and experienced sentiments of Sheila Kitzinger from her book, *Ourselves as Mothers*:

'To be a mother is to take on one of the most emotionally and intellectually demanding, exasperating, strenuous, anxiety arousing and deeply satisfying tasks that any human being can undertake. Becoming a mother is a biological process, but it is also a social transformation and one of the most dramatic and far reaching that a woman may ever experience in her life. It is a task that shapes and changes you so that you see yourself and other people see you in a different way. It also entails commitment that, in one form or another, lasts for life. There is a great sisterhood out there – a celebration of the diversity, ingenuity, the energy and the courage of mothers.'

The Literature Of Motherhood

Lynn Knight

'If a man had a child and he was also a writer we should have heard a lot about it'. Enid Bagnold's caustic remark rebuffed those critics who were scandalized by her 1938 novel, *The Squire*, a hymn to motherhood that crescendoes with childbirth: 'a silver, whistling hub of pain'. Even liberal thinkers were shocked when she addressed this taboo subject (and used the word 'nipple' in print). [1] *The Squire* is but one in a line of such novels by women who have offended the decorum of their time.

Their work features among the short extracts that accompany the interviews here and that offer beguiling expressions of love alongside those of ambivalence and uncertainty. Like Mrs Ramsay's daughters in *To the Lighthouse* [1927] each generation hopes for 'a wilder life' than the previous one; they share the desire to 'shoot off in all directions . . . like the coloured arrows from a Fourth of July rocket' so dazzlingly evoked by Sylvia Plath, but are often grounded by reality, with pregnancy forestalling their plans for education and independence. In *The Millstone* [1965] Margaret Drabble's heroine speaks for many who understand her journey from ignorance to knowledge: 'I was trapped in a human limit for the first time in my life, and I was going to have to learn how to live inside it.'

The parallels between art and life are striking. Moving from the passive pleas of the 1920s to the outspoken voices of the 1990's, the literature of motherhood traces social progress. Although the heroine of Elizabeth von Arnim's novel, *Love* [1925] asks why she has been a daughter, wife and mother, but has never been 'herself', she does not ask that question out loud. Contemporary heroines, who dare to 'have-it-all', are by no means so reticent.

The decade that was to introduce the Pill – hailed by Angela Carter as 'the most significant invention since the wheel' – finally broke the tyranny of whispers and ignorance. In 1960 Lynne Reid Banks caused a furore with *The L-Shaped Room*. A novel about illegitimacy, it cut through the reigning hypocrisy of the 1950s that sex was bartered for a wedding ring and that 'nice girls don't'. Other novelists, including Margaret Drabble, also confirmed that they did, writing with a candour and lack of sentimentality unimaginable to their predecessors. Further controversy followed with *Up the Junction* [1963] and *Poor Cow* [1967]. Nell Dunn's young women were not only far more audacious and exuberant but they were also working class. Fay Weldon neatly underlined assumptions about class difference – as great a divide as time in *Down Among the Women* [1971]: 'Getting married and not pregnant? There's posh for you'. Pat Barker took realism much further in *Union Street* [1982], a novel that will remain a rebuke as long as mothering is undermined by poverty.

The courage to confront socially-awkward truths and to challenge the conspiracy of silence that long surrounded sex and maternity are as much a part of the rich history of motherhood as the eloquence with which women writers have conveyed its joys.

1. See Anna Sebba, Introduction to *The Squire*, Virago Press 1987.

CHAPTER ONE

————•◦•————

Family Histories: Childhood Expectations and Aspirations

'The natural vocation for every woman is that of wife and mother, and in the training of every girl, provision should be made for the acquisition of definite and accurate knowledge of the essentials of domestic economy and mothercraft.'
Mary Scharlieb, THE SEVEN AGES OF WOMAN, 1915.

————•◦•————

Violet Stevenson-Hamilton [born 1902]

My father felt, as his entire generation did, that marriage was the future for a young woman. But he was quite prepared for me to have an art school education or anything else I fancied, while I was growing up and getting ready for matrimony. I decided to do a general nursing training. I was terrified of sickness in any shape or form. I felt the only thing to do was to grasp the nettle. I enjoyed nursing very much. It was a wonderful life. We were not well paid, we had £20 the first year as juniors, £35 the second year and as staff nurses we went up to the magnificent £50. We were fed, we were clothed, we were housed. There was not much social life; my old father and I would play golf on my days off, and he would give me a rattling good dinner in the evening before returning me by 10pm to the nurses' home.

Janet Stewart [born 1904]

I was brought up in Alloa, Clackmannanshire. My father was a mill-worker, but when I was a child the whole family went over to Canada, my parents and four children. We were six weeks on the ship. Life there did not work out and my parents were told that my youngest brother would not survive another winter, so we returned to Scotland. My mother then became an invalid suffering from asthma. I left school at fourteen and trained as a secretary. My parents had no expectations of what I could achieve. As the eldest of four children, I had to do the housework and help my mother in many ways as she was so ill. I myself had no idea what I could do with my life.

Susan Curtis [born 1905]

After boarding school, I went to Bristol University from 1923 to 1927 to study philosophy and English literature. My aim was a career in journalism but I could not find paid work. I then got engaged and I was forced to take up teaching as my father expected me to earn my own living by this time. Father's word was absolute in those days. I was able to joke about his Victorian attitude – he was over-caring – but my elder sister hated him because she thought he took advantage of my mother's devotion.

Eileen Brown [born 1908]

I was expected to help at home until I married. My own wish was to get married and set up my own home. I was not clever but I was a good cook.

Patricia Rogers [born 1909]

My maternal grandparents came from little villages in Lancashire. My grandfather was the village blacksmith and he was very fond of natural history. As a boy he had played truant and had gone bird-watching and rambling and never learnt to read or write. My grandmother, Caroline, kept his accounts on a hinged slate which always fascinated us when we were children. Every evening, after their meal, she would read the *Liverpool Echo* from cover to cover and then she took down one of the classics and she read to him – the whole of Dickens, for instance. She read to him every night while the daughters washed up. They had five daughters, one being my mother. There were also two sons who had both died in infancy.

As far as I know my grandmother never had a holiday in her life but she was the happiest person. Her favourite sayings were 'Yes Tom' and 'Of course, Tom', and she sat at home with this wonderful, kind smile.

Every Sunday, she would prepare the Sunday dinner, which had to include rice pudding, always firmly made so that the spoon stood up in it, because that was the way Tom liked it.

My grandmother always wore a bonnet – she was a traditional Victorian woman and the loveliest, kindest person, and I don't think it ever clouded her happiness that her husband was definitely the boss. I mean that was the order of things. My mother was the fourth daughter and in many ways she was like Caroline, although my mother had more spirit. On moral issues she was very strong and stood up for what she believed in.

My father was Irish and reckoned he had no real education from the age of eight. The one thing my father wanted to do for us was to give us a good education. For him that was an important thing and they expected me to have a 'safe' profession. Although I was the eldest of four and they weren't well off, I went to university. I took my degree at Liverpool University, and then a diploma in education and taught for five years. Marriage was a goal for me though.

Mary Maclennan [born 1911]

I was born in Birsay, the northwest corner of Orkney. I lived on a small farm with my two sisters and parents. I had an ideal childhood, running about the farm with complete freedom, and went to the village school. From the point of view of hard education and grammar, this was rather neglected so that I went on to secondary school in Stromness, ten miles away. It was too far to cycle every day so I had to get lodgings in the town and came home for weekends. I think I went because my father – poor man – was saddled with three daughters; he didn't have a son to take over the farm. He wanted one of us to have the chance of secondary education and going on to university if they wanted to. My older sister was rather lame with a bad foot and my little sister was very wee and my mother's darling, so I was the only one to be pushed into being semi-educated. I worked hard and went on to Aberdeen University in 1929. I studied arts and science, a double degree, an MA BSc which was quite common to do at the time. I wasn't sure what to do then, just to earn money. Teaching was an obvious career.

'We missed [Lucy] when she went away to Chicago to study music. She was eighteen years old then; talented but too careless and light-hearted to take herself very

seriously. She never dreamed of a "career". She thought of music as a natural form of pleasure, and as a means of earning money to help her father when she came home.'

Willa Cather, LUCY GAYHEART.

May Stephen [born 1911]

I was brought up in Aberdeen with my two sisters, one elder and one younger. My grandfather came to stay with us when I was six until I was eighteen, so that made our family life a bit restricted in terms of going on holiday and being quiet around the house. My father had a printing press, the Caxton Press in Aberdeen. He had left school at eleven and been a paper boy at the *Press and Journal*, and got interested in printing and learnt all about it. He saved up and bought his own business. He was a most widely educated man; we had books, all the classics, and he knew his Shakespeare even though he had left school at eleven. My sisters and I all went to the fee-paying high school – our parents wanted us to have a good education. This was a very sad time because the First World War was on and I just remember all the sad news each week in church of the death of another young man.

My older sister contracted pneumonia as a young girl, and we spent many months away from the misty, foggy dampness of the city and lived in the country in a rented cottage. I would be driven to school in a pony and trap. I left school at eighteen and went to university to read chemistry. My sisters both did Latin and Greek. I then went south to London to try and find a job in teaching as it was not easy to find work in the north of Scotland.

Emily Heggie [born 1912]

My father was a policeman but he was a lot older than my mother, and I was eight when he retired; my mother had to bring up two of us on two-thirds of his salary, on the pension, so we were really very poor.

My father's view was that a daughter was only fit for housework and that sort of thing so, when I was fifteen, it was his idea that I become a nursery nurse. It so happened that a lady near us needed a nursery maid and it just fell into place and I went to work for her for a year after I left school.

The second post was with Sir Archibald Edmonson and his wife who had a baby girl. They spent six months of the year at their home in Scotland, Duntress Castle, and six months in Leicestershire. There was a nanny who was in charge but I had to see to the meals which came up to the nursery. I looked after the washing and care of the baby's clothes, took her for walks and really was a general dogsbody. It was a big estate in Scotland and they employed twelve gardeners, cooks and maids. It was a beautiful place and I loved that job. I used to travel with them everywhere the family went, travelling first class. We used to come to London for a month each year and stay in Grosvenor Square, and I would go shopping in all the big stores – Harrods, Harvey Nichols – to get clothes on appro for Nanny to try them on the baby. I was paid ten shillings a week and was given my uniform and all my food. But I didn't even need to spend this on private clothes or anything, because I was given very little time off.

Eileen Watkins [born 1912]

My father was in the Stock Exchange and my mother never worked outside the home but was involved in a lot of charity work. I was sent to a private boarding school and at eighteen went to university to study English but I failed it. I then took a secretarial qualification. My parents expected me to work for a bit before marriage. My aspirations were a university degree [!] and then marriage and a family.

'What I rebelled at chiefly was the dependence implied in the idea of "destined" marriage, "destined" motherhood – the identification of success with marriage, of failure with spinsterhood, the artificial concentration of the hopes of girlhood on sexual attraction and maternity.'

Cicely Hamilton, LIFE ERRANT.

Alice Wands [born 1912]

It was very happy, my childhood, very secure but I was the youngest of a large family of six children, so we were very poor. I had a lot of hand-me-downs, but I was very spoiled by the rest of the family. I think my mother was shocked when she found I was on the way. But it was happy, we didn't want for anything, we didn't have luxuries or expensive holidays. We had to behave ourselves. We were not allowed out at night until we were quite old and we never had a key to get in. We simply dared not defy or disobey my father.

We lived in a small village in Derbyshire and all the other families were the same. They had to do as they were told. They knew right from wrong and we learnt to help people: fetching water for the old folk who didn't have water laid on or shopping would be a Saturday job. When I left school I didn't have a lot of choice because we didn't have a lot of money for doing anything except starting work. Nursing was supposed to be ladylike without costing money. My sister, who was one above me, had done nursing and had enjoyed it, so it was more or less automatic that if I could get into nursing, I would do that. There was no question of going to university or college. All of us children were expected to get jobs and contribute to the housekeeping.

Nancy Beaty [born 1914]

I was brought up on a farm with mother, father, grandfather and three brothers. I was the youngest. My mother died when I was eleven and thereon we had housekeepers to look after us. When I left school at fourteen I had to keep house for my father, you see, and look after my brothers. I couldn't have the education I would have liked to have had – I had the qualifications to go to a higher school but it was essential to help at home – but the experience was good.

Ethel Hay [born 1914]

I can remember all about my childhood. This was in the East End of Dundee. We lived in an old stone house which even had a toilet inside: so many folk just had a toilet in the garden. In my childhood, I never had no kisses, cuddles, stories, loving, nothing. I was the youngest of three girls. My mother lived with us for a while but she was ill. I remember her being in bed. We had a daily woman to do the cleaning but then we got a housekeeper who made us do most of the work. Believe me it was hard work in those days. I was even dumped in the dolly barrel – a great big barrel drum used to wash blankets and clothes. When the wash was done, we had to do the mangling. We had to lug all this damp washing about, you can imagine the weight. There were black ranges to clean, to black lead the ranges and get the brushes and clean the soot down the chimney. We were made to do a lot of the cleaning, a lot of steel and metal rings which was very hard on my hands. I remember coming home from school, crying with pain in my legs. I was told it was growing pains, but it wasn't. My knees were all swollen up because of all the heavy washing and housework. My mother was there when I was tiny, then she was ill in bed for a long time. I just don't remember her being there after that. No one told me where she was or what had happened and I was too young to understand.

I had no ambitions, I was so cowered down. I just accepted things as they were. There was nothing expected of me at all. I learnt later that my parents separated when I was young; my mother left my father and went to London and eventually went to America.

Doris Melling [born 1914]

My father died in the First World War, when I was about two years old, and so I was brought up in Blackpool by my mother alone. I left school at sixteen and went into the Civil Service for five years until I left to get married. There was a marriage bar then and no married women could work in certain jobs and professions. I think my mother just wanted me to be happy. After school, I had no career expectations and looked forward to marriage and a family. I could have gone to teaching college and I later regretted this as I could have returned to teaching later on.

Mary McKerrow [born 1915]

My mother was a doctor's daughter from Dumfries and she had been used to a house where there were maids, a cook and a coachman, and where all the washing was done below stairs in the very early morning and never seen. My grandmother's cook was paid £20 a year and once was in tears when my grandmother forgot to ask her at the end of one year if she would stay on. So my mother had certain strict ideas about how people ought to live and behave and we also lived in rather comfortable surroundings. It wasn't seen as extravagant for the period, just normal middle-class life. I had one older sister and we were brought up in quite a big house, with a cook and a housemaid and somebody who came to clean the floors and do the sewing. We had a big garden looked after by two gardeners, with a tennis lawn, an orchard and two greenhouses so in that way I suppose I had a very good start in life. We weren't spoilt, we didn't expect to have a lot of extras or treats, and we lived a normal life.

We were then aged ten and twelve. My sister loved the cinema and would go weekly, sitting in the sixpenny seats, and ardently following the careers of the film stars of the twenties.

Life went on in this idyllic fashion through my childhood until my mother died rather suddenly. She had been ill with pernicious anaemia, for which there was no cure. She was forty-five when she died and it was decided my sister and I would go to boarding school. And so in September 1928, the summer after she died, my father saw us off to school. A week later our headmistress called us to her study to tell us the tragic news that our father had also died. He had died of septicaemia and, with no penicillin in those days, the poison raced quickly through the body of this big, strong man.

Our lifestyle drastically changed. My mother's sister, a spinster lady, brought us up and we lived with her during the school holidays. She wasn't strict but insistent that we toed the line. The death of our parents was certainly a traumatic experience but, looking back, I think we were fortunate because we were at boarding school. We were being cared for and made a lot of good friends, friends I have kept all my life, so that it was like a second family. So in that way, there is a lot to be grateful for. I was very jealous when my friends had their parents coming down at weekends to take them out and I found it difficult to explain what was wrong. I didn't think they would understand my misery. I was eleven when my mother died and I had no more experience of a mother's love until I could give it to my own children.

But before marriage, further education was seen as a good thing. My mother and aunt's family had regarded professional people as God, so there was no question of leaving school and just finding a job. I had done suitably well at school, so I went to university to study English and classics.

Joan Counihan [born 1915]

My father was a pretty successful writer, who managed to keep his wife and six children in comfort and send us all to private boarding schools. At our peak, in the 1920s and 1930s, my mother had two domestic staff and two nurses to look after four children. Once or twice she engaged a governess to look after the older ones during the holidays. Several times she would keep us at school during the holidays, perhaps if the younger ones were ill. We were on the whole a very happy family. Our parents were strict with us about going out to events when we were older, wanting to know which families we were visiting. We had to toe the line. They were never very positive about what they expected us to do when we left school, though my father did hope some of us would take up writing, which I have done but not to any extent while he was alive.

I drifted into teaching, in private prep schools, and was going to take exams to qualify as a Montessori teacher, when the war broke out and that altered everything. By then my ambition was to marry and have a huge family, without realising what it would entail. We had a very sheltered upbringing, had never learnt to cook or do much in the way of housework.

Emily Hagues [born 1916]

I had a very happy childhood. There were six children – I had twin sisters, two brothers and another sister. We lived in Port Elphinstone and my father worked in the joiner shop at the locomotive works. He worked so hard right through the war from six in the morning and it must have been quite a struggle keeping us all. I left school at sixteen and went into domestic service. I went to Sir Thomas and Lady Jaffrey and we entertained Lloyd George and Winston Churchill when they came to Aberdeen. I had a happy time there meeting all these people. I stayed for a while and then moved to Mr and Mrs Dickson in Queens Road, Aberdeen, to work as the house table maid. When Mr Dickson died, the cook and I joined Dr and Mrs Duffy, and I was there until I married. I was hoping to go on further at school. I was very good at maths, not so good at English but I had a good report and took my Scottish certificate, but the thing was, with the other four children coming behind me, my parents couldn't afford to continue my education. I could have gone into the paper mill but my mother wouldn't allow it, and she said I'd be better off going into service.

Elizabeth Grey [born 1917]

I enjoyed my childhood in Blairgowrie, and I believe life was far better then than it is now because you learnt to stand on your own feet. To begin with, when you were no age at all, we all had wee jobs to do. There was none of this sitting around watching television; we had to do a wee job before school, at dinner time and when you came hame from school, you had another wee bit to do and you didn't get out to play until you had finished your chores. I had a brother who died when he was six months old. I had four sisters – Jean, Greta, Willis and Matilda.

We had a good childhood, but we had to be in at eight o'clock at night, say when you were nine or ten. That was the latest, eight. It was the same for all of us. There were no bairns running about the streets as they are now. We were all in 'cos we were up early in the morning.

My father was a jack of all trades, mostly plumbing work, but after 1910 he started all these raspberry crops. He and his people were among the first to bring in the raspberries at that time. That was a great time for the raspberries.

We all knew that we couldn't waste money. We were given tuppence each week, but a penny of that had to be saved to buy what you wanted at Christmas. When we were older it went up to threepence and then sixpence. But then you were away to work at fourteen. We all went to work when we were fourteen. I went into domestic service. I had a job all sorted out for me at the big house, Ashford down the road here. I lived in and was given five shillings a week. I got up at six o'clock in the morning but you never thought anything about it. I did the housemaid duties and worked hard all day, right up to the evening, and served the suppers. My parents didn't say what I had to do after school. It was up to me what I did.

Lucy Firth [born 1917]

My father had been wounded in World War I and lived on a hundred per cent disability pension. I was brought up with one sister in Skegness, Lincolnshire, and sent to a grammar school until I was eighteen. My parents just expected me to marry and have a family and I felt that my intelligence and education were wasted due to the lack of parental money to put me through university. During the war I worked as a chemist's assistant and then married at the age of twenty-three.

Milicent Woolner [born 1917]

When I was five, my father was killed in a freak accident, when he was umpiring a local cricket match. My mother was only thirty-six at the time, and expecting her sixth child. I left school at seventeen and trained to be a nurse and later as a midwife. My mother encouraged us to seek our own chosen path.

Catherine Begg [born 1920]

My father was a gardener and forester and I was brought up near Kirriemuir, Angus. I left school at fourteen as my parents couldn't afford to keep me on till seventeen years, as all books had to be bought in those days. It was considered a waste to educate a girl. I passed the bursary exams entitling me to go on, but my father suffered ill health. I went into domestic service.

Joan Hill [born 1920]

I was brought up in Yorkshire and had one brother who was killed in action in 1942. My father was a textile agent and had his own family business. I went to a girls' high school and left at sixteen but had no further education. Other than the professions, medicine or teaching, girls in my time were encouraged into the secretarial world. It was not done even to go into my father's business. I opted to train as a hairdresser and beautician. My mother wanted me to go into teaching, my father wanted me to be happy and thought that marriage would come in due time. For myself, in 1936, everything looked possible – except being a textile agent – but then three years later my life took a very different turn, as it did for most of my generation.

Jean Charleson [born 1922]

I was born in St Mary's Street, off the Canongate in Edinburgh, but was only there a year or so before my parents moved to Easter Road and I was brought up there. I loved my school days. I left school in February 1936, almost exactly to the day when I was fourteen, so I only had two years at my high school. I don't know why really, because I loved school. Parents somehow then wanted you to leave school. Everyone had to go out to work and bring in money and I suppose that was the reason. I had done commercial work, taken Pitman's shorthand, and I wanted to go into an office there and then. But my family was in the printing trade, they were lithographers, compositors, book binders. They were good wages in comparison to office work and that maybe is why my mother arranged it that I would go into the printing trade. I served my time as an apprentice for three years, but never liked it. Then the war broke out and our lives changed.

———•———

'You little girls, when you grow up, must be on the alert to recognise your prime at whatever time of your life it may occur. You must then live it to the full.

If only you small girls would listen to me, I would make of you the creme de la creme.'

Muriel Spark, THE PRIME OF MISS JEAN BRODIE.

———•———

Joyce Macpherson [born 1923]

I was brought up in Hertfordshire and had a traditional two-parent family. My mother had been a teacher until she married. I left school at sixteen just when war broke out as my mother didn't want me to continue going to school, near Hendon Airport. I began to train as a nursery nurse when I was seventeen. Both my parents thought I ought to train for something. My father actually wanted me to go into banking because that was a nice, safe job with a good salary, and it was seen as a classy career. He wasn't keen on my going into nursery nursing but my mother thought it was ideal as she knew I loved children. I loved babies and had always wanted a baby sister but never got one. I did two years training and then chose a war day nursery, otherwise I would have had to join the forces and I wasn't keen on fighting. I am a Quaker. I was a nursery nurse throughout the war and then went and did teacher training and worked in a nursery school which was nice. I did that right up until I married.

Jane Ward [born 1924]

Both my parents were elementary school teachers, and when I left school at eighteen I went to university to study economics. My mother wanted me to train for a well-paid career, while I suspect marriage and a family were my father's expectations. At seventeen I wanted to be a meteorologist in the WRAF. When I was nineteen, after one year at university, I did wartime army service.

Joan Longmuir [born 1930]

My father died when I was three and my mother was a secretary. I left my grammar school when I was seventeen and went on to a commercial training school. My mother certainly wanted me to have a good career, to do something with my life which my birth had denied her! I simply wanted to get married and have a family.

Barbara Henderson [born 1931]

Looking back at my family history has been very interesting, to see how women's lives in particular have changed. My grandmother, Catherine Webb, was born in 1882, and as a girl she kept house for an uncle. When she was fourteen she had a baby by him but this was hushed up and the child integrated into the family. She later married James Stewart, a master baker, and they lived in the Aberdeen area, later in Keith, Banffshire. There were seven children of this marriage but my grandmother was plagued by miscarriages for many years. Her husband died when he was forty-two, leaving her in dire straits with five children at home, the youngest aged three. The eldest boy, aged fourteen, supported the family off a farm worker's wage until he went to Australia. My grandmother died in her sixties in an old people's home.

My mother, Catherine Webb Stewart, was born in 1913 and went into domestic service at fourteen to give her mother her monthly wage of a pound in order to help support the family. She became pregnant one month before her fifteenth birthday and was subsequently forced to marry the father of her child that September. The child was born in October, but was a blue baby and lived only a week. My father proceeded to make my mother's life hell. Previously, at the age of nineteen, he had made a girl pregnant but her parents had not given permission for her to marry. He agreed to pay five shillings a week for his son, James, until he was fourteen. So every four weeks, my mother had to place £1 on the dresser with a quarter of sweeties. His good suit had to be pressed and he cycled over to see his son James and his mother. This woman then married and her husband was known as Uncle John and a tea of scones was baked in his honour. Because of this arrangement my mother and her children – I had six brothers and sisters – existed in poverty. My father was a farm worker. Until I was twelve years old, my mother never had any spare money till the family allowance was paid in 1947. I was brought up in the Morayshire district, going to schools all over the area. I left after third year certificate exams, but then went to night school to study accountancy. I trained as a student nurse for a year or so, but then I married at seventeen. I would have liked to have been a vet and worked with animals, but this was not possible at the time – perhaps if I had been born twenty-five years later.

Margaret Cruikshank [born 1933]

I was brought up in the Nairnshire area mostly. My father was a farm labourer, my mother a full-time housewife, and in my childhood money was scarce as I had four brothers and two sisters. As well as no hot water, there was just a dry toilet outside. Meals were wholesome: broth, tattie soup, mince, a stew, sometimes stewed rabbit. Mum baked girdle scones, pancakes and clootie dumpling – all food was homemade. Porridge – twice a day, and if we were lucky half a boiled egg. If Dad had a boiled egg after his porridge, there was no egg for us and Dad gave one of us the top of his one. We had to take it in turns, with seven of us, so it was a long time before it came round to your turn again! I remember when my brother was in the army, he wrote home and said he wished he had the top of Dad's egg. For enjoyment we used to sit and sing hymns round the fire. I left school at fifteen with the *Dux* medal. I wanted to be a hairdresser or do office work but I trained in tailoring.

Sheila Brown [born 1934]

I was born in Peterhead, and was an only child. My father was a fisherman and my mother did not work and was at home with me the whole time. Before she married she had been a nanny. When I was in my teens, my father had to give up going to sea because of an injury from the war, so he set up a business in Peterhead, called the Harbour Cafe and my mother helped him out in that. There was no babysitting in those days, so I trotted along with them wherever they would be going. I left school at fifteen and became an auxilary nurse in the local cottage hospital. I loved it and didn't want to come off duty on my first day. I was accepted for nursing training in Aberdeen Royal Infirmary when I was eighteen.

Mary Anderson [born 1934, daughter of Janet Stewart]

I was brought up in Alloa and after school went to Miss Simpson's secretarial college in Stirling. My parents did not speak about further education or a career for me. I wanted to go to art college but that was never entertained by the family.

Jennifer Harper-Jones [born 1939, daughter of Lucy Brown]

My parents expected me to marry and have a family. I left school at eighteen and began a degree course at the Sorbonne University, but left due to ill health. I became a secretary but I really wanted to marry and have a family. I was not ambitious even though I was given the opportunity to have an education and career.

'A flurry of reports in the late fifties and early sixties discussed whether the curriculum for girls should be different from that of boys. They were concerned about girls leaving school in order to marry early. The post war industrial boom needed women as workers as well as mothers. [For her report, "Half our Future"] Dame Kathleen Ollerenshaw was appalled by the apathy of the girls she interviewed. By their mid teens they had completely lost interest in school and were dreaming of wedding dresses, fitted kitchens and prams. Their urge to marry was fostered by romantic fiction in teenage comics and advertisements for three piece suites, frilly bedcovers and gleaming grills . . . far more exciting than the classroom.'

Angela Holdsworth, OUT OF THE DOLLS HOUSE.

'Carol' [born 1942]

I was adopted by a middle-aged couple and sent to a convent at the age of eleven. I left school at eighteen and went to a teacher's training college. My parents expected me to have a good career but to stay at home. I wanted to write and to travel, but felt it my duty to support my parents.

'I wanted to be an actress, and anyway I was bad at almost everything at school and so hated it. Several of my friends wanted to leave early too, and aggrievedly compared notes about their parents' reactions – which were all along the lines of how much we would regret not getting a proper education. I boasted that my father was different; he would understand that I was an artist and that to stay on at school would be a fruitless waste of time. But when I confidently put my theory to the test, I got a terrible disappointment. Father refused to understand. His reaction was the same as all the other parents. I was ashamed and angry and from then on nothing went right.'

Lynne Reid Banks, THE L SHAPED ROOM.

Sheila Davidson [born 1944]

I left school at fifteen and my parents expected me to do some sort of training or job until I married. I wanted to work with children and then one day marry and have children of my own. I had an elder brother and a younger sister but she had severe asthma so I was always the one to help Mum and tried to please everyone. My parents were very strict – no alcohol at all was allowed and we had to be home by a certain time or there were rows about it. But we respected everything our Mum and Dad said. In 1960, when I was sixteen, I began to train as an NNEB nanny in Aberdeen.

Jenni Smith [born 1946]

My own upbringing was loveless and although I was bright my mother was determined I should leave school and get a job. She was not prepared to support me financially beyond O level. I had wanted to stay on at school and train to be a teacher but this was not to be. I therefore left home at the age of sixteen to start a career in nursing. I was not able to complete this for health reasons and I tried other jobs before I married. I consequently had no training or career structure, and nothing but secretarial experience behind me.

Vivienne Leighton [born 1947, daughter of Emily Hagues]

I remember my childhood being very happy, going for country walks with my dad, looking at the birds. I can't remember any time when I was miserable as a child. The only thing was I was fat, really fat, and I think when I got to the age of twelve it was difficult for me, it was a nuisance. I was brought up in Aberdeen city, in the top flat of a tenement house. We were there until I was eighteen when we moved to Dyce. My father worked for the Civil Aviation Authority and my mother didn't really have a job outside the home, but helped out her friends in the hairdresser or fish shop when I was young. I don't think we were well off, but I don't remember wanting for anything, but then in those days we did not have the desires for clothes and things. Perhaps it was because there wasn't so much to buy, in terms of records or games which children hanker after today.

I left school at eighteen and went to train as a medical scientific officer in the hospital laboratory at Foresterhill, Aberdeen. I had wanted to be a vet but I don't think I'd have managed that academically. At school I never thought of marriage and having a family.

Motherhood

'I never wanted to get married. The last thing I wanted was infinite security and to be the place an arrow shoots off from. I wanted change and excitement and to shoot off in all directions myself, like the coloured arrows from a Fourth of July rocket.'

Sylvia Plath, THE BELL JAR.

Mary Law [born 1949, daughter of Davina Thorpe]

I am the eldest of four children; we were born within five years of each other between 1949 and 1954. To explain a little of my family background, my father had very much enjoyed his life as a soldier in the cavalry and after the war was very unhappy as a mill worker. He then joined the army again as a captain. When he had to retire from the army he worked in a factory for the last seventeen years of his life. My mother had been a secretary and gave up work when she married. She had wanted to train as a nurse but her husband wouldn't let her which made her very unhappy. In later married life she took up part-time office work in which she was contented.

My parents wanted me to have a good, reliable job which would make plenty of money, and therefore they believed in good education so that I could pursue a professional career. They also wanted me to have the opportunity to travel and see the world. For myself, I couldn't wait to leave school. Four years at secondary school nearly killed me but what kind of a job could I do with four O grades? I didn't want to live at home. It was actually my main aim in life to marry and to be a mother.

'My prime concern is that, back at the childhood stage, parents and schools should not encourage girls to be competitive with males if that is going to make them dissatisfied with raising children, their most creative job in adulthood, whether or not they go to work too.'

Dr Benjamin Spock, A YOUNG PERSON'S GUIDE TO LIFE AND LOVE.

Ailsa Gray [born 1953]

My parents believed that a good education and a career were very important but I think marriage was also assumed. I was very unclear what I wanted to do, thought vaguely about teaching, but was undecided. I did go to university but left before completing my degree as I developed anorexia nervosa. I later took a secretarial training and joined the BBC where I worked for fifteen years.

Trudi Barnet [born 1954]

My father was actually twenty-five years older than my mother and I think, looking back, I was a bit of a Daddy's girl. I went to a private fee-paying girls' school but I left school at fifteen. I was not very academic and all I wanted to do was ride horses. So I did that, riding and showjumping until I was twenty. I had never been interested in going out with boys. I was very young and immature – naive in a way – and when I met this man, who was fifteen years older than me, I perhaps looked upon him as a father figure (my father had died when I was seventeen). I thought, why not just get married, have children and live happily ever after. I got married within ten months of meeting him. I was twenty-one.

———•———

'The lover in romance is a man of masterful ways, clearly superior to his beloved in at least one respect, being older, of a higher social rank or more intelligent or au fait. He is authoritative but deeply concerned for his lady whom he protects and guides in a way that is patently paternal. He can be stern and withdrawn but the heroines of romance melt him by sheer force of modesty and beauty and the bewitching power of their clothes. The original for such characters is in fact romantic in the historical sense for perhaps the very first of them are Rochester, Heathcliff, Mr Darcy and Lord Byron.'

Germaine Greer, THE FEMALE EUNUCH.

———•———

Winifred Fyfe [born 1955]

My father was a train driver and my mother was a shop assistant, later promoted to a manager. I was brought up on a busy street, in a tenement in Aberdeen. We were not far from the bus depot and so the corporation buses would often be burling down the street. As well as my family – my sister, mam and dad, we had an aunt who lived nearby and my grand-parents lived downstairs. So we were quite close as a family. I had cousins too who lived on the street.

My mother did tell me that I would probably have had ten brothers and sisters had it not been for her doing the contraceptives, because my father wasn't very good in that department. So I dare say it was my mother who decided on the two children. In fact there's only a year and four months between my sister and I. My mother told me that when she heard she was expecting me, she tried things like jumping down the stairs, and hot baths, because I don't think she was a very maternal person. She really didn't enjoy pregnancies and babies. I remember as a child she had a box with a rubber thing with a hooter on the end. This must have been some kind of contraceptive device, a douche. It used to fascinate me as a child. I daresay I wasn't supposed to have seen it. Anyway, after she had had two children, she'd obviously decided she was having no more.

My parents' marriage began going wrong when I was about ten, and I remember some rather sad times. They separated for a time when I was thirteen and my father moved to Glasgow but he did come back at weekends. My sister and I often spent time at our gran's house because we were happier there. I was a very sulky, sullen, morose teenager. I just hated everybody. I didn't enjoy secondary school – it was a very tough school, even the girls were tough. This was back in 1967, 1968, at the time of the change to comprehensive education. I couldn't wait to leave and I got absolutely no career assistance, nothing. What they expected of us was to go straight to the paper factory. I left school at fifteen; my parents, I think, just wanted me to have a better life than they had had. In fact my mother told me, 'If you think you are going to work in a factory with those girls, you're not', and that was that. No alternative was given.

When I first left school, I worked in a chemist's shop, which I hated, and got £4 a week. After three weeks I moved to a music shop and I was happy there for a while. I had no clear idea about what I wanted to do, but always felt I would like to work with children. When I was sixteen, I began a three-year course to train as a nursery nurse.

My parents were finally divorced when I was nineteen so it was a long haul for my mother. She went through a hard time even after that and I couldn't understand it at the time because all I could think of was that he had gone and that was what she wanted so why was she miserable. It was difficult at that time to get a divorce, there was a shortage of money and for a while we had to sleep on the floor in my granny's small tenement flat. Really when you look back you wonder how you survive all these things, but you do. I admire my mother. I think she survived because of the family unit.

Jano Rochefort [born 1955]

I was brought up in Cornwall with one sister. My father was an oil engineer but later a postman, and my mother was a nursing officer. My parents were very keen that I should aim for a good career. I was certainly keen to go to university and find a good job as I had decided I would not marry or have children.

Roma Young [born 1956]

Basically where I grew up in Cupar, Fife, it wasn't the in-thing for girls to go on and have an education or a big career. You just left school, got married and had a family. That is just what I expected at the time. When I was at school I had thought of going on to art college, that was one thing I quite fancied, but when the crunch came it was a case of deciding whether to work and earn your pennies or whether to stick it out for three or four years. So you just didn't do it; I've no regrets of not going to college or whatever.

Didi Hopkins [born 1956]

My parents separated when I was just eighteen months old so I was brought up by my mother, who was a very enthusiastic and hard-working parent. I was very ill at nine months from a smallpox vaccination which caused severe eczema and I was in and out of hospital for nine months. My mother was, in fact, the first woman to campaign for parents to stay in overnight with their children, because in those days they were not allowed to. My mother was a teacher at art school and basically never stopped working, and she was a painter, writer, researcher, so I grew up with the image of the woman, the only person in my family, who earned the money and worked full-time.

I had always veered towards the arts and trained as a classical musician but gave that up when I found it too insular, and branched out into music generally. She did her utmost to find educational grants for me, and was dedicated to help me get through music college and go to the Guildhall. She never expected me to have a bottom drawer, which I would line with little bits and bobs for my wedding, and certainly I suppose being brought up in a single parent family, we were quite ahead of our time in a way.

Most of my friends had two parents. I was unusual, growing up in an alternative family.

Jo Davidson [1960]

As my father was a merchant seaman, he was away for long periods of six to eighteen months at any time during my childhood in Southampton. My maternal grandfather lived with us and we lived close to my mother's sisters and their families. My mother was in effect a part-time, single parent once my grandfather died when I was ten. My mother then treated me like a confidante, and I felt significant responsibility for her, which I feel was too much for me.

I went to university and teacher training college. I am not sure what my father expected I would do in life. My mother wanted me to have a good career, such as in medicine or in the media. She also wanted me to marry and have a family. I wanted to work for the BBC and travel abroad.

Sue Rook [born 1960]

I spent my childhood in South Yorkshire, with a brother and a sister; my father was a civil servant, and my mother a school secretary. I took an English and history degree and then went on to a postgraduate diploma in personnel management. My mother, very career-orientated in her day, had joined the civil service in 1939 and did very well as a high-flyer. I was always encouraged to complete my education, which is what I wanted as well, so that I would be in a position with a degree behind me, to choose what I wanted to do in life.

Lucy Owen [born 1961]

I went to a private day school and then a boarding school from 13 to 17. My father wanted me to take a safe secretarial course and expected that I would then marry. My mother encouraged me to go to university, and I studied English literature and language for four years at Edinburgh University. I always wanted a career of some sort but was unclear at school. I then trained 'on the job' as an editor of a publishing house and worked as a bookseller's assistant. I expected to marry at some point – I was very romantic!

'I hadn't really been doing anything in Paris. I had gone there immediately after coming down from Oxford with a lovely, shiny, useless new degree to fill in time.

To fill in time till what? I thought about jobs, and seriousness and about what a girl can do with herself if over-educated and lacking a sense of vocation. Louise had one answer, of course. She was getting married. It seemed to be one way of escaping the secretarial course-coffee-bar degradation that had been creeping up on her ever since she too had left the esoteric masonic paradise of Oxford.'

Margaret Drabble, A SUMMER BIRD-CAGE.

Diane Connelly [born 1961]

My father died when I was nine and my mother was an auxilary nurse. I didn't enjoy A levels at school so I left and the careers officer found me a place on a pre-nursing course. I still made no real efforts with A levels and failed. I was always much more interested in boys. My mum was not firm enough with me in terms of studying for exams. She always emphasised the fact that I would get a job after school rather than a career as she could not finance me through university. I had always had little jobs from the age of eleven and had an early understanding of the need to earn money. I suppose I always wanted to be a carer and at eighteen I began training as a State Registered Nurse and mum was delighted.

Angela Blanchard [born 1962]

I have two older sisters and my father was a vicar, my mother a school teacher. We all felt that religion was rammed down our throats as children, with church every Sunday, even on holiday, and lots of preaching from my father at the dinner table. Unfortunately much of it was of the 'Do as I say not as I do' variety, and it has left us all with mixed feelings. I was sent to a Church of England school as a boarder, from the age of 11 to 18. I sat three A levels and went to Aberdeen University to read Celtic studies and English. My parents expected me to fulfil my intellectual potential and work until I married. I too did not believe that it was possible to combine a career and marriage – how old-fashioned! – but as I was sure no one would want to marry me, I thought I would have a career. I wanted to be a writer – and still do.

Rachel Lockey [born 1967]

I am the youngest of five children and my parents are from Newcastle. I was brought up in Italy and New Zealand because my dad worked for an American company. My parents had come from a working class background but were able to bring us up as a middle-class family. I took my A levels and was then expected to go to university. But I didn't. I had my daughter Bella instead.

Andrea Duffin [born 1970]

I lived with my mum and brother. My dad had left us when I was eighteen months old. We lived just along the road from my Gran and Grandad and they were like second parents; my grandad was like a father figure. We lived in a council house in Fife and my mum never had any money at all. The whole area didn't have any money so it didn't really matter. My mum had to go out to work when I started school. When she had studied at college I went to the creche, I remember that. When I started primary school, she was going to her first job as a typist. My grandparents looked after us after school and I never felt I was missing out or felt upset that she wasn't there all the time. I didn't feel like a latchkey kid, to coin a phrase! I was always proud of her going to work, struggling to look after us with so little money.

Then mum remarried when I was about ten and we moved to another house because my stepfather had two other children. We didn't really get on at all. I remember being so happy until I was ten and then things changed so much and I was very unsettled.

When I was a teenager I felt rejected because of me not getting on with my stepdad; this upset my mum and all that. I rebelled a bit, staying out late, and coming back a bit drunk. I dyed my hair red and blue and I was always generally making a nuisance of myself in front of mum – just to get attention I suppose. We had a lot of conflict plus we had very different ideas about lifestyle. She wasn't willing to accept my views and I couldn't accept hers. We fell out and I went to live with my gran for a year.

I sat my O levels and although I stayed on to sixth form, I bungled my Highers and decided to leave school. I did have high aspirations for myself – I did want to go to university to study English or go to art college, but I never had the confidence to carry it through. I just gave it all up, what with the stress at home and everything. But it was something my mum and I had always presumed I would do, to study something. I had no plans when I left school and my mum wasn't pleased. I had no idea what I wanted to do. So I had to go on a Youth Training scheme and I asked if I could work with children, so I helped out at the local school. I also had to go to college once a week, but they began with the one times table, and I thought 'What is this all about? I am not thick'.

So I gave up the college part of it, as I wasn't learning anything, and then they chucked me out of the YTS, which was a shame because I really enjoyed working with children. So then I looked around for a nanny's job and I loved that, living on a farm, looking after two little boys. I never thought much about having children of my own until I cared for these boys, but I realised then how much I enjoyed looking after little children. I had always thought I would have a career and ignored the prospect of marriage or babies.

CHAPTER TWO

———•◆•———

Relationships, Marriage and Family Planning

'*The only secure basis for a present-day State is the welding of its units in marriage. Today marriage is far less really happy than its surface appears. Too many who marry expecting joy are bitterly disappointed and the demand for freedom grows. It is never easy to make marriage a lovely thing: and it is an achievement beyond the powers of the selfish or the mentally cowardly. Knowledge is needed and, as things are at present, knowledge is almost unobtainable by those who are most in want of it. I have some things to say about sex which, so far as I am aware, have not yet been said, things which seem to be of profound importance to men and women who hope to make their marriages beautiful.*'

Marie Stopes, MARRIED LOVE dedicated to young husbands and all those who are betrothed in love. [1918]

———•◆•———

Married Love was an immediate and influential success. It sold 2,000 copies in the first fortnight, and over 400,000 in the next five years. It was later regarded as among the twenty-five most influential books of its time and continued to be used as a source of advice on marriage well into the 1950s.

Violet Stevenson-Hamilton [born 1902]

We sort of had boyfriends only after we left school. I would stay with relatives during holiday periods and long weekends when one would be introduced to suitable young men, and I eventually met one whom I married after I'd finished my nursing training. I married in 1924 and looked forward to having two children comfortably spaced. Marie Stopes in her widely read *Marriage and Parenthood* booklets gave us every encouragement to plan and control our child-bearing. Her's was really the only sex education book available, so we read it. There may have been improper books but they didn't come our way in those days. However, contraceptives were not reliable. Condoms were known as French Letters and were clumsy and off-putting to use, while the Dutch cap required a high degree of internal manipulation. These methods were not inducive to sexual pleasure.

I had my first baby within the first year, and a second and third child within five years.

———•———

'Marie Stopes described Married Love as "crashing into English society like a bombshell . . . its explosively contagious main theme that woman has the same reciprocal need for enjoyment and benefit from sex union in marriage distinct from the experience of maternal functions – made Victorian husbands gasp." Stopes was a rationalist and a proselytiser. She deployed the authority of science to divide sex from procreation, to enshrine mutual sexual pleasure, and to counter ignorance, particularly about female sexuality. She launched a campaign to make birth control respectable, and to alleviate the poverty and suffering women experienced through excessive and involuntary childbearing. She embarked on her work in the spirit of a moral crusade to improve women's lives and their rights in marriage and as mothers.'

Kate Haste, RULES OF DESIRE.

———•———

'22 March 1921

Dear Dr. Stopes.
I read about the Mother's Clinic that you have opened. What I would like to know is how I can save having any more children as I think that I have done my duty to my Country having had thirteen children, 9 boys and 4 girls.'

'B Castle, Scotland
August 3 1930

Dear Marie Stopes,
I have among my tenants a woman who at the age of thirty-four is the mother of six children. Just recently, a serious miscarriage has nearly cost her her life. Her doctor will not tell her of anything to avoid pregnancy. Her husband does not consider her position, as she would wish. I would like to be able to advise her by your help so she could look forward to a happy future without the constant dread which has always been before her.

Yours truly, Miss SB'

Ruth Hall [ed], DEAR DR. STOPES.

Janet Stewart [born 1904]

I married at the age of 29 and had our first child the next year. It just happened really, unplanned and unexpected. I was ignorant of the facts of life and contraception.

Susan Curtis [born 1905]

I was engaged to be married but this was broken off as I met my future husband – although marriage was not immediately possible. I married at the age of 31 and I had my first baby at 32. I was reasonably intelligent about contraception although I had no help from my parents. I had picked up bits and pieces from life at boarding school. Our reason for starting a family immediately was because we wanted children.

Margaret Dixon [born 1905]

My aspiration as a school leaver was to marry and have a family. I married at 28 and had our first child when I was 32. I had an adequate knowledge of birth control when I married. It was certainly seen as a custom to have children and my view is most people don't like children until you have some yourself!

'By the thirties birth control became more respectable after a ten year campaign by Marie Stopes. In 1924 the Worker's Birth Control Group began a campaign to

make birth control a state responsibility. It was led by Labour Party women. Dora Russell, one of its feminist socialist leaders, saw birth control as an issue of women's right to control their lives. Women had a right to decide how many children they should have, and to receive contraceptive advice as an integral part of the state's maternity and child health service.'

Kate Haste, RULES OF DESIRE.

Patricia Rogers [born 1909]

When I was teaching I joined a rambling club and met my husband on one of the weekend outings. He worked for a big furniture company and made long journeys during the week. We would meet up at weekends and go for long walks. It was a romantic five years for me, teaching and making friends. I was engaged for two years – we got engaged when I was 25 and I began to fill my bottom drawer; the other teaching staff embroidered linen for me. Of course I had to relinquish my job when I married. That was the law. Only women teachers in a rural district were allowed if there was no one else available to teach in the local school, but otherwise you had to leave.

We married when I was 27 and we had our first child the following year. I considered a family as the natural and desirable result of married life.

Mary MacLennan [born 1911]

I had lots of boyfriends but I wasn't looking that far ahead towards marriage and a family. We all had lots of friends at university. You didn't get serious at that time, we always went around in a crowd. Because I had been brought up on a farm, I knew a bit about the facts of life, so I wasn't as ignorant as some girls.

Then I met Chris, my husband to be; I think we met at a hockey hop, a dance. I was captain of the women's team and I think he was teaching at the Grammar school in Aberdeen at the time and happened to come along. There was no prospect of me getting a job. I waited at home for a year and there was still no hope of a job, so we decided, well he decided, that we would get married. The 1930s was a dreadful time, with hunger marches, there were no jobs anywhere; it was impossible to get a job, far worse than it is now. It was hopeless.

So we got married when I was about twenty-one; it was common then to marry quite young because if one person had a job, well there wasn't much point waiting until I found work because it would likely be nowhere near where he was living.

———◆———

'The 1930s were a lean time for women. There were not enough jobs for men, let alone women so they were encouraged to remain at home, firmly tied by their own apron strings. Although some girls were going into professional life, mostly as teachers, it was more important to be able to hold elegant conversations, based on a sound education, to play a useful voluntary role, or to dish out low budget meals for the family. Like their mothers and grandmothers, they were trained to be adaptable seconds-in-command, but the crusading zeal that had surrounded the early years of girls' schooling was missing.'

Angela Holdsworth, OUT OF THE DOLL'S HOUSE.

———◆———

Eileen Watkins [born 1912]

My husband and I were married with all the trappings on a lovely June day in 1939, the reception being in my home. He was 28 and I was 26. We had been acquainted for about five years, 'going steady' for about two to three years, and officially engaged for nine months. Since 1937 I had lived at home with my parents having given up work to be a companion to my mother.

Attitudes in those days were very different from those prevailing today. For instance my mother once said to me that she would rather see me dead in my coffin than the mother of an illegitimate baby! I trust she didn't really mean it – it was in the nature of an Awful Warning! – but I am and always have been of the opinion that chastity before marriage and faithfulness within it is the only way to live. This is the Christian ethic in which my husband and I were both brought up, and to which we have adhered in faith ever since, for 54 years of happy married life.

Alice Wands [born 1912]

I finished my general nursing and midwifery training at the end of 1936 and got a job as a theatre sister in a private nursing home. When war broke out I was on the territorial list and I got my papers at three o'clock in the morning of September 3rd. So of course there was no question of marriage then, although there were plenty of opportunities. I was a

Queen Alexandra Sister and went over with the British Expeditionary Force to France, where we had a tented hospital. Belgium was invaded and the Nazis came flooding in and we received orders to get out as quickly as possible. So we were evacuated and later on we got orders to be sent to Greenock and then out to the Middle East, where we had a tented hospital on the banks of the Suez Canal. We got a lot of nasty casualties from tanks and filled up pretty quickly. After six months we set off to Java but had to travel on to Ceylon because Singapore fell to the Japs. I then worked for a time in Poona and Bangalore in India. More diseases there than wounds – malaria, dysentery, things like that. Some of us were sent up to the North-West Frontier, and that is where I met my husband.

He was in the army and there was a very large training camp for officers. So we met there – social life was pretty good at the club and there were always dances and gatherings. We married but he wasn't stationed there very long before he went south. Later on I was transferred back to Bangalore and we were very happy there. By then I was getting a bit tired of being in the army; if I went north, my husband was posted south. It was so very awkward and we didn't see a lot of each other in India. It was quite a short courtship really but there were a lot of wartime marriages and we thought [married life] would go on for ever and ever, blissfully happy with no ups and downs. Of course there were a lot. Quite a lot of girls got married out there and of course the choice of men, as you can imagine, was pretty wide! I told my parents I was going to get married and by then I was thirty so there was nothing they could do.

Emily Heggie [born 1912]

I joined the police force in London in January 1940 and I was there for three years. It was interesting, plenty of bombs. I was working in Kennington, Southwark and Tower Bridge. We dealt with children quite a bit as that was a policewoman's work in those days. We worked with the NSPCC a lot of the time, caring for children. I had known my future husband, a policeman, for three years before it became serious. One day he said to me, 'What would you say if I said I was getting married?' I said 'I wouldn't like it very much.' Some days later he rang me up at two in the morning when I was working night duty at Southwark, and he said, 'Shall we get married?' I said, 'Yes, please', and that was that: we married in 1943.

━━━◆━━━

'*Parental control of women's behaviour was backed by the threat of social ostracism for transgressions. Ignorance was widespread among the working class, and sex was still obscured by secrecy and taboo. Unmarried sex was wrong and it wasn't talked about.*

'*Parents controlled their daughter's movements and their choice of partner and expected to meet their young men within the first few weeks. This did not stop courting couples meeting secretly, but the unspoken social rules on women who went the whole way were strong. It was part of the code accepted by both sexes that women risked losing respect if they gave in to male demands.*'

Kate Haste, RULES OF DESIRE.

━━━◆━━━

Nancy Beaty [born 1914]

When I was growing up I was told very little about sexual matters. My aunts told me not to have sex before marriage; the rest I learnt from friends. It was never discussed in the open and contraception was a dirty word and not for single girls.

I married a farmer's son in February 1936, when I was 21, and we moved out to our own farm where we had cattle. This was at Bewcastle, on the Scottish Borders, a deserted place, quite outlandish. There was just the church, a little pub and farm houses around. We had to travel nineteen miles to Brampton for food but in those days there were vans distributing bread and groceries round the farms. The farm was very, very old, with no electricity and just one cold water tap. Water was heated on the old black range. When the fire was on, the boiler heated the water and that was the only hot water we had to wash all the nappies and everything. There was no bathroom – just an outside toilet. It was a lovely old house, old stone steps up to the bedrooms, little windows, thick walls and a huge dairy. There was no fridge, of course, no Hoover or washing machine. All washing was done by hand. It was very primitive but we were very happy. The neighbours were lovely people, very friendly, and we all helped each other. We went to dances and had some lovely times.

'I am glad it cannot happen twice, the fever of first love. For it is a fever and a burden too, whatever the poets may say. They are not brave the days when we are twenty one. They are full of little cowardices, little fears without foundation and one is so easily bruised, so swiftly wounded, one falls to the first barbed word.

"I wish" I said savagely, throwing discretion to the wind. "I wish I was a woman of about thirty six dressed in black satin with a string of pearls.".

. . . He felt for the brim of my hat, and took hold of it, throwing it over his shoulder to the back seat, and then bent down and kissed the top of my head. "Promise me you will never wear black satin." I smiled then, and he laughed back at me. . . .

"I've come to say goodbye." I said, "we're going tomorrow morning."

"So Mrs Van Hopper has had enough of Monte Carlo. She to New York and I to Manderley. Which would you prefer? You can take your choice."

"Do you mean you want a secretary or something?"

"No, I'm asking you to marry me, you little fool."

Daphne Du Maurier, REBECCA.

Ethel Hay [born 1914]

I was a very shy, ignorant and innocent young woman. I didn't know anything about anything. The only pleasure in life was going to the pictures. That was my one and only pleasure. To see the romantic scenes. But the romantic scenes then were always at the end of the story, the happy ending. That was your role model. In films you saw how things would happen between men and women. That kiss was the end of the story. I remember one of my friends and I would practice kissing each other. I mean no thought of lesbians or anything – we didn't know about them, but we we wanted to practise kissing before we could find a boy.

I knew one or two folk, but we weren't allowed to have anyone up to the house, bring any friends home or anything like that. We used to go to the park. There was nowhere else to go. I had one or two friends and we went about together for a chat and that was it. Then with one of my friends we knew some lads by this time. It was all so naive. We would go out in two couples, just friends. I would then say to my friend, 'He is no good, let's swap over.' Silly things like that. Nothing serious, just playing about.

But I did get married. Unfortunately I was looking for a father figure

I think. I had known him years and years and years. Anyway, I stupidly agreed to get married, it was at a registry office. I was thirty by this time – perhaps I should have known better, I don't know.

It was all very difficult in those days. People talked about me as if there was something wrong with me, for not marrying earlier. In those days you just didn't sleep with boys, not like nowadays.

The marriage lasted three weeks. I just packed up and went away. I hadn't really known him properly beforehand and then I realised I had made a dreadful mistake. I think I married because I wanted to be looked after and because I had known him all these years and he seemed to be keen on me. We shouldn't have done it. He was looking for a mother figure and I was looking for a father figure so it was no use. I had no sex with him, that was the thing. In those days I was so naive. I did not know that I could get a divorce because the marriage was unconsummated. Anyway he wouldn't divorce me because I left him. I only got divorced thirty years ago, when I was sixty.

Doris Melling [born 1914]

I was married at 22 and we had our first baby, planned after a few months of marriage, when I was 24. I had no knowledge of sexual matters when I married and was rather ignorant of contraception, but my husband was five years older and he knew more about the whole business so that was fine!

'Supposing he had started to have an emission while he was still inside her? Or if he used one of the rubber things and it had broken when she had jerked like that and that was why he had pulled so sharply away? She had heard of the rubber things breaking or leaking and how a woman could get pregnant from just a single drop.

"Dick," and she shut her eyes in shame, "Do you think I should take a douche?" "A douche?" he repeated in a mystified tone. "Why? What for?" "Well in case . . . you know . . . birth control," murmured Dottie. Dick stared at her and suddenly burst out laughing. He dropped on to a straight chair and threw his handsome head back. "My dear girl," he said, "we just employed the most ancient form of birth control. Coitus interruptus, the old Romans called it."

Mary McCarthy, THE GROUP.

Mary McKerrow [born 1915]

I went to university in 1934 and it just happened that someone else was doing a science degree; we lived close by and travelled on the same bus each day. This was my future husband, Sandy. I left university in 1937 and he stayed on to do his MSc. I had various jobs working as a medical secretary and then a school secretary until the war broke out and I joined the WAAFS. Sandy and I were still very friendly during this period. During my leave we visited each other but it was very difficult to decide to settle down and marry. You had to find a house or somewhere to live, which wasn't easy. Financially things were very tight. In the WAAFs I got £2.10s a fortnight and Sandy was earning just a bit more than that. But we found a little place we could rent and we married in 1943. It was very much a case of being thrown in at the deep end. I was not a housewife, by any means, and we had a lot to do: decorating, finding our way. We had very little furniture. No bedroom curtains for a long time, because of war rations. You had to use your coupons for getting material. Most of our furniture came from our kind families or was second-hand. But we were very happy.

Emily Hagues [born 1916]

I had a few boyfriends beforehand, you know, but I was twenty-five when I got married. My birthday was on the 14th and I was married on the 18th August 1941. I was a house table maid, living with Dr and Mrs Duffy at the time. I got married from their house and a year and a half later I became pregnant. My mother had told me nothing about sex and having babies and all that. I remember on my honeymoon in the morning there was this mess of blood, that shook me! I can't remember what I thought about it at the time but I just remember being frightened about that. It wasn't very pleasant, I can tell you. The next time was much better, you know. When you think back, you wonder what you did think about it all. I didn't know anything before I married.

Elizabeth Grey [born 1917]

I never much worried about marriage. I was thirty when I did marry and thirty-two when I had my first baby. I didn't really think about it much when I was younger. I was never running after folk to get a man. I was engaged two or three times, but I got fed up with them. I don't like people telling you what to do, or who think that they are better than you are. I always had answers for them. I think it was because we had no brothers that my sisters and I believed we were as bold as the boys. We were as good as any of them, we stood on our own two feet. We knew lots of boys in the town, but the man I married was in the army, and was twelve years older than me. His sister and I had gone to school together. He had been in the hospital, where I worked, and we thought we would get married.

Experiences
Some men break your heart in two,
Some men fawn and flatter,
Some men never look at you:
And that cleans up the matter.

Dorothy Parker

Lucy Firth [born 1917]

I married at the age of twenty-three in 1941, knowing very little about sexual matters or birth control. Fortunately I married a pharmacist who was rather better informed! I was unaware that men had testicles, being a nicely-brought up girl and only having a sister. I had never seen a man undressed before I married.

Mary Sparrow [born 1921]

I was working as a clerical officer in the Ministry of Transport in London from January 1939 to October 1940, and then I transferred to the Admiralty, Bath, where I worked until March 1945, when I left to be married. I was very happy in the office, being involved in work about ships in the war, but happy to get out and marry.

I married when I was twenty-three. We did want a family but our three girls really arrived unplanned. We tried the rhythm method of contraception, which didn't work as I was so irregular. After the third child the family planning clinic advised a diaphragm. It was all very hush-hush. Only my husband and I knew and I never told my parents or any friends. If we had a baby-sitter in while we went to the clinic, we pretended we were going out for a meal. It was something no one talked about.

We didn't receive any knowledge of sex or facts of life from school or parents, apart from biology lessons, which I think stopped at frogs. My husband and I obtained quite good books which gave us the basics, and we were very much in love and have had a very happy sexual relationship for nearly fifty years. Our parents never discussed sex even after we were married. I do remember that when my father lived with us he used to listen to the radio, and one day there was a programme about the Pill and he said he didn't think it was suitable for me to listen to this. He was then 74 and I was 39, with three daughters aged 14, 12 and 10. I was most amused.

'The Birth Control clinics met with considerable official opposition and even in the late 1930s still only a quarter of all local authorities provided parents with information about contraception, fearing that greater knowledge of birth control would encourage immorality, liberate women from their "duties" as mothers, and reduce the fertility rate in Britain to such an extent that there would be a population crisis.'

Steve Humphries and Pamela Gordon, A LABOUR OF LOVE.

Jean Charleson [born 1922]

I had served as an apprentice in the printing trade and, when I was eighteen and the war broke out, I went to work in the Naafi offices in Colinton, Edinburgh. I was there for a while and then my friend Greta and I, without my mother's permission, went to the offices in George Street and joined the WAAF. And I was in the services for four and a half years. The years before the war were really happy times. We went dancing and enjoyed ourselves as young girls. And then I met Jack just after the war broke out. He went overseas almost immediately and I was later in the WAAF. He came back just before VE day, 1945, and we got married that very week he came back and I hadn't seen him for four and a half years! I don't why we were rushing all this, why we didn't wait a few months and get to know each other again. But mother arranged this quite big wedding, with all her relatives and all Jack's family – about a hundred at the wedding I think there were. There was the business of coupons for food so mother had a lot of trouble trying to find extra coupons, and father was out there trying to get bottles of whisky under the counter, things like that for this wedding.

So it was a strange kind of courtship, of course. Well, we didn't really have much of a courtship at all. I had only known Jack such a short time and then he went away. He just seemed to come into my life and then went out of my life. But we wrote to each other. We wrote a letter to each other every day. So I felt I knew him very well through the letters. I think we wrote to each other solidly for four and a half years. We had little airmail letters, aerographs I think they were called, which you got from the post office. I can't remember if they were free or not, but they didn't cost that much, that's for sure. They were for the forces, and they were very small – you could only write about twenty lines on it and then you sent it off. And he would send me long letters, and then not long after he had gone abroad, he wrote to say he wanted to be engaged. I suppose it was one way of ensuring he tied me up [so I] waited for him! Of course, when I joined the WAAF he was not very pleased and that was a bit of a stumbling block, but he got over that. After four and a half years he came back on leave and we decided to get married. Jack had been so full of this in his letters, that we would marry whenever he came back. I was up north in Fraserburgh, stationed at the time, and I got leave as well. We had to borrow a white wedding dress, and my girl friend, Greta, was there. Our best man, who was in the Royal Scots, had to come home on leave, and so they were all in uniform. I remember we stayed at the Tartan Hotel in Royal Terrace on our first night, and I found the receipt a few months ago. It cost us twenty-one shillings for the night, for the two of us! Then we went on a little honeymoon to Northumberland.

I often wonder – it just seemed right at the time, but looking back I'm sure we should have taken more time, to get to know each other. 'Why didn't we wait until his next leave, what was the rush?', but we didn't wait. We just swanned off and got married. And of course it was our fiftieth wedding anniversary in June this year.

Joyce Petchey [born 1922]

Neither my husband nor I considered any relationship outside marriage. We were engaged for eighteen months before we married when I was 26. We had our first baby a year later.

Pamela Worthington [born 1923]

I married at the age of nineteen and our first baby, unplanned but very welcome, was born when I was twenty-one. Looking back I was somewhat uninformed about the facts of life at the time! I did have an abortion once we had three children, who I felt were enough to care for and educate properly.

Jane Ward [born 1924]

Planning a family in 1950! We were engaged for nearly three years, and by the time we married I was 25 and my husband 29. Our first baby was born the following year. I probably knew more about sexual matters than most as I had been in the army for three and a half years, but I knew nothing of contraception. There was never any question of family planning. When I married I had every intention of having a baby and I was never going to put any child of mine through the sort of life I had led, being an only child, and, in any event, I looked forward to having my husband's children.

———◆———

'My prime destiny was to look after a husband and children and knowing how to cook and wash up was far more important than anything I might learn at school. Birth control was a veiled secrecy and was not part of either school or home education; [in fact I came to conclusion that my mother scarcely knew a thing about it herself, other than that it did not work.] It became clear to me that I was a new sort of woman, quite unlike my mother's generation. I had intellect, I had ambition, and I had no intention of turning into a domestic drudge'.

Eva Figes, A CERTAIN AGE.

———◆———

Davina Thorpe [born 1927]

I married at twenty-one and had my first baby eleven months later. I think I knew about the facts of life when I married – I had done Red Cross classes and worked as a volunteer at the hospital – but contraception was pretty well unheard of. I remember my eldest daughter telling me that I hadn't told her anything about this side of life. In fact, I had told her more than I had known myself until I married.

Barbara Henderson [born 1931]

My mother was seventeen when I was born and thereafter practised breast feeding birth control. She couldn't understand why it never worked for me but whereas she never menstruated when she breast fed, I menstruated regardless. After four more children, my mother fell pregnant again when she was thirty-nine, after I had had my first child. She blamed that on the fact that my father then started to claim his rights again.

I married a farm worker when I was seventeen. We were informed about contraception to a certain extent, but we took risks and wanted to start a family. My husband and I were sexually attracted to each other and wanted children. Large families were the norm in those days; my husband was number six of a family of twelve and the government was encouraging large families after the war losses. We had seven children and after the last baby, I was sterilised. This was regarded as a sin at the time and I really had to push the medical authorities to have it done.

'Contraceptives. It is the days before the pill. Babies are part of sex. Rumours abound. Diaphragms give you cancer. Marie Stopes says soak a piece of sponge in vinegar and shove it up.

There is a birth control clinic down in the slums. You have to pretend to be married. They ask you how often you have intercourse – be prepared. They say it's for their statistics, but it's probably just to catch you out.

Every month comes waiting time; searching for symptoms. How knowledgeable we are. Bleeding can be, often is, delayed by the anxiety itself. We know that. It's the fullness of the breasts, the spending of pennies in the night, the being sick in the mornings, you have to watch out for.

Try hot baths and gin. There's an abortionist down the Fulham Road does it for £50. But where is £50 going to come from? Who does one know with £50? No one.'

Fay Weldon, DOWN AMONG THE WOMEN.

Sheila Brown [born 1934]

I had made up my mind as a young girl, that I didn't want to marry too young for some reason or another. I wanted to see a bit of the outside world and not always be stuck in my little town of Peterhead. However this was not to be. I met Ian when I was eighteen, at the students' union in Aberdeen. I was rather innocent and I think I knew less about the facts of life and all that than I believed I did. But I got by, the same as the rest of my friends. I had no truck with sex before marriage. I used to say to any boyfriends who – how shall I say it? – had wandering hands, I would say, 'No, a little ring here is what is wanted before I do anything like that'. However that was never the case with Ian. We got engaged and then six months later we got married when I was twenty; we had our first baby at twenty-one.

Now there was an element of selfishness in me. Being an only child and having the advantage of more or less getting what I wanted, I suppose I was selfish. And from the day I got engaged, I was so excited, just absolutely over the moon, I knew this was what I really wanted in life. We were studying for exams at nursing school and I simply could not concentrate on the lectures because I kept looking at my little ring here. I was so thrilled. It cost £25 and I think Ian had to borrow £12 from his father to buy it. I think it is worth about £300 now.

As I say, I was terribly excited getting engaged so I left my nursing course. Ian was doing his National Service in Derby and I just up-tailed and left, much to my mother's horror and disgust because I hadn't finished my training. There was still six months to go before the final examinations. That took quite a bit of forgiving and I think it was the only time in my life that I had actually displeased them, you know, to do something very much against their wishes. Mind you we were happy, and this year we will have been married for forty years, so there you go.

Liz Sanderson [born 1938]

I was sent to boarding school from the age of eleven to seventeen and was certainly expected to earn my own living and train for some kind of career. Since hospitals fascinated me and I also loved using my hands, in those days – 35 years ago – occupational therapy was very much a craft and science career. So I started at the Astley Ainslie Hospital, in Edinburgh, living in the hostel in Morningside, thinking, 'This is me for the next three years.' But I got engaged after a year and gave up my course after two terms – I was what they termed 'marriage wastage' – and came to live in the Borders. In those days it was quite the norm to give up a career and get married as marriage was the next career. Now it seems very odd I think, but in those days my mother took the view that anything you learned would never be wasted and if you found a nice young man to marry, fair enough.

I was married at twenty and had my first child at twenty-one. We had four children so that I had completed my family by the time I was thirty.

Jennifer Manning [born 1944]

I had my first baby unexpectedly, when I was 19 and single; I was not very aware of sex and contraception at the time. I then married when I was 23 and was a little more informed by then. My second child was planned after a few years of marriage.

'He said again, his eyes trying to meet hers: "We're just the best friends in the world, aren't we?"

"That's right, Rowley. Best pals in all the world, we are darling." Knowing then, with pain like sudden blindness, that he didn't want to be friends – knowing that what he wanted was something else, but no responsibility. Just why is it so appallingly difficult to get what one really wants from life? Selfish swine, men were.

"I'm going to have a baby," she told him, without preamble.

"Not mine?" There was a glory and an intimacy alive now in his voice.

"No, oh no!" Mary lied primly.

Molly Keane, TAKING CHANCES.

Vivienne Leighton [born 1947]

I went to work as a medical laboratory scientific officer when I was eighteen and I worked there for seven years. At school I never really thought about marriage or having a family. I met my husband when I was about twenty-one and we got married in August 1971, when I was twenty-three. Even then, we never discussed the prospect of having a family – and in fact we were careful about contraception from the start. Because my sister had been on the Pill and had developed thrombosis, I decided not to have anything to do with the Pill at all. You see my sister died when she was twenty-three. It was a deep vein thrombosis; a blood clot developed in her leg and part of this went to her lungs. She couldn't breathe and she had a venous coronary. She was taken ill on the Thursday night and died on the Friday. It was so very quick and a terrible, terrible shock. And the cause we believe was because she had taken the contraceptive pill.

I took advice from a consultant in the hospital and he suggested I had a Dalcon shield put in – a contraceptive device, shaped like a flat fish, plastic with hooks on the side. He did say there was a slight risk of becoming pregnant because my uterus hadn't reached its proper shape. It was seen as 99% protection with a 1% chance that I *could* become pregnant. And so our first child was an accident in a way. My son was born in September 1972 with the Dalcon shield embedded in the placenta. So it happened and the decision to start a family was out of our hands. We had taken precautions but it didn't work. After the shock of becoming pregnant passed – it had been such a surprise – I was very pleased, you know.

Wendy Walker [born 1949]

I left school at fifteen and my ambition was simply to marry and have babies. I am English and married a West Indian man when I was eighteen, although my parents were disgusted that it would be a mixed marriage. My husband's family in the West Indies were very proud. We planned to have a baby straight away. I have always been totally against abortion and contraception all my life although I am not religious.

Mary Law [born 1949]

I married when I was twenty-four. My husband is a primary school teacher and we met at Dundee College of Education, where we were both taking a Diploma in Primary education, and we graduated in the same year, 1974. After three years of marriage we decided to start our family. I felt I had done what I wanted to do for the moment in terms of my career. I was desperate to have a family. Our first baby was born a year later when I was twenty-eight. We now have three children.

Janice Mackenzie [born 1950]

Having completed my teacher training course, I married at the age of twenty-one. We decided to wait a bit – I wanted to have a teaching career before starting a family, and five years later I had a spontaneous abortion when an ovarian cyst was discovered. However I was pregnant again quite soon after, and I had my first baby the following year.

Sheila Gray [born 1951]

I met my future husband when I was eighteen and, because I was far too embarrassed to discuss contraception, I became pregnant. Since he was still a student and we were not ready for family life, I had an abortion. We then married when I was twenty-two and, as my husband was in the oil business, we went out to Brunei. There was no work for me there, or friends, so we decided to have a baby.

Ailsa Gray [born 1953]

A year before my partner and I decided to get married, I found out I was pregnant. We felt very unprepared for this and it would have been a mistake to go through with it at that time, so I had a termination. We married the next year when I was thirty-four and then planned to start a family. We had five children in extremely quick succession: Stuart is five, Laura four, Douglas three, Robert two and Heather a year old.

Liz Hodgson [born 1954]

I started adult life very ignorant of the facts of life and contraception. But during my time working as a bookseller, I became extremely informed with so much access to the right books. It was very much a joint decision a couple of years ago, when my partner and I believed it was the right time for us to try for a child. My partner's mother had recently died and he wanted to continue the love from her. I felt very emotionally drawn by a mother and son I happened to meet at the same time and I wanted what I felt I saw – that image of motherhood – for myself. Our urge to have children had never coincided so cleanly before. I was thirty-nine when I had my baby son, Toby. At my age I doubt whether we will have another child but he is lovely enough!

———— • ————

'In Western culture there is a common assumption that every woman has a right to a child. To deny that right is to take away her freedom. Coupled with this, there is a sense that a woman who has never had a baby must be emotionally unfulfilled, and is therefore less than a woman. Women are under great pressure to bear children.'

Sheila Kitzinger, OURSELVES AS MOTHERS.

———— • ————

Winifred Fyfe [born 1955]

I had a serious relationship for two years when I was nineteen, with a Chinese boy, Ronald. My parents were wonderful, they didn't make any difference at all with him, they liked him. In fact my mother asked if I was on the pill. I remember being quite shocked and I said, 'Mum!' and she said, 'What's wrong? You won't be the first girl to be carried away in a frenzy and you certainly won't be the last.' She was very good, asking about contraception.

I must have been quite prudish really because I remember being at a party with some girls from college when I was about eighteen and they were sitting around talking about being on the pill. I was amazed when I heard they were on the pill but they told me about the family planning clinic around the corner. Well, I was round there the next week to get myself all geared up.

But the relationship with Ronald was doomed from the start because his family were very strict, and so the relationship had to finish after a couple of years and it broke my heart. I was twenty-one by then. He had to go back to China and it really did devastate me. And then just after we separated, I realised my period was late and although I had been on the pill, I was absolutely mortified to find out I was pregnant. He had left by that time and was going back to Hong Kong. He never knew I was pregnant. It was a very sad tale but I had to deal with it because I had no intention of having the baby; I just didn't want it – it was a mistake. I remember feeling very grim during the whole awful business of having to be examined to find out whether I could have an abortion or not. I remember going into this room at the hospital, with this shift on, and the nurse behind me. I hesitated at the door because the room was full of people: the nurse pushed her fist right into the small of my back, pushed me forward, and I had to lie down while all these medical students had a poke and a prod. 'This girl wants an abortion; she says she is only ten weeks pregnant, but she has to be more than that.' But he decided, this awful man with his bifocals on, that I could have an abortion. And I was dreading going into hospital, because I thought they were going to treat me badly – 'I'm in for it, like'. But I went to Foresterhill Hospital in Aberdeen, and the treatment was just wonderful, they really were nice to me.

Motherhood

'It is a favourite saying among women of my type that if men could have babies, then abortion would be as readily available as light ale.'

Angela Carter.

My mother was the first to know in fact. She was a bit upset when I decided to have an abortion and I remember my mum saying the night before, 'You can have the baby'. And my grandmother knew about it and so they both came in to see me afterwards. My mother and grandmother were very supportive.

Looking back I know I could have married him if I really wanted. I think this is why it is so dangerous for girls of that age getting involved, because when you do meet someone, he is the first love of your life. He was my first boyfriend, I didn't go out much with boys when I was younger. So I could have married him, but I doubt it would have worked. My mum said a few years after the event, when I'd started going out and enjoying myself more and meeting lots of people, she said, 'Can you see yourself now, standing in a Chinese carryout, washing dishes at the sink with two babies strapped to your back. I canna see it can you?' When she put it like that, I thought no, I can't see it right enough. But at the time I was heartbroken. But I think it all goes to enrich your life. I think every girl should experience that, that feeling of heartbreak. .

I don't regret the abortion at all. When I was over to see my mum a few years ago, she did say to me, 'Sometimes I think about that baby', and I said, 'Well, mum, I don't'. I never think, 'Oh, he or she would have been this age now.' I think I did the right thing and I did get over it. Two of my friends at work knew about it, and we have remained friends for years and they never mention it at all. It's a thing I keep to myself. My husband knows, he knew before we were married. And I'll tell my daughters when they are old enough because I think they should know.

So I had a couple of wild years and it was great and I'm glad I had them. My sister married when she was young and she says, given her experience, she regrets it, and if she had the chance would never do it again. I then met Steve at one of those awful parties where everyone brings their own booze in a bag. Steve and I just seemed to get on and that was it. I lost a leather jacket at that party and never got it back.

I married him about a year later, when I was twenty-three. I'm not sure why really. We didn't have to and, looking back, perhaps we shouldn't have. Our first year of marriage was awful, it was grim. I used to sit on the bed and sulk, and think this is bloody grim this. And he felt the same. I don't know why, we had no reason. Once we got over the first year, we were fine. I think it was me, because I hadn't given myself a chance to heal after my previous relationship. I think it just happened too quickly really. We shouldn't have been in such a rush. I'll often say, 'It was you who wanted to get married', and he'll say, 'No, it was you', and we'll have this argument about it. But anyway, we just went to the registry office and that was it.

I never actually thought I'd ever marry. I remember thinking, 'Oh, no, not for me', but of course I'm not the first woman to say that and I won't be the last. As for children, I hadn't really thought about it at all. It happened quite naturally. My husband never thought he'd be a father and he left the decision up to me and said he'd back me up whatever I chose. We didn't sit down as man and woman saying, 'Let's start a family'. I always find it very strange when men want to have a child because I don't think they are naturally in tune with babies. Well, we'd been married for a year, and again there was no definite sense of 'I want a baby now'. I can honestly say that it was probably the whole social thing, that I was married a couple of years so I'll have a baby. I fell pregnant very easily.

I had been on the contraceptive pill, as my mother had done before me. She began taking it back in 1967, and hid them in the wardrobe so that my father would not know.

'The contraceptive pill influenced the steady loosening of constraints, although it was probably not the only factor and its most dramatic impact on behaviour was in the early 1970s. Attitudes to pre-marital sex were becoming more flexible in the sixties before the pill was widely available to single women. On the market since 1961, its use spread rapidly among married women: by 1968, 28 per cent of women, predominantly middle-class had used the pill, increasing to 75 per cent by 1975, when its use had spread to all classes. It was not so easily available to single women until the Family Planning Act of 1967 when clinics for the first time made no distinction between married and unmarried women. Before then the only sources had been the few Brook Advisory Clinics which after 1964 provided advice to single women over 16. Some Family Planning Clinics continued until 1969 to

provide advice only to married couples, and to engaged couples, if they had a note from the vicar.'

Kate Haste, RULES OF DESIRE.

Jano Rochefort [born 1955]

Having been extremely feminist in my views as a student, adamantly deciding that I would not get married or have children, in fact I married at the age of 22. Well, we all change!

We did plan to have a family but this would not be until I was really ready to settle down as a mother. So it wasn't until I was thirty that I thought the time had come to have a baby.

Roma Young [born 1956]

So instead of art college, I got married instead! It was a whirlwind romance – we met and married within six months; at the time our mums were wondering if it would last, we got that kind of reaction. But it has lasted.

We had thought of having a family, obviously, but it all started accidentally. After the first one came along, we thought we would have them one after the other very quickly and that is what we did. Or rather, thought we did. We had four children in five years, with a miscarriage in the middle. By that time I was twenty-three years old. Then under parental guidance my husband had a vasectomy done, and then later on, under wifely pressure, he had it undone.

So we went on to have Oliver, who is now three, but that was ten years after the last baby. I decided to have another. I became very broody, unbelievably so. I never would have classed myself as broody when I had the first lot of kids, because it was a baby a year, it was just like churning them out, but as your own children are growing older, you begin to miss having a little baby around.

Didi Hopkins [born 1956]

It never occurred to me to do anything else except work and be independent, having been brought up in a single parent family with a working mother. However I did marry, when I was thirty-four.

I had known Oliver as a friend since I was thirteen – in fact my mother and his mother were at school together. I believe we first met when we were four. We drifted apart and met again when we were twenty-four and did a peacock dance around each other. We were a bit on and off for a while. I think I felt I was waiting all my life for the right time to marry him. I looked upon marriage as a liberating experience for me, because I suppose if I hadn't married him, I would be a little worried or anxious that one of us might stray. And for whatever reasons, my profession as an actress, the way I am socially, I do attract men, and I don't want to have to keep saying, 'No, it's not that I don't like you, but I am busy tonight.' I could now say, 'No, sorry, I am married.' Once you are married, men tend to see you as a closed shop. It gives me a firm base, I feel.

The other thing that drew us together was the desire to create a family of our own. Oliver's father had died recently. My mother died six months before that, so within two years of us getting married, we had each lost a parent. Because I had not had a normal family life, Oliver felt I had missed out and that I had not been dealt a good hand of cards in the family stakes, so to speak. Oliver had always wanted us to have a child. The baby was not planned – we were not ever using any contraception – it just happened.

Deborah Holder [born 1959]

At the age of twenty-three I accidentally became pregnant and decided to have an abortion because I was on the verge of starting my degree course, having been out of the country travelling for five years. I suppose at the time I was fairly knowledgeable about the mechanics of sex and contraception, but emotionally inexperienced.

I then had my first child when I was thirty-one; I was unmarried but I just felt the time was right for me as an individual and that I was in a stable relationship with someone who also wanted children. After we had two children, within three years, I became pregnant again but decided to have an abortion because I already had the two children which was enough for the moment, and the relationship was under strain.

———◆———

'Most women decide to have abortions reluctantly and with trepidation, as the lesser of two evils. No woman has an abortion for fun. They do not see why they should take on the responsibility of an unwanted child after the method of contraception has let them down . . . their circumstances – bad housing, lack of money, ill health – are such that they cannot cope with a new baby.'

Joan Smith, MISOGYNIES.

———◆———

Lorna Reid [born 1962]

I had always wanted to have a family but decided to do something with my life first and develop my career. During my ten year relationship with Geoff he used to view marriage as the M word. He couldn't bring himself to face it – he was not somebody who was in favour of marriage at all. That went totally against what I'd always believed in, which was that I didn't want children outwith marriage. So that is why it took us so long, ten years, to get round to thinking about marriage. We got engaged and married, and had a baby straightaway. I was thirty-one when I married. I think that Geoff's attitude stems from the fact that he has been best man to the same chap twice and now this man is on his third relationship. I think he felt that marriage should be for life, yet these days it is so very expendable and he found that very hard to come to terms with. And the thought that if we got married, what if our feelings changed, what would we do? But by the time we got engaged and then knew the baby was coming, it just all seemed like the right thing that could have happened.

My parents were a bit 'iffy' when I began living with Geoff but they liked him a lot; they also knew I was getting older and perhaps I passed a bit of a watershed in my mother's eyes when I got beyond the age she was when she married, twenty-four. So when I reached twenty-four she reckoned I was old enough to make up my own mind. After that, if she didn't approve, she didn't say so although she might occasionally say, 'Well, I was married by that time'.

———◆———

When Zoya met Vladimir he was stunned. Or well, at least pleasantly surprised. And wanted to see Zoya very often. But not constantly. And that saddened her.

Zoya stuck her photograph into Vladimir's wallet: whenever he reached for his train pass or money, he'd see her, so beautiful, and cry, "Ah, why don't I marry her?"

She wanted to be married before she hit twenty five – it was all over by then, no more youth, you lose your place in the queue, and others run to take your place: swift and curly haired. In the mornings they drank coffee. Zoya was hostilely silent, staring at his forehead, sending telepathic messages: marry, marry, marry, marry me!

Tatyana Tolstaya, HUNTING THE WOOLLY MAMMOTH.

———◆———

Carol Ziyat [born 1962]

When I was twenty-six I became pregnant just before leaving London to live in Amsterdam with my boyfriend. We decided this was not the best time to have a child so I had a termination. We then did get married when I was 29 although we didn't plan to start a family immediately. Our first baby was born three years later when I felt 'ready' for motherhood.

Angela Blanchard [born 1962]

After cohabiting for two and a half years, and at the end of my final degree year, I married at the age of twenty-two. My husband and I both envisaged having children but it was always something we would do 'in a couple of years', and of course we would never have been ready. It is such a momentous decision to make! What happened in the end is that I came off the combined pill, after three years of marriage, for health reasons, and we used the sheath instead but increasingly took risks and eventually got caught out.

It's funny really, I had started a new, promising job three months previously and thought myself terribly important when I had my first business meeting ever in London. In fact I was so carried away that when it was fixed for January 10th, it did not occur to me that it was my husband's birthday. I duly went to London for the meeting and felt so guilty that I missed a train trying to buy my husband a lavish and unsuitable present, and rather than wait till the cheap rate trains later in the evening, paid double fare to travel at peak time to Leeds, and found I'd just missed the local train, so paid almost as much again for a taxi to our village some thirty miles away so that I would be home in time to go out for dinner.

We went out to a local wine bar, drank a lot, and went home to make love. Because I felt so guilty about messing up my husband's birthday, I did not insist he use a sheath even though I knew we were pushing our luck. When I started suffering from morning sickness, a few weeks later, I had no idea what was the matter with me!

———◆———

'Of course there's no need to worry. Six, seven days late. I am worried. But it's happened once before; the first year Ivor and I were married, over a week then. I was beginning to be sure – but it was a false alarm. . . . That was in August too,

so I expect it's the time of year. I'm sure I've heard it does happen sometimes. Falling for one, Mrs Banks calls it. "When I fell for our Doris. . . ."

I feel a bit sick. Train-sick, I expect. I've never been train-sick in my life. This morning when I got up, suddenly retching as I began to wash. Nerves. Lying down like this I feel fine. Be all right tomorrow. Sleep. Thank God for lying down, a sleeper to myself. Supposing I'm sick when I get up tomorrow? That would clinch it. No, it wouldn't. A long journey like this often upsets people.'

Rosamund Lehmann, THE WEATHER IN THE STREETS.

Rachel Lockey [born 1967]

I couldn't say my baby was planned – that I had decided to have a baby – or that it was an accident. I was eighteen and involved with this guy who was my boyfriend. We were both doing voluntary work in Africa. It was very exciting there, and I think being away from home I felt very free and confident with myself and when I became pregnant I was very happy. But it was my decision to be a single parent. I couldn't see how this teenage relationship was one that I could have forever.

So after I knew I was pregnant I took myself off for a few days to think what I would do and I decided to keep the baby. I thought about abortion, it was a choice between abortion and keeping the baby – I felt adoption would be too difficult for me. Deep down, I do believe I allowed myself to become pregnant. It was really exciting. I couldn't do it now, but then at eighteen, it was what I wanted. I was very idealistic and it was a side of me that I wanted to explore.

I was very much into being a woman and I saw it as a very feminine thing I wanted to experience – it was a challenge for me.

CHAPTER THREE

———•———

Pregnancy

To Expectant Mothers

*'One of the most wonderful things in life is to be the strong and healthy mother
of a strong and healthy baby. If expectant mothers will take reasonable care of
themselves, they will be able to lessen or remove most of the dangers of childbirth,
and will save the lives of thousands of children. Of every thousand children born,
a hundred die in the first year of life. Expectant mothers must have plenty of simple
nourishing food. Meat should be taken once a day, but green vegetables, peas,
beans, brown bread, cheese and milk puddings are useful foods. Fresh fruit and
oatmeal porridge help to keep the bowels regular. Plenty of fresh water is good to
drink, also milk and cocoa but tea in moderation. Beer and spirits should not be
taken. The expectant mother should wear clothes that do not fasten by tight bands
round the waist, but which hang from the shoulders. She ought to do no heavy
work during the last month of pregnancy, but light home duties are not harmful.
Eight hours sleep at night is needed by every pregnant woman. She should also
lie down for at least half an hour in the middle of the day.'*

Association of Infant Welfare, TO WIVES AND MOTHERS, 1917.

———•———

Susan Curtis [born 1905]

There were no antenatal classes in my day. This was in 1939 and I had
excellent doctors and intelligent friends [one is still extant at 84]. I never
smoked during pregnancy and had no medical tests for abnormalities.

Eileen Brown [born 1908]

There was little advice for pregnant women. I just visited my GP from time to time to check all was well. Perhaps it was all just treated as very natural in those days and doctors and hospitals were not involved as if we were ill.

Patricia Rogers [born 1909]

I think antenatal classes were limited in the 1930s but more information and meeting other women was certainly helpful. I don't remember any organised classes or anything. I had check-ups. With my third baby, I was worried because it felt peculiar. My mother had four children and she thought she was pregnant with a fifth when she was thirty-two. But it was a growth, and because everything was much more serious in those days, and the state of medical treatment wasn't the same, she was a month in hospital. She had a hysterectomy to remove the growth – and she was only thirty-two.

So when I felt this lump and I knew this pregnancy did not feel normal as the previous two, I told my doctor. She said it would be very bad luck indeed if I had the same as my mother. So I was X-rayed, and they thought it was twins. It was Christmas Eve and they were thinking I was expecting twins! But actually it was a breech baby. I knew it had felt different. I had no other tests as such when I was pregnant, although I had an examination before marriage to check that all was in order, that I'd be able to have children, following a worrying experience by the wife of a pharmacist friend.

Peggy Wilson [born 1911]

Before my daughter was born in 1934, my husband and I, both actors, were working in repertory in Plymouth. I was able to work on and off till a few weeks before she was born, mostly in costume drama and, finally, in a play in which I was only seen in the dock, draped in fox furs, being tried for murder.

Antenatal classes or exercises were unknown, I had no relatives around, so my pregnancy was advice-free, except for two suggestions from a woman's magazine. Hot lemonade made with half a lemon was recommended before getting out of bed, to avoid morning sickness. This provided vitamin C of which I had then no knowledge. I also ate a lot of small herrings, costing four a penny, brought to our door on a handcart.

An excellent diet, [eggs for breakfast, meat and two veg and puddings] could be provided for eight shillings a head. The other magazine tip was to rub my tum with olive oil to avoid stretch marks. It worked.

May Stephen [born 1911]

Our babies were not exactly planned – to tell you the truth, it was difficult. There were no tampons in my day; we just had towels and because it was found I had a very tough hymen, the marriage was not consummated for about a month. Girls these days using tampons usually break the hymen. We hadn't had intercourse before marriage so I didn't know there was a problem. We got engaged when I was twenty-one, and weren't able to get married, because of our careers, until I was twenty-seven. My granddaughter is so surprised at this. She says she has a boyfriend now and knows they wouldn't wait until marriage, as we had done, without really loving each other. It is so different now.

Anyway we married in September 1938 and Ruth was born in February 1940. When we discovered that Ruth was deaf at fourteen months – we had suspicions before then, but we knew now definitely – we blamed the birth, the forceps, the blackout and conditions in the hospital when she was born. It was not known in those days that German measles during pregnancy might cause deafness or blindness. I had had German measles a few months before, but I hadn't really felt ill and we had no idea how dangerous it was. And my husband is a doctor, a surgeon. It wasn't until Ruth was five, when an epidemic of deafness in babies in Australia was connected with an outbreak of German measles a year before, [that] the whole thing came out. In America they began aborting babies if women had had German measles during pregnancy.

Eileen Watkins [born 1912]

I became pregnant within a year of marriage. We had hoped for children straightaway and allowed it to happen. I don't think there were any antenatal classes in those days, the 1930s, and I remember going to my doctor when I was two months pregnant and he said to come back in seven months time. I read a book about what to do in pregnancy but otherwise carried on normally.

Ethel Hay [born 1914]

I was told many times I was frigid and so on. I suppose after I left my husband, three weeks after the marriage, I got paranoid about it. Anyway there was this one man after that I went out with, and I liked him. He was very kind to me even though I wouldn't agree to go with him. So in the finish we had sex once. You may not believe me but to me it was loathsome. The actual intercourse, the experience. I had been brought up that you didn't let anyone touch you. I never had anyone touch me or even kiss me when I was young. It was incredible but that is what happened. I didn't know anything about it. He was supposed to have used a sheath or something but I don't think he did. I fell pregnant after that one time.

I had known him a little while. He had wanted to go with a married woman because there would be no comeback on him. He knew I was still married but not living with my husband. I didn't want a child. I just wanted to know that I was a normal woman who could go with a man.

When I knew I was going to have a baby I was just stunned and I went to the doctor to prove it. I didn't want it and somebody told me to throw myself down the stairs to lose it. But to me that was wrong. It was abhorrent and if it is there, it will have to be there.

I just thought this was meant to be. I had to have the baby. I couldn't get rid of it. The baby was born early. I wasn't going to have her adopted either; it was meant to be, for me to have her. The father had disappeared and he didn't want anything to do with me. He knew I was expecting his baby but that didn't do any good. He just said I was the wrong person for him, and I just didn't know any better. Nowadays they grab the fathers and make them pay for it.

'She hated her motherhood. Motherhood that was thrust cruelly upon her while she was still a child. Motherhood, robbed of its honour and covered with shame; motherhood and its pains stripped of the love that makes its agony a glory. This was the motherhood Bella knew, and her head was bitter against it. She felt trapped.'

' "I have no call to shelter a wanton and unrepentant woman; if Bella Tocher is minded to face the elders and made admission o' her sins . . .'

"Her sins!" Jessie broke in. "It's no' her sins Drummorty is punishing her for; it's the evidence. It's the bairn. There's them that ken more o' sin than Bella Tocher, but they dinna get found out; their sillar in the collection plate blinds the minister." '

Lorna Moon, THE SINNING OF JESSIE MACLEAN.

Constance Küenssberg [born 1911, student Doctor in Edinburgh 1936–37]

Abortion was illegal, a criminal act, and that was quite firm. There were always police on the watch to see that doctors were not practising as abortionists. Also any discussion of contraception was seen as infradig, taboo. There was still very little precaution available. When we were studying medicine, the only contraceptive advice we had was from a lecturer in public health. The lectures in midwifery and gynaecology did not mention a word so if we as doctors were fairly ignorant, pity the poor women. We were shown a display of what looked like sweets – fancy little things that the women inserted before intercourse, and decorative condoms with fancy heads on. And of course these got whipped by the students, they proved very useful. But it was only this splendid chap, an ex-army man, who saw fit to give us this information. No-one in midwifery did.

———◆———

'Concern to improve standards of health and the quality of marital life figured in campaigns to liberalize the laws on abortion and divorce. The abortion controversy was prompted by official concern about the role of criminal abortion in the persistence of disturbingly high maternal mortality rates despite improvements in childbirth techniques. This link made by the Ministry of Health in 1930 was strengthened as more shocking evidence of the extent of illegal abortion accumulated. Marie Stopes was fully aware of the scale of demand. In 1932 she published in a letter in The Times the staggering facts that "in three months I have had as many as twenty thousand requests for criminal abortion from women who did not apparently even know it was criminal."

One woman from Preston recalled how common abortion was. "They push needles up. They take washing soda, quinine, all that sort of thing. Mrs Hesketh's mother had nine children and sent her daughter to the chemist for potions. Mrs Dickinson tried to stop one or two – Epsom salts, hot baths, and things like that . . . Everybody tried." '

Kate Haste, RULES OF DESIRE.

———◆———

Joan Counihan [born 1915]

I was having my babies during the war and there were no clinics for pregnant women. I did have German measles during my seventh

— **69** —

pregnancy but this was at the time when the dangers were hardly known. My child was born with no defects, fortunately.

Elizabeth Grey [born 1917]

I never had an unwanted pregnancy – I was of that generation, you just accepted what came along and that was it. When I was pregnant I had a lady doctor who was a good friend. She was so nice. There was no antenatal advice really. But we knew about picking rosehips which were good for babies. We believed in old folklore. What your mother did, we did. Mothers knew best. We didn't have any books or anything; you just seemed to know yourself what to do. You didn't stop and worry about it because even if you were pregnant, you had to get on with the work just the same. Not like a lot of them now, they just sit down all the time. My husband Willie was a painter, and I minded the shop of our painters' business. You just got on with it. Och aye. I remember the Nisbets. They had a farm and a lot of cattle and she had a bairn and was working up to the day it was born and up and away the next day seeing to them, away in the fields. We were all like that. But now they get maternity leave and they even get paid to be off work for six months or whatever it is. We got nothing if you stopped work.

Milicent Woolner [born 1917]

I married at the age of thirty-two and we had decided to have two children but delayed starting a family for a few years because I had a prolapsed disc. As I had trained as a nurse and midwife, I actually taught the parent craft classes as part of my duties in public health work. I attended the antenatal clinic which mostly gave reassurance that all was going well. Since I was thirty-seven when I was expecting my first baby, and forty for my second, I was regarded as an elderly primapara! I had no medical tests done, except the usual blood pressure and urine monitoring. At thirty-six weeks my first baby had to be turned as it was in the breech position.

Joan Hill [born 1920]

We hadn't thought of having a family so soon after marriage but I suppose I was not as well informed as I thought in terms of contraception and so on. I thought I knew it all but found I was woefully ignorant. The pregnancy was unexpected and as my husband was in the army and we were living in digs, it was quite a shock. I don't remember there being any classes for pregnant women, to give advice or anything. I did smoke at the time, as no-one knew the dangers of smoking during pregnancy in the 1940s. I had married at twenty against my parents' wishes, but my parents continued to give me unstinting support when I became pregnant at twenty-one.

Olive Banbury [born 1920]

There were no advice classes as such but relatives passed on information and my elder sister was married with children and she was able to help me. I had one or two checks to see when the baby would be ready to be born. It was turned by a specialist six weeks before the birth.

Mary Sparrow [born 1921]

I didn't go to any classes but visited my doctor once a month.

Joyce Petchey [born 1922]

I went to the local clinic once a month and had an internal examination each time.

Jean Charleson [born 1922]

I think the antenatal care was good. This was about 1946 when I was first pregnant. Nobody went into great lengths to explain things. We just went to the doctor at the start of pregnancy and he arranged for you to go to the hospital. I went to the Simpson Maternity Hospital in Edinburgh, which was a brand new modern hospital. I think it had opened in 1939. I went to the clinic every so often. But the horror of all that would be all these internal examinations. It was like a nightmare. I used to hate it. I often wonder how we didn't lose the baby with all that going on inside you. When Elizabeth was born, twelve years later, it was all very different. Doctors used to feel your tummy and they would say, fine, fine, and you'd go away. But in the old days, every time I went up to the Simpson, you had to get onto this bed and all this paraphernalia would start up. I must say I hated all that. Fortunately you only went two to three times in the nine months.

Mary Boulcott [born 1922]

During my second pregnancy I had undiagnosed twins! I went into hospital four weeks premature and it was only then that twins were suspected. An X-ray confirmed this and they were born six hours later.

Pamela Worthington [born 1923]

I was married in 1942, and our first baby was unplanned but very welcome when he arrived in 1944. I did attend a clinic for pregnant women run I believe by the Ministry of Food, which was responsible to ensure mothers-to-be kept healthy and received cod liver oil, orange juice and vitamin pills. There were no antenatal classes for information or advice. I do not think much fuss was made at all. I had my pregnancy confirmed by our family doctor and did not see him again until I had the baby. I gave up smoking when pregnant with the third baby in 1950 because by then we knew about the possible damage to health.

Joyce MacPherson [born 1923]

I suppose at the time I felt I had quite good pregnancy care for the first one, but later on, compared with how I was dealt with and looked after when I was expecting Katherine, Graham and Heather, I think it was very cursory during my first pregnancy. I went to the doctor when I knew I was pregnant and was told to come back in three months time for a check-up and then six months for a check-up. For later pregnancies there was more attention: I was weighed regularly and had my blood pressure taken and was given good advice. For my first baby I was recommended the book by Grantly Dick Read, which was full of relaxation advice and breathing techniques. I did practice this and it was a tremendous help I must say. I would have been very nervous and this book gave me confidence.

———◆———

'Dr Grantly Dick Read worked for many years among mothers in slum areas in London in the 1940s, and his work there convinced him that there was more to motherhood than the aseptic, anaesthetised conveyor belt system that hospitals were offering. The theory he came up with became known as the fear-tension-pain syndrome.

"Fear and anticipation have given rise to natural protective tensions in the body, and such tensions are not of the mind only. Unfortunately the natural tension produced by fear influences those muscles which close the womb and prevent the child from being driven out during childbirth."

Dick Read's teachings about natural childbirth were a revelation to millions.'

Jenny Carter, WITH CHILD.

———◆———

Jane Ward [born 1924]

I never attended any antenatal classes but I saw my doctor regularly and I knew the local midwife – a fantastic tower of strength to so many. She had 'her' thousandth baby not long after seeing mine into the world. I read books instead, and I enjoyed with much appreciation a book on natural childbirth; I think it was by Grantly Dick Read. I was already good at relaxation and I liked the advice this book gave. As regards smoking, there was no question in 1949 about the dangers of smoking. I had smoked since I was seven, albeit not regularly until 18. I continued to enjoy the occasional drink or two as well – barley wine in those days I seem to recall!

Davina Thorpe [born 1927]

The first time I was pregnant I went to a few classes but didn't find them very useful. We learnt about childcare and practiced bathing babies by using a doll. We were told about suitable clothes for baby and mother.

I also went to the clinic and was weighed regularly. For the second baby, I remember going to the hospital and we all had to queue up in the corridor. For the next two pregnancies I kept well and hardly visited the doctor.

Grace Rae [born 1928]

Although my husband and I intended to have a child as soon as possible after we married, I had to wait eighteen years to become pregnant.

After ten years of hoping for a child and eight years of being resigned to the fact I wasn't going to have one, I was thrilled to find myself pregnant. I wasn't all that surprised because inwardly I had never given up hope. Way back in 1947 a gypsy read my hand and told me I might have one child but never any more than one.

I had a great pregnancy: no sickness, no aches and pains, just a *huge* appetite and a longing to sleep all the time. I took raspberry leaf tea – an old wives' remedy for an easy pregnancy and childbirth – and I just relaxed. I felt the way I think a contented cow must feel.

Having said that, I was also very scared and apprehensive. I wondered if mother nature was maybe going to kick me in the teeth and give me a less than perfect baby. I don't believe in counting chickens before they're hatched, so I refused to buy anything but the absolute necessities beforehand.

Joan Longmuir [born 1930]

I was very lucky – my doctor told me to read Grantly Dick Read's books and I found them immensely helpful. There were no antenatal classes until my fourth baby was due in the late 1950s. I found the classes very interesting and in fact I was a founder member of our local National Childbirth Trust branch. I had six children between 1953 and 1963.

'The National Childbirth Trust founded in 1956 offers information and support in pregnancy, childbirth and early parenthood and aims to enable every parent to make informed choices. The NCT is Britain's best-known charity concerned with education for parenthood. It is run by, and for, parents through its network of 350 branches and groups.'

National Childbirth Trust.

Barbara Henderson [born 1931]

All the women in my family have been extremely fertile and enjoyed healthy pregnancies. My grandmother had seven children, four girls and three boys. My mother was seventeen when I was born, and I was the eldest one of seven children. I married at seventeen and also had seven children myself. There was never any thought of special tests and worries about diet, because the farm diet was wholesome. Apart from smoking, I think the poor diet of mothers today is a bigger hazard. The supermarket trollies are filled with what I see as dead foods.

My second daughter married at eighteen and had her first son the next March, a second son a year later and a third a year after that. Then the doctor put her on the pill, till she got sterilised.

Sheila Brown [born 1934]

Before I had my first daughter, I was a bit apprehensive. I was totally ignorant about what would happen during pregnancy and childbirth. I didn't have a sister or friend who had produced, so I asked my mother; she said it was so long ago she couldn't really remember, to which I said, 'Well, that's a fat lot of good to me!' People would tell me some dreadful stories and my mother kept telling me, 'Don't believe any of it.' But I did hear a lot of old wives' tales about pregnancy and childbirth, some with foundation but a lot of it rubbish. They would say that if a cat crossed your path, or if you got a fright, your baby would have a mole or a disfigurement. But I didn't pay any attention.

I did read books and one by Grantly Dick Read was very fashionable at the time. He said to detract attention from your expanding stomach, wear a cutie hat or something. Of course we all wore hats in those days but I can assure you, if I had worn a monkey on my head, they would still have looked at my stomach! That's how I felt. When I first became pregnant I thought I would feel awful, so big and ugly that I wouldn't want my husband to see me, but it wasn't like that at all. We shared the whole experience; he would be able to feel the baby if it was kicking.

The strangest thing happened to me during each pregnancy. Long before the warnings about smoking, I always wanted to stop smoking – even before I knew I was pregnant. I suddenly wouldn't be able to put a cigarette to my mouth. I also liked an occasional gin and tonic, but I couldn't drink either during pregnancy – all of a sudden I couldn't bear it, as if my body was telling me what to do.

During my pregnancies, when I went up to the clinic for a check-up, they always thought I was going to have twins because I was enormous. I was like a ship in full sail, at six weeks. My varicose veins were always bad and I had high blood pressure but, apart from that, I soldiered on. My skin and hair were always in good condition and I enjoyed the pregnancy. I must admit when I turned up at the clinic for each pregnancy, they would first of all ask, 'Intentional or accident?' which I always thought was a bit odd. But I was always able to say, 'Intentional. We want this baby.'

———◆———

'One hears much about the beauty of a woman with child, ships in full sail, and all that kind of metaphorical euphemism, and I suppose that from time to time on the faces of well-fed, well-bred young ladies, I have seen a certain peaceful glow, but the weight of evidence is overwhelmingly on the other side. Anaemia and exhaustion were written on most countenances. The clothes were dreadful, the legs swollen, the bodies heavy and unbalanced. Even those who had no evident complaints, and who might well have been expected to be full of conventional joy, were looking cross and tired.'

Margaret Drabble, THE MILLSTONE.

———◆———

Mary Anderson [born 1934]

I found the antenatal classes very basic and all I can remember is long waits in a clinic corridor and then, after all that, little advice was given.

Jennifer Harper Jones [born 1939]

I thought the antenatal classes were excellent and very useful. I was given good advice and so, when the time came, I knew exactly what was going to happen to me. I also had routine check-ups but it was before the era of scans and other tests.

The classes were marvellous and I would say they were fun in the way I could share my feelings and worries with the other women. I had to have an early examination because of bleeding. It was diagnosed as a fibroid growing with the baby.

Sheila Davidson [born 1944]

The pregnancy clinics in 1964 were very simple. A urine test and blood pressure was taken. There were no scans or father involvement.

Barbara Bryan [born 1946]

When I was much younger I became pregnant but I chose to have an abortion because I didn't want to marry the man and single parenthood was almost unheard of in those days.

I married at the age of thirty and had my first baby at thirty-three. During my first pregnancy I did go to antenatal classes and they were useful in terms of getting advice, learning how to relax and, equally important, meeting other pregnant women. I chose not to have any tests to check for abnormalities.

Jenni Smith [born 1946]

I don't remember any organised classes but in terms of medical care, for both pregnancies I had to have radio istopography for placenta checking. I had very high blood pressure and all in all, I suffered really quite bad pregnancies.

Vivienne Leighton [born 1947]

I knew very early on that I was pregnant because I have very regular periods. I was very shocked, really devastated because we hadn't planned to start a family so soon. I don't know, I think it is very, very hard to plan to have children. Do you suddenly decide, 'Now this month, we will try to start a family'? How does one know when the best time will be? It is a natural thing and perhaps what happened was for the best in my case. I don't know.

I went to the National Childbirth Trust classes which I found very helpful because you were meeting other women in the same position, having a first baby. Unlike the others, I hadn't been trying for a baby, and I hadn't wanted to be or hadn't expected to be pregnant. In the first pregnancy, I don't think I even had a scan. I would have had the alpha-foetoprotein test, to say whether the child might have spina bifida, because everyone gets that, and blood tests obviously. I was extra apprehensive about it as, working in a hospital, I knew about the obstetric emergencies when women have died in childbirth, and you start wondering, could this happen to me? I sometimes would come out in a sweat at night, thinking, 'How am I going to get through this? What have I done?' but, as the pregnancy progressed, I became more calm and it was inevitable that it was going to happen anyway.

Janice MacKenzie [born 1950]

I did not find the National Health Service classes very useful but for my third baby I went to National Childbirth Trust classes and enjoyed these, meeting other mothers.

I had ultrasound scans during all three pregnancies and an amniocentesis for the third baby.

Sheila Gray [born 1951]

During pregnancy with my third child I was thirty-nine, and was offered an amniocentesis to test for Down's syndrome. I refused this because of the risk of miscarriage.

Ailsa Gray [born 1953]

I found the medical attention to be really excellent. I felt well looked after, perhaps because of my age! I had a CVS [chorionic villus sampling] for each of my five babies as I was older than thirty-five. This checks for any risk of Down's syndrome. I really enjoyed the antenatal classes because they provided a good opportunity to meet other mothers-to-be and share all the excitement of a first pregnancy.

＊

'OK, I got pregnant. I was really pleased. I was so happy I can't even tell you. I was over the moon. You know how it feels, something valuable and special tucked up inside you, growing there, filling you up, ripening secretly. My truffle, I used to think, my precious under-ground peanut. When the baby moved, I could feel it like a fish; my lovely troutling I would sing to my stomach. There was the baby rising perfectly like a souffle.

Sarah Maitland, APPLE PICKING.

＊

Liz Hodgson [born 1954]

I went to some antenatal classes which I found put too much emphasis on birth plans, where we had to choose our preference for labour and so on, which became irrelevant for us. There was also too much pep-talk of ideals. Other classes were realistic and acknowledged the postnatal period and didn't just focus on the birth.

I nearly had an amniocentesis because of my age then decided not to because the risk of miscarriage was higher than the risk of Down's syndrome. Once a breech position was discovered I had two extra scans so I think I was well looked after.

Trudi Barnet [born 1954]

Something I noticed when I had my third baby, in the early 1980s, was the difference in what we wore in pregnancy. For the first two babies, during the 1970s, we all seemed to wear these floral gowns, which were very full and loose, hanging from the neckline and out. When I got to my third pregnancy, people started to show their bumps, which was all very new and different. So your clothing was tighter and shaped your new body rather than hide it – trousers, sweaters, and so on.

Barbara Buckley [born 1954]

The pregnancy classes were reasonably useful but the most benefit I had from them was a feeling of belonging, being with others in this state of transition, and that we were all together and sharing the same imparting of new information.

Because I was expecting twins, I had lots and lots of scans.

'Cathy' [born 1955]

Our baby was planned at once on marriage and our son was born eight and a half months later. I did not attend antenatal classes as I am sceptical, physically ungainly and don't like the way women swap grisly birth tales like men at the bar discussing sport or war.

Winifred Fyfe [born 1955]

The classes were good for the advice given but also it was something to do in the last three months of pregnancy, which can be boring after working full-time. It's the one time in life when you can be a bit of a slob, put on weight and relax a bit.

I eventually went to antenatal classes, not any of those breathing things, though, I went to the clinic. I think there was a botch-up though because I went to the clinic to see the doctor and I think they were supposed to notify me about these classes but they didn't. And I remember going to the clinic when I was six months pregnant, and there were all these women in the class speaking about the last meeting they had had, but I had not been told about them. So I think I must have slipped through the net.

Also I only knew a week before the birth that I would have to have a Caesarian section. I knew nothing about it. I think it was because I am only 4 foot 10 inches tall but I wasn't really told. So once I knew I would have elective sections for each baby, I didn't bother with the classes after that.

I didn't read Dr Spock or any books like that. Well, you see I'd trained as a nursery nurse and had worked with babies so I just thought I was the bees knees. In the daycare nursery where I'd worked they used to bring in babies aged six weeks, so I'd experienced the care of young babies. Still it's not like having your own. So I didn't read books and just went on with life like I wasn't pregnant. I did what I had to do and that was it.

I don't remember being very health conscious or worried about my diet and so on. I didn't smoke and I didn't drink. I remember it was Christmas time and so I had the odd glass of wine. I walked everywhere because my husband and I have never had a car, and I have always been healthy. It was a very lucky pregnancy. I never felt any different. I felt the baby move around, but that was it. I never had any heartburn. I was very lucky not to feel sick. You feel a bit nauseous from time to time but you just get on with it. I worked up until I was six months. Very unremarkable pregnancies, on the whole.

I took a binge for cola with Lesley, I remember that. I had this awful urge and it's something I never drink and I had to have it. In the first pregnancy I never had any craving to eat things, but with the middle one I remember being up in the middle of the night, with the cola bottle up to my mouth!

———•———

"Cressy and her cravings" Midge explained to David, bringing to the table a bread and butter pudding smothered in nutmeg.

David had at first been amused by the cravings, and had himself gone to some trouble in London to buy lychees. Any stray fancy that came into her head at once became a craving: liquorice allsorts, tinned grapefruit, black treacle; nothing very expensive, like strawberries out of season, for she was an unspoilt, undemanding girl – but oddities, and eccentricities. Now this nutmeg, the latest of the whims.'

Elizabeth Taylor, THE WEDDING GROUP.

———•———

Jano Rochefort [born 1955]

As I was a qualified midwife I didn't need to worry too much about classes but I did go to the NCT meetings. I found these especially useful in meeting other women, and I'm still in touch with many of them.

I had the routine ultrasound scans for the first and second pregnancies. I requested an alpha-foetoprotein test for my second pregnancy, to test for spina bifida and other malformations. During my third pregnancy, I was given absolutely nothing in the way of tests.

Sue Rook [born 1960]

I found the classes to be very informative and they also provided me with the opportunity to ask questions. The physiotherapy was extremely good. I used to smoke but stopped when I was trying to become pregnant. As yet I have not started smoking again!

I had all the usual tests and a second scan at twenty-four weeks as I became unwell.

Jo Davidson [born 1960]

Our baby was planned after a few years of marriage. I thought the antenatal classes were useful, giving advice on what would happen in labour, and it was good to meet other pregnant women. They were useless in terms of being a parent and what that involves. Everything seems to stop with the birth and then you are on your own to muddle through. I need someone to visit me everyday now to check how I'm doing with my toddler, rather than come during the early days with a baby.

Lucy Owen [born 1961]

I went to antenatal classes for my first pregnancy only. I enjoyed the yoga relaxation and advice. We were taught how to handle very young babies – we looked after the babies of mothers who were doing postnatal exercises! The classes focused the mind on pregnancy and birth, giving practical information and providing a secure support group. I got to know all the midwives well which was a great comfort.

'Once you are pregnant, you have an unbreakable appointment to meet a stranger. Mostly I was living off a sustaining solipsism, contemplating for hours tiny changes in my body, ribbons of silvery stretched skin on my legs and arms, blue stars of exploded capillaries, little junks and caiques of white beneath my moony nails. I watched the plundering of my own body for minerals by the miner within. I wondered, indulgently, which part of myself I would find missing next. A sense of the self has never been my strongest suit; I deemed it no dishonour that I was being dismantled.'

Candia McWilliam, A LITTLE STRANGER.

Carol Ziyat [born 1962]

I found that the pregnancy advice given was generally helpful although some women were more anxious *after* some classes than beforehand. This was due to the explicit diagrams and explanations given when describing the use of forceps and having to cut the mother to avoid ripping.

'FORCEPS: These are really tongs which fit round the baby's head and can be used to help lift the baby out or turn him if the head is in an unusual position. If the baby is very small, premature or showing signs of distress, forceps may be used'

'EPISIOTOMY: This is a small cut in the skin of the perineum to enlarge the vaginal entrance just before the baby is born. There is a good deal of controversy

surrounding the practice, which used to be almost routine for first time mothers in some hospitals.'

Tessa Hilton, BABY AND CHILD CARE.

Angela Blanchard [born 1962]

With my first pregnancy I attended hospital-run NHS classes alone, as my husband, who was a trainee doctor, was always on call on the night of the class. I thought they were useful at the time, but looking back, they filled me with more misinformation than useful or relevant information. I made no friends through these. With the second pregnancy, my husband and I attended NCT classes. These were invaluable: excellent range of relaxation techniques, first class information, lots of life skills – like assertiveness, plenty of opportunities to explore individual fears and hopes, and I made real and lasting friendships. Continuing support long after the babies were born [came] through the NCT network. Like many women here I found that the NCT replaced the sort of sisterhood or kinship that women must have enjoyed in previous generations and certain rural communities, and of course still do in many countries. My antenatal group still meets regularly and we confide in each other, bolster each other's confidence, compare practical notes and tips in a way that I could not with any other group of women.

Lorna Reid [born 1962]

I wasn't married when I became pregnant. Becoming pregnant was a big surprise. Well, it was and it wasn't. I was thrilled to bits. Geoff couldn't put the television off because there was sport on – and I wanted to beat him about the head. I think he was just so shocked he couldn't talk about it, and so watched a football match instead. We both couldn't really believe that I was pregnant.

When you have been practising contraception for so long – and Geoff and I had been together for ten years, you sort of think conception wouldn't work anyway, that if you weren't always careful, it wouldn't matter. I think we had unprotected sex once and that was it. It was also the same day we got engaged, and the two events seem to be closely intertwined.

A lot of the feelings you experience in early pregnancy are similar to those when you are expecting a period. So here I was expecting my period and ironically I had decided that because we had given up using condoms, I thought I should go back on the pill. So I had been to see my doctor and got three months supply of some oral contraceptive with a name that sounded like an outer space alien – Mercylon or something. So I got my three packets of Mercylon and was awaiting my period and it never came. The days were going on and on but because I never have a regular cycle I wasn't too worried. But by the end of January I counted the weeks and it did seem curious. We decided to get a home pregnancy kit. I couldn't wait to use it and raced home. I read and re-read the instructions but there was the blue line on the indicator stick. I came downstairs to show Geoff that it was indeed positive. He couldn't think of anything to say except, 'Oh, ff . . . ff . . . oh God . . .', and I think we just sat about, mesmerised and in shock.

I did another test the next day and it was still positive. I then went to the doctor and he didn't bother testing me, because I had had two positive tests. He suggested I go to the chemist and get some folic acid, which is supposedly a good dietary supplement, helpful for spine developments. This should be taken for the first twelve weeks of pregnancy and even before conception if you are trying for a baby. I immediately felt some of the symptoms of pregnancy. Did I feel nauseous really or was this just because I knew I was pregnant?

My mother was distinctly lukewarm about the whole thing. Not impressed at all, she did not sound pleased. But I was so thrilled with the news, and this exciting event happening inside me. It was like my own very big secret and you are holding on to it. We went out to the bookshop in Inverurie and bought the Johnson and Johnson book of pregnancy and child care. This book charts your weekly development with photographs of what the average foetus will look like. It tells you how you will feel and things you might want to do. I tried to read as much as I could about pregnancy because I was really enjoying it and wanted to know all about it.

I got advice from my doctor's surgery and had regular antenatal appointments for the first couple of months. I actually had bleeding early on which I know is not all that uncommon but consequently I had a scan when I was seven weeks pregnant. The doctor kept a close eye on me after that.

I was very, very conscious about my health and diet during pregnancy. I thought constantly about the baby before I put anything in my mouth to the extent that the people at work used to laugh when I brought in my healthy packed lunch. I think the day I had carrot and butter bean soup – I work in a very male oriented office – this soup was the end. One of the men said, 'What are you trying to do to that child?' So yes, I was very careful about looking after myself.

I hadn't started going to the antenatal classes because they don't start until week 30. I never made it to week 30 because my baby came at week 26.

Linda MacPherson [born 1962, interviewed in August 1994, in eighth month of pregnancy]

I had worked for nine years before I married and have now been married for just under two years so we basically decided on trying to have a baby straightaway. The pregnancy was therefore planned so I was very happy. I was extremely unwell for the first four months, which made me swear that this was going to be the only time I would ever go through this. But then things got better and you begin to feel fine again. I'm feeling very well now, with the baby due in four weeks or so. I'm looking forward to the birth now, because I am tired of being pregnant. I've gone to antenatal classes run by the hospital as well as NCT groups. I have read any literature that comes my way. I just want to be informed about what will happen. I find to a certain degree there is too much information, which makes pregnancy more of a worry than I feel it should be. But that is my personal view. There is all the advice about what you can't or shouldn't do. That really bugs me. All the things you can't eat. Especially the rules about what you can't eat. Because I feel there is slightly too much concern; the chances of something happening to you because you eat some soft cheese are pretty minimal. If you go to someone's house and have some salad, it makes you wonder if they washed it properly. I feel all this is overreacting and the risk is so minimal, compared to all the other things that might go wrong in pregnancy or during labour. It causes unnecessary concern. But then you don't want to disobey the rules.

———◆———

'If you are pregnant, it is best to avoid the following: soft cheeses such as Brie, Camembert or mould-ripened cheeses such as Danish Blue and Stilton because of the risk of listeria; raw or lightly cooked eggs because of the risk of salmonella which includes foods such as homemade mayonnaise and icecream; patés and raw or lightly cooked meats.'

Tessa Hilton, BABY AND CHILD CARE.

———◆———

I have been careful and not had paté and things, but I do have soft boiled eggs because I don't like hard boiled eggs. When I meet other girls at the antenatal class or the aqua-natal swimming club I go to, this is something we talk quite a bit about – what we should be doing, eating, not eating. 'You haven't had smoked salmon!' one will say. 'You shouldn't eat that'. And the worries start all over again. I am really looking forward to a normal diet once again I can tell you.

You are given a choice about how you wish to give birth and what pain relief you would prefer. It would be better if someone else took the decisions for me, because if you have never given birth before, how are you to know what is best for you and the baby? And you would think the doctors and midwives know best. I suppose in some respects it is nice to be given the choice in childbirth, but I'd quite prefer it if people advised me and explained what would be best.

I had a miscarriage at twenty weeks in a previous pregnancy so they have been checking me quite carefully. I had two scans to make sure everything was alright. I had the normal scan at ten weeks to see the size of the foetus as everyone does, but also a detailed scan at twenty weeks to check for abnormalities.

I wanted a hospital birth because I haven't had a baby before and I want all the help from qualified people to be on the spot if something goes wrong. I hope to have the birthing pool and will be allowed to have the first stage there, but not the delivery. My husband is going to be there – there is certainly a lot of pressure on fathers to be there but I feel if I have go through with it, why shouldn't he? The whole point of him being there is to support me. He is not meant to be down at the grisly end with the midwife, but by my side holding my hand.

So it will be interesting to see how it all works out!

Liz Suttie [born 1964, interviewed in July 1994 in eighth month of pregnancy]

My husband and I wanted to wait a couple of years before starting a family. I was only twenty-six when I married so there was no rush. However, I had trouble getting pregnant. I came off the pill and then found I did not have a regular cycle. It would be fifteen days, then twenty-one days, then thirty days. It was like that for eighteen months. We were just at the stage when we were about to have tests done to see if there was anything wrong, when I became pregnant. I was careful about looking after myself, I was very fit, and my diet was good. I was having shared care, the hospital for scans but the doctor for basic monthly check-ups. I have been very impressed with the Simpson Maternity Hospital. There was one time I had a scare when I was at work and couldn't feel the baby moving. My husband suggested we go down to the hospital and get it checked out. We just walked in without an appointment and I explained what the problem was. And they could not have been more helpful, giving up a lot of time to do the scan. And this was actually the midwife's lunch hour. They did a full scan and ultrasound on the baby and told me it was all fine. They said if it happens again, make sure to come in if there was anything worrying me. I was really impressed by that because to begin with I felt maybe I was being silly and overreacting. But they made me feel that I had done the right thing.

At Simpsons you are asked to complete a birth plan, which means that you choose from various options which will suit you for the birth – position, pain relief and so on. Now I have not filled this in for the simple reason that I do not know what to expect when I get there. I might change my views completely. If contractions are not as bad as I think they may be, then I can say, 'I don't think I'll have any pain relief yet.' But on the other hand I am quite prepared to just say, 'Give me everything!' I don't think you can plan for it, for the first birth especially, because you simply don't know what to expect. Natural childbirth is all very well in principle, but I don't know anyone who has actually gone through with it. So I don't think for one minute I will.

Rachel Hanks [born 1967]

I had just completed one year of a degree course when I became pregnant. I was twenty-five and it was unplanned and unexpected, having only known my partner Rory for about six months. I enjoyed the antenatal classes for good advice on relaxation. They made me feel very special, as if I was part of a new club. The information was pretty basic and not so important. I was just keen to submerge myself in all things natal.

Without being mean to my son, becoming a mother is a little like being disabled. I did not choose to be a mother. It happened as a result of faulty contraceptives; first the condom and then the morning-after pill let me down.

Because I am a fertile woman, I am now having to pay the price for these few moments of pleasure and I have regretted getting pregnant many times. I feel that it happened at the wrong time of my life. A relationship cannot live on love or lust alone. So with the loss of freedom and the loss of the people we were before becoming parents, there have been a lot of problems coping with the baby. But we've made the first birthday mark, we're still together and I live in hope.

'Early in my pregnancy I had become aware of a discomforting sense of dependency on the father of my child. We could no longer go our separate ways as simply, if love ran dry.

But this feeling of dependency was incomprehensible to women who had never been pregnant. As they spoke confidently about politics and their work, fear gathered in my throat, and muffled my words. I wanted to shout – I may never work again.

For the first time in my life, I could not speak about my feelings. I wondered if I would ever think of anything but my child again. My friends told me of back packs and assured me that they would babysit while I worked; I suspected it would not be true. They didn't understand, nor did I have the courage to explain, that I did not fear not being able to work again so much as never wanting to work again.

Jane Lazarre, THE MOTHER KNOT.

Carol Walton [born 1943, trained as a midwife in 1966–67; now involved in parentcraft and early pregnancy classes]

We don't have strict rules or advice but we try to encourage pregnant women to go to parentcraft classes, but as usual the uptake is the educated, intelligent girls who could learn it from the book anyway. They have probably read the books, seen the video and bought the T-shirt! But the younger ones who need it don't come, and they say they don't need advice and it is rubbish anyway. Parentcraft classes are voluntary, unfortunately; you can't frogmarch them into coming.

We also have an early pregnancy class to teach women about diet and minor illnesses of pregnancy and how they should look after themselves. It is a continuing battle trying to advise the women who need the help. Some midwives who are very committed to helping these young girls will even arrange to see two or three in their own homes if they won't come to the hospital, because they are so concerned about the lack of knowledge some young mothers have.

One of the things we do is to check their blood sugar which is just a random blood test, but to see that it is accurate we have to ask what they have had to eat. Well you would be amazed what some of these young pregnant girls have for breakfast: a pork pie, half a packet of crisps, or a cup of tea and three biscuits. It is quite rare to find a girl who has had a bowl of cereal and a slice of toast! And we get these enormous girls who are extremely overweight, who say they haven't eaten anything. And you say, 'Nothing at all, no sweets?' and they say, 'Oh yes, I've had a Mars bar and a Twix, crisps and three Opal Fruits but nothing to eat at all.' And they tell you that with the diet they are on they should be fading away! Completely unaware that they have had about a thousand calories before elevenses.

But you can't persuade them, just the same with the smoking. They sit there under the No Smoking signs, smoking. And you can't tell them that they are harming their baby, they simply do not believe it. It is very difficult. Again the girls we should be getting at with advice, are impervious to it. It is very sad.

———◆———

Some thoughts on being pregnant

'I woke up with a start at 4.00 one morning and realised that I was very, very pregnant. A few times a day the information actually causes me to gasp . . . how on earth did I come to be in this condition? Well, I am beginning to put two and two together. See there was this guy. But this guy is no longer around, and my stomach is noticeably bigger every few days. So I am going to have a baby pretty soon, and this has raised some mind boggling issues. For instance, it occurs to me over and over that I am much too self centred, cynical, eccentric and edgy to raise a baby, especially alone.'

Anne Lemott, OPERATING INSTRUCTIONS.

———◆———

Rachel Lockey [born 1967]

When I decided to have the baby, I knew it would be a nightmare having to tell my parents. I am not as close to my dad as I am to my mum. She is quite old-fashioned – she has a different set of expectations to me. So I told her first. I just said the usual, 'I've got something to tell you, Mum – I'm pregnant.' And she sort of threw herself around me, and was crying, and she said, 'Do you love him?', and I said, 'I don't know if I love him, all I know is I am having a baby.'

Her immediate reaction was that I was going to tell her I was getting married as well, which of course I wasn't at all. She came to terms with it very well, but she was very worried about telling my father. All he said was, 'Look what you've done to your mother. She is going to be left to look after your baby.' And I said, 'No, that is not what is going to happen. I am having a baby.'

And I stayed away for some time, and visited occasionally. But in time, their expectations of my going to university weren't as important as they once believed now that they saw how I was leading my life. They have been very supportive.

It was very difficult having to tell them. I actually hid it from them for six months. I remember vomiting in the first few months when I was living there and not being able to tell them what was wrong. It was fine in the end, but I was very scared having to tell them. I could tell friends, and I could tell people who were their age, who were friends, but I just couldn't tell my parents for some time.

Only then could I walk down the street proudly, and not have to try and hide my pregnancy.

Andrea Duffin [born 1970]

Just when I was going back to college in Glasgow to study for two Highers, I fell pregnant and that is when a new life started for me.

I had known Barry for a while – we were both eighteen. He lived along the road and we saw each other every day. It was a very intense relationship and I know this sounds corny but I knew I had fallen in love with him. Within a fortnight we went away together touring with a band, The Stone Roses, around the country. We were like a couple of groupies, travelling to concerts, sleeping here and there, on buses. We couldn't afford anything else. It was a great adventure. So we got on really well. He was about to go to Manchester University but he decided to put it off for a year, and stay with me in Glasgow. But I fell pregnant. It was a surprise but we had no qualms about this. We knew we would keep the baby. It wasn't such a tragedy as some people thought. We knew what we felt about each other. We may not have known each other very long, about three or four months. We met in the June and I was pregnant in September. But we had spent so much time together, it felt right.

It was more of a shock to his parents because he had only come out of school. I was not very well at all to begin with, dreadful sickness. My mum was so good about everything, although I was ill; even the doctor suggested I had a termination for the sake of my health. I continued living with my mum and Barry lived at his home just for practicalities. When I got to sixteen weeks I was feeling fine again. Then we began to look for a place to live and we got a house about a month before I was due. I was in such a hyper about it, I was shifting wardrobes about and bookcases, even though I shouldn't have been. I was huge by this time. It was a very hot summer, a real heatwave. That was May 1990. I remember I wore this big sunhat and I was so fat and hot. Barry said I was like this big, bouncing ball of happiness.

'There is a fatuous state in pregnancy when you know all is well, not only with yourself but with the world. You know that a species which has evolved this miraculous system of reproducing itself, the natty idea of containing the future empursed within, cannot allow destruction to obtain, will not short-change us. You know that, by placing your gravid body between the light of ugly fact and the undefended of the race, you can cut out the glare. I knew, because I had been pregnant before, that it is a fleeting sense of beneficient glowing power, preceding almost invariably a certainty that all shadows are black and all breaths our last, a time during which tears – selfish tears of easy altruism – are never very far away.'

Candia McWilliam, A LITTLE STRANGER.

CHAPTER FOUR

Labour and Childbirth

' *"Oh this is terrible, I am dying . . . I shall die!" she cried and the same unearthly shriek echoed through the house.*

"It will soon be over now," said the doctor. And the doctor's face was so grave as he said it that Levin thought he meant that it would be soon over with Kitty and she was dying.

He saw the midwife's face looking more frowning and stern than ever. Kitty's face was not there. In its place was something fearful – fearful in its strained distortion and the sounds that issued from it. He let his head drop on to the wooden rail of the bed, feeling that his heart was breaking. The terrible screams followed each other quickly until they seemed to reach the utmost limit of horror, when they suddenly ceased. He heard a soft stir, a bustle, and the sound of hurried breathing, and her voice, faltering, vibrant, tender and blissful as she whispered, "It's over!"

"Alive, alive. And a boy too. Set your mind at rest." Levin heard the midwife say as she slapped the baby's back with a shaking hand.'

Leo Tolstoy, ANNA KARENIN.

Up until the end of the first world war, the vast majority – over 95 per cent – of women had their babies at home. By the late 1920s, home births still accounted for 85 per cent of all births in Britain. The middle class mother would be able to afford professional medical supervision throughout her pregnancy and was attended by a doctor and midwife at the birth. A maternity nurse was often employed to live-in for a month afterwards. Private nursing homes became common between the wars.

However the working class mother, who was often in paid employment as well as looking after a large family, would often be doing heavy manual work up until her due date. The cost of employing a midwife would have been around ten shillings, almost a week's wages for the low-paid worker, and therefore few families could afford to pay the two pounds or more for a doctor to attend the birth. This resulted in the age-old tradition of the 'handywoman', often a neighbour or relative, who was untrained but who was able to comfort and assist during childbirth. Hospital confinements were reserved for those women whose home circumstances were unsuitable, who were having their tenth or eleventh child, or were medically at risk for some reason.

While the 1902 Midwives Act made it an offence for unqualified persons to attend women in childbirth "habitually and for gain", although this provision came fully into force in 1910, there are records of some handywomen delivering babies unsupervised twenty-five years later. No wonder. Community life and culture take time to adapt. For generations, women had been attended by family, friends or any other person they wished to be with them at the birth. Unqualified practitioners were far less expensive than doctors or even midwives, and being of the same social class, were probably more welcome in some of the poorer homes. Case histories and registers often record that the baby was born before the arrival of the midwife or doctor [BBA], perhaps deliberately, to save on the fees.

Poor housing conditions meant that the home was not an ideal place to deliver a baby. Even though many mothers worked tirelessly to keep their homes clean, fleas, bedbugs, dampness, one or two room flats with no sanitary facilities or running water could create serious problems for the midwife.

Violet Stevenson-Hamilton [born 1902]

When I was training as a nurse as a young girl, there were no intensive care units in hospitals, so underweight or terribly deformed babies took their chance of survival with the normal care expended on the newly born. Aged 19 I was serving my first spell of night duty in the Labour ward at Bristol Royal Infirmary, when I saw on two occasions the birth of 'monsters'. As the first, hideously deformed baby appeared, Sister wrapped it up in an all enveloping towel and laid it on a trolley while coping with the mother. No effort was made to aid the start of its breathing and it was mercifully spared from the limitations of care in a slum. Maternity wards were never empty of the wives of the poorly paid and unemployed in their annual pregnancies. Treatment was free in the superbly well-run hospitals run by Matron. Caesarean sections were so rare that when one was scheduled, any nurse who could be spared was allowed to watch the miracle birth from the gallery of the 'gynie' theatre.

The well-to-do middle classes in the rigid class distinctions of those days either had their babies at home or in a maternity home. A month was reckoned to be the right period for lying-in but according to how Mother and Baby thrived, three weeks was the minimum of stay.

I had my three boys in a nursing home, where one was marvellously looked after for about £15 a week, run by retired nurses. In those days we weren't too badly off. In fact we married on £350 a year and we were still able to run a small car on that and have a live-in maid. But even so it wasn't too easy to have a child at home and, with my nursing training, I felt it would be easier to go into a nursing home. As I've always been very energetic, I rode and walked and swam until the ninth month; I had babies as easily as a cat has kittens.

Janet Stewart [born 1904]

I had my first baby at home and it was all completely natural. I did not even know the baby was about to be born and I went to the loo and the child started to be born. It was retrieved in time and the midwife eventually arrived.

'It is interesting to have lived through successive fashions of childbirth. In the early twenties it was still thought of with some alarm and excitement; one was so to speak going into battle, and, for those who could afford it, every possible ally was brought in. As far as I was concerned this meant having a Harley Street specialist, a woman gynaecologist.'

Naomi Mitchison, YOU MAY WELL ASK.

Margaret Dixon [born 1905]

I was in a hospital maternity unit for the first baby and a private nursing home for the other two births. The first birth was completely natural and I had a little pain relief for the second and third. In the hospital I had a sadistic nurse but in the nursing home, the nurse was quite alright. I stayed in the hospital for two weeks afterwards.

———•———

'If the mother is to have a labour free from anxieties and risks, she ought to make certain preparations beforehand.

A few days before the expected confinement, the room should be thoroughly cleaned out, preferably not by the mother herself. The furniture should be moved, and dusted with a damp cloth. The floor should be scrubbed and any carpet taken up and beaten. The paint should be washed, the pictures taken down, and the glass polished. The bed should be a single one, if possible. It should have no curtains or valance, as a free current of air should be able to circulate all round and under the bed. In order to protect the bed, a simple maternity sheet can be made at home. It consists of a large sheet of new brown paper, the edges of which are turned down and stitched over five or six layers of clean newspapers with a further covering of an old sheet which has been well boiled.

A kettle and saucepan, with means for heating are necessary, and a supply of clean sheets and towels. A clean nightgown for the mother as well as clothes for the baby should be aired and put ready.

A supply of sanitary pads, to be burnt after using, can be made from old linen or calico. They should be boiled for 20 minutes and afterwards ironed on both sides with a very hot iron. At least a dozen should be prepared and they should be kept wrapped securely in freshly ironed brown paper.

The doctor or nurse will need two wash-stand basins and jugs, a bedroom slop pail, two chambers and two good sized pudding basins and a zinc bath put in readiness in the lying-in room.

The doctor or midwife should be sent for as soon as the pains begin, or if the waters break without pains.

After the confinement the mother must stay in bed for ten days, at least, so she should arrange for a woman to come in and do the housework while she is laid up.'

Association of Infant Welfare, TO WIVES AND MOTHERS, 1917.

———•———

Susan Curtis [born 1905]

Most people had home confinements. I was attended by a midwife, a doctor and my live-in monthly nurse as we called them. She was the maternity nurse who looked after me for the month afterwards while I rested for two to three weeks. During labour all I had was a whiff of choloroform at the last minute. I remember the doctor and nurse sat on the bed and chatted while we waited. I never murmured, to their surprise, but a tough schooling had taught me self-control. I had two healthy boys, in 1939 and 1943.

Eileen Brown [born 1908]

The first birth took place in hospital and was traumatic. The baby was in the wrong position and I was in labour for 28 hours, frequently left alone for long periods. I was not given any information or help and was in terrible pain but the nurses were very unsympathetic and told me not to make a fuss. The baby was delivered very bruised indeed. There was not much help offered afterwards either – it all seemed to be just considered part of having a baby. I can remember the trauma and pain vividly after sixty years. The second birth was at home and the labour was over within a couple of hours. It was a very easy birth with only a midwife in attendance.

'A great deal of the success of a home confinement depends upon the services of a good maternity nurse, so it is worthwhile taking great pains to choose the right woman. Maternity nurses have two main duties: 1] the obstetric care of the mother, and 2] the training and care of the baby. In my experience it is much easier to find a nurse who is competent in dealing with the mother than one who is good at managing the baby. Interview the nurse before engaging her, make sure you like her and have confidence in her.'

Dr John Gibbens, THE CARE OF YOUNG BABIES, 1941.

Patricia Rogers [born 1908]

I have had six children, three born at home and three in hospital. I had my first baby at the age of 28 and it was a home delivery. It seemed the right thing to do at the time; we had a maternity nurse, privately paid, living in for a fortnight looking after me, doing the housework and caring for the baby. We had the same nurse for the first two babies which was nice. There was also a doctor in attendance – very good doctors for all the births. I was given pethidine, or a whiff of something. I had read all sorts of books on labour, and listened to friends and taken lots of exercise during the pregnancy – I was very active. I was really looking forward to it. It's lovely to have a baby at home. Neighbours are always so good and lend a hand. I was kept in bed for two weeks and I remember my husband brought in four of the children who lived next door to see the new baby. I can see them now, sitting on this blanket box at the end of the bed, eating Bournvita biscuits and drinking milk, staring in wonder at this little baby. That was how neighbours and children welcomed a new baby into the street, into the community.

By the time we had five daughters, we thought perhaps that would be our family. My husband loved children and he loved our girls and he never said anything about being disappointed at not having a son. But I remember this Christmas we felt that if we had another child we could cope. It didn't matter if it was a girl or a boy. So we decided to have another baby. By now I was forty-six, but the pregnancy was fine.

I remember it was a hot summer when I was pregnant and I was wearing this rather fetching duster coat. People would say to me, 'Are you going for a boy?' I think because of my age they must have assumed we were desperate for a boy and having one last chance. This annoyed me but somehow I wasn't able to say, 'No, I would just accept what we have. I accept what life gives me.' I didn't disillusion them, if that's what they thought. As if that was the only reason to have another child. But I had a boy. It was early Sunday morning and my husband had gone to church, where all the maiden ladies kissed him for luck. Later that day I had a little boy. And despite my age, the labour and birth were absolutely fine. But all we wanted was healthy children. I wouldn't like to choose the sex or know beforehand. I think the nearer you can live a natural sort of life, the better. That is my opinion.

May Stephen [born 1911]

Our daughter Ruth was born in February 1940, at the beginning of the war. I had gone into the hospital on the Monday morning for a check-up and the doctor advised that since I was beyond my due date, we ought to speed things up a bit. So I went home and took a spoonful of castor oil and that started labour going. Of course it began in the middle of the night, in the blackout. The ambulance couldn't find our house and my husband, being a doctor, was all prepared to deliver me himself. He was pulling sheets out and getting everything ready. But I went into hospital for the second stage of labour. I didn't have an easy time, and they used forceps and gave me an episiotomy.

Peggy Wilson [born 1911]

A week or so before the birth of my daughter in 1934, we moved to Leeds because of our work in the repertory theatre. I booked into a nursing home. I must have arrived at an awkward time because I was shown straight into the delivery room, where I had to wait alone for a few minutes till someone was free to deal with me. There were some fearful instruments set out, which I found very frightening. I comforted myself by remembering various twittery dimwit mothers of my acquaintance and told myself that I was surely as brave as they were.

At that time it was routine to give women castor oil at the start of labour, presumably expecting that it would work while they were still in the early stages. I had not taken opening medicine since I was a small child, and argued uselessly against it. But my daughter arrived unusually fast, for a first baby, and through the haze of whatever gas was used, I could hear the grumbling down the other end, and thought, 'Serve you jolly well right!'

After we had both been cleaned up, the doctor stood at the end of the bed as the baby was put in my arms, saying sentimentally, 'Now this is what I like to see.' But in farming language, the family breeds true and with her then bald head, and fringe of black hair round the back, she looked so like her great-great-uncle Willie, that my reaction must have been a disappointment to him.

New mothers were not allowed out of bed, even to go to the loo, for at least a week, so that when you did, you were weak and wobbly, with a poor sense of balance, and it took a few days before you felt safe coming downstairs.

Both before and after the birth, we wore a bra in bed, and after the baby had arrived, our tums were bound with a stiff new strip of roller towelling. Not comfortable but worth it, for we regained our pre-baby figures and were able to go home in our pre-pregnancy skirts, with nice flat tums.

Mary Maclennan [born 1911]

I had my first baby in 1935. In those days, even if you had a difficult birth, you didn't go into hospital. We were not allowed into a hospital, which was reserved for poor people. My husband being a teacher with a reasonable salary, we were expected to go into a nursing home and pay for it. I found childbirth horrible, it was very painful but I just accepted it. You accept that there are these trials and tribulations in life. I was in a nursing home for about eight days for each of the four births except the last one, when there was a problem before the birth; I don't know the details, but I had to have a Caesarean section. I was quite ill after this but I got through it. I didn't want any more children after that; we didn't want any more than four anyway, but of course in those days we might have had another because no one bothered much about prevention. You just took what was coming in these days. It was natural.

'The main intervention to attempt to make childbirth safer – especially from the late 1920s onwards, – was hospitalisation. Before then, most hospital provision was archaic; many maternity wards were attached to Poor Law infirmaries, charity hospitals, or workhouses and were mostly used by poor or unmarried mothers on the verge of destitution. The death rate for hospital births were generally higher even than in home births, but in 1929, when local authorities took control of Poor Law hospitals, conditions changed rapidly.
                    Steve Humphries and Pamela Gordon, A LABOUR OF LOVE.

'There she lay, beached for a moment, panting, quivering, aware. With a touch of the anaesthetic from a gauze mask to help her she went forward. Her mind went down and lived in her body, ran out of her brain and lived in her flesh. Now the first twisting spate of pain began. Swim then, swim with it for your life. If you resist, horror and impediment! If you swim not pain but sensation. Who knows the heart of pain, the silver, whistling hub of pain, the central bellows of childbirth which expels one being from another? Wild movements, hallucinated swimming! A little more, a little more a little longer. She was not in torture, she was in labour; she had been thus before and knew her way. The corkscrew swirl swept her shuddering, until she swam into a tunnel – the first seconds of anaesthesia.

Now the shocked and vigorous cry of the born rang through the room. Faces smiled over her.

"What is it?" Nine months of wondering in one second solved.'

Enid Bagnold, THE SQUIRE.

Eileen Watkins [born 1912]

I went into a private nursing home for the first two and had my third baby at home. They were all very normal and natural deliveries, and fairly rapid. The first labour was eight hours and then two hours and five hours respectively. I only had a little chloroform, I think, at the last moment. I had a doctor and a nurse for the first two and a doctor and midwife at home for the third. It was lovely being at home, as suggested by my doctor. I stayed in hospital for three weeks for the first two, one week in bed, and two weeks learning how to care for the baby.

Alice Wands [born 1912]

I began my six months' midwifery training in 1936 at Leeds Maternity Hospital. The fee to be a pupil midwife was £25 but I got a scholarship which let me off paying. There was the labour ward and the lying-in ward where the women who had had their babies rested while we helped them feed and wash them. Also the isolation ward where we had the women who had miscarried and the dirty cases – people who went a bit septic, or women who were too ill or infectious to be with the others. We loved the babies, but not so keen on the mothers. We kept the mothers in bed for ten days and kept them well fed and clean. So many poor women did not have a change of nightie so we had a supply of hospital gowns for them to change into.

Nancy Beaty [born 1914]

My first son was born in 1936. I visited the doctor twice during pregnancy but nothing more. The midwife came to the farm and did everything – I just lay there in state for ten days. That was the first one. A year later I had twins. They were a month premature and when the doctor had visited me beforehand, he didn't even know I was having twins so it was quite a shock when they arrived. I really wanted a little girl because I had been brought up with brothers and my mother had died. The first twin was a boy so I was a bit disappointed. But the Scottish midwife who was attending me said, 'Just hang on there Mrs Beattie, there is another one coming.' And half an hour later, a little girl was born.

I stayed in bed for ten days. They wouldn't let your feet over the bed. But I had to get up then, there was too much to do with three little ones under three years old. It was quite an experience.

Doris Melling [born 1914]

My son was born in 1938 – I was twenty-four. Those were the days when we stayed in the maternity hospital for fourteen days. The old wives' tale was that if we put our feet on the floor under ten days we would drop down dead. That's the truth! So we came home after fourteen days, weak as water, and never having seen the baby bathed.

I was given chloroform for this birth, which was the doctor's choice. The babies were kept in the nursery and I was terrified of it being mixed up and I would get the wrong baby so I insisted on going into a private ward. That cost £20 and my husband's wages were £3 and 15 shillings. As it happened the maternity ward at the cottage hospital was empty the whole time, so there wouldn't have been a mix up of babies.

For my second baby five years later, I was offered gas and air but found it useless and pushed it away. But I was only in labour for an hour and a half with my daughter, so it cost us just £1 and 6 shillings for the medical treatment.

Mary Lewis Brydon [trained as a midwife at Glasgow Maternity Hospital, 1937]

My mother had trained in 1902 at the Glasgow Royal Maternity and Women's Hospital when it was just a four month training. Now it is about eighteen months. She never talked to me much about her work when I was a child because in those days it was considered unsuitable to talk about it. We weren't meant to know about such things! But I decided to go into nursing and in my day, unless you had done your midwifery training, you could not be promoted to Sister. It was the thing, you had to do your midwifery when you finished your basic training and my mother was keen for me to follow in her footsteps to Rotton Row in Glasgow, which I did. It was pretty awful because we had to pay for the training – there was no salary – and for our own books and uniform. We did six months without any leave or holidays. We didn't have any time off.

Labour and Childbirth

I did enjoy my training very much but I got very flea-bitten. This was because the women I attended and their homes were so dirty. I saw bed bugs one time when I was with this woman all night during a difficult labour. I saw them climbing up the wall. They were very poor indeed. You took a deep breath before you went up the stairs to get to whichever flat it was, because there was only one toilet in the middle of the building and everyone used it, but no-one cleaned it. Oh, it was awful.

We did get used to it and many homes were cleaner and better. Some women were delivered on a piece of brown paper, to keep the sheets clean for afterwards, so that when the neighbours came in they would see the mother in a lovely clean bed with her new baby. Women were much tougher in those days and there was always a neighbour to help, not so often a mother, and one or two women would send for us but not until the baby was born, because it was cheaper. We were always cross because we had to have twenty-five deliveries before we could sit our exam. There were hundreds of us there training in Glasgow, nurses came from London and the Midlands too, because it was a very good training. And we witnessed some difficult births; because of the lack of calcium in the water, a lot of women were bow-legged and this caused a contracted pelvis and with that it is difficult to deliver.

One question we had to ask each woman was when was their last menstrual period and many of them just couldn't remember. It had been years before, because they had had their babies, one after the other. A lot of them were Glasgow Irish, and of course good Catholics, so they produced babies all the time. They would look so tired and weak by the time it came to the tenth or eleventh baby.

The husband would come to fetch you to attend a birth, if it was in the evening, and then walk three or four yards behind you – 'Nothing to do with me.' kind of attitude, because there we were with our bonnets, with a bow under our chin, and our black bags.

When we went to the slums in the Gorbals, sometimes the police would escort us so far and then leave us at a certain corner and say they couldn't come any further. There were street gangs with knives in those days. Yes, it was a rough and dangerous area, but as nurses, with that uniform on, they respected us. They weren't likely to harm us.

I remember one occasion when the woman was beginning to shake and shiver, with the loss of fluid, and I asked for another blanket. But what did they bring, but my coat! All ready for the fleas to jump on to.

Then I would ask for a cup for the Dettol, for tying the baby's cord, the ligatures, and then after it was all over, I was offered a cup of tea – in the same cup! It was washed I presume.

A difficult birth I encountered was a breech birth, when the bottom is coming first. You could send for a doctor if you were out in the district, and the husband should be hovering around so that he can help out. But often they were hovering in the pub, and there were no phones of course so it was the greatest problem for us. I don't remember a doctor coming to any of the births because the message never reached him.

So we learned the hard way, coping on our own, and we had to take the placenta back to the hospital after the birth for the staff nurse to inspect, to see that it was complete and no membranes had been left inside which causes sepsis afterwards.

There were often some sad cases when women were very ill. I remember two mothers dying, one of a kidney infection after the birth, and another of eclampsia. People suffered poor health and there were a lot of abnormalities in Glasgow in those days. Everything has improved so much. I do think midwifery was very stressful then, with all the home births. It was a long time ago. You either loved it or you didn't. I was able to do it.

Glasgow Royal Maternity Hospital Case Histories

MRS D., 9 Shaw Place, Paisley Road. 44 years old. 8th pregnancy. Admitted 24.6.37; 2nd stage 15 hours; 3rd stage, 5 minutes. Boy born dead, 5¼ lbs.

J. W., St. Gerards Home, 218 Renfrew Street. 18 years. Admitted 28.6.37; 1st and 2nd stages, 7¾ hours; 3rd stage, 10 minutes. Girl born alive, 8 lbs.

MRS C., 28 Stratfield Street, Gallowgate. 35 years old. 3rd pregnancy. Admitted 14.6.37, labour started 2.7.37. 2nd stage, 4 hours; 3rd stage, 10 minutes; girl born alive, 6½ lbs.

MRS K., 34 Vine Street, Partick. 29 years. 6th pregnancy. Admitted 4.7.37, 1st and 2nd stages, 11 hours, 5 mins; 3rd stage, 10 minutes. Boy born alive, 7½ lbs.

Glasgow District Case Histories

M. S., 330 Forge Street, Ganniston. 25 years. 4th pregnancy. Roman Catholic. Husband unemployed. Girl born alive, 4.15pm, 6.7.37.

J. M., 1 Portree Street. 33 years. 12th pregnancy. Roman Catholic. Husband unemployed. Boy born alive, 12.15 am, 11.7.37.

A. C., 54 Hogganfield Street. 25 years. 5th pregnancy. Roman Catholic. Husband unemployed. Girl born alive, 13.7.37.

J. V., 7 Gardiner Street. 22 years. 1st pregnancy. Protestant. Husband, soldier. Boy born alive, 7.40pm, 14.7.37.

L. C., 644 Gallowgate. 23 years. 2nd pregnancy. Protestant. Husband, LMS railway. Boy born alive, 7am, 16.7.37.

M. M., 53 Dunrobbin Street. 37 years. 11th pregnancy. Roman Catholic. Husband unemployed. Girl born alive, 5.50pm, 16.7.37.

J. C., 17 Lenzie Street, Springburn. 28 years old. 5th pregnancy. Protestant. Husband's employers, Smith and Co., Possilpark. Girl born alive, 5.5pm, 18.7.37.

Joan Counihan [born 1915]

I married in 1939 and had three babies in quick succession during the war years. They were born at home with only a midwife attending me. No doctors were involved in any births. They were all born naturally with no pain relief. We were evacuated to a farmhouse in Shropshire where life was very primitive. My husband was in the army from 1940 to 1947 and abroad for a good deal of the children's growing up time. After the war I had five more children between 1948 and 1954, three born at home and two born in hospital. The fifth, sixth and eighth babies were about six weeks premature. The fifth baby died after a week but the other two grew up to be perfectly sound. The last birth was a breech birth.

Mary McKerrow [born 1915]

I went into a nursing home for all my three babies and was given some kind of anaesthetic, for the first baby, which was a very quick labour. I had pethidine for the others. I was mainly attended by nurses as the doctors were not there all the time. I stayed in the nursing home for about ten days each time, perhaps a bit less.

Dr Ekke Küenssberg [born 1913, General Practitioner, Edinburgh, during the war years]

I qualified in 1939 and started general practice work that year in Granton and Pilton, suburbs of Edinburgh, where families had been resettled from the overcrowded tenements of the Old Town. A large part of my work was dealing with women in childbirth because it was very common to have babies at home if you were in that social class. There were a lot of hurried marriages during the early war years and, with housing shortages, there were often two or three families in one house, with parents sharing the house perhaps. That was often when you could get a hospital bed, if the house was overcrowded, but otherwise the women were guaranteed a delivery at home as the common method. Women booked me as the doctor for their confinement and there would be a fee of £1 and 30 shillings I remember. This covered my costs for anaesthetic and all sorts of other things I needed to supply. I used pethidine and triline (which had just become recognised at this time and was extremely useful and helpful), although when I started many of my colleagues were still using the old chloroform. When used properly it is hard to beat, but often it is not used correctly. There were always these horror stories about some doctors saying to these poor labouring mothers, 'If you want chloroform, it will be an extra three pounds.'

It must have been awful to have to worry about the cost, because most of my patients couldn't afford it. In fact normally in Leith, Granton and Newhaven, these districts, it was thought rather feeble to need any anaesthetic for a normal childbirth. If a woman took it, then something must be seriously wrong. But this was not the case of course. Many a time I would use an anaesthetic if it was necessary, but if the woman couldn't afford it, then I would not send in a bill.

A woman who could not afford a GP to attend her would have the district midwife, together with a student doctor or pupil midwife perhaps, as they had to gain the experience of home confinements, and for these I don't think there was a fee charged.

———— • ————

'There was no pain relief for the working classes. The rich had anaesthetics; the poor, a knotted towel to pull on.

The babies they delivered were often a source of worry as of joy – another mouth to feed, a danger to the mother's health. Women begged in vain for advice on preventing future births. Midwives had little information and the best doctors could do was to warn the husband he should "make sure" his wife had no more children . . .'

Angela Holdsworth, OUT OF THE DOLL'S HOUSE.

———— • ————

Constance Küenssberg [born 1911, doctor in East Anglia, during the Second World War]

My experience of delivering babies was in the blackout, during wartime in East Anglia. I travelled around a great deal by bicycle as I could not always get petrol for my car. As antenatal care was almost unknown, we never knew when women would be expecting – we had no record of their due dates. So what would happen would be a pebble was thrown at your window in the middle of the night by the husband who had rushed out, perhaps on his bicycle, perhaps on foot, to fetch a doctor for the delivery. If I had my car, I would put his bicycle in the back and we would drive off across the countryside. Sometimes they were very remote cottages. We would come to a fence, abandon the car, and clamber over the stile and across the fields in the pitch black. Eventually we would come to the house which would be very primitive and broken down. They had been good cottages but no repairs had been done and these families were very poor people. Then I would clamber up a vertical ladder to the attic bedroom and find the labouring woman on a mattress up there. I then had to bring hot water in a bucket up the ladder and deliver the baby up there with no facilities to hand at all. Some houses were appalling, with no plumbing and filthy unhygenic conditions.

If anything had gone wrong, heaven knows what we would have done. Ipswich was about twenty-five miles away, in the black out, and there was no telephone for miles. But I was very lucky. These rural people were tough country folk, and solid with good hips. I remember one wee, thin woman, who hated eating and lived on lettuce and tomatoes. When her time came, I was really very worried about the health of both mother and baby because she was so small and thin. The labour took nine hours and then this enormous eight pound baby was delivered. I was very surprised!

But these women had a great belief in raspberry leaf tea as an analgesic and it really helped them. I believe it was later revealed that there is something medicinal in raspberry leaves. These women were strong; childbirth just went on, year in, year out. And if you weren't pleased, you tholed it.

Emily Hagues [born 1916]

When I knew I was pregnant, my husband Douglas was already away off to the War, to Gibraltar and then on to Africa. He was there for two and a half years and Jennifer was three and a half before she saw her father. But it was good because I was staying with Dr and Mrs Duffy, the people who I had worked for as housemaid. They said they wouldn't hear of me going home and I stayed with them right up till I left to go to the maternity hospital. I kept working all the time; I've always been a very active person and so I just carried on. I was very neat, I didn't show much. I was very lucky being with Dr Duffy so I knew exactly what was going to happen. Mrs Duffy was also able to tell me about it. The first pain was at seven o'clock on the Saturday evening, I think it was, and I remember Dr Duffy saying, 'Now you take note, your pains will come at regular intervals.', and the second was at ten past seven, and there it went on. My daughter Jennifer was born at twenty past ten on the Tuesday morning, 5th January 1943, so it was a long labour, and I didn't have anything to help me. My waters didn't break until just before she was born. I remember this student I had at the end of the whole business, who said, 'Top of the class, no sedatives, not anything.' I was attended by Professor Bard, because I had to have stitches.

I wasn't really scared beforehand. I remember I went to the clinic and this lady said something about 'If it's a dry labour, it's dreadful.' She was an older person. That was the only time that I ever heard anyone say anything about childbirth. I'd read this medical book, and nothing that happened really shocked me in any way. It was all very natural.

With my second baby, Vivienne, I was a fortnight overdue and I saw the doctor on the Tuesday, and I says, 'I'm not coming back again', so what did I do on the Saturday? Douglas was home at the weekend, so I took two cupfuls of castor oil, one after the other, and at five in the morning I woke up and she was born at ten past five on the table at Queens Cross Hospital. The castor oil did the trick, didn't it? The doctor had said 'Don't go home and do anything' but I did.

Elizabeth Grey [born 1917]

For the first birth, I went into a nursing home and I was attended by my woman doctor, Dr Stewart. What happened was that my waters broke and so I had a dry birth. I mind her head was quite swollen where it had been in the one position, with no fluid round it. We had to pay for the nursing home; it wasn't a lot of money but I couldn't go to the cottage hospital because they didn't have a maternity ward. Janice was born in 1949 and Alice was born in 1952. The second birth was much easier, much easier.

Lucy Firth [born 1917]

I had no choice about the birth. I had the first baby at home and it was a forceps delivery with an open ether mask. The second was in hospital, as I was thirty-five by then, and I had no problems really. I had a little gas and air and a pethidine injection. Both births were not well managed when I think about it. In hospital I was alone in a single bed ward until just a few minutes before the baby was born. I stayed in hospital for thirteen days afterwards.

Milicent Woolner [born 1917]

For my first baby I went into hospital and was attended by a midwife, a doctor and a specialist. It was a forceps delivery. I was given gas and air and pethidine. I stayed in hospital for about three weeks because the baby had a cold, which was quite unusual, but both midwives had colds. I do think they should have been off duty. For the second baby I stayed at home and it was just a natural birth. I was going to be attended by a midwife only, but the doctor was called because an earlier prolapsed disc caused some difficulty.

Mary MacDonald [born 1920]

I had five daughters in all! Three were home births with a midwife and a doctor looking after me. I stayed in bed for ten days after each birth as this was the habit during the 1930s and 1940s. I had two hospital births for the last two girls and stayed in for a week in each case.

Jill Rowe [born 1920]

My mother has told me in great detail about the day I was born. She calls it The Great Surprise!

'I think we've got another one here.' said the young doctor, who was sweating freely having just delivered a baby boy. He was absolutely right, another baby was delivered a few minutes later. This time a little girl – that was me. I don't know who was most surprised, my exhausted mother or the young GP. For him the thrill was the fact that they were the first twins he had delivered. Jack and Jill had arrived.

My mother was so pleased to have a daughter at last as she already had two small sons; Allan, born in 1916 and Norman, born in 1919, and now twins in 1920. The bedroom, known as the spare room, had been prepared for the event with, of course, a fire alight in the grate. What to do when two babies arrive and preparation had been made for only one? One baby was put in a drawer of Mother's best mahogany chest of drawers, after making it comfortable. Nurse Morrow, the village midwife, attended all the confinements and without doubt it was she who kept me alive all night, as she wrapped me in a warm blanket and cuddled me in her arms in front of the fire. She was in fact to me what an incubator would be in hospital today.

The GP, Dr Cliff-Hodges, who was in his first practice in Godalming, had a speedy method of travelling using his Douglas motorbike. He pronounced the baby boy fit and well, but the little girl small and weak. Multiple births were not so common in 1920, so the arrival of twins caused quite a sensation in the village.

In 1948 I gave birth to our first baby and it was in the same room as my birth, as I was staying with my mother. It was a home delivery which did not go well.

I attended no antenatal classes, there were no such things. I just called to see my GP who confirmed that I was pregnant and we worked out the date of the expected baby.

My mother thought it good for me to have my baby at my old home. She was so kind but in no way prepared me for the birth of my baby. I knew nothing and nobody told me anything!

I remember being very wet 'down below' and mother said, 'Oh dear, your waters have broken.' I had no idea what that meant. Later the village midwife came, and my GP. I remember having pains and quite severe backache. I did not know that I was expected to take any part in the birth of the baby. In the end I was very exhausted and the GP told me that he would put me to sleep and that when I awoke 'it would all be over'. It was a forceps delivery, as my baby had a large head. When I awoke the GP was stitching me where I had been torn. I was very emotional and I cried for no particular reason. Blood was spattered around, even on the wallpaper!

I was on my mother's divan bed and the doctor told me so much bending had made his back ache. It was taking place during the night so my husband and my parents got no sleep that night. The baby was a healthy boy but he cried a great deal. After his birth I vowed, 'Never again!'

But three years later, I had my second baby. He was born in a maternity hospital in Guildford and I had two excellent nurses. They told me exactly what to do. He was a small baby and it was much easier, all so different from the ghastly experience of the first baby.

Joan Hill [born 1920]

My baby was born in a maternity hospital and it was all quite natural, with only gas and air as pain relief. I had a midwife only for the labour and then the doctor came in just before my daughter was born, which seemed to be the normal practice. I stayed in for two weeks and my mother, who had been flat on her back for three weeks when we were born, was amazed at the 'new ideas' of the 1940s. Now I am the one who is amazed.

Jean Charleson [born 1922]

I had my first baby, Kenneth, at the Simpson Maternity Hospital in Edinburgh in 1946. Everyone wanted to go to Simpson's. I remember I was very ignorant when I went in to have the baby; we had had no classes to tell us what to expect in labour. I didn't expect it to be such a dreadful pain. They had advised me to take castor oil and this was just awful. I got these dreadful pains and I didn't know if that was because of the castor oil or the labour starting. I was up half the night and then in the morning, about 8 o'clock, my husband and I went up to the hospital. The pains were coming quite regularly and they said I would have no problems. But at 8 o'clock that night I was still in labour, still in terrible pain. So then they decided to use the forceps because I was getting very weak. Kenneth was born within seconds.

With the birth of my second son, Ian, the labour was fine. Of course by then you know a bit more so I was not so apprehensive and I relaxed which made it much easier.

I was not well at all after the births. I took a very high temperature, a really high temperature, and it was the Sister who recognised the symptoms and called it nursing fever, or what used to be called childbirth fever. Long ago a lot of mothers would die of this, without any way of bringing down the temperature. But the drugs they had when Kenneth was born helped. But I had the same fever with the next baby, Ian, and even twelve years later, after the birth of Elizabeth, I had this fever. I was at the Eastern General with this last baby, and my temperature went up to 104°F and I was shaking all over, like a kind of malaria. Well the nurses didn't know what this was; they were panicking, putting me in a private ward and not knowing what this fever was. I was trying to explain that I had this every time, but they couldn't understand this. Then an elderly sister came in and I explained to her and she knew what it was. It must have been very uncommon by then. She said 'We'll have to get rid of your milk.' That is the cause of the fever, my body not accepting the production of milk. So I always had this problem but after a week I was fine, once the temperature came down.

It must have been a busy time for the hospital, with so many women having babies right after the war. I remember the queueing up to visit the mothers at night from 7.30 to 8. The fathers would be queueing right along Lauriston Place, three or four deep. You only had half an hour each night, so there was this mad stampede, the men all pushing and shoving to get in quickly so as not to waste a minute of this precious visiting time. I think there was also a Wednesday afternoon when your parents could visit but it was all very strict.

Joyce MacPherson [born 1923]

We decided to have a family right away because my husband had been married before and had lost his wife in childbirth. I felt the longer we held off having a baby, the more this tragic memory of his first wife and child would hang over him. It was quite normal to have babies at home. My mother came and looked after the house and propped up my husband so that was nice. For my first baby I was recommended the book by Grantly Dick Read which was full of relaxation advice and breathing technique. I did practise this and it was a tremendous help I must say. I was very nervous and it gave me confidence.

Labour and Childbirth

It was actually an easy birth – but the first stage was very drawn out. I was getting up and walking about and very uneasy all day, but by five o'clock in the evening things had really started and that was when the nurse and doctor arrived, and they stayed until Neil was born at ten past eleven. I had a pethidine injection because I was in terrible pain, and that really helped. Towards the end the doctor wanted me to have gas and air, and I tried it but found it an awful nuisance and pushed it away. However the nurse encouraged me to use it because the cord was round the baby's neck and she didn't want me to go on pushing, so the gas would relax me a bit and then they could cope with the problem. I didn't know about the cord at the time: they only told me about it after the birth!

When he was born, he was so blue and limp but I didn't know if there was anything wrong. I was so exhausted by this time and just glad it was all over. He didn't cry at all and the nurse picked him up and swung him about, which I thought was terribly cruel, and smacked him and eventually he cried. My mother told me afterwards that she was petrified because the baby just flopped onto the bed and didn't move. But he was alright. I had a midwife and a woman doctor for the birth. She was very modern for the age, but she was excellent and I was very pleased to have the two women with me.

from MORNING SONG

Love set you going like a fat gold watch.
The Midwife slapped your footsoles, and your bald cry
Took its place among the elements.

One cry, and I stumble from bed, cow-heavy and floral
in my Victorian nightgown.
Your mouth opens clean as a cat's.

Sylvia Plath

Jane Ward [born 1924]

I had five normal births, three born at home, two in hospital. I was conscious throughout all of them and found it was nothing as bad as the dysmenorrhoea I had suffered for years: that was pain without reason; childbirth was pain and hard work, but with something at the end.

Son number 1 (6 lbs) arrived at home after a long time and with the cord round his neck. I could not understand what the nurse meant when she said 'Push!' The product was red, wrinkled, very small, and not at all happy.

Son number 2 (7½lbs) took only three hours from start to finish, also at home. That was one Saturday morning. I was ticked off because my first question when he arrived was 'Is it perfect?'; the nurse thought I should have asked 'Boy or girl?'

Daughter number 1 was born in hospital, a completely painless arrival, smaller than her predecessor and with a small head. One of the delivery nurses was a nun, and considering I only knew her for a couple of hours, a truly remarkable woman. She made a tremendous impression on me and was certainly responsible for a stress-free delivery.

Daughter number 2, at home again, was tiny, but I was very tired and it was a hard night. Three small children, and rather more than my fair share of illness had not helped.

Son number 3 – hospital again. 'You can't have a child at home with four young ones running around.' They would have been farmed out, but authority won. This was not a happy time.

It was two weeks in hospital, or ten days in bed if at home. My mother had enjoyed the luxury of a live-in nurse for a month, and always had a daily help, anyway!

Grace Rae [born 1928]

In the event my fears and apprehension were groundless. After waiting nineteen years to have a child, I had a 9¼ lb beautiful baby girl. I had a whiff of gas and air, but I never got to the pushing stage – I think my womb gave up at the last moment and I had to have a forceps delivery. I was attended by a doctor and midwife, as well as a gallery of students looking on. One leaves one's dignity on the doorstep on such occasions! They took her off for peace and quiet for a while because of her sudden entry but I saw her for a moment, just to stroke her chin and say, 'Hello Isobel'. She turned her eyes to me – I don't suppose she could really see me – and she gave me such an old-fashioned look. I'll remember it for ever.

Rosemary Walker [born 1929]

I had my first baby in hospital and it was just a natural birth with no painkillers given. I was not too happy in hospital. For a start I was hungry and I was left on my own for a lot of the time, during labour, with no clothes on in a very public place. It was also cold. I could not believe that the sanitary towels were burned in an open fire in the ward. It was horrible and I still remember the smell. I stayed in for ten days so I was glad to get home again.

Joan Longmuir [born 1930]

I have had six children, the first in 1953. Numbers 1, 2, 3 and 4 were born at home, and the last two in hospital. I was given pethidine as pain relief for most of the births although the third one was very natural. Number five was a Caesarean section as I had a placenta praevia which meant it was all rather dangerous as the placenta came away first with a lot of heavy bleeding. I was attended by a midwife only for them all except for the fifth, when a surgeon had to deal with me of course, and I stayed in for three weeks after that. I much preferred my home deliveries!

Barbara Henderson [born 1931]

I have had seven children, two born at home and the rest in hospital. The first was a very natural birth, with no pain relief, and for the others I had some gas and air. For the sixth birth I had an injection to induce me as I had very high blood pressure. In fact for the last two births, I was inclined to haemorrhage and afterwards I was told I would have possibly died if I had stayed at home for the births.

Sheila Brown [born 1934]

In 1955 I had my first baby. When the time came I was getting these pains, and I immediately felt that this was a familiar discomfort, and therefore something I could cope with, rather like a period pain. And then when things really got going, time passed very quickly. Then I shrieked to the nurse, 'Oh, I've wet the bed.' And she said, very calmly, 'No dear, that's just your waters breaking.' How naive I was then. Although I'd been told it would happen I didn't realise what your waters breaking really meant and had expected some kind of warning. It happened so suddenly and forcefully, I felt I was in a loch, swimming I was!

It was all very quick really. I was induced about 7.30 or 8 o'clock in the evening and I produced Susan at twenty-five to two in the morning. Well I was totally euphoric. Some people have their miseries, but I was as high as a kite. If there had been light to do so, or if I was allowed, I would have written letters there and then to every friend I possessed. I was so over the moon with this child. I felt so important, as if no-one else had ever had a baby. I couldn't wait for Ian to come in and see her. I was tremendously proud. While I was in hospital I remember saying, 'I'll be back before long to have a son', and the nurses all fell about laughing.

Well I came back for my son, a second, third and fourth time, and I said to my mother, just before Jennifer was born, 'I think I'm going to shed a wee tear if this is another girl.' But I was delighted when she arrived. It didn't matter a bit. It wouldn't have mattered if she had been a small horse. Well, she felt like a small horse, the way she kicked and thumped her way into the world. And she arrived in just two and a half hours; it was a perfect production. She was a gorgeous baby.

I never had much bother at the actual deliveries. I had quite a good pelvis, so they said. They were all delivered at Foresterhill Maternity Hospital, Aberdeen. With Alison I had high blood pressure and they took me in and tried to settle me, but it went soaring again so they induced me. I was induced for each one, except Gillian. For this one I remember my Aunt Mabel had come in to see me on the Saturday afternoon. I was put in a private room because of my high blood pressure, and I was meant to keep quiet and rest. So Aunt Mabel arrived with a great big pound of black grapes. And after she had gone, I felt very lonely and bored so I ate the grapes, all of them. I know they say castor oil is the best inducement but these grapes did the trick and by twenty to eight, I was on my way. I said I was euphoric for the first birth. Well, it was the same each time. I was as excited and delighted each time.

I think I was more frightened beforehand, thinking about it. It was slightly different with me because I was taken in to hospital before the labour began, due to the high blood pressure. One fear I did have was getting halfway to the hospital and giving birth in a taxi or the car. I was always glad to arrive early at the maternity hospital, well ahead of time, so that I was in the best hands.

Daphne Laing [born 1935]

I had no choice about where I would have my babies: in hospital. One was a natural labour and birth, and three were induced. I had gas and air for the first three and an injection of pethidine for the fourth. Apart from a doctor being present for the induction I was delivered by midwives only. I had no problems.

—————◆◆—————

'[By the 1960s] the surgical procedures began as soon as the mother to be arrived in the hospital, when her pubic hair was shaved and she was given an enema. These measures were designed to protect the patient from any dangerous infection. The delivery position recommended in hospitals reflected the greater emphasis on surgical techniques; medical attendants insisted that women should lie on their backs with their feet secured in stirrups, to make obstetric movements easier, and physical intervention with instruments became normal practice.'

Steve Humphries and Pamela Gordon, A LABOUR OF LOVE.

—————◆◆—————

Liz Sanderson [born 1938]

We decided we didn't want a home birth which we could have had, living in the Borders, but it wasn't so common by then, so I just went into the Galashiels Cottage hospital. Russell, my husband, was never with me at the birth of any of our children because it wasn't the norm and really wasn't his scene. And I took the view that it was my job to have the babies, so I just got on with it. Luckily I had a lovely midwife with number one; when I had the second one the midwife wasn't so good but, because I felt I knew what I was doing, I just did it my way and there wasn't a problem. With the first baby I was in hospital for ten days. I'd never seen a newborn baby before – and they taught me how to bath it and got me going with breastfeeding and then I was on my own after that.

Baby three arrived terribly quickly. I'd only been in hospital for an hour and in those days you had a regulation shave and a regulation bath. When I thought I was going to have the baby in the bath, I staggered out into the passage and said to the midwife, 'I'm about to have my baby!' Then she took one look and said, 'Oh yes, you are. I will deliver the baby and telephone the doctor afterwards.' So that's what happened with baby three.

Four years later I was pregnant again and I cheekily said to the doctor 'I'm giving you the last chance to be there this time for the birth' – and he was. And after the baby was born he said, 'I'll ring your husband.' But I said, 'He won't be at home because he's about to go on the stage at

Melrose for the annual Gilbert and Sullivan week.' So he said, 'Oh well, I'll drive to Melrose and tell him.' I gather they had a great party after the show – but he came and saw me the next morning.

Jennifer Harper-Jones [born 1939]

I had two hospital births, and with the first one there were some difficulties in delivery. The monitor showed that the baby's heart was in distress and so a lot of equipment was wheeled into the room. I had wonderful care and very sympathetic treatment. The second birth was an easy delivery. I stayed in hospital for two weeks each time.

Carol Walton [born 1943, trained as a midwife at the Simpson Memorial, Edinburgh, 1966–67]

When I was training, hospitalisation was certainly becoming more recognised but we still had a lot of home deliveries in actual fact. I don't think many women were given the choice whether it was a home or hospital delivery. I think a lot of women had babies at home because they were not told they must go into hospital. Women had a hospital delivery if there might be something wrong, high blood pressure or something, otherwise you had your baby at home. But slowly by the late 1960s, the whole childbirth business changed almost without anyone really being aware of it, I think. Hospital began to be regarded as the safe place to have your baby, after generations of home births. And by the early 1970s, everyone was going into hospital. It is funny because it is only in recent years that most of us have realised women have a right to choose. That never entered into it before.

Women stayed in for a week for a normal delivery, five days minimum. Seven days for a forceps delivery and ten days for a Caesarean. We allowed them up out of bed but only after twenty-four hours, to go to the loo if things had gone normally. After a Caesarean they would have complete bed rest for three or four days. Now mothers are lucky if they get four or five hours after a normal delivery and are hauled out of bed, poor things, and often home within a day or two.

There is one practice that was carried out at the Simpson which people might not believe today. The mothers had to go in the bath twice a day so you had two student midwives for each end of the ward. One would get them up and take them to the bathroom. One nurse had to be in the bathroom all the time, in case they fainted or something. We had to get all these women bathed and their beds made in the morning. They could only move at a snail's pace because they were sore, but you had to get something like twenty women processed through the bathroom, otherwise we got a row from Sister. So one would be hauling them out of bed, one in the bathroom on guard duty and swabbing out the bath afterwards, and another in the ward making beds. It was so ridiculous looking back, that these poor women weren't allowed to have a bath at their own pace or when they felt like it. They were processed like machines.

'Within an hour of clocking in, Mrs. Dempster had been rinsed, scrubbed, scoured, shaved, tranquillised and produced a faeces to order. She was then trolleyed back to bed, prior to being started off in the morning. The phrase "starting off" was new to Sadie, it made her sound like a consumptive car, with attached jump leads. It turned out to be the in-hospital jargon for artificially induced childbirth ... the countdown for take-off.'

Sheena Blackhall, THE CONVEYER BELT.

I do believe that women accepted the doctor's decision at that time. They assumed without question that if one is ill, or having a baby, one trusts the doctor and he makes the decision. Women put themselves in the hands of the professionals and they sorted them out in their way.

We did not have monitors in my day, but we were inducing them more and putting them on drips. We kept women in the first stage of labour up and wandering around although many wanted to stay in bed. Maybe we would have half a dozen women in the first stage room all moaning and groaning together. Then as they progressed we wheeled them round the corner and put them in the delivery room. The only way to monitor them in those days was to listen in every half hour with a stethoscope.

Delivery tended to be the traditional method of lying flat on their backs. I actually saw some mothers being delivered on their side but that was rapidly going out of fashion and most mums were delivered on their back. There were certainly none delivered in other positions – squatting, standing – none at all. We only used stirrups for instrumental delivery.

Fathers were tolerated in the father's room and nowhere else. I don't even remember them being allowed into the delivery room afterwards. Later on it was beginning to be the case that they could stay in the room during labour but only if they didn't get in the way. They would always be turned out during an examination or a forceps delivery.

During my training the midwife would be left in charge of the delivery quite often. We only called the doctors if there was a problem. I remember the midwives' rule in those days. Everything seemed to be prefaced with Call Medical Aid. 'If this happens, Call Medical Aid'. But I don't think doctors would stick their nose into the delivery room unnecessarily. I think we had a better relationship in those days. If there was something going on where they might be needed, they might sit in the office, or hang around, just in case, but they wouldn't interfere with the midwife's care and attention.

The Simpson was a training hospital so there would often be a number of medical students observing a delivery. Especially if something exciting happened. I do remember being present on one occasion when triplets were born and the place was like the Odeon on a Saturday night, you know, standing room only! Millions of people in the room and I don't think the poor woman was consulted about it either. I think she was incidental to the whole procedure.

I think the biggest change since my day is in the status of women. In the 1960s, we had a few unmarried mothers but they were always called Mrs so they wouldn't feel out of place. It was a stigma, a serious embarrassment then.

———— • ————

'The midwife was a pretty lady with smart ginger hair and small features and blue eyes. "Hello Mrs Stacey," she said warmly extending her hand from behind her desk. "I'm Sister Hammond, how do you do?"

"How do you do?" I said, thinking I had reached civilisation at last, but feeling compelled to continue. "But I'm not Mrs Stacey, I'm Miss."

"Yes, yes," she smiled, coldly and sweetly, "but we call everyone Mrs here. As a courtesy title, don't you think?" '

Margaret Drabble, THE MILLSTONE.

———— • ————

Nowadays if you call them Mrs, they stand up and say, 'Actually it's Miss', quite boldly. So there's been a great change there. And of course we had many babies for adoption, some very sad cases, where you would have young girls and you took their babies away and they didn't see them after the birth, or else the girl might look after the baby for a week and then went home and left the baby in the nursery. It was heartrending and nobody knew how to deal with them properly. Here were all the mothers sitting happy and pleased with their babies and on the other side of the ward were these girls crying. We tried to put them on their own but it was not always possible. I think there was also an air of disapproval which hung about them as well.

I did my community midwifery practice in Paisley. Many women had their babies at home because there weren't enough hospital beds. Hospital beds were kept for women who had had eight or nine children already or were seen to be at risk for some reason.

Some of the home circumstances were quite appalling. Some of the deliveries I did were in the most disgusting places. You just wouldn't want to wash your hands because the bathroom was so revolting. I remember one flat, the bedroom was clean and tidy, they had done their best, but you couldn't get into the kitchen for unwashed dishes and things all over the place. The husband then said to me that he would have made me a cup of tea, but he wasn't expecting me! His wife was nine months pregnant but he wasn't expecting the midwife to call. I was actually quite grateful because I didn't want to drink out of any of their cups. Very poor circumstances and I was shocked by the housing areas I had to visit. One evening I once came across a child sitting in the gutter, eating out of dustbin. I thought I had come to the last outpost in the British Empire. People living in one room, a single end, up these stone stairs, with one loo for three flats, halfway down. The one room with the sink, which did duty for the potatoes, and the washing and the baby's bath.

Infant mortality was certainly much higher then, although I did not myself deliver any particularly small or sickly babies. They were all quite healthy but premature babies did not have much of a chance thirty years ago.

My home deliveries were actually all fine. One woman got up to go to the loo and the baby shot out and landed in a bucket, before I had arrived. We had been called and were on our way but it was born before we got there. The baby was fine, but the cord had snapped and the baby was quite cold. I bathed it in front of the fire and warmed it up. We would be horrified now at the cold home conditions in which we used to deliver babies. A lot of these were big families and I delivered babies to many women who already had eight, nine or ten children. I do remember visiting a young mother who had had her baby in hospital and had just come home. She was still wearing the same sanitary towel she had been given in hospital and she had no nappies for the baby. She also had a toddler which was sitting in this cot with the baby. She had nothing at all for that little baby.

'Carol' [born 1942]

I had a natural birth in hospital. The labour was just two and a half hours although the pain I felt for around fifteen minutes was nasty! My husband was present for the birth, but he was threatened with expulsion from the room because he kept making me laugh. It was a wonderful experience.

'A fad called Natural childbirth' was going the rounds about the time I gave birth to my first child. I remember seeing a short film in the cinema about a woman giving birth with this ecstatic look on her face; not a cry, not a whimper, passed her lips. I bought this hook, line and sinker, and went into the labour room, confident and smiling. The smile was soon wiped off my face as I went through the worst twenty four hours of my life, during which I realized childbirth was natural all right, but it was red in tooth and claw and had no respect for my person. My vision of life changed utterly in those hours, and I knew now that whatever I might be as a person, as a woman I had simply become a vehicle, a pod to be used and perhaps discarded after the event.'

Eva Figes, A CERTAIN AGE.

Sheila Davidson [born 1944]

My first baby was born in 1965 in hospital – I had no choice. It was an induced labour and I was given pethidine. The labour lasted from Friday evening until Monday at 4 am. I was in a room all on my own with a buzzer to press if I needed attention. The doctor came in at the moment of birth. My second son was born in 1970 and the birth was even worse.

In fact from day one of my second pregnancy I felt ill. Then when the time came, I was in labour from the Wednesday afternoon until Friday at 6 pm. It was very traumatic. I was given pethidine and doctors, midwives and children's doctors, came rushing in and out of the delivery suite. Paul was rushed off to the special care unit after a forceps delivery. I only got to see him through the window in the door, when my husband came to visit. I never held him in my arms until he was five days old. I cried most of the five days.

Barbara Bryan [1946]

I had a hospital birth with my first baby in 1979, although that wasn't necessarily by choice; actually, I had tried to arrange a home birth and had contacted several doctors in Edinburgh, but eight out of the ten doctors were utterly reluctant to contemplate home birth and thought that it was the most irresponsible thing for me to ever even to suggest, let alone to contemplate. They were extremely arrogant and extremely rude.

With my second baby, I had a home delivery. This was not so difficult to arrange because they are more amenable with a second birth, and because I had had a successful birth before, there was no problem. I remember how relaxed I was. The good thing about a home birth is that you are allowed to go through labour at your own pace. The midwife was not concerned about the contractions stopping and starting or that my waters had broken. I know that in hospital they are very keen to start the whole induction process once your waters have broken. I was able to take my time and go with my own rhythm and pace. There was no hurry. I play the piano and halfway through the second stage of labour I was playing the Chopin Preludes and thinking how wonderful this was. And then after that it really got going, and she was facing the wrong way round, so it was extremely painful. I was offered gas and air, but didn't really know what to do with it. Although I was having contractions fast and furious the baby wasn't coming out, so they had to give me a big episiotomy. It was quite a big slit and the baby simply flew out. And that was the second birth.

With a home birth, you have to be confident with your body. I truly believed that there would be no problem and it would be fine. Now some people may say that is ignorance or naivety but actually you have to have trust and confidence in what you are doing and the midwives are doing.

The change in attitude seems to be extraordinary. In the 1940s, it was still normal to have a home birth, yet in two decades, say twenty-five years, the transition has been from a perfectly natural environment to one of total unfamiliarity of medicalisation and technology. Women are pushed into hospital, slapped onto foetal monitoring machines, or being induced and whatever, and the whole birth process has become dehumanised. And that is a tragedy. And with the appalling proportion of women having Caesareans, it certainly seems to me, in this era of doctors now being in control of childbirth in hospital, that the midwife during the 1980s and 1990s has almost become redundant.

The night before my third baby was born, I had an inkling it was about to begin. I was sitting knitting furiously, listening to Beethoven's Choral Movement, the finale, at top volume . . . and I felt something was up.

So things began that night and since I couldn't sleep I came downstairs and lay on the couch in the sitting room. But as Katy's birth had stopped and started, I wasn't worried in the slightest. So the next morning I sat around, lying sedately, knitting away. Friends called in and I thought this is fine, 'Nae problem', the fabulous labour. But by six o'clock, I had a seering pain and my waters broke. It was a rush of water, like a Scottish burn. And I thought, 'Oh my God, the baby is going to be born **now**!' I had been dilating for days and I knew I was fully dilated. So I thought the baby would be born on the bedroom floor, with no midwife or doctor in sight.

I was very calm and got into a very comfortable position with my back against the loo. Contractions were coming every single minute. I was like that for three hours and twenty-five minutes. And although it was a great well of pain every minute, you can let your body go with it, and tell yourself 'Relax, relax', and I did feel very relaxed. I hadn't actually read many African, Caribbean or Chinese women writers, but for whatever reason I completely locked into what I believed was the Third World experience of childbirth. I thought, now these women have traditionally gone into a field and given birth and it is not a problem. If they can do it, I can do it. It was quite extraordinary, but I got into this vision and fantasy.

The midwife eventually arrived about an hour later, followed by a second midwife and the doctor. By now I was exhausted because I had been three hours in transition, fully dilated.

I was actually standing up when I gave birth. It is a much more natural position. And I learned later from a friend that that is how women in India give birth, they stand holding on to a pole. And that is what I wanted – a pole. I was leaning over a chair but I wanted something higher up.

So the baby was born on the sitting room carpet at twenty past nine, that night. Then I collapsed on the couch, where the cat had been lying, totally unhygenic, but it didn't seem to matter.

It was a fabulous experience. The only real pain was when the head came through. As someone has said to me, 'it is rather like giving birth to a melon – a water melon.'

Vivienne Leighton [born 1947]

I really read up about the birth itself beforehand. And going to these National Childbirth Trust classes told you what to expect. But I was still very nervous and apprehensive. I remember I could never think past that birth. He was due on the 15th September 1972, and I know I could never plan anything or think beyond that time. I didn't think I would get through it somehow. I don't know what I was thinking.

Anyway on the 1st September, my husband had gone back to Lossiemouth, he was in the Navy, and my waters broke. There was no one else in the house, so I phoned for a taxi to take me to hospital. I had started contracting but nothing much at all. By a quarter past three I really did start labour properly but all the pain was in my back. It was very swift but very painful. The midwife couldn't feel the strength of the contractions at the front. He was born at five minutes past five so it was really only two hours in actual labour. So that was it!

I had read a book about natural childbirth, which was recommended at NCT classes, and I really read everything about childbirth. But everyone has different ideas about what is best, and the classes suggest you hum tunes that you know to get over the contractions. But at the time I must admit I didn't think about tunes, I just concentrated on what I was doing, and all that good advice on how to relax and cope with the pain just went out the window. I just tried to breathe over the contractions using the gas and air, as they told me. My husband was not there which I was quite glad about. I don't like people to see me if I am in pain as I find it harder to bear. I wouldn't want to see him upset. Maybe in childbirth it is different because so often the husband is there nowadays. I am sorry he missed the actual experience of it, but for me I preferred it that way.

The second birth in 1975 was not so easy. I saw the obstetrician a few days before my date and he gave me an examination and said, 'Well, if nothing has happened, come in a week on Sunday.' I persuaded him that I should come in on the following Sunday instead and be started off with an enema. So that is what happened. They gave me an enema, prior to actually inducing me, and that started me off. Because I was so quick with the first baby, they rushed me to the labour ward expecting this to be as fast. But everything slowed down, and I didn't contract or anything. That would be the Sunday night and by the Monday morning, nothing had happened. So they put me on the drip which is something the NCT would not have wanted me to have, to induce contractions. Again the pain was all in the back and they couldn't tell how far on I was. At 12 o'clock the doctor was going to examine me and by this time I was wanting gas and air, but the midwife was not happy about this. The doctor came in and I remember shouting at him, as he began washing his hands, and I said, 'Do you think you are God? – come on, I need gas and air.'

He had one quick look and I was three fingers dilated and he said, 'Right, give her gas and air.' And at ten past twelve I wanted to push and the midwife said, 'No, you can't push. I haven't got my instruments out yet.'

Anyway I said I couldn't wait, and I pushed. And because it was all so quick, I tore, and Emma was born at twelve minutes past twelve. Just twelve minutes after I was given gas and air. I can still feel her head going down. Despite this last minute panic, all in all, I thought the medical treatment was first class – the midwives were excellent, couldn't have been better.

Mary Law [born 1949]

For my first baby I wanted a home birth, but my husband didn't agree. In the end, the baby was in a breech position and I had to have an elective Caesarean section, so that put paid to that idea. I had to go into hospital in week 37 and had the baby one week later. For the second baby, I was induced and given an episiotomy and it was all very unpleasant. I came home after two days. For the third birth, I only used gas and air and I needed no stitching. It was a lovely experience and I stayed in for six days because I needed a rest from the home and family!

Wendy Walker [born 1949]

Having had eight children I have experienced every kind of childbirth I would imagine! I had six babies in hospital and two at home. I didn't want to have a home birth but my GP insisted. I expect it was because of a shortage of beds and, since I had previously had several children normally, they must have seen me as a low risk mother. However I did have high blood pressure during one pregnancy and I had to stay in hospital for seven weeks and have the labour induced. I also had to have one Caesarean section. But the other births were all quite normal and natural with just a little gas and air for pain relief.

One tip I would recommend is for women to take raspberry leaf tablets

– they are excellent. Raspberry leaf tea has been a remedy for generations and whatever is in it, it works miracles.

Sheila Gray [born 1951]

I had my babies at the midwives section at Aberdeen Hospital with no doctors around. They were very homely rooms, but close to medical help if needed, but I was attended only by midwives. I was just given gas and air and, very traditionally, I lay flat on my back for all of them.

Ailsa Gray [born 1953]

I have had five babies within five years, all born in – or almost in – hospital. The first three were fairly high tech, constantly monitored births and I was given an epidural for all of them. With the first baby I needed a Ventouse – also called a vacuum – delivery, which is more common in the rest of Europe rather than in Britain, where forceps are more often used. My third baby hadn't arrived by forty-two weeks and they wouldn't let me wait another day, so I had to be induced. By the time baby number four came along, I think my body was getting used to this annual labour, and he was born in the front seat of our Ford Escort en route to hospital!

I think if I had experienced this with my first baby I would have been extremely frightened but as it was my fourth I knew what to expect and tried to keep very calm. But it was still a great surprise because I had no warning that labour had actually started. I was woken up at about four in the morning, but I didn't think I was in labour, and I know that sounds daft because if you've had a baby before you should know but this wasn't the same; this was just a niggling stomach pain, and I took a paracetamol and thought it would go. It was just like a sort of period pain. But then suddenly, as I stood there on the landing, my waters broke and I knew that I had to get to hospital. So I pulled on some dungarees and we quickly put some emergency plans into operation. Our other three children were in bed – so my husband rang his mother to ask if she could come round immediately by taxi while he took me to the hospital. I then realised that things were speeding up quickly and I had to go to the hospital straight-away so we left the children in bed – we hadn't woken them up – and informed a neighbour that we had to leave and that Alan's mother would arrive in about ten minutes. We set off in our Ford Escort.

We live in Milngavie, in Glasgow, and we were heading for Queen Mother's Hospital. We knew we would be passing the police station and thought it might be sensible to stop off there to see if they could offer any assistance, perhaps give us an escort so that we could reach the hospital at top speed with blue lights flashing, the lot! But we found when we got there that it was a daytime police station only and it was shut.

We carried on as fast as Alan would dare go, along the Dumbarton Road. By this time I knew the baby was definitely on its way and I was in great pain. It was extremely painful and I am someone who cannot tolerate great pain and have always requested an epidural. So I kept apologising to Alan and I was saying things like, 'I'm sorry but I'm going to have to scream', to warn him what was coming, and I was clutching at his arm, while poor Alan was endeavouring to concentrate on driving me to the hospital. By this time it was getting on for five in the morning, and as there was no traffic to speak of on the roads, we had driven through a couple of red lights. Having had three babies before, I could tell what stage the labour was at and quite quickly I felt the baby's head coming down and then actually appearing. I did not tell my husband because I think he would have crashed into a lamp-post or something. This was not the moment to tell him the baby was being born *now*.

We got to the hospital and we parked right outside the main entrance and Alan dashed in to get some help. By the time they had taken me into the vestibule they found Robert, our fourth baby, had been born and was inside my dungarees. I think it was then that they cut the cord. I'm sure they did that immediately.

At this point Alan had to be literally sedated as he sat there in the reception area. He was a bag of nerves and no wonder, having driven us in such a panic to the hospital. But I felt wonderful as I was wheeled up to the maternity ward with my baby, who had been wrapped up in a towel and placed in my arms. I then enjoyed my tea and toast, knowing that it was all over. Robert was whisked away to be checked over and he was absolutely fine. There was no problem. He was 9lb and 14 ozs. I didn't even need any stitches. They actually told me that a very quick labour and delivery is fine for babies because they don't suffer so much compared with a long drawn out labour. I think I must have missed the first stage completely in my sleep and woken up as I was going into the second stage, and within less than an hour he was born.

I think in some ways it had been an even worse experience for my husband who had to witness me being in pain, hearing my screams, as he desperately tried to drive carefully but quickly to the hospital. I was in great pain but there was nothing he could do to help me. Looking back we wonder whether we should have stayed at home, phoned for a doctor or ambulance for help and delivered it ourselves. It might have been safer to have stayed there. But I couldn't have predicted it would be such a swift labour and so going to hospital was the obvious decision at the time. Our three other children never woke up and never knew we had left the house and their grandmother arrived very soon afterwards.

Having survived this incident with Robert, when I was going into labour with my fifth baby the following year, I felt I could cope without much pain relief. I was always the first to say, 'I'm here for an epidural' but now I felt in control and wanted a more natural birth. I had a little gas and air, and Heather was born within seventeen minutes – and this time I was safely in the labour ward, in hospital. I was absolutely thrilled because I so much wanted a second daughter – and Laura had always wanted a little sister.

———◦———

'This is what I'm going to have when I have a baby,' the nurse said, sliding the needle into a vein and taping it down on to the skin. 'Speeds things up no end. You set them off at breakfast time and the babies are here at tea-time. It's far and away better. You never get the cases of real exhaustion now like you used to get. Some poor girls, you know – they used to go on for days.' She watched the clear golden liquid flow along the pipe. 'No, this is what I want. Either that or not come in till the head's there.'

Pat Barker, UNION STREET.

———◦———

Trudi Barnet [born 1954]

I had very normal deliveries for my first three boys. Then some years later I had my fourth baby. I went into labour in the early morning and when I got to hospital I actually wasn't too sure whether it was a false alarm or not. Nothing much was happening. I was on the mobile phone to my sister-in-law and I had just switched this off when the midwife came in to examine me. I got on to the bed and I knew exactly what position to get into for this. I put my heels together and let my legs flop sideways. And as she was washing her hands, I suddenly felt things begin to happen and I gave birth, just like that. So I had a labour of about one minute. This in fact was not exactly very clever. I knew instinctively the baby was coming and I just helped to push him, and out popped Jack. My insides were very sore. I didn't rip on the outside but I definitely ripped the birth channel. It was incredible. I think I was only learning about this childbirth business with number four.

For the birth of my fifth baby, I had a planned induction because I was in severe pain. The doctor thought that at thirty-eight weeks, I should have an induction. Just beforehand a midwife was explaining to me how one mother had been helped to deliver the baby herself and that there was a great feeling of partnership, a lot of weeping and happiness, the women together. And I fancied this. I thought 'Well, I had had such an easy birth the last time, it should be fine.'

So I went in on the Monday; they put a lot of gel inside me but they wouldn't put the drip on yet because I would go very fast into labour. They didn't want me to go so fast this time. They told me to keep walking up and down the stairs. The midwives on duty were really pleased because a woman that morning who had four girls and was having her fifth, had just had a boy. Here was I, the mother of four boys, so would I have a girl?

So they put the drip up to get me going. I had never had a normal labour before and, after an hour, I thought 'I am getting fed up with this, this is longer than all of them put together. It must be a girl.' Graham was saying 'It's not that long, just be patient.' I think really it was because my body was getting lazy, because it had had so many births. I was standing over a chair at this point with my husband massaging my back. The midwife suggested I go on all fours, like a dog, and they would be able to see how things were going. It is not the most elegant position, but it was nice because you could rock back and forwards.

Things progressed slowly. I was on the delivery table by this time, and really got to the end of my tether. I was sniffing some gas and air, and the room was spinning a bit. And then I thought 'I am not going to get any medals for this', so the midwife said she would get me something else for the pain. Just as she left the room my cervix opened. It had only dilated one centimetre but suddenly it opened completely. But that is what happens when you have had lots of babies, because the body goes from one stage to the next very quickly.

So the midwife came back in. She told me not to push yet, and I was concentrating hard on panting as she explained that the cord was round the baby's neck quite a bit, so that I would have to keep panting to slow down the delivery. I was aware of her hand right up inside me, holding this baby's head, as it was coming down. That wasn't painful at all. She had explained to me that if I was going to deliver the baby myself, I would put my hand down and hold the baby's head as it came out. So she was saying, 'I'll just tell you when to help it out', and I thought, 'Maybe I shouldn't do this.' Then she said, 'Now it's all yours. The head is out.' So I put my hands down, I can remember feeling this baby, and drew it slowly out and put it down on the delivery bed. But because I had sort of closed my legs no one knew what it was. I had to peek between my legs to see what sex it was. And it was a girl! It was a very easy birth. She was quite small, about seven pounds, and I didn't have a scratch. The midwife was so pleased with herself. Everything intact, not a tear, not a scratch. The moral is, don't push and get yourself a good midwife who knows what they are doing! And it was just an hour and forty minutes in total.

And I had the birthing tape on in the background – the sound of dolphins and water. It was very relaxing and soothing. Some people think you must be a bit fruity to have background sound effects, or music, but I think it was wonderful.

'Cathy' [born 1955]

My first baby was very big indeed, around 12 lbs at birth. A Caesarean section was mooted for my second one, but she turned at the last minute. She was 9 lbs. The third was very sick at birth and only the amazing intensive care of the hospital saved him. To show the comparison, the first two babies had a score of 20/20 on the APGAR test when they check breathing, heartbeat, reflexes, etc. after birth. But the third baby had a score of just 3/20, which was very worrying. He is now fine six years later.

Winifred Fyfe [born 1955]

I had very good pregnancies and perhaps because I am only four foot ten, I never showed much of a bump, and could wear jeans until I was six months gone. I never wore maternity clothes. Because I am so small, it was decided some months beforehand that I would have to have an elective Caesarean. They just give you a date to go in. The eldest girl, Sarah, was born in 1980, under general anaesthetic, and the last two using an epidural which I found quite an ordeal as I had no feeling in my limbs. With the second baby, Lesley, in 1982, I actually went in to labour on my own, and during the night I thought 'This is it' and then I thought, 'Surely not?' and went back to bed but it kept on going. So although I had to have Caesareans for all three babies, at least I'd experienced labour a little bit. After a section it is quite unpleasant because you can't move for two days. I mean you rely on everyone so much, the nurses down there were just great. I stayed in hospital for ten days which was quite a long recuperative period but I needed it.

I was quite happy to have the sections and with the last two I had an epidural so I stayed awake when the babies were delivered. I didn't like this at all. I hated it. They put up a screen so that you can't see anything and I remember feeling very claustrophobic and I wanted to scream and yell. I found the sensation very difficult to cope with. So when I had Amy, my third, I told them about that and so they gave me some valium. You could see them lifting up your leg but you couldn't feel anything, it is a horrible experience. Although, on saying that, if a woman is having a Caesarean it would be well worth having the epidural if she can stand that sensation. But the doctor said to me that some women find it enjoyable, to be conscious through the childbirth as in a natural birth. It was a quicker recovery as well compared to a general anaesthetic.

After Amy was born I haemorrhaged which put me back a bit. I had to have a transfusion, it was all very unpleasant, and I was glad it happened with my third one because if that had happened with the first I don't think I'd have had another child. It was really very nasty because I was sterilised at the same time and I think that probably caused the haemorrhaging. I found out afterwards that many doctors will not do a sterilisation after a section because your blood vessels are so full. It was very unpleasant anyway, but I'm here to tell the tale, so I survived.

In fact our third daughter was a great surprise. I had two girls and that was what I had planned, two children. I never went on the pill again after Lesley was born, because I didn't like it, and we were using various methods which obviously didn't work. Well, I had a four year gap, right enough, and once I thought I was pregnant again, I remember walking about for a fortnight thinking, 'A baby, oh heavens above!' and after that I just thought 'This is silly. It's a baby, big deal, what difference is it going to make?'

However, my husband was made redundant when I was five months pregnant with Amy, and I then walked around almost suicidal for a fortnight. But it all worked out, and she's just wonderful, and I'm so glad I had her. I've enjoyed that baby so much. I think it's because with having two children already, she just had to fall into the pattern of our lives, and the two older ones just adored her. So it is nice to have three girls and I think I'm very lucky to have three healthy children.

Jano Rochefort [born 1955]

My first baby was born in a maternity home and, while I wanted to be attended just by a midwife, I ended up with a Caesarean section. For my second baby I went into hospital and it was a planned Caesarean section, but in this case I had chosen a female obstetrician who was going to be looking after me. For my third baby, I was living in the United States at the time, I chose a local male doctor with seventeen years experience of home births. I had excellent care and had the baby at home. It was a perfectly natural birth, with no painkillers or monitors or anything.

Roma Young [born 1956]

I was nineteen when I had my first baby and I was really terrified! I went into the Craigtoun Cottage Hospital at St Andrews, which was a nice, small maternity unit and the staff do try and put you at your ease. If you are young and frightened it's not easy. You don't know what to expect and they didn't seem to give me good enough explanations as to why they were doing things and what not.

I had a long labour so I was induced and, because it was my first, I was happy to get it over with as quickly as possible. I was absolutely exhausted through the whole thing and the doctor had to do a forceps delivery on her, which meant she was very black and blue. She had black eyes for about a fortnight but she was OK apart from that. I stayed in for a full week.

When I had my second baby, we were staying near Lossiemouth and I was going to go to a cottage hospital but I started bleeding and they thought my placenta was going to come first, so they whipped me by ambulance to Aberdeen. The staff there were a lot better in the sense that they told me more. It was a big teaching hospital and I was surrounded by student nurses and student doctors. Basically the midwife was telling the students what was happening to me, so I heard what was going on too!

In 1990 when I had my youngest little boy, after a gap of ten years, attitudes towards childbirth had changed enormously. I read about water births when I was expecting Oliver. I decided to have a home birth as I wanted a more relaxed and natural birth. I was told if the pregnancy went fine there was no reason not to have a home delivery. I was close enough to a hospital if complications arose, and it would only take ten minutes to get there so that was our back up. Our trust in the midwife was total; I trusted her and she trusted me in the sense that if I felt something was not right, I would tell her and if she said medically there is nothing to worry about, then we would stay at home. But if she had a problem then I agreed to go into hospital. I had got to know the midwife for some months. She conducted the first antenatal check up at the very start. She popped in every couple of weeks to see how I was as she would pass the end of our road on her way to the hospital. During the last six weeks or so she came to see me once or twice a week. She became a very, very good friend and we still keep in touch.

The whole thing was a different experience, knowing the midwife so well by the time of the birth, instead of going into a hospital environment and not knowing who will attend to you.

I felt so relaxed because there was no one popping in and out to check an instrument or monitor. I had no monitors or anything; the midwife had an ear trumpet and a stethoscope and that was about it. I had no pain relief except for hot water. I sat in a hot bath during the first stage of labour and Allan massaged my back with aromatherapy oils which helped a lot. And it turned out fine. Oliver was the biggest baby I had and yet it was the easiest birth. I don't know if this was because I had no medical intervention but, deep down, I think it must have been why it was so easy.

June Williams [born 1960]

Although I trained as a midwife myself, I don't think this made the whole process any easier! When I had my first baby, Alexander, in 1990, the early stages were as I expected and I think I coped quite well with the pain because I got to hospital and he was born two hours later which was good for the first time. But I didn't anticipate the pain would be quite as bad as it was. Because it was such a quick labour, I didn't have any pain relief. I just had gas and air, that is all I could have. I remember thinking this cannot be happening to me, it was such a painful experience, but you get through it.

Labour and Childbirth

While I am a midwife and knew what to expect, and also went to antenatal classes for advice about breathing and so on, when it comes to it, it is usually different to what you may have planned or anticipated.

For my second baby, I chose the domino scheme which is a good halfway system between home and hospital birth. A team of four community midwives looked after me antenatally and when I went into labour, I phoned them all and then was able to stay at home with the midwife until the last stage. We went to the hospital together and she and a student midwife delivered me so I had the same midwife throughout my pregnancy and labour which was so relaxing and comforting, being looked after in your own home. I never saw a doctor which is not unusual as you only really need a doctor when there are complications.

I decided to go into hospital for the delivery itself but opted for a twenty-four hour stay. I would not opt for a home delivery, because you don't know what might happen and the baby might need resuscitation. It is the best of both worlds. I knew the midwife who would deliver me, and I knew I'd be home the next day, whereas if you just go into hospital at the start of labour by yourself, you don't know which doctor or midwife might be attending to you.

The natural birth campaign and the use of birthing chairs and pools is now taken seriously in most hospitals; it is good that women have a choice now. Lying on a bed is the most uncomfortable way to have a baby and so this time the midwife suggested I stand up. Although Jonathan's delivery was still painful, it was much easier standing up. The delivery bed converted into a chair, so some of the time I was sitting, relaxing, and then I was leaning over the chair, and it all seemed much more natural and gravity was really helping me to give birth. I went home the next day as planned, and the same midwife came round to see me for a postnatal checkup.

I do think that the so-called 'Natural Childbirth' is quite hard to carry out in practice; for a lot of women their experiences are far from what they believed after reading the book or going to the antenatal class. When the labour begins, you often do need some pain relief and in this day and age, excellent pain relief is available and it is safe to use; I don't see there is any harm in it and it is silly to be a martyr.

Now that I have experienced childbirth myself my work as a midwife will be different. I am sure to approach it more subjectively, but at the same time, you have to be quite tough even if you know what the woman is suffering; you still have to ensure that she breathes properly and you do have to be very firm otherwise they don't concentrate on what they are doing. But I think I would be more sympathetic.

Jo Davidson [born 1960]

I had both my children in hospital although I had considered a home birth but backed out in fear of something going wrong. As it happened it would have been fine. Both were monitored, the first with a scalp monitor on the baby's head as it had passed meconium and this indicated foetal distress. Because of this I seemed to have an entire football team of experts in the room with me, which was strangely comforting as they were all rooting for me to push the baby out. For the second birth, I had a student doctor as well as the midwife. The student was doing her second delivery and that was lovely because it felt special for all of us.

'Childbirth can be the best or worst moment of your life – most likely both. You can give birth at home, in the bed where the child was conceived; in the back of a taxi on the way to hospital; on a bean bag surrounded by flowers and candles and friends; or in an operating theatre amid state-of-the art technology.

A waterbirth is seen by many today as the Holy Grail of maternity. Michel Odent, a follower of Frederick Leboyer's 'birth without violence' principles, first used a tank of water as a birthing bed because it eased a mother's labour in many cases. He soon discovered it was an excellent way of providing a baby with a gentle door into this world.'

Cassandra Eason, A MOTHER'S INSTINCTS.

Lucy Owen [born 1961]

I had always wanted a waterbirth, since seeing Michel Odent's programme when I was aged about fourteen. So I went to Yehudi Gordon and Faith Haddad at the Garden Hospital, where natural childbirth or active birth is encouraged. My first baby was ten days late when labour started naturally. I laboured for thirty-two hours, sometimes in the pool, which was wonderful, just as good as an epidural, sometimes out of the pool. My husband massaged me with oils for twelve hours solid. I did not dilate more than half a centimetre but really wanted to do it myself. The baby was never in distress, but I was. So I had my waters broken and was given syntocinon to speed up the third stage and I dilated to full in half an hour. I pushed for two hours but the baby's head was stuck. So I had an emergency Caesarean under epidural. There were no screens, my husband was present, and I watched it all. I was very disappointed not to have had a water birth but thankful to have had Archie.

For the second birth, I was ten days late again. The baby was huge, and [we] decided on an induction after much heartsearching. It was the same team of midwives, which was very comforting. It was a short, five hour labour, mostly in the pool. Again the water was a blessing as a pain reliever helping me to cope. I was in the dark with whale and dolphin music playing. It all seemed right at the time. I was much more confident and knew I could do it. I had to get out of the pool for the birth, sadly, as I am very small pelvically and the baby only just got out. She was 8lb 10oz. The sense of achievement was fantastic as this slippery bundle shot out at about 100 mph onto the floor; it made me feel a real woman and mother at last. I needed to do it myself even if only once. I have never felt such euphoria, even with 24 stitches. I had one midwife, Faith Haddad, and my husband so it was a team effort. I was with people I knew well and I think that's what made the difference.

Diane Connolly [born 1961]

As a midwife I gave birth in the hospital where I worked, with a consultant of my choice. I was augmented for prolonged rupture of membranes at thirty-nine weeks. I had a long labour with an epidural as pain relief. I had a three hour second stage with no descent of the head, which proceeded to a Caesarean. I had a very experienced midwife during labour who was in fact a good friend. She came on duty at 7 am and looked after me until after 9 pm, when she was emotionally physically exhausted. My delivery at 10.30 pm was witnessed by her and my husband through the theatre door.

I can remember opening my eyes and focusing on my husband Andrew holding a baby, and the realisation dawning that it was ours. The midwife shoved him under my nose and I apparently nuzzled him. I loved him from that first moment.

I was keen to have an elective Caesarean for my second child as my pelvis is quite narrow but my friends encouraged me to drink copious amounts of raspberry leaf tea, and I eventually presented myself to my consultant at forty-two weeks. Sixteen days after my due date I had an elective Caesarean under spinal injection, with my husband holding my hand and best friend as midwife keeping me calm, and out came a 10 lb 10 oz boy. All my colleagues had said this would be a smaller baby! He screamed from the moment of birth and I asked Andrew to take him out of the theatre. I thought he was so ugly and fat and bald and didn't like him at all for nearly a week. I don't think it helped that he cried such a lot!

———•———

'Next morning at six the door was thrown open and a cot wheeled in. "Here's your daughter" the nurse said.

The baby was curled up asleep, mouth and cheek pressed out of shape by the mattress, bottom stuck up in the air. Lisa worked herself across to the side of the bed, grimacing as the stitches pulled, and stared at the child. Her hair was reddish, almost auburn, and yes, it did look as though it might curl. She saw blood pulsing across the opening in its skull and drew back. There was nothing about this baby she recognised as hers. If she had been an animal she would have rejected it, would have sniffed at it and turned away, at once and finally.

Instead she read the label on the cot. She read the label on the baby's wrist. Her mind told her that it was hers. She found herself dreading the moment when it would wake up and demand to be fed.

There was nobody she could talk to. She listened as her mother and the nurses said what a beautiful baby it was. And prayed for the moment when she would be allowed home, when she would no longer have to lie in this little cell of a room, pretending.

Pat Barker, UNION STREET.

———•———

Angela Blanchard [born 1962]

My blood pressure fluctuated and rose towards the end, as is common in first pregnancies, but I felt well and had no other signs of pre-eclampsia. However the consultant got very twitchy and once I had gone to term plus two days, he asked me to come in for a check-up. He said I ought to be induced and I was devastated. There was I, vulnerable, lying down on a bed like a sick person, being told by a consultant that he'd like to keep me in for observation and, if I was going to be in, I might as well have the baby. Anyway, he was going to a conference in London on Monday and he'd like me to have the baby before he went! It was not what I wanted, but I was powerless to resist. Once I was in hospital, I was on a conveyor belt. I spent a miserable night and hardly slept as the hospital was so noisy; I missed my husband and was not comfortable. On the Saturday morning, the midwife came to insert prostaglandin pessaries and when she monitored me found I was having mild contractions. I had severe pains all morning and then was given a second lot of pessaries. Labour actually got going by that evening and at about 11.30 pm I was taken down to the labour ward. At 2 am I think the midwives thought the baby's heartbeat was speeding up, indicating distress. I was being constantly monitored by electronic devices. They tried to attach a monitor to the baby's head but this did not work. The midwife then told me she was going to give me an episiotomy and I wasn't in a position to argue. I bled profusely; my husband told me afterwards that he thought she must have nicked an artery as there was so much blood, although I was unaware of this at the time. I had gas and air as a pain relief and Clare was born normally at 5.56 am on the Sunday. My blood pressure then plummeted – I had a postpartum haemorrhage and was given an emergency transfusion. By now I was exhausted and it was my husband who had my portion of the customary tea and toast!

Pregnant with my second baby, I made the decision to have a home birth. It no longer seemed such an outlandish thing to do. This meant that much of my antenatal care was at home, which saved the stressful trips to the clinic with a toddler in tow. When I was nine days overdue I went into labour, and the midwife came and checked me over but said it would be a while yet. I felt no fear, nothing but excitement about the coming event. By 9 pm the contractions were beginning to change and the midwife came back at about midnight and stayed the night. I laboured in various positions – standing, crouching over the bath, over a bean-bag, on the bed and on all fours. I kept my strength up by eating toast and honey, but I was beginning to tire. I used gas and air for pain relief. At 6.30 am the second midwife joined us and I finally gave birth, lying on my side, at 9.20 am. He was delivered on to my lap, still wet, bloody and blue but very much alive and well. Then we all had toast and jam and champagne, myself, my husband, my mother and the two midwives, sitting in the bedroom together. It was wonderful.

Linda MacPherson [born 1962]

I felt contractions from nine in the morning but they were very weak, and I knew things would take time and I wanted to stay at home for as long as possible. At eleven I called my husband, and he came home from work. We stayed home together all day, resting and relaxing. I kept calling the hospital, to see what they thought I should do and they said as long as I felt in control, I was better off at home at this stage.

At four o'clock the contractions began to get stronger and I went into hospital at that point. I was examined and they put a monitor on to check the baby's heartbeat and contractions. Ten minutes later the waters broke and after that things really began to move quickly.

I had put my name down for the birthing pool, so I was brought up to the labour ward with the pool. I went into the pool and was there about twenty minutes, but I found it didn't give me enough pain relief. It didn't help me much at all. So I came out of the pool, and was put into another ward and given dimorphine. I had tried gas and air, and it did nothing for me. Dimorphine was wonderful. Two hours later he was born. It went very well, and I was only in for about five hours and he was born at 10.30 that night. Although I thought I was going to die at the time, looking back, and having talked to other girls, I was lucky and it really wasn't that bad.

The pain was far worse than I had expected because I have friends who have done it with nothing but gas and air. But I thought the pain was horrendous when the contractions got really bad. I certainly cannot imagine doing it without pain relief. At first I thought I might have managed it without drugs, because when I was at home the contractions were just like a period pain, and quite gentle, and I thought even if they got worse it would be alright. But when the contractions were really painful, I couldn't cope with it or relax because you were just waiting for the next one. The dimorphine was wonderful because it took your mind off it. And because it was over so quickly it wasn't bad.

But the baby was in a bit of a bad state, because there had been meconium staining in the waters. He was slightly off centre when he was coming out, so it was a bit hectic in the end and he was rushed away for a suction thing on his lungs. But he revived quite quickly.

Immediately afterwards I was just so exhausted. My husband held him up to me as they were doing my stitches, but I wasn't really impressed at that moment in time. I was really hungry, and I just wanted something to eat, and wasn't interested in Magnus at all. I was glad it was over and just wanted to be stitched up.

After that, when I had had time to relax, it was fine. I think his dad was far more emotionally touched by the whole experience than I was. He was sitting there holding him with tears in his eyes, and I was just lying there saying, 'Where is my tea and toast?'

I stayed in for five days and could have stayed on but I thought if I don't get home now, I'll never cope on my own. The midwives were wonderful, and it was so nice to have people to look after him and people there to ask if something worried you. But I thought if I don't get myself together now, I'll never leave.

The antenatal classes were good. I think I knew theoretically everything that was going to happen to me. I knew all the technical words and processes so that I understood what they meant all the time. The one thing they did not prepare me for was the pain, but I don't think you can describe pain. And pain thresholds are different for everyone and so it is a different experience. But they will never prepare you for the pain. It was as if someone was cutting me open with a knife, it was just horrendous. But it is so individual, some girls don't feel it at all.

Liz Suttie [born 1964]

I expected the birth to be very painful and it was very, very painful. It was quicker than I was led to believe, as for a first baby it could be anything up to twenty-four hours if not longer. It actually happened within five hours and was very intense.

About three o'clock on the Saturday morning I had stomach pains but I wasn't quite sure if this meant it was starting. I lay for a while but by five o'clock my waters broke – not in a flood as I expected, but very gradually. We went down to the hospital and the midwife said as this was my first baby it was unlikely things would happen quickly and I was advised to go home and relax. I went home again and had a hot bath. I was fine in the bath but when I got out I was in sheer agony. So we decided to go back to the hospital. They examined me and I was three centimetres dilated; it was happening very quickly. I was taken to the delivery room and they were timing my contractions. Strangely I was not getting any gaps in between the contractions. At eleven they asked if I wanted an epidural and as I was in so much pain I said yes, please! I was continually monitored and at about three o'clock the midwife and doctor were telling me that they expected me to deliver sometime that evening. But all of a sudden it all happened. The baby was in distress but, because I had the epidural, I couldn't feel the pushing. They asked me to push through five contractions and if I couldn't push her out, then they would use forceps. So of course I couldn't push her out. I didn't have the energy so they pulled her out. And that was it. The whole thing, the real pain, had really started at ten in the morning and she was born at half past three. I was cut and stitched but I didn't feel that because of the epidural.

Having had the epidural, after they put that awful needle in my spine, I couldn't really feel very much. I had always thought I would have an epidural if it came to it. I am glad I had it. What was strange was that people had told me that gas and air would help me through it, but the gas was of no help at all. It made me lightheaded and made me sick.

I think what did surprise me was the number of midwives and doctors floating around. Perhaps they were changing shifts. It actually became quite irritating, because people kept coming in and out all day to introduce themselves, and to be perfectly honest, I really couldn't care who was there, or who would deliver me. I just wanted the whole thing to be over. The staff were actually very good so I am not complaining.

I had gone to antenatal classes but I don't really feel they prepared me for the birth at all. Definitely not. My whole labour was so different. What I was led to believe was that I would have three stages of labour. Now I completely missed out on the first, the pain building up, the sore back and so on. I just went straight into contractions every four minutes and then one massive contraction. I wasn't ready for it. It was quite a shock because they had warned me it would take a long time, that I wouldn't deliver until the evening.

The antenatal classes were good in one respect, that they showed us round the labour ward and we knew what to expect in terms of the baby monitoring. It didn't prepare me for what would happen to me though! We were even told the baby would be checked ten days after the birth so it was very much from the baby's point of view not the mother's. The classes were interesting but in hindsight they didn't help me during labour.

When I did hold my baby for the first time, to be honest I felt tired and awful. So many people had told me I would feel euphoric and fulfilled. I didn't feel that because I had a really bad headache from the epidural. It was like my brain was popping out of my head. I had felt sick after I had my tea and toast. After the birth I felt so dehydrated and hungry I just wolfed down the toast but then wished I hadn't. So the last thing I wanted was to be left in a room to bond with this little baby. I just wanted half an hour on my own to get rid of this headache and then for her to be brought in.

I did get the sense of euphoria about twelve hours later, once the effects of the epidural had worn off. Then I thought this is my wee baby. And I thought she was gorgeous. She was smaller than I thought she would be, six pounds and six ounces. I just remember thinking she was beautiful. She was a perfect wee doll, so tiny and a quiet wee thing.

It is difficult to explain because it is a mixture of emotions. There is relief that it is all over and that she is OK, but at the same time you are so physically and emotionally drained that you want to sit down and cry.

Rachel Lockey [born 1967]

I wasn't so very aware of what would happen to my body or of the actual process of labour. It wasn't until I had told my parents after six months that I did not need to try and hide my pregnancy, and it wasn't until then that I began to go to NCT classes. They were very helpful but in the end the birth was completely different to how I had imagined. They ended up inducing me, and if I had been more educated on the subject I would have resisted, but at the time I was just keen to have her born safely. Being induced just led to a lot of problems to do with timing. I had to have an episiotomy, a large cut. I didn't realise what effect this would have on how I feel. I was so young that I hadn't come to terms with how I felt about my body. I was just eighteen and having a baby. I hadn't explored sexuality and things like that. So it was scary.

I was also treated like a teenager, an ignorant young girl; I was aware of that. Perhaps a lot of other young women would not realise this attitude but I am relatively well educated and they treated me very differently from other young mothers. I was quite happy about going into hospital because that was the normal thing to do, but I had never been into hospital before. Now I would be much more apprehensive about the whole process. There are advantages, of course, but it does change the whole relationship between mother and medical staff. There is a whole power structure going on there. I was planning to have a birth without drugs. I thought I could withstand the pain and just have gas and air. But they believed I had high blood pressure and made the decision to induce me, so the whole natural experience was taken away from me.

Induction means you go straight into full contractions, you have no control over it. Often you are not dilated properly and this meant I had to have a cut and an epidural as well. It was very much a case of their timing, their way of doing things.

A midwife delivered me attended by another midwife. My mum was there as well and she was absolutely fascinated because although she had had five children herself, she had never really seen a birth! She was totally amazed. Although things didn't go according to plan, it was lovely having the four of us women – it was a good group. And then the doctor came in to sew me up. He was late and I spent two hours waiting for him. He came charging in and proceeded to pour saline water over me at which I screamed. And he said, 'You've had a blooming epidural, why are you screaming?' I said 'That was five hours ago, and it's not working any-more!' Then he blamed the midwives for not telling him that. Everything was everyone else's fault: the scissors were blunt, the stirrup was broken – so he shouted at everyone. He really was quite horrible so that spoiled things a bit.

I had to stay in for five days because I had this third degree tear and I was in such pain with the stitches.

After Bella was born I went to sleep and Bella was put in the nursery. I woke up at five in the morning and suddenly thought I had to see my baby. So I got up and went to the nursery and there was this enormous, long baby. But the staff didn't like the fact that I had gone to see my baby. They put in my notes that I was restless and too active. Ridiculous! I mean, if I hadn't wanted to see my baby and stayed in bed, they would surely have thought I didn't care and was depressed. So they had some funny ideas in that hospital.

Bella was 10 lbs when she was born. I think that was because I was very aware of my health and diet during pregnancy and went over the top eating healthy raw foods!

I had read books about birth: Sheila Kitzinger, Michel Odent and Frederick Leboyer, and at the NCT classes we learnt about breathing, but in the event all this went out the window.

So having the baby was OK, but psychologically I wasn't prepared for going through the whole process in hospital. After the birth I had to backtrack in a way, to learn what it is like to have a woman's body in our society. I needed far more preparation but I imagine that is the same for a lot of women, that they feel they don't know very much of what is going on.

———•———

*'Because birth is a medical event, the woman is supposed to be a "good patient",
quiet, placid, polite, appreciative of what is being done to help her. . . . Problems
in the relationship between women patients and doctors are not only a matter of
psychological stresses, or because women find it difficult to be assertive and to
negotiate skilfully. The management of pregnancy and childbirth is a political
issue. . . . One consequence of this powerlessness is that women are denied their
own definition of pregnancy and birth.'*

Sheila Kitzinger, OURSELVES AS MOTHERS.

———•———

Moyra Heggie [born 1950, tutor midwife, and daughter of Emily Heggie]

A lot of the problems in the relationships between midwives, doctors
and the mothers are due to the power issue, the gender issue. Most
obstetricians are male, most midwives are female. The few female
obstetricians are very male in their attitude, perhaps more male than
the men in a way. And because most births are in hospital, women
have to be booked under a consultant, and he has the ultimate
responsibility even though the birth is normal and 75 per cent of
deliveries are safely managed by the midwives, so most women do not
even meet their consultants. It is the system. Since the 1930s, most
midwives have trained as nurses first, and the relationship between
doctor and nurse or midwife is that of superior and subordinate. The
nurse carries out the doctor's orders. We now have to re-educate nurses
and midwives but you cannot easily change attitudes and the culture
of 'the doctor says I have to do that'.

I think we are moving away from that. In the 1970s, childbirth was
doctor-dominated; they were in the powerful position and there were a
lot of induced labours. Women were told what to do whether they were
the midwives or the mothers. Women are more questioning now and the
new breed of midwives is significantly different.

The Winterton Report of 1991, which re-evaluated midwifery and
childbirth, was an absolute sea change. In the 1970s, the dominant view
was that every birth should be in hospital. The Winterton report has
turned it all round, saying 30 per cent of women should have midwives

as their main professional carers, that midwives can admit women to their own 'beds' and they do not need consultants. It's a total reversal and a golden opportunity for midwives.

Our main aim is for choice, continuity and control for women. Groups of independent midwives have been forming over recent years because they want to give women the continuity and choice of care, which they couldn't do within the Health Service. They mostly deliver women at home. There are still very few home births, but with the idea of 30 per cent of midwives being the leading professional carers, that might change but it depends on the local health authority. The difficulty is insurance cover for home births, because the underwriters for the policy which governs our profession have suddenly realised they might be at risk of large claims which could cripple them.

'Home births are as safe as hospital births and may lead to fewer complications, according to the National Perinatal Unit. There is no evidence to support the claim that the safest policy is for all women to give birth in hospital, and for some the risk of complications associated with a hospital delivery may outweigh any benefit.'

THE TIMES, 7 December 1994.

A statistician, Marjorie Tew, has been comparing the perinatal mortality rates and the risk factors for women who delivered at home with those who delivered in hospital; the ones who had a home birth actually did better than those in hospital. There is more intervention if women are lying in bed in hospital, plugged into a monitor so they can't move for hours, the physiological processes may not happen so quickly and this can result in what is called a cascade of intervention. But at home they can move around, they do what they choose, and are more relaxed with the midwife whom they know well and trust. It is a sharing of positive feelings, working together for the birth of this baby. The woman has chosen to have her baby at home with her selected midwife. In hospital everything is geared towards something going wrong; you think of hospital as the place you go if you are ill; so it is much more negative.

Technology has changed to a certain extent; in the late 1970s and early 1980s, there was a great deal of foetal monitoring, putting electrodes on babies' scalps but because the machines have now improved and the quality of traces using abdominal scans is much better, there is less intervention of this kind.

Most labours these days are expected to be completed within a certain time. If the mother is two hours behind, for example, they might want to stimulate her labour to hurry it along. Midwives have done that in the past but research shows that while it speeds things up, it might not really be good, so there is a great deal of debate on this point.

The mother is offered a great deal of choice: alternative positions, birthing chairs, water births, mobile epidurals, etc., but surprisingly few women will choose an alternative position for delivery. Leboyer's approach, with a darkened room, massage, music, and use of water, influenced us as midwives in the late 1980s and we wanted to use it. We believed in this apparently ideal environment and it seemed the right way, the new way for birth. And as for shaving, we had always shaved women but after some research by midwives, some stopped the practice, others then followed suit, and the change sort of just happened.

Many women will still rely on the medical profession in the old way, rather than want to make their own choices and decisions. It is the culture that the doctor is seen as the epitome of knowledge while the midwife is referred to as the nurse. Awareness of the potential of the midwife is still limited and perhaps that is our fault because we don't let women know of our skills. If we publicise our professional skills and let mothers know our role, then attitudes will gradually change.

I like women to feel that they are in control of their bodies and of the birth. I remember one woman who had a fairly traumatic first birth, using pethidine which hadn't agreed with her. You do get some women who have read so much about the whole thing and want it to be natural that if it doesn't end up as a normal delivery and there has to be an epidural and forceps, they are totally disillusioned.

I think there is much more common ground now between the aims of the NCT and midwives. I think a lot of us felt their expectations were unrealistic, whereas now they teach women that it will not be a bed of roses but if they sing 'Ten green bottles' and do their breathing, they will be in control and relax. And I think that is better.

And there are acupuncturists coming in and complimentary therapies coming on board. Some midwives are trained in acupuncture and so the whole area of childbirth is changing. It is still only a relatively small minority of women who are taking the opportunity of full choice; the more educated middle class women who read the books and attend classes will generally opt for a home birth or midwifery care. If we can work together it will improve and women will learn to approach childbirth their way and not do only what the doctor orders.

Rachel Hanks [born 1967]

I had my baby in a cottage hospital so that it was not a high tech birth as such; they didn't have epidurals on the premises for instance. It was a natural birth really, with a little pethidine and gas and air. The hospital was run by midwives as much as possible. Doctors were called in for emergencies only. As my second stage had been going on for so long, the nurse called in the doctor. She had given me the preliminary injection to prepare the doctor to cut me. But the thought of the snip, and the sight of those huge forceps, gave me that last bit of energy to push a healthy 8 lb 12 oz baby out, without so much as a stitch. At dinner the next day, with the other new mothers, I discovered how much of a feat this was, not only because of my ability to do it, but also because I was allowed to try. Most women it seems are given the dreaded snip as soon as possible, which is very sad.

————————

'Sadie was elastic at the limit of its tension; mind or body would snap at any minute. A second injection of pethidine was administered and then, the bliss of splitting in two of consciousness. But the bubble of safety was dissolving, she was being pulled back down into pain. The surgeon slit skin.'

Sheena Blackhall, THE CONVEYOR BELT.

————————

Andrea Duffin [born 1970]

Lauren's birth was very scary. I was a fortnight over my time, which I hated because everyone phoned up every day to see if I had the baby. I suppose I was frightened and nervous. I felt wary about not really knowing what to expect and because I had read so much about it being so painful, but having not experienced it before I did feel I would be able to cope that I'd be fine. As young as I was and as little as I knew about things, I had read quite a bit about the whole thing, and I had a few ideas about how I wanted it to go. I wanted to squat, I didn't want to lie down. I didn't want pain relief if I didn't need it. I didn't want an epidural. I wanted to feel it. But when it came to the crunch I felt instinctively that I wasn't scared at all. I was up at my mum's this night, and I stood up to go home and my waters broke. I went into the bathroom to clean up and I remember looking at myself in the mirror and I just felt so excited. I had read the book *Sunset Song*, about a woman who had just gone into labour, and I felt so like her.

'Chris found herself sick, a great pain came and gripped at her breast, at her thighs, she cried "Ewan!" and nearly fell and he ran to her. They stared in each other's faces, hearing the rain, and then again the pain drove through and through Chris like a heated sword, and she set her teeth and shook Ewan free, she knew the things she'd to do. "It'll maybe a long time yet, but get Chae to drive for the doctor and nurse. He'll bring the nurse back from Bervie, Chae."

Ewan stood and stared and his face was working, she smiled at him then though the pain of the sword was as nothing now, iron hooks were tearing in her body instead, rusty and dragging and blunt. She held up her face to be kissed and kept her teeth fast and said, "Hurry, though I'm fine." ... Then, white, in a daze of pain, she began to walk backwards and forwards on the kitchen floor, as she knew she must do to bring on the birth quick, everything else was ready and waiting in the room upstairs. And after a while the pain waned and went, but she knew it would soon be back.

So she filled her a hot-water bottle and almost ran up the stairs to put it in the bed ... she smoothed out the sheets, brought out the rubber one she'd had bought, and tied that down, firm and strong, and set the great basin on the rug by the window and wondered what else there might be. Then she saw her face in the glass, it was flushed and bright and her eyes all hot; and suddenly she thought how strange it would be if she died, like the many women who died in childbed, she felt well and strong, they had felt the same, strange to think that her face might be dead and still in another day, that face that she looked at now, it couldn't be hers, it was still the face of a quean.'

Lewis Grassic Gibbon, SUNSET SONG.

Motherhood

I couldn't believe I was looking at myself and I was just about to go into labour. I was on a high. But of course by that time I hadn't had any contractions. That was why I was smiling.

My mum drove us into the hospital, and she left us. We went in and got settled in. It was about midnight by this time and I had my first few really bad contractions, and I thought I had had enough and asked for some pethidine and had to lie down. This was two or three hours on, mind you. Then she looked to see how far I had dilated. She said two centimetres. And I thought, 'Hold on, this pain must mean I am nine centimetres!' So I did my breathing. It was a very white room and doctors kept coming in and out. I had a monitor on my stomach the whole time, which I didn't really like. It seemed too clinical to be in this white hospital room, with monitors strapped to my stomach, and because the contractions are so tight, the last thing you want is tight belts around you, it just makes it feel worse.

I got through it alright though, and just did the breathing with the gas and air, and she was born at fourteen minutes to nine in the morning. I was over the moon like everyone is, very high, phoning people. She was taken away for a few minutes to get her lungs cleared out. She had swallowed meconium but she was fine. I breast-fed her straight away; I was adamant I was going to breast-feed. The first five days I remember as a fight to get her to eat, but then she ate nonstop and became a chubby wee thing. I loved the whole thing. Friends said I was glowing.

I had been to antenatal classes to learn about the breathing. It really helped. I felt in control, except for just one moment just before she was born. I suddenly felt I had had enough and I had lost control of the situation. I remember crying out and saying, 'Oh no', and holding on to this nurse's hand. I really tensed up, but it was only for about two contractions. I knew I had to get back in control, which I did and I felt better and was able to cope with it.

I adored Molly's birth. I could go through it all again tomorrow. I had had a terrible pregnancy again, I felt rotten all the way through – kidney infection, urine infection, you name it. I was supposed to have a domino birth, with the midwife coming here so we would go into the hospital together and then both come home again. I had wanted to have a home birth but Barry was so uptight and nervous we decided to have this compromise of the domino system. However my haemoglobin was so low that I was at risk of having a blood transfusion when delivering, so

Labour and Childbirth

I was told I would have to have the baby in hospital. That shook me up a bit, because I was prepared to have it my way. I knew the midwives who would have been with me, and I felt ill at ease knowing I would just have to go into the hospital, which I hadn't dealt with before. I had only been dealing with the community midwives. And then I went into a false labour a week before. I was getting contractions every minute, and they kept saying I would be going into labour soon, and I was five centimetres dilated. Then I went to the loo, and suddenly the contractions stopped. And I was so depressed for the rest of the week. I felt I should be having my baby by now and I haven't.

So then I went into labour the following week. I adored it. It was in the middle of the night; the lights were dimmed and they asked me if I wanted to have some music.

It seems odd my saying this now but I decided that if I really concentrated on the pain, not just where I felt it in my stomach, but if I closed my eyes every time I had a contraction, and visualised it going right down to my feet and travelling round my body, I wouldn't feel it so much, and could let it rise up and out through my head. I would rock back and forward with each contraction.

I felt so at ease between contractions, so relaxed and happy. Then they got a bit stronger, so I asked for some gas and air. I had been standing around for a bit, and then they took me in a wheelchair to the delivery room. And I felt so comfortable in the chair and I asked if I had to get on the bed. And they said, 'Are you comfy?' But I was. And it was so calming and relaxing, with the lights so low. The midwife just kept coming to see how I was. She was so nice, so cheery. They put this tube in, in case I needed a transfusion. But I was alright, I was coping with it really well.

When she was born I was screaming, not so much in pain. The nurse said to Barry to tell me not to tense up, but I shook my head and said I wasn't tense. I just felt the whole experience was so natural, a real natural birth – so that was why I was giving voice to it, shouting out, but I really did enjoy it. I didn't have pain killers except gas and air at the very end. It was much better than having painkillers.

She was born at 12.32, just past midnight, and I was in all the next day and came home the following day.

———◆◆◆———

Motherhood

Ambition

'When people inquire, I always just state,
I have four nice children, and hope to have eight.'

Alice Murray Kilmer.

CHAPTER FIVE

— ◆•◆ —

Trauma and Tragedy

May Stephen [born 1911]

We discovered that our first baby, Ruth, was deaf when she was fourteen months old. We had our suspicions before but we knew then, definitely. We blamed the difficult hospital birth in the blackout, with the forceps. But it was not known in those days that German measles during pregnancy can cause deafness, blindness, or heart trouble. I had had German measles but I hadn't felt ill at all. We had no idea how dangerous it was.

When she was older, this haemotologist said he could test Ruth to prove the deafness was caused by German measles and not hereditary. He tested blood from both Ruth and myself, and he proved that I had had German measles, just a mild dose, but Ruth had had a massive dose of the German measles virus. She had had it as a foetus. So that is why she is so deaf, completely deaf.

When she was a baby, I went to the Ear, Nose and Throat specialist to check how bad Ruth was. She was bright and began lip reading at a very young age, so it was difficult to prove to doctors that she was deaf.

On one occasion when she was being tested, and the doctor said to her 'Where is your teddy?', she picked up her teddy to show him. So she was lip reading at one year old. As a baby she babbled normally but all deaf children do; they babble, playing with their mouth even if they cannot hear the sounds. It doesn't lead anywhere, and they go silent.

When she was proved to be deaf, we had a serious problem to deal with: what was going to happen to her in terms of education? So we found out a lot of things. Manchester University did a course for teachers of the deaf. Because I had already been a teacher, I was taken but, of course, as I wasn't going into a school afterwards, but just wanted to teach Ruth at home, we had to pay for digs, fees, etc., while I did the course in Manchester.

That was a year's course and Ruth was sent to a school for the deaf in London, although they were evacuated out of London during the war. My husband stayed in London working in the hospital. Then I brought Ruth home and began to teach her. It is very different today, when they learn finger spelling, I don't agree with it. With my training, children didn't use fingers, the whole idea was to teach them to speak and read. I gave her slips of paper with words on them, like household items, and she could match the names on paper to objects round the house by the time she was three and a half.

The speech was very slow; she was bright mentally and it was easy to teach her. I was amazed how quick she was. It makes me so concerned that today, normal children leave infant school and primary school unable to read; that is awful. Here I was with a deaf child and I taught her to read.

There were books from Woolworths – pictures of houses, trees, etc., so I bought two books, cut out the pictures from one and the words from the other, and the first thing they do is to match a picture with the word underneath.

Perhaps she was intelligent. She went to an ordinary girls' day school, and obtained top prizes and exam marks. She went on to study dentistry and was a very successful career woman before marrying and having two children of her own.

'If a woman has German measles in the first three months of pregnancy it can cause devastating damage to her baby. This is easily preventable because a simple blood test can show if a woman has immunity from the disease. Girls have been routinely vaccinated in schools since 1970, but sadly many women still slip through the net for various reasons, with the result that hundreds of babies are still born deaf, blind and mentally and physically crippled because the mothers were never protected.'

Tessa Hilton, BABY AND CHILD CARE.

Mary Sparrow [born 1921]

After having had two healthy daughters in 1946 and 1948, both born in a nursing home, I had my third child at home in 1950. We had just moved house and I was being attended by a different doctor. He didn't seem to realise that she was face presentation until well into the second stage of labour, when it was too late to go into hospital. We then waited until his partner came to give me an anaesthetic. Eventually the other doctor delivered the baby with forceps. She was brain damaged possibly due to lack of oxygen.

The next day the nurse told me they thought they would have to cut her up to save me, which didn't help my recovery very much.

I stayed in bed for three weeks after this birth. I had a very good home help who lived in and coped with all the cooking, – on a black range which she cleaned better than I did! – the washing, ironing, bed pans and looking after my husband, who was busy on the farm, and our two daughters, aged four and one.

I think I probably had postnatal depression after the third baby, but it wasn't recognised then. I used to cry a lot. I knew the baby would be backward but the doctor and nurses wouldn't agree on her prognosis. When we moved to Cheshire the doctor there said, 'She won't be able to earn her own living.' She was eighteen months old then and very ill. The paediatrician said she would recover mentally when she was fit. But I knew she wouldn't. She recovered wonderfully physically.

She went to normal day school, despite various struggles with the authorities, and then a day centre. Since 1977, she has lived in North Wales, with our eldest daughter who is married and has six children aged between twenty and five years old. We visit when we can.

Mary Boulcott [born 1922]

Our first baby, a healthy boy, was born in 1950; his was a normal, natural birth in hospital, attended by a midwife. Two years later I had twins, both girls, who suffered from asthma and eczema. Just before her third birthday, one of the twins was taken ill on the Wednesday and admitted to the children's ward of the East Surrey hospital, Redhill. In those days [1955], visiting the children's ward was allowed on Wednesday and Sunday afternoons only. We therefore did not see her again until the Sunday, although she was very ill. We saw her for maybe an hour on the Sunday and she died that night.

Looking back it was a cruel practice both to the parents and to the children, and it is incredible that we were so submissive that we, as parents, allowed it. I think we were always in awe of the medical fraternity.

Three months after this unhappy experience, our surviving twin was seriously ill with asthma and was admitted to the Great Ormond Street Hospital in London. The consultant who had been called in [Sir Wilfrid Sheldon] insisted that I accompany her and stay in the hospital, where I was given a bed in the nursing mother's accommodation. On the ward I was received initially with great hostility. Parents were not welcome as they were deemed an upsetting influence on the little patients.

However I stayed, looked after my daughter, cuddled her when she was out of the oxygen tent, read to the children, helped feed them, mended sheets and clothes, and above all was there when my little three year old needed me.

After a few days I was accepted by the nursing staff and when my daughter was discharged eight days later, the ward sister said that she had never known a child in my daughter's condition to recover so quickly.

Maybe that was the start of the change of heart in the hospitals with regard to visiting hours!

In 1957 we had another boy, who also suffered from asthma and eczema but not too seriously so we were able to cope.

———◆———

'The lady in charge, a lady in white whose title was not clear to me assured me that all was well, that all was progressing, that the child was as comfortable as could be expected. 'I'd like to go and see her' I said then, summoning up a little courage.

'I'm afraid that won't be possible,' said the lady in white with calm certainty, looking down at her file of notes. 'Why not?' I said, 'I would like to see her. I know she'd like to see me.'

The lady in white embarked upon a long explanation about upsetting children, upsetting mothers, upsetting other children, upsetting other mothers, justice to all, disturbing the nurses' routine and such topics. 'Really Mrs Stacey, you must understand that it is of no practical use to visit such a young child, she will settle much more happily if she doesn't see you. Mothers never believe us, but we know from experience how right we are to make this regulation.'

Margaret Drabble, THE MILLSTONE.

———◆———

Alice Finigan [born 1920]

I had one son born in 1945. Three years later I lost a baby. It was full term but survived only a few hours due to a Rhesus factor, haemolytic disease. The cause was that my blood group is Rhesus negative and my husband's Rhesus positive, and the baby inherited the Rhesus positive. A first baby is rarely affected by the Rhesus factor. My body began reacting to these foreign blood cells and produced antibodies, destroying the baby's red blood cells. Because I had been given no blood tests during pregnancy this problem was not known in advance and the baby became extremely anaemic and died a few hours after birth.

I received an explanation from the Radcliffe Infirmary with regard to whether my husband and I could have another healthy baby, unaffected by this disease. They could do further blood tests to see if my husband had two Rh positive genes or one positive and one negative. If both were positive, all our future children would have the disease. If one was negative, half our children would be at risk. I was advised to wait five years or more before planning another baby. This would ensure that my anti Rh antibodies had died away, but also the doctors suggested that they would know a good deal more about the disease in a few years time.

We waited a few years but decided not to risk having another affected baby.

———◆———

Today, a pregnant woman's blood is tested automatically at the first antenatal check up, so that the Rhesus factor problem can be detected early on as there is now a way of preventing the disease. This has been one of the great success stories of obstetrics. An injection is given to the mother within seventy-two hours of the first delivery, which stops her making antibodies for this and future pregnancies. The baby can also be given a blood transfusion in the womb, either injecting blood directly into the baby's abdomen, or through the umbilical cord blood vessels. This may be done several times during pregnancy, and then a Caesarean section is typically carried out when the baby is mature enough.

———◆———

Mary Anderson [born 1934]

We did begin to plan a family four to five years after our marriage. I had had a serious illness at the time and did not particularly want children then, but when I was completely well I knew I wanted a child. I had two healthy children but, during my third, wanted pregnancy, I started bleeding and had to have an abortion because I couldn't hold on to the baby. I went on to have another baby but, afterwards, I suffered severe postnatal depression. We had just moved from Scotland to England when the baby was three weeks old. I had been out of hospital less than a fortnight and I just could not cope. What a nightmare! I kept this depression within our immediate family. My parents were not aware of the problem.

Daphne Laing [born 1935]

I was born at home, which was normal at the time, but it was a difficult forceps delivery. I still have a small scar above my eye from the forceps. My mother lost a lot of blood so, to help put that right, she was made to eat raw liver. However the nurse took pity on her and cooked it slightly. It seems a disgusting way to get iron!

My sister was born at home with no complications in 1940. Then my mother gave birth to twin boys in December 1943. The doctor did not know she was having twins and her due date was February 1944. So they arrived two months early. Although the doctor and midwife were phoned at the same time, the midwife arrived before the doctor and she had walked two miles to get there. One twin died at birth because the cord was round his neck; the other, who weighed about 3 lbs, only lived three days. Today, these babies would have had a far greater chance of survival, but then there was very little hope.

I myself married late. I was thirty-five when I miscarried after three and a half months while staying in Scotland with my parents-in-law. My mother-in-law did everything that was needed; the doctor was in the middle of surgery and could not come at once. When he came he cleaned me up and checked me over, and his first words to me were 'Oh, you poor lamb.' This might not have been applicable but very comforting. I was kept in bed for a week, and treated like royalty. The district nurse came in every day and I was very well looked after. When I returned home, I had a D and C.

My first daughter arrived in 1972 when I was thirty-six. I had been put on a very strict diet by a consultant, who gave me a lecture telling me I was far too old to have this baby. I had another daughter two years later after having the same diet and the same lecture but this time I was told, no more children.

However, a few months later, in late 1974, we moved north to Scotland, to Aboyne, and soon after I found I was pregnant and was, to be honest, horrified. It took time to pluck up the courage to see a doctor but I was treated nicely with not one word about age. I had a son in 1975, no bother.

Shortly after that I found I was pregnant again, but started having problems. I was kept in bed for a while but this proved to be extremely difficult with two small girls and a baby. However I had to go into hospital as I was starting to miscarry. I remember a lady doctor came into the room, sat on the bed and held my hand. She said, 'I'm sorry, your baby is dead.' I had already guessed this might be the case but asked if it was possible to have another baby. She said, of course, as many as I wanted! I was stunned after what I had been told down south by the previous consultant, who had advised me to have no more children. I did have another baby, a perfectly healthy boy.

After that the doctor said I should have no more, not that I was incapable but it was too much for me to carry babies and look after the others. So with great reluctance and a lot of pressure, my husband signed the consent form for me to be sterilised as other forms of contraception had not worked and the pill made me bleed all the time.

I was extremely lucky and had four healthy children, with no complications. I doubt very much whether I would have had four children if I had stayed in England!

Liz Sanderson [born 1938]

We lost our youngest son two years ago. He was just in his early twenties. I knew I was lucky having had four healthy children, and I think that when Andy was ill, that year was awful, and what came after, but I think one learns a lot from it, and hopefully becomes a more understanding person towards other people.

A great friend of ours, her daughter died of cancer the other day. She was just thirty and of an age with our younger daughter. She'd fought it for thirteen years and I can't help saying that my gut feeling to cope with the death of a child is to realise that that person is no longer suffering. As long as you put that at the top, the fact that we then have to pick up the pieces and go on living, and everything, that is grim, but you somehow get help to do this one way or another. When I could understand that our son was no longer suffering then I could cope with losing Andy, and this is the advice I would give to anyone else. And I also feel, having lost a child, that we all have to die sometime – and some live a long time, some a short time. I believe we mustn't think we are immortal and go on forever. I think it is a good thing to battle against it for a while if it will do good, but that it is also important to realise that the end is inevitable and let's be peaceful about it and not grieve so much. I know that when our daughter Claire was studying medicine in South Africa, she found the African women accept death when it looks inevitable. There was a woman dying of cancer, and she said the family all just supported her but they weren't fighting against it. They accepted what was to happen and were more peaceful with it.

I think maybe we battle against illness too hard in this country. I think that if I needed a transplant, I would question whether I have a right to someone else's organ. I sort of feel that we are born into this world once, and that some wear out more quickly than others. Having lost a child, I perhaps have a different view of death, and to me it holds no terrors. But hopefully one can learn from one's experiences and be more supportive to other people.

I've got one friend who had one child that was born severely mentally handicapped, another child who died as a young man, and her husband has just had a stroke, but she battles on and she is one of my closest friends. And when we lost Andy she was one of the first to come round and say, 'I know it's devastating, but there is light at the end of the tunnel, and life goes on.' And in time, I was able to believe that.

———— • ————

'John is a physician and perhaps [I would not say it to a living soul of course] but perhaps that is one reason I do not get well faster.

You see he does not believe I am sick!

And what can one do?

If a physician of high standing and one's own husband, assures friends and relatives that there is really nothing the matter with one but temporary nervous depression – a slight hysterical tendency – what is one to do?

But these nervous troubles are dreadfully depressing. John does not know much I really suffer. He knows there is no reason to suffer, and that satisfies him.

It is fortunate that Mary is so good with the baby. Such a dear baby!

And yet I cannot be with him, it makes me so nervous.'

Charlotte Perkins Gilman, THE YELLOW WALLPAPER.

———— • ————

Mary Law [born 1949]

I suffered depression after each of my three children was born. It really began during my first pregnancy and I have just learnt that a bad pregnancy may show up as postnatal depression. Things began to go wrong when, at nine weeks, I had a threatened miscarriage. This was after two years of trying to have a baby and attending a fertility clinic. Already I was failing as a woman. I was admitted to hospital for five weeks and felt lonely and bored yet, when I did get home, unable to do anything. It was a time I should have been happy. I was not. I was distraught. I'd waited for this all my life and it wasn't what it was cracked up to be. I felt cheated. My husband didn't understand and told me not to overdo things. He was in charge of my life and I hated it. I felt life had stopped for me.

After trying every method on earth to get pregnant, using a thermometer, having sex on the appropriate day and then lying in bed for one hour after with a pillow under my bottom, I now felt like a machine trying to make a baby. At 32 weeks the consultant said the baby was in the breech position and unless it changed position, I'd have to have a Caesarean at 38 weeks. Well, I burst out crying. I had wanted a home birth, no episiotomy, no intervention.

So I had to go into hospital at 37 weeks and was prepared the night before – shaved, given an enema and catheter and so on. I wanted to be awake and have an epidural but that wasn't common then in 1978 and I was anaesthetised. I had fourteen stitches but the top section didn't heal for ten weeks. A stitch was left under the skin and it was very painful.

The next problem was that I found breast-feeding difficult. Another blow because I thought it was natural. In fact my baby girl was sleepy with jaundice, she had a urine infection and an eye infection and was disinterested in feeding. I was up the wall, and felt very alone. I felt I was being judged as a very bad mother. When I got home again, my husband would come back from work and find me crying. He couldn't understand why. Why was I not thrilled to bits with our lovely baby?

I was a nervous wreck; I had forgotten how to cook and shop even if I had the opportunity to do so. I was tired and felt very lonely. I couldn't cope with anything – not even the baby who was my only occupation. But things picked up: Fiona began breast-feeding well and I got involved in the Open University by the time she was five months old. I would get up at five o'clock to feed her and carry on reading. I was happy again even if my husband did not involve himself in any part of the baby's care. I felt he was jealous of her and resented the time and attention I gave her.

I had my second baby, Douglas, when Fiona was two. By this time I had done nothing for over two years except look after my child. I used to be such an active person but my husband wouldn't let me go anywhere now. He was out all day and most nights, at the football and meetings. He seemed to hate the children. The baby suffered from colic and would cry all day and all night. I would fling him onto our bed. I couldn't cope. I would get out of the house as much as possible. We would go to the park and feed the ducks, sitting on a park bench in the snow. I would visit friends every day, but still I felt lonely.

I became pregnant again when Douglas was just over a year old and I continued breast-feeding him right through my pregnancy. When I came out of hospital with baby number three, Gavin, I was breast-feeding both of them. The health visitor was not pleased but it was the only thing I could do and I was in charge of it.

Having three children under school age was very tiring. Many days I didn't get dressed. I didn't want to cook meals, particularly irregular ones for my husband who was not around much of the time. We were not getting on at all well. He would give me £8.00 a week so, although I had the family allowance, it was not enough and I was hard up.

I asked my doctor if I should take Vitamin B6 or something for depression – I'd read about it. I knew I was feeling bad but didn't want them to send me to the mental hospital, as they'd take the children away. David wouldn't have looked after them. I started walking out into the road without looking for traffic, but I was pushing a pram with the three of them. I thought 'I don't mind killing myself, but it's not fair on the children.'

I saw the doctor who fixed me up with a psychiatrist. I didn't tell David. He was awful and just called me a bored housewife and said it couldn't be postnatal depression as the youngest was now one, but I was still breast-feeding him although my husband didn't think about that.

I wanted to die but I didn't want to leave my children. At this point I was at my worst: Gavin was 1¾, Douglas was 3 and Fiona 5. The health visitor and Child and Family Centre helped; the children went there and I got involved, reading stories. I will always be grateful for their kindness; we were always welcome.

My youngest boy was very ill from the age of three. He got pneumonia, was hospitalised, and nearly died of a closed stomach. After three weeks in hospital in Dundee, he was sent to Great Ormond Street Hospital – that was three years ago. He was too ill to talk or walk. He was tube fed for four months. We now know he has a rare condition, a genetic hormone deficiency, and will never be right.

Now the children are older, David and I are happier. Fiona's career ideas are shaping up and she's a lovely, happy girl. Gavin is at secondary school; he will always be frail but is happy. Last year I began a three-year course, a diploma in midwifery. I would like to do my third year research project on postnatal depression so I shall have to read a lot more on the subject.

From my own experience it is difficult to know what is postnatal depression and what is depression.

Janice MacKenzie [born 1950]

I married when I was twenty-one and we planned to start a family after a few years. My first pregnancy, when I was twenty-six, ended with a spontaneous abortion because an ovarian cyst was discovered. But a year later I was pregnant again. I had a very high tech hospital birth, with lots of medical interference. The labour was induced and after a fourteen-hour labour, I had to have an emergency Caesarean section. The baby, our daughter Wendy, was normal and healthy.

My second child was born in 1980. During the pregnancy there was really a lack of accurate monitoring, despite my GP's concern. At thirty-nine weeks it was discovered that the baby had an enlarged head. I tried to have a normal labour and delivery, but again this resulted in an emergency Caesarean section. My baby boy was born with hydrocephalus – his brain cavities were enlarged with fluid. With constant treatment, Matthew lived for eighteen months. He died in 1981.

With my third pregnancy I had an ultrasound scan and an amniocentesis testing at sixteen weeks to check that all was normal. I had a normal pregnancy and planned an elective Caesarean at thirty-nine weeks. Our third baby, Richard, was normal and healthy. Our surviving children are now eighteen and twelve years old respectively.

Sue Gammerman

I have three children. My eldest child, Julia, is seven and is profoundly handicapped by cerebral palsy. Physically and mentally she is like a small baby and, of course, she will stay like that for the rest of her life. Four years ago we decided that we could not continue to look after her within our family for much longer, and we started to enquire about alternative forms of care. About eighteen months ago Julia was placed in long-term foster care with a family in Fife. The social workers and foster parents would prefer us not to see Julia at all, but in fact we see her for a few hours once a month.

As a mother I have chosen to put my healthy children – and myself – first. It was not an easy decision because current thinking emphasises that handicapped children have the same emotional needs as normal children and are best cared for by loving parents in their own home. I have had to recognise that I wasn't able to be a very loving mother to Julia. I resented the enormous physical and mental pressures she placed on us all. Although I tried very hard, I was never able to accept her for what she was: ultimately, I did not love her enough to want to keep her.

Most people are very polite when I tell them that Julia has been fostered but I often feel that underneath they are thinking 'How could she? I could never do that to my own child.' Funnily enough, parents who have a handicapped child of their own seem to have most difficulty in understanding my decision, perhaps because subconsciously they would like to do the same thing.

Twenty-five years ago attitudes were quite different. I am sure that a child like Julia would have been put in a residential home or hospital until she died, probably in early childhood. As her mother I would have been encouraged to put the whole tragedy behind me and have another child as soon as possible. These attitudes were, of course, very unfair to children with single handicaps or with milder multiple handicaps. But they may have been more realistic for children with gross multiple handicaps.

Undoubtedly our current attitudes mean that Julia has a better quality of life, and a longer life, but I do wonder whether this has been achieved at the expense of the quality of life of the rest of her family, and particularly of her normal, healthy brother and sister. At any rate, I think that our current attitudes to handicap are just as intolerant and inhumane as the old ones. The difference is that we now focus on the needs of the handicapped child instead of on the needs of other family members.

The whole experience of having Julia has made me rethink my role as a mother. In a way I failed her because I wasn't able to give her my unconditional love. At the same time, I was a good mother to my other children because I recognised that my negative attitude would ultimately affect them and I removed them from a situation which might have made them very unhappy later in life.

———•——

'Researchers have compared low-risk women delivered at home with low-risk women delivered in hospital. They found that more complications occurred among the women in hospital. They concluded that simply because the emergency equipment is there, it is used too often and too soon in perfectly normal labours in hospital. [Over the past thirty years] home births were phased out as hospitals were then seen as safer places for mothers and their babies. it has been assumed that medical interventions are beneficial. The advantages of intervention have been thought to outweigh any disadvantages.

Marjorie Tew has looked at figures for babies with breathing difficulties at birth. She found that more hospital delivered babies were transferred to Special care units with breathing difficulties and more died because of breathing difficulties, than babies born at home.'

National Childbirth Trust, GIVING BIRTH AT HOME.

———•——

Roma Young [born 1956]

In 1992, two years after Oliver, our fifth child, was born I was pregnant once again. The pregnancy was fine and we had opted for a home birth having had a very successful one with Oliver. After a lot of pressure from us on the doctors at the Simpson, they agreed. I must stress that the midwife we had was excellent. She was very good and again, like the midwife I had for the previous home birth, she became a good friend. We saw her regularly through the nine months.

When I went into labour I phoned her up, and she came out and checked me over. Everything was fine. She went away for a while and came back to wait with me for the duration. The labour was going fine and things had niggled on all day and it hadn't bothered me, but by ten o'clock at night, things actually started to happen and the baby was on its way. The first stage had been completed and I was into the second stage. I began pushing but nothing was happening. This lasted about two hours and the placenta suddenly ruptured. There was blood going everywhere. An ambulance was called immediately; I was rushed into hospital and I was given an emergency Caesarean section.

The baby's heartbeat was fine until we got into hospital. There had been no stress monitored or anything. But the baby died, he just didn't make it. They said they couldn't save him despite a great deal of resuscitation and the best medical care; it was too late.

Looking back now, we have in some ways to be thankful that he didn't make it because he was without oxygen for goodness knows how long, while they did the operation on me. Now as everyone knows, if the brain is starved of oxygen you don't know what might happen, and had anything been wrong with him, whilst we would have got on with it, I don't think it would have been fair on Oliver. If this new baby had been brain damaged or anything, he would have taken so much more attention, so much more care, in some ways Oliver would have suffered. It wouldn't have affected the older children so much, the ages they are, and perhaps they would have helped me as well and been more understanding about it.

We don't know if our wee baby was affected because he died. But we look back and think that he might have been, you just don't know, and as I say, perhaps it was for the best that he didn't make it. It was meant to be like this, for the sake of the whole family as well as myself.

Didi Hopkins [born 1956]

My baby is called Alice Ann Claudia; and she was born on the 8th February 1993, after 52 hours of labour, in which we both nearly died due, I feel, to hospital negligence but it is very difficult to prove. I am not interested in pointing a finger, but I was obviously very angry and upset by the whole process of giving birth.

I chose the domino system, to have the baby in hospital. I certainly did my homework and read various books on pregnancy and childbirth. I don't think my husband Oliver was prepared. He looked at the books and saw pictures of men with glasses and beards and didn't feel this was for him.

I had been trained as a dancer and so I am quite physically fit, and I didn't have much problem imagining I would have a natural childbirth with a lot of groaning and a lot of squatting.

But in the event, they didn't really check which way round she was. Not only was she back to front, she was a forehead presentation, which is a textbook Caesarean; apparently the chances of successfully coming out of the birth canal from this position are something like one in four hundred, because they can break their neck on route as they are completely the wrong way round. No one bothered to check for sure.

There was blood going six inches back up the drip I had, and nobody noticing. They sent someone in to give me an epidural who then had to ask the midwife to look for tubing. They couldn't find the right size forceps and the doctor had an argument in front of me with a nurse, which went on for about five minutes, about not finding the right forceps. He was in fact a very good doctor in the end, it was fine. He was a very good stitcher-upper, thank God.

No one ever told me that cutting me would sound like cutting liver for the cat and that it would take forty-five minutes to sew me up afterwards; nobody in any book ever explained what it would *really* be like. No one had shown me a pair of forceps, and I was convinced they were there for a horse! I was convinced they had got the wrong instrument.

A couple of other things that happened in labour were that they gave me sleeping tablets on the Saturday night, after having been in labour since the Friday, so after about thirty-six hours they gave me sleeping tablets in the middle of the night. They put me in a ward called the Marie Celeste with twenty-eight sleeping women. I was contracting every two minutes and, because the baby was back to front, it was very painful. The best way to deal with it is not to lie on your back but to crouch over. However they put me in bed, on my back, with these heavy duty sleeping tablets; that meant for two minutes I would fall asleep and, instead of preparing for a contraction, I'd wake up in the middle of one. So I woke the entire ward up and they were really annoyed, quite rightly. There were women there for all sorts of reasons, some to be induced and so on.

And another thing was that one of the junior doctors came up to me and asked me how old I was and whether I had had an amniocentesis test. I didn't know why they were asking me this now, when the baby might be born in a few minutes.

They didn't know that I was not dilating because I had had cancer of the cervix fifteen years ago, and this was not in their notes for me.

And I just found this whole attitude to be very frightening. As an educated woman, I just fear for other women, and how they are treated, in these hospitals.

We suggested that they did a scan; the equipment is around but it's a hospital that doesn't approve of scanning all the time. And I just feel that it was a massive mismanagement: there was no consultation, there was no opportunity just to confer together – the midwife, my husband, my girlfriend (who was my birthing partner) and a doctor. Never, at any point, was there a meeting of minds to discuss the situation, however much I demanded or screamed. That was distressing, really distressing.

Alice seemed to be alright; there was no foetal distress. I was on gas and air and these two drips, and I was becoming rather distracted – unconscious and then awake – and I couldn't stand the pain any longer. My girlfriend and birthing partner, a National Childbirth Trust teacher with two children, knew what was going on. She kept saying, 'Wake up, breathe, breathe, breathe!' And I did.

This went on for some time – I had lost track of how long this was going on for – but the midwife just didn't take any notice.

After Alice was born, much later, I asked my girlfriend what had happened. And she said I had suffered a serious trauma: labour is traumatic enough but emotionally and physically I had had to cope with this critical situation.

We are not taking legal action, because it is very difficult to point a finger. At the end of the day it was not any particular person's fault.

I really can't go through the experience again because it was the most dangerous moment of my life.

———— • ————

'You almost died,' a nurse told her. But that was nonsense. Of course she wouldn't have died; she had children. When you have children, you're obliged to live.'
Anne Tyler, DINNER AT THE HOMESICK RESTAURANT.

———— • ————

'After the first, I didn't ever want to have another child, it was too much to go through for nothing, they shut you in a hospital, they shave the hair off you and tie your hands down, and they don't let you see, they don't want you to under-stand, they want you to believe it's their power, not yours. They stick needles in you so you won't hear anything, you might as well be a dead pig, your legs are up in a metal frame, they bend over you, technicians, mechanics, butchers, students clumsy or sniggering practicing on your body, they take the baby out with a fork like a pickle out of a pickle jar. After that they fill your veins up with red plastic, I saw it running down the tube. I won't let them do that to me ever again.'
Margaret Atwood, SURFACING.

———— • ————

'The nature of antenatal care has changed very considerably in the last thirty years as the technology available to the doctor has grown. Central to the improvement

of the detection of foetal genetic or growth problems has been the development of cell culture from amniotic fluid, and the invention of ultra sound. Picking up on submarine detection work during the First World War, a Scottish doctor, Professor Ian Donald, began to use the technique of targeting ultrasonic frequencies at the foetus in utero.'

Jenny Carter, WITH CHILD.

———————◆·◆———————

Most hospitals do scans routinely around 16–18 weeks and some do one at the end of pregnancy. Very high frequency sounds we cannot hear are directed into the uterus; the echoes bounce back off the tissue and bones of the unborn baby and are converted into a black and white picture.

Moyra Heggie [born 1950, tutor midwife]

The ultrasound scans today are very good but there are advantages and disadvantages about them. It depends whether you want to know if the baby is OK or not; they can even tell you what the sex of the baby is. For some women they feel very pressured into having the screening, and terminating the pregnancy if the baby isn't normal. I was speaking to a woman a few weeks ago who is having a baby in her late thirties and she said, 'I suppose they'll want me to have an amniocentesis, to see if it's a Down's syndrome. I don't think I will, because it is not going to make any difference.' And I said, 'Good for you, because if you are happy to have the baby, whatever, then why not? It's your choice.' She is going to have a bit of pressure to have the test.

It is true that women over the age of thirty-seven are automatically screened for Down's syndrome, but in fact most babies born with this are born to women under that age, so there is a new test called the Bart's test, developed at Bart's Hospital, which is a blood test on the mother that identifies if she is at risk of certain congenital abnormalities. But the interesting thing about this test is that the women being tested have to pay for it. A lot of women do want to have this done but, if they can't afford it, they have no choice so there is a dilemma there about that. It is the modern equivalent of only the middle classes being able to afford doctors and midwives before the National Health Service.

But I think the technology in general reproductive health and fertility is moving ahead so fast that the ethical issues aren't something we have spent time on. Issues like, do you terminate a pregnancy because the baby has a cleft palate? It has happened. I think the mother should have more choice, and if we have got the technology and they wish to avail themselves of it, then that's fine, but if they don't want to, then why should they?

Lucy Owen [born 1961]

I suffered very bad post natal depression after my first baby was born. It had been a Caesarean section and the scar got infected and burst ten days after the birth. So I was back to hospital. The only thing that kept me sane was breast-feeding Archie. It was the only thing I could do for him, as I couldn't move. For months afterwards I felt I was living in a black morass of endless nappies and no sleep. I wanted to do it all myself but finally had to get help. I had also suffered from ME and it recurred after the baby, hence the depression and tiredness. It took a long time to get back to normal. I was overweight, sex was horrible and became a big problem which needed sorting out later. But once we sorted out Archie's sleeping routine at five months, I started to recover.

So far, at the time of writing this, five months after our daughter was born, I have had one bad day of post natal depression, two weeks ago, when I got totally hysterical. Otherwise no sign, so fingers crossed. I have had more help this time and learned my lessons the hard way. Being a mother with ME was never going to be easy as an option, but I am coping well, I think. It also helps that the baby, Tabitha, is an angel!

Lorna Reid [born 1962]

I was six months pregnant. Things went wrong one particular evening when I was laughing at something on television. There had been a Channel 4 programme, *Baby it's you*, about a baby's learning and development, and there was a small child systematically cramming household items into a video recorder. I laughed out loud and felt this small release of fluid, but when you're pregnant you do lose urine from time and time, through sneezing, coughing, laughing, running, and it just means that your pelvic floor muscles are not so strong, or maybe the baby is leaning on your bladder, so I didn't think anymore about it. Geoff, my husband, was working offshore. I was in the house alone. When I stood up to go to bed I had another release of fluid, which was enough to make me look for my pregnancy books, to read what I could about incontinence.

I went to bed and – looking back now it seems stupid – I was surprised that the baby moved more than it usually did when I lay down to sleep at night, and I seemed to lose even more fluid. So I ended up getting a bath towel and lying on this towel in bed. I did snooze, I wouldn't say I slept. After I had got my third bath towel because I had soaked the first two, I began to realise that the amount of fluid I had leaked was in no way the contents of my bladder. I knew the fluid didn't smell, it had no colour, but I didn't want to admit that there was anything wrong. I was really desperate to phone someone for reassurance but it was the middle of the night so I didn't. I did get out a booklet which I had been given from the maternity hospital in Aberdeen, and I read it from cover to cover. It talked about if your waters break, but I still didn't know that is what had happened. I didn't want to cause a fuss so I didn't do anything until the morning.

Looking back now, I stayed in bed, I kept warm. If I had gone to hospital, I would have done the same and been kept in bed so I didn't in any way accelerate what happened.

In the morning, at the earliest time I could, I phoned my mum. She told me to ring my doctor and ask for a house call. I phoned the surgery and the doctor asked me about the fluid, whether it had a smell and colour. He said he would phone the maternity hospital and that I was to make my own way there.

I rang Geoff's parents and, at the merest mention of the word hospital, they cancelled all their plans for that day and were with me within half an hour, so all credit to them. And they kept cool and calm though none of us felt like it.

We were taken to the admissions room of the labour ward where a student midwife monitored the baby whose heart beat was as strong as ever. A lady doctor came and did an internal examination to ascertain whether or not my waters had broken. She then said I would be in hospital for the remainder of my pregnancy. Once the baby has no fluid around about it, no sac, there would be a risk of infection, so I would have to stay in hospital. I remember crying, because I would have to be in hospital for fourteen weeks, during the summer when I had planned to do all these marvellous things, like make baby clothes and decorate the nursery. My sister-in-law was also pregnant, and we were going to gad about the countryside, two fat wifies, eating scones for afternoon tea. All my expectations of what I was going to do were now absolutely shattered. It now seems so very selfish, because I didn't have any real thoughts for the baby – here was I thinking about myself. I didn't realise properly that I was on this rollercoaster that couldn't be stopped. My waters having broken, there was nothing to suppress labour if it began.

The only thing the hospital could do was to insist on complete bed rest to try and prevent labour from starting prematurely.

As soon as she knew I was going to have to stay in hospital, my mum began to arrange to come up to Aberdeen. I now felt abandoned. I had only been in hospital less than a day but I felt so institutionalised I sat on the end of my bed, wondering what to do. Should I put on my nightie, should I get into bed? Should I just sit there? I didn't know how serious it was.

I was able to have a steroid injection, which is the only thing they can do if the baby is born early; I was going to have two steroid injections each week, for as long as they could keep the baby inside me, to try and mature the baby's lungs to cope with breathing. At 26 weeks, the lungs are the most immature part of a baby's system.

Not very much had been explained to me because I don't think the hospital staff wanted to alarm me, by telling me how precarious my position was. Babies live from 24 weeks; babies which weigh less than mine live from 24 weeks.

The registrar on duty said in his experience women whose waters had broken tended to have their babies within a fortnight. This was a real shock. In fact the majority of them have their baby within a week. I was quite stunned by this but he was trying to prepare me gently. I asked him if my husband should come back from offshore and I was told that would be a good idea.

I remember asking him why my waters had broken. Even now, no one can give a reason why my waters broke prematurely.

But everyone was very jolly about keeping me bed rested. I was not to go further than the door of my room. I was allowed to wear leggings and a T-shirt during the day, to break the monotony of being in bed. I could alternate between the bed and the comfy chair, and I had to ask if I wanted to do anything else. I was being monitored regularly like the other women: blood pressure, baby's heartbeat, temperature, routine observations. I didn't know this but once you lose your amniotic fluid, your body continues to make it and, because the sac was broken, I would have continued to leak amniotic fluid for the rest of my pregnancy. I had to wear sanitary protection all the time and if the fluid turned from clear to pink, this might indicate the onset of labour.

I was given my supper, and my mother had arrived by this time. She was going to find out about Geoff, where he was and if there was any word of when he might get home. That night, I didn't think I would sleep.

It had been a long day and there had been a lot to take in, but I wouldn't say I was unduly worried. I was gently worried that this was not normal but had no real idea of how things might develop.

I woke up at four in the morning; it felt like I had a period pain, and I don't know how many waves I went through before I realised these were contractions. Because I was only six months pregnant, I hadn't been to any classes. I had been reading the books but hadn't tempted fate by reading all that far on to labour. I had concentrated on the stages I was going through. I didn't time the contractions but they weren't that far apart. I rang my buzzer, and the nurse came and put me on the monitor which monitored the baby's heartbeat and my contractions, the reason being that the baby could be distressed by the contractions because it had no amniotic fluid to act as a cushion, so the muscle contractions were quite hard on it especially since it was so wee. We spoke about premature babies and she said that the next day, presuming the contractions stopped for a bit, I could go in a wheelchair to the neonatal unit. I think the idea was that seeing another woman's baby in an incubator attached to drips and tubes, is not as upsetting as the first time you see it, when it is your own.

After about an hour of monitoring the doctor came. She let me know that this was not a good sign at all. I asked her what can you do the stop the labour? And she said there was one drug but they didn't use it in Aberdeen because the maternal death rate was too high. I digested this information and spoke again about premature babies.

Anyway the contractions continued until half past six but they were getting weaker, not stronger. I was cheered by the news that my husband was getting home.

Later that morning I asked to have a shower. I was really needing a wash and I was told to be careful. When I came out of the shower, I realised the contractions were starting again. I got dried and on to my bed. They started to get more frequent, so I was watching the clock by the side of my bed and trying to gauge how frequently they were coming, because they were much stronger than the ones in the night. Those had been like mild period pains; these were serious business – strong pains, really sore. Ten minutes apart for a bad contraction and five minutes between those which were not so bad, and the frequency appeared to be increasing. I knew that the midwife was on her own, and there was this feeling of not wanting to make a fuss, so I didn't ring the bell.

Lunch appeared and, for some reason, I thought it might be a good

idea to have something to eat. Immediately I had finished it, I felt really
sick and I rang the bell. Just by looking at my face the midwife knew the
contractions had started again. She put on the monitoring equipment
and asked me how frequent they were; she could hear the baby's
heartbeat, so obviously things were alright; it was alive.

Very quickly they wheeled my bed down to the labour ward. They
asked who they should contact and I gave them my home phone number,
where my mother was.

My bed was put into this horribly stark, clinical room, with a lot of
scary looking equipment. And a great big clock on the wall. I crawled
across on to the labour bed, which had plastic sheeting on it and a big
bean bag at my back, to lie against. The midwife who had brought me
down from the ante-natal ward explained what had happened to four
midwives, none of whom spoke directly to me.

Two midwives were left with me. They tried to get me into a comfortable position, as they helped me get through the contractions. The pains
had begun again at around 11.30 and I had been brought down to the
labour ward at 1 o'clock and they were now increasing in frequency. I
was already dilated four centimetres, which surprised them; labour
seemed to be happening very, very quickly.

They told me that in order to give birth to this baby, I would only need
to be dilated about six centimetres instead of the usual ten because it
would be so small. They tried to put the monitors on again but both the
baby and I were moving about so much that they were not getting any
kind of serious reading. I was holding both their hands. One girl was large
with a lovely soft American accent; she was called Anne. The other nurse
was a young, slight girl called Tracey, and they talked me through what
I ought to do, telling me it was really important to breathe slowly, so the
baby would get oxygen. When the pain started to get really, really bad,
they gave me the gas and air mask. This was a great help because I was
able to breathe really deeply to help me ride through the pain of the
contractions.

In between the contractions I was introduced to about half a dozen
different doctors, one of whom was the registrar and one of whom was
the consultant paediatrician. I knew that there was a team on standby,
ready to help the baby when it was born, but the registrar was trying to
prepare me for the fact that the baby might be born dead. When he told
me that I said I didn't want my mother into the labour room. I thought
it would be easier if only I knew.

Trauma and Tragedy

I continued to get through the contractions with the gas and air mixture. But at about three o'clock – this great big clock was facing me, so there was no doubt about the time – I felt things change and I had this very strong urge to push. And I was kind of thrashing about and got exhausted very quickly partly because I had had very little to eat and my mouth was very dry. There was still talk of a Caesarean so they didn't want to give me any drinks of water because of the anaesthetic. Eventually they gave me an ice cube to suck on, which was good.

At the pushing stage the midwives had to show me what to do because I hadn't been to any classes and I didn't know what I was trying to do or meant to do. I remember shouting at them, 'You'll have to help me because I don't know what to do.' And they were helping me as much as they could. Sister appeared from time to time and there were alarm buttons behind me so I knew if I got into trouble, or they were worried about me, the midwife would alert the doctor immediately.

I don't know but I must have pushed for an hour. To help me they said they could see the top of his head. The head was coming and that the baby had dark hair. I knew they were telling me good things to encourage me to keep going, but I was exhausted and the baby didn't come. I had lost the notion of what to do; initially when I began pushing I felt my body was telling me what to do, but as I got more tired I lost out on this impulse. And I just got more and more tired. I think it was about four o'clock, and they said if I put my hand down, I would be able to feel my baby's head. I had in my mind a picture from one of my pregnancy books, where everyone is smiling and everything is going fine. The picture in the book shows this mother giving birth to a full term baby, and she is fully dilated and there is a very large cervix with this lovely rounded baby's head just appearing, and I thought I would feel this. But I put my hand down and felt this tiny opening, with this even tinier little head which felt as if it was being squashed. I remember shouting out, 'I am squashing the baby, I am killing it!'

The midwives were trying to help me by saying the baby was OK, and everything was OK. But I don't know if they knew as they couldn't monitor the baby at all. They can monitor full term babies by putting a clip on baby's head, but my baby's head was too soft. They couldn't put a clip on it, so they didn't know if he would be born alive or not.

I was panicking, and I could tell they were panicking too. They said they would have to do an episiotomy, and I had read in my books that when you have an episiotomy the skin is so stretched that you don't feel anything, so there isn't any need for an anaesthetic. Well that might be true when you have been fully dilated and gone through a normal labour, but this wasn't a normal labour and I felt every cut of this girl's scissors. And I was screaming, 'You are cutting and you are hurting me!' But I knew that they just wanted to get the baby out the best way they could. I heard one of the midwives say to the other, 'It would have helped if my scissors were sharp.'

Anyway, the baby was born very quickly after that and Ann had told me that I had to pant like a dog when the head came out so that the body wasn't born too quickly. I remember that because I was in a position that I could see the baby's head coming out; I saw him being delivered into a little green cloth which Sister was holding, and then she cut the umbilical cord very quickly and bore off this little bundle. She disappeared out through the double doors. I think they said I had had a little boy. I was very surprised because I really thought we were going to have a girl, and we had chosen half a dozen names suitable for a girl.

Immediately following the baby's birth I felt the sense of euphoria that other mothers feel, as well as deep, deep worry about what was happening. I was so pleased the baby was alive, but I couldn't really hold out an awful lot of hope. The midwives asked me what I was going to call the baby and I immediately said Martin Ewan. I had liked Martin and Geoff had liked Ewan but we couldn't decide which should go first. But I said if I was going to give birth to the baby, I should have the first choice. I remember we had laughed about this.

They asked me if I'd like my mum to come in. She had been waiting outside since three o'clock. Ann went off duty because she had stayed longer than her shift so that she would be with me through the birth, which was great. My mum came in to be with me while Tracey stitched me up. I had to have nine which I don't think is an inordinantly huge number but it was pretty painful. My mum was laughing gently, helping me through it, trying to keep both of us going.

Fifteen minutes after the baby was born – Martin had been born at twelve minutes past four – the registrar came back to say the baby was struggling a bit. We were more subdued after that but still a bit hopeful and we knew that Geoff would come soon, which was comforting. Then the consultant paediatrician came in to tell us that Martin had died at a quarter past five; that they had done everything possible to help him live but his lungs weren't strong enough and that they had to ventilate him. He then had a brain haemorrhage and after that they could do nothing more, but he had lived on his own for about fifteen minutes. My mum was sitting beside me and I knew she was weeping. The consultant said he would come and see me again soon. I remember asking the Sister if she could make sure Geoff was told the news before he came in to see me, because he would arrive, smiling and happy, and I knew I couldn't explain what had happened myself.

I was asked if I'd like to see the baby and I said yes. And quite shortly after that, a nice nurse or doctor, one of the staff who had been trying to save him, brought in this little bundle wrapped in a shawl and placed him in my arms, and I was able to look at my baby and see his beautiful wee face. He was wearing a beautiful knitted blue bonnet and a really pretty white smock with blue stitching across the front. It must have been specially made for premature babies, because it fitted him. My mum held him and I held him and I think she told me then that she felt it would be good if I cried. I said, 'No, not until Geoff comes.' Then they came to take Martin away again.

My mum then telephoned my father and I called some friends who were due to visit me that evening.

At six o'clock Sister came in the door and Geoff came in behind her. I will never forget his face. It was so, so sad. Of course the last news he had had of me was that I had been sitting up in bed that morning, quite chirpy. He said he had delayed coming to the hospital because he wanted to buy me flowers, chocolates and books to read, because I would be in hospital for such a long time. I think that was what finally made me cry, thinking of him buying me flowers and things. And he was sorry that he had missed the birth and missed the death, but I kept saying to him the outcome would not have been different had he been there, and he wasn't to worry about that. Of course it would have been nice if he had been there; it would have been easier for him to cope if he had shared it all.

We had some time alone together and then we asked for Martin to be brought back, and we spent a few minutes together as a family with him. We both held the baby. We did open the shawl but we didn't want to look too closely in case it was distressing. We didn't want to disturb this poor wee soul.

While we were there with Martin, Mum came in with the hospital chaplain, and Martin asked if he could christen the baby. He said he could not christen him because he had died, but he could give a blessing and use words from the Christening service. So we sat and prayed together, the minister, my mum, Geoff and myself, and our baby son was blessed.

And then the nurse took Martin away.

Dr. Bernard Lunan [Clinical Director, Obstetrics, Royal Maternity Hospital, Glasgow]

Scanning was just in its infancy when I was training in the 1950s and it has come on in leaps and bounds. The sophistication of the equipment has improved enormously. We can confirm that the woman is pregnant and make sure there is only one there. We can get an idea how far on it is, and that the pregnancy is viable, that there is a heartbeat. By eighteen weeks we can see the structures fully formed and if there are any problems they will be picked up at that stage. It has made other prenatal testing possible. If we are doing an amniocentesis, drawing amniotic fluid from the baby, that is possible under ultrasound. While tests and scans can give a mother a lot of reassurance, I think one of the issues that has been raised is an unmitigated blessing.

In the early days of scanning, we were getting information but weren't sure whether to act on it. Another test came along, the spina bifida test for alpha-fetoprotein, which can then be confirmed by a scan. If the woman is agreeable, we could perform a termination. Now often these cases were very severe and would be incompatible with survival. I must say at the time I thought this was a tremendous breakthrough – this was preventing the need for a woman to continue to term and deliver a baby that was seriously handicapped and was going to die. We were now able to terminate the pregnancy at around eighteen or twenty weeks and the women were grateful for the diagnosis and treatment.

And then it gradually became apparent that what we were doing in cases like that was taking away a pregnancy which a woman wanted. It was often a planned pregnancy, and often by the time a termination was carried out, the mother was aware of the baby moving. Very often these women had a grieving over the loss of that pregnancy which wasn't appreciated by those around them; even their husbands and family would believe that they should be glad the diagnosis was made and the pregnancy stopped. The woman often had to bottle up her feelings, because her family would be saying things like, 'It is now two months since the abortion and it was a good thing, and you should get over it.' It took the medical profession time to realise that this was a far more complex process than we had understood, and that a woman's reaction to the loss of a pregnancy in these circumstances was quite different to a woman who has chosen to have an abortion. We now understand that she might need many months of counselling and support and that it will take time to heal.

Another corollary to that was a reappraisal of the conventional advice of the past, namely, 'Go away and get pregnant again soon.' It was thought this would help the woman get over it. Now we can tell women who have had a miscarriage or termination to wait until they have recovered, physically and emotionally, and to come to terms with their loss before embarking on another pregnancy.

In the past families were perhaps stronger, and people were far more accustomed to dealing with miscarriage or the very common death of a child. Nowadays people are vulnerable; they live in nuclear families and they don't have the support of extended families. They rarely have personal or close experience of the loss of a baby. I think these issues are better appreciated by medical staff today. Happily, such tragedies and traumas are less common than they used to be but babies still die and pregnancies are still lost, and women have to cope with that; our ability to give counselling and emotional support has improved as has our understanding of women's feelings.

Andrea Duffin [born 1970]

I had a miscarriage between the births of my two daughters. It was a rotten time for Barry and me. I had a molar pregnancy which they couldn't really explain to me properly. It is not very common, a rare condition when the embryo fails to develop and the placenta grows abnormally and quickly. There is no foetal heartbeat and the sign is heavy bleeding. This false embryo is referred to as a mole.

At the start of the pregnancy I was really ill again, like I was at the beginning of my time with Lauren. I kept getting scans to check it wasn't twins or an excessively big baby, because you can be sick with a big baby or twins. I was being kept in hospital because I kept being sick. They kept shaking their heads and I thought there is something going wrong here. And I was put back to bed. Eventually the nurse came in and explained that there was no baby there any more. I'm not sure why but it was because the foetus hadn't been properly formed that something explodes and you are left with bits floating in your womb, not a natural foetus. And I was so ill at the time. I was taken down to have a D and C to have it cleared out. I was calm about it all. My mum came in and Barry was working so I hadn't wanted to ring him and tell him the news over the phone. I knew he would be devastated. And he was when he came in at visiting time that evening. He was a wreck. I was fine and he couldn't understand this and felt I was being hard and cold about it. I wasn't. I just couldn't feel emotional about it.

It wasn't until I got home and, some time later, my mum took me to go Christmas shopping and everywhere I looked there were prams and newborn babies, and then I really was upset after that.

Some months later, I also felt a great loss. I felt very sad, at the time when the baby would have been due. I had no counselling or anything, and it caused a lot of problems. I instigated a break up with Barry because I couldn't handle the relationship anymore. He had got a new job and seemed to have changed. Perhaps we were trying to blame each other for the loss of our baby, because we couldn't cope with it emotionally. Then my brother's marriage broke up and I thought perhaps we ought to be more mature and sort this out. And we got back together and it worked better than ever. Barry regained a bit of his old self. I think it had been very difficult for him, learning to be a dad and be respectable, and I don't think he understood that he could still be a person in his own right as well. My parents respect us for what we did. So we got back together and we planned to have another baby.

CHAPTER SIX

———•———

Nourishing and Nurturing

A woman's milk is not her own. It is created for the baby, and the first duty of the mother is to ensure a proper supply of the only perfect food – the baby's birthright. Hence every mother should if possible fulfil her maternal duties.

As soon as the mother has settled down comfortably after childbirth, always within twelve hours of birth, baby should be put to both breasts to stimulate the secretion of milk. For a day or so baby gets scarcely anything – only a few teaspoonfuls of creamy fluid called colostrum but every drop of this is precious. The normal baby should be fed only five times in the twenty-four day, at 6 am, 10 am, 2 pm, 6 pm and 10 pm. With clear intervals of four hours between feeds and with eight unbroken hours at night, the mother has opportunities for sleep, rest, housework, and recreation. The giving of food to a baby between 10 in the evening and 6 o'clock the next morning is a great mistake – it encourages an unnatural and bad habit.

It is of the utmost importance to ensure regularity of the bowels. Try to get them to move at the same time every day. Place a tiny chamber pot between the nurse's knees. Hold the baby on this, its back against the nurse's chest and its body firmly supported. After a few weeks, the bowels will move as soon as the infant is placed on the chamber.

A baby cannot be expected to thrive if his mother is not regular and punctual in his daily routine.

Stick right and stick to it.

Sir Frederick Truby King, FEEDING AND CARE OF BABY.

———•———

Violet Stevenson-Hamilton [born 1902]

We brought our children up during the 1920s and 1930s, in the Truby King Method. Truby King was a New Zealander who had just published his book on child rearing and his ideas were taken up and practised all over the country. From birth, the baby was started on a by-the-clock routine which in a sense initiated them into self-discipline and a consciousness of time, because you stuck rigidly to feeding times, playing times, cuddling times, bedtimes and getting up times. Potty training began within the first week. I breast-fed, of course, for three to four months. One wouldn't dream of bottle feeding. Providing the infant was not underweight, feeds were four-hourly from the start, at six, ten, two, six, and ten with no night feeding.

The baby was expected to sleep from 10 pm to 6 am. If there was excessive crying between feeds during the day or at night, the baby was lifted out of the pram or cot, given a nappy change and some cuddling, and a few drops of warm boiled water were dribbled into its mouth with a spoon. They were never fed in between the set times.

After four months I introduced a more solid diet: a milky porridge with the 10 am feed, progressing to milk puddings or baked custard at six months. Mashed potato with beef gravy varied with minced chicken, fish or scrambled egg became the midday meal from about nine months.

Babies and young children had a good sleep daily either in a pram outside or in their cots. Exercise was taken in a playpen when the baby would kick about in a warm room. No central heating in those days, but healthily warmed rooms with coal and wood fires. A walk was taken every afternoon. Tea time was followed by play and reading time, and I taught the children early on to play simple card games. They learned their numbers from nursery rhymes, 'One, Two, buckle my Shoe', etc., and they learned to read at a very young age.

All parents were entirely responsible financially for their children from birth to the age of twenty-one. This was in the days before state benefits or child allowances. A pound went a long way, but my husband's income at the beginning of family life brought us just £400 a year.

We lived in the country in the Cotswolds, and I found I could make a little money at home by letting out rooms in my rather biggish country house. I started a poultry farm, I had an orchard and made jams and jellies. I made cakes and I earned quite a bit of money to help out and to pay for our sons as they were growing up. I was also lucky in that I had a mother's help whom I had engaged at the very start, and she stayed with us for seven years. Doris was the eldest daughter of a local farmer and, on leaving school, had helped her mother with the younger children. She knew the basics of simple cookery and she was able to cope when I was in the nursing home having another baby. She would deal with the cooking, cleaning, childcare, the poultry and the garden, and she took it all in her stride for a pound a week!

And so life continued; it was a hard working life but it was a very rewarding one.

Janet Stewart [born 1904]

I had similar attitudes to my own mother who was a strict disciplinarian. I breast-fed my two children for nine months. 'Breast is best' was our motto, with strict feeding times, and bottles were frowned upon. When they were growing up it was war time so that food was rationed but the babies and children got the best that was available despite a shortage of vegetables, fruit and eggs.

Susan Curtis [born 1905]

My first baby was born in 1939 and my doctor rushed off to join the forces when my son was barely a fortnight old. But in a few weeks a pleasant health visitor called to see how I was getting on. She admired the small baby – he was a month premature – and told me not to roll him in so many blankets, *never* to put him to sleep on his back or front and to use *no pillow*. Truby King had already advised something of the sort. Cot deaths were unheard of in the 1930s and 1940s and this might be the reason. She also said, rather severely, that laying him down alternately on his left and right side would help to keep his ears nicely flat!

The baby was *hell* at night, and though my husband took his turn at walking him up and down the bedroom floor, he eventually had to occupy a separate room. My second son slept all night and woke about 7 am with an angelic smile. Was it because I was generally more relaxed? I read in my Truby King 'Bible' that babies cried more in their mothers' arms as they sensed the anxiety and tension. This was proved as one child was immediately quiet when his father took over.

I breast-fed for about nine months as it seemed customary and labour saving to do so. In my parents' day dummies were taboo, but recognised as a palliative for overworked mothers, with large families, of a certain class. When my children were born, dummies were scarcely seen. No self-respecting mother would be seen dead with a child sporting one. All classes were taught that they could be germ-laden, jaw distorting or the cause of bad habits, eg smoking, in later life.

I was very much responsible and in charge of bringing up the children when they were small, because my husband was a chaplain in the forces until he was demobbed in 1945. The children did not know him. But I was lucky to have a live-in cook/housekeeper/companion from 1938 until 1951. I followed Truby King and still do not regret doing so. I was a disciplinarian but no iron hand was necessary. My two boys were taught to be obedient, good mannered and truthful but allowances were always made for traits of personality.

———◆———

'A Good Mother breast-fed her baby and stuck to carefully prescribed feeding routines. How often she should feed her baby was a matter of changing fashion. Before the first world war, Eric Pritchard, a specialist in infant care, recommended three-hourly feeds, but nothing at night. Sir Frederick Truby King, who became chief guru on infant care in Britain between the wars, preferred a four-hourly schedule. Truby King's reputation was made in New Zealand where his scientific approach dramatically reduced the number of babies' deaths. In his eyes, mothercraft was more important than motherlove which hampered routines. Nothing should be allowed to excite or spoil babies; they were not to be given much love or attention.'

Angela Holdsworth, OUT OF THE DOLL'S HOUSE.

———◆———

'According to Truby King, feeding on demand when baby cried and night-time feeding could have dire consequences on character formation. The child would be spoilt and spineless, a terrible burden on the mother and, later, on society.'

Steve Humphries and Pamela Gordon, A LABOUR OF LOVE.

———◆———

'We had our book – in those days, Truby King – which meant four-hourly feeds, and that baby must be allowed to cry if it stupidly began to be hungry before the clock struck. Nor must there be any stray pickings up and pettings except at the authorised play period. I don't know why all this was accepted but worried mothers have a habit of accepting authoritative books by doctors.'

Naomi Mitchison, YOU MAY WELL ASK.

———◆———

Margaret Dixon [born 1905]

Breast-feeding is the natural way and I kept going as long as I could. With food rationing during the war, we were given special allowances of milk and cheese for mothers and children. I read the Truby King book on childcare but did not feel this was good advice. Truby King was the 'Stick the baby in the pram and let it cry' school of thought, which I did not agree with. My own mother probably thought I spoiled my babies because I was a more loving mother than Truby King would have advocated. I had a fairly strict routine but this was always flexible.

Eileen Brown [born 1908]

I did not read any baby care books but just brought them up in my own way. I breast-fed them for about six months or more with no problems. When they went on to solids, I simply mashed the same food as we ate. I had a very strict routine with an afternoon walk and regular meals of good, plain, home-cooked food, eaten together as a family. Discipline and good manners were important, but the children respected their strict father.

Patricia Rogers [born 1909]

I wasn't able to breast-feed my first baby. I had wanted to but found it difficult, and I actually put this down to the fact that back in the 1920s we had brassieres made of satin and, as it wasn't fashionable to have large breasts and I was a big girl, we wore bras to flatten them. A boy's figure was fashionable.

So the worst time, much worse than having the babies, was trying to breast-feed them. But I didn't give up. I did feed the third one, which was a good thing because it was war time and there was a shortage of tinned baby milk.

But you really were pressurised to breast-feed. It was terrible. I remember one nurse, a big, brusque girl who would say to the baby, 'Oh dear, love, your mother is no good to you.' I always remember that: 'your mother is no good to you.'

And to encourage the milk I was given hot milk, boiled with the skin on the top, and I had this by my bed, to drink during the night.

I did have help looking after the children. When I was expecting my second baby, I was very lucky to find an eighteen year old girl, an old-fashioned type, who had trained as a nursery nurse. I employed her from 9 am to 6 pm and I had her for a year.

Every morning Annie would arrive and help with the feeding and care of the children, and in the afternoon I was able to go out if I wished, often taking the toddler, while Annie cared for the baby. So for a whole year I was a complete lady of leisure, having all this help. It was wonderful. Some people might see this as very superficial, looking back now, and laugh at how I had it made easy for me. But we did live a kind of magazine style of life. Married women did not have jobs. You went out for tea with your friends and took it in turns to have people to tea. You went to the park and met other mothers and nurses and their children. For a whole year I lived this idyllic existence, it was the year before the war, 1938 to 1939. Then the bubble burst. Annie was called up and we decided to move to the country, a few miles outside Leeds. No one knew what would happen. Then I managed on my own with the children.

Mary Maclennan [born 1911]

I never had any postnatal depression after having the babies. No. I was always so busy, I just had to get up and get on with it. If you have four children and have to get the oldest to school, and cope with the little ones, you haven't got time to be depressed.

There was a fashion to follow the advice of Truby King, but I never paid much attention to it. I took what he said with a pinch of salt. I didn't bother with fads – I was very old-fashioned. I just used my instinct and during the war you didn't really have much alternative with food rations. There was no one I could leave the children with, because I was so far away from relatives, so you just had to get on with it. It was really quite interesting bringing up the family during the war. I breast-fed them for about six months and my doctor was a great advocate of weaning them early. You had to give them sips of things when they were quite wee to teach them to use a spoon.

I was advised by a friend in the medical profession to keep a good stock and boil it every day. Use this stock to mix with cereal meals and make a porridge with it. It was very important she said to use a stock and not just milk. So that's what they were fed on. Then they were given orange juice, which the government handed out free during the war for children, which was a great treat.

We had ordinary nappies of course, which had to be washed and dried every day. We had to make the nappies ourselves, out of towelling; there were no ready-made ones but it was cheaper to make them. I washed them every day by hand, there were no washing machines. It had the advantage of making you get cracking as soon as possible with a potty. It worked. I used to put a potty on my knee and put the babies on the potty when they were very little, first thing in the morning and after meals. It used to be quite successful and saved another wet nappy.

'Early training is of great importance. From the third day the nurse should have a small chamber on her knee and the baby should be held with the back against the nurse's chest for no longer than two minutes; the cold rim should just be allowed to touch the child at the back of the anus, and very soon a reflex is established. Many nurses train their babies so that they have no soiled napkins after the first week or so, and very few wet ones.'

Mabel Liddiard, MOTHERCRAFT MANUAL, 1928.

Emily Heggie [born 1912]

When the baby was born, in 1944, my mother was not keen that I stay in London and she suggested I go up to Leicestershire and stay there for a few weeks.

My husband was stationed in this county and while transport was bad, he would walk miles to come and see us on his days off. I think he was jealous of little David. Perhaps he had come too early really, and the time for us together had been so short, with him being in the services. It was a traumatic time one way or another really.

The baby would only need to cry for an instant and my mother would be rocking him, and of course they get used to that. I wouldn't do that, and if I knew he was clean, dry and fed, I used to leave him and I wouldn't pick him up every time he cried. That was the Truby King idea which I had been trained to do as a nursery nurse. Strict routine and it worked.

With the second baby, Stuart, I would put him outside at ten in the morning in his pram, in the snow, in all weathers, [as Truby King recommended].

'Keep the baby in the open air as much as possible. Pure cold air is invigorating, and prevents "catching cold". There is no danger, but actual safety, in free flowing air.'

Truby King, FEEDING AND CARE OF BABY.

Motherhood

I would bring him in for his feed, and back out again at two o'clock until four o'clock, when I would bring him in during the winter, when it was dark. And there wasn't an atom of trouble. They didn't ail or anything. He never wore a bonnet, and I would just put him outside in the pram all day. With Moyra, my third baby, she used to sit out there in her pram until she was three – and when she was older she would chat to passers-by. You couldn't do that today; you wouldn't dare in case someone takes them, but then it was the most natural thing to do, to put babies out all day in the pram in the garden.

We believed in smacking when they were naughty. We always had a cane hanging above the picture, because Stuart was a bit of a devil. He was never wicked but we never used the cane; we only needed to point to it to warn them. And they would go to bed at set times, when they were little.

In my day people waited to save up until they could afford to marry and support a family. In fact when we married we had exactly £33 to our name, but my husband did get on in the airforce and we were able to save. It was a hard struggle. We had to pay for everything we wanted or needed for the children. So much so that when Stuart went to the senior school and had to wear a blue blazer, there was only one place in Streatham where you could buy that and it was almost a week's wages! Six months later it had worn out, because he was growing so big, so this time I bought the material and made him one and it lasted a year. I went to tailoring classes and learnt to make coats, so that kind of thing saved money. I made Moyra's coats and my own coats. I bought material at Dickens and Jones; it was £9 something a yard and a coat cost me something like £30 to make. An identical coat off the peg was £108. So that is what I mean; if you do things yourself, you can earn as much as if you were going out to work, except I was there for the children.

I think people can save a third or two-thirds on all purchases if they made them at home. And that applies to jams, cakes, biscuits. I still do. All these tinned baby foods. I never bought one in my life. I used to get a marrow bone to make a good stock for soups, and I sieved all the food. And it hardly cost anything at all to feed the children, because they just had a little of what we were having. We had an allotment, it was a case of economy again, and we grew our own vegetables.

And we washed all the nappies, none of these expensive disposable ones. I mean what is nicer than a nice line of clean nappies?

————•————

'I wanted to fish Octavia out of her small white cot and hold her, to comfort her, but it was not feeding time and I did not dare. I had been taught to get her out only at the correct intervals, and although I knew this method was outdated I did not like to break the rules. Authority, the War and Truby King. I was reared to believe that the endurance of privation was a virtue, and the result is that I believe it to this day.'

Margaret Drabble, THE MILLSTONE.

————•————

Eileen Watkins [born 1912]

During my three weeks in the nursing home in April 1940, I learned how to breast-feed, with a lot of patient help from the sisters, and bath the baby. Babies were put outside to sleep in prams all day, and were laid on one side and then on the other. They were tightly – too tightly I now think – wrapped in shawls. There were no disposable napkins, one used a Harrington's muslin square with a towelling square over it. No plastic pants either. They wore woollen vests, Vyella nightgowns and woolly jackets if necessary. The one complaint I have to make is that no night feeds were allowed, and a strict four-hourly daily schedule of feeds had to be adhered to. This inevitably meant bad nights for everyone, as the suggested sugary water in between feeds was considered by the unfortunate infant as an insult at two in the morning. And certainly no substitute for nice warm milk. However, somehow we survived. Weaning was done with the aid of a cereal called Farex. The Government provided cod liver oil and orange juice – a far sighted measure indeed. I fed my first baby, a girl, for six months – I never thought of any other way to feed my children, and it was the most marvellously satisfying thing that ever happened to me.

My second daughter born in 1943 and I breast-fed for eight months. With my son, born in 1945, I disregarded all the nonsense about no night feeds and fed him when he was hungry; he slept like an angel and throve, and I was able to breast-feed him for nine months.

Washing was all done by hand and with no detergents; soapflakes were used, sometimes with soda to soften the water. We had a coke boiler, which provided constant hot water. At times I had domestic help for one morning a week, but this was erratic. Our income when we married was £250 a year, of which I had thirty shillings a week for housekeeping.

Our family holidays, three weeks each August, were spent for eleven consecutive years on the Norfolk coast. We found digs with a delightful landlady and we had three rooms and the use of a bathroom for twenty-five shillings a week per room. The beach was beautiful, never overcrowded, and we had no worries of polluted seas. In 1949 we acquired a very second-hand car, which widened our horizons a bit.

A short time after the war, my father gave us our first refrigerator, a great luxury, and some time after that a single tub washing machine. We had no television thank goodness. During the war years we derived so much pleasure from the radio and we sang around the piano. We used to take the children cycling on Saturdays, for picnics, blackberrying, etc. There was hardly any traffic on the roads for a number of years post-war, and it was a lovely, happy time to bring up our children.

'Marie Thérèse was Daphne du Maurier's first grandchild and she was full of sympathy for her daughter Tessa who "looked white and washed out – who wouldn't be . . . the baby was 8½lb as against my babies of 6½lb." Then there was the ease with which Tessa breastfed Marie Thérèse. Watching her and feeling unexpectedly moved by the sight, Daphne recalled what a disappointment it had been to her when she had failed with Tessa – "Sister Rhead was so contemptuous too, whisking the baby off to a good go of Cow and Gate while I fell back limp on my pillow".'

Margaret Forster, DAPHNE DU MAURIER.

Mary McKerrow [born 1915]

Our first son was born in 1945 and so we brought up our family, three children, in the late 1940s and 1950s. I breast-fed them for as long as possible, and then went on to Cow and Gate baby milk, which you mixed up; that was the main food I gave them. There were mothers' clinics where we went to collect a supply of free orange juice and cod liver oil, which were excellent, they really were. In fact, when I gave children's parties, I used the free orange juice and they all loved it. And our children had a spoonful of cod liver oil after dinner every day. It probably makes some mothers curl up when they think about giving children cod liver oil now, but I do think it gave them a good start. Everyone was doing it.

After that they just had fresh food, home-cooked meals, pureed and mashed. The bought baby foods were so expensive and I have always believed that home-cooked vegetables, soup, potatoes, meat, gravy, are ideal. They are all still fond of gravy, even to this day.

I remember it was Chivers who made the tins of blackcurrant puree, which they liked on top of semolina or rice pudding. If you put a dollop of fruit puree on top of milk puddings, that went down a treat. Just good nursery food. Shopping was easier in those days because the grocer and butcher would come round to the house delivering orders and the baker would call: I remember a large loaf cost a shilling. And although everything was much cheaper than it is now, but even so, it wasn't always easy to manage on £20 a month. Rationing was still on of course, until the early 1950s, but I remember a very kind grocer who felt sorry for us, bringing up the children, and we would be given great hunks of cheese when in fact we should have been given a very small ration each. As a young girl I'd never been encouraged to go into the kitchen or taught to cook, so I had to learn with the cookbook propped up in the kitchen. It is a wonder how they've all survived.

We thought we were not too badly off with facilities really. We did have a Calor Gas washing machine outside in the yard where I washed the nappies. I really enjoyed hanging out the washing, it was nice on fine days. What you don't have you don't miss: no one had fridges, we had a larder for the first seventeen years of our married life. Neither were there lots of electrical gadgets. The children dried their hair in front of the fire at night, and at tea time in winter we often made toast in front of the fire. There were no duvets or electric blankets. We always had hot water bottles so there was quite a business each night to fill five or six bottles.

Television times were carefully restricted and only children's programmes were allowed. Reading was encouraged throughout my childhood, when our parents saw that we each had a Bible and started us on the classical authors and Arthur Mee's Encyclopaedia. And I encouraged our own children to read, with bedtime stories from a young age: Beatrix Potter, *Wind in the Willows*, and so on, until they read for themselves.

I do believe a routine is a good thing but I think because the war was just over, it was a time of great change and settling down to a fresh start; it was perhaps the time to say, out with Truby King, and in came a looser, more liberal and relaxed attitude to bringing up children. And it has steadily become more and more relaxed since then.

———◆———

'When the war was over a new approach to babycare began to come into vogue. Mothers were told to form close, warm and loving relationships with their babies. The motto was "enjoy your baby" and "have fun". The new guru of this more permissive approach was Dr Benjamin Spock whose Common Sense Book of Baby and Child Care, published in 1946, became a best seller outsold only by the Bible. Mothers wanted to enjoy their babies and their families after the horror of the war; many were no longer prepared to put up with the regimentation of the past.'

Steve Humphries and Pamela Gordon, A LABOUR OF LOVE.

———◆———

Joan Counihan [born 1915]

I brought up seven children in the 1940s and 1950s and I had no outside help with childcare, no nanny or mother's help. My husband was away for most of the war and after that his work took him abroad a great deal of the time.

I used towelling and gauze nappies. I breast-fed for up to about five months and then gradually moved on to mixed food. There was never any question of not breast-feeding. My mother always had and I considered it the only normal thing to do. I started weaning them with Farley's rusks and Oster milk and then gradually progressed on to mashed potatoes, eggs, vegetables. There were no tinned baby foods about for the earlier babies in the 1940s. An advantage of having a large family is that the older children join in the care of the younger children.

Emily Hagues [born 1916]

My first baby, Jennifer, was very ill with a terrible sickness when she was very young. There was this locum doctor who didn't really know what was wrong. So I contacted my old employer, Dr Duffy, and he said, 'Bring her in. I'll admit her to the sick children's hospital.' So he said that she had this blockage, that the food wasn't getting down. She was in the hospital for about a month and I didn't know her when I went in to get her, she'd put on weight. I then tried all sorts of different baby food because of this illness, and things settled down again. With my second daughter, Vivienne, I put her on Oster Milk. By the time she was born, babies were quicker onto solids and I used to mash up the potato, you know, and some gravy and feed her that. Well, my mother wouldn't have done that. She said, 'You can't give the baby that!' But I did.

When Vivienne was three months old, Jennifer started school and very soon developed whooping cough. Then Vivienne took it and, before she got better, she took chicken pox off Jennifer. What a time we had! Vivienne was that bad that the doctor would come over in the middle of the night, and just put his jacket over his pyjamas to come and see her. 'Well, if there's no improvement in the morning, she'll have to go to the City Hospital.' However on the Sunday morning, she was better and we carried on.

Elizabeth Grey [born 1917]

I didnae bother reading any books on childcare. We used to say, 'Who's got time to do all that?' I mean there's no twa bairns alike, so how can someone say, 'This is what you must do to your bairn,' as if all bairns behave and feed and sleep the same.

I wanted to breast-feed her; there were not many people bottle feeding in those days. Well, she went down and lost weight, from seven to six pounds with me trying to feed her. They said I didn't have enough milk for her. We had strict routines. We didnae let them off with anything. I had a young lassie who would come in for the morning and help me in the house, and she would stay up to dinner time. She was a good help and the bairns liked her. But it wasn't just my bairns she would look after. Friends that I knew, they would bring their bairns in the pram, and leave them with her to go shopping.

I made all their clothes out of all sorts of bits and pieces of material. I started making wee breeks when wee Alice began walking, but once I didn't have an elastic and the breeks would fall down and she would walk away, leaving them on the floor. But they didnae make baby clothes now. They go and buy new ones. I could have made six pairs for what they pay for one nowadays.

Milicent Woolner [born 1917]

We realised we had to make the pennies go round and that anything outside that limit had to wait. One neighbour told me that her budget for that week would not stretch to a tin of treacle and she would have to wait until next week's housekeeping was due. This was usual. It was really a time of living within one's means and we did not use credit.

I didn't follow any rigid pattern like Truby King but believed in flexibility, common sense and loving care. They were fed every four hours or so, and I dropped the 10 pm feed as soon as possible. We played with the babies and we put them out in their prams in all weathers, suitably protected. The babies learned to amuse themselves – playing with their fingers and toes, watching the leaves on the trees, and they generally got on with being babies and being loved. We did not use dummies and had nothing between feeds except boiled water.

Bathtime, bedtime and story time gradually became the province of their father, because he worked permanently on night duty as a printer. He would sleep during the day and get up at five-thirty so that he could devote this time to the children, and have a meal before going out to work. In this way we shared the responsibility and care of the children, because I was largely on my own, with him being a night worker. It was our way of life.

Lucy Firth [born 1917]

I breast-fed my first baby for a few weeks but he lost weight as I had insufficient milk, so I swallowed my pride and went to the Welfare clinic who advised a bottle of National Dried Milk. The Clinic was considered working-class in those days! A few years later, I found it easier to breast-feed my daughter. Both children started on Farex and then Heinz tinned foods. From about fifteen months they shared suitable family meals.

Olive Banbury [born 1920]

Seventy years on, we look back. The Great War was just over and women were having to adjust to a peaceful world. My own mother in her late thirties had three children in as many years. I was born in 1920 and mother told me I was fed on Betty milk, probably the condensed type that Nestle's produced. The man of the house was called the breadwinner, who brought home his weekly wage to a working-class house. It was up to the wife to manage her housekeeping, which some did very skilfully. Looking back I now realise what a talented mother I had. She could make lovely dresses for us, sometimes out of hand-me-downs; she always made a first class dinner, and her puddings would make any chef envious.

I can only speak for the working classes – my father was a motor mechanic, always trying to better himself! What the upper-class mother was like I know not, but even in the 1930s there were many nannies about, who I know were regarded with great respect by the children before they went on to their boarding schools.

In my day we couldn't afford to be constantly at the doctor's surgery as there was no National Health Service, so home-made remedies had to suffice. Whooping cough, scarlet fever and measles were prevalent with no innoculations for infants in those days. Maybe a mother then was more resourceful and confident in coping with children's illnesses.

The second world war brought great changes. I had my first baby in 1944 with men away in the forces, which made women more independent. 1947 saw the birth of our second child and motherhood in that year was very popular. I think we were very, very happy, despite all the postwar hardships, when we got our men back home.

Mary Sparrow [born 1921]

I didn't feel it was all my responsibility at all to look after the babies and children. My husband said they were his family too and he could cook as well as I can. All washing had to be done by hand; we didn't even have a wringer to begin with as there was a shortage of metal after the war. My husband often washed nappies after a very long day on the farm. He would often be the one to get up in the night if one of them cried; he would read them stories and had great fun with them.

I had no experience whatsoever of babies so with the first one I started off with Truby King's book; I think our present Queen was reared on his ideas. The poor little soul would cry in between feeds and could only be given boiled water, so by the time the second one came along I became less rigid. Fresh air was a great feature. I used to put them outdoors in the big old-fashioned pram in all weathers and seasons. Of course in those days, with no central heating, we were not used to warm houses; bedrooms were often not heated at all, and plenty of fresh air was normal and healthy.

I had great difficulty having enough milk and supplemented each feed with a bottle. I wouldn't do it again as babies don't like the difference between bottle and nipple but breast-feeding was considered best and no mistake. I used to read 'Mother and Home' baby care books which advised on weaning and suitable foods. They had groats, prune and apple pulp, sieved vegetables, coddled eggs, potato and gravy, semolina pudding. Later they had fish, vegetables, steamed puddings, bread and butter and Marmite. With rationing it was not easy and we had no custard powder for years! I couldn't afford bought biscuits but used to make them.

When they went to school, they always had cereal and a cooked breakfast: bacon, egg and fried bread.

We did not have television (we still don't) but listened to the radio – 'Listen with Mother' and schools' programmes when they were under five, and then 'Children's Hour'.

Jean Charleson [born 1922]

When we first married housing was very difficult to get, and we lived for a time with my husband's mother and had one room in her little house. We then managed to get a single end-with one big room, down at Newhaven. It was about four shillings a week, for this one apartment, with a toilet downstairs and out at the back. We were six months there when Kenneth was born. But the problem of space was a nightmare, coping all together in this one room. You had to keep moving the pram backwards and forwards if you wanted into the sideboard or the sink or whatever. And we all slept and lived in this one room. So I kept going every day to this lawyer for advice. And he was wonderful, because he advised us to buy a wee house. We had about £200 to put down, and in time he found this flat for us. So we got a mortgage with the Leith Building Society. The lawyer said the interest was 3% – it had been 3% all his lifetime and he said it would never change, so he said not to worry about that. And so we bought our first house, and it cost £750. We now had a big kitchen with an open fire and a recess where we could eat, a boxroom, a bedroom and a really big bathroom. It was wonderful.

In the kitchen I had a double sink and my mother got hold of a wringer, which was great. In those days, we had to boil up the nappies because you wanted them really white; you daren't hang them out unless they were really brilliantly white.

It was certainly the thing to do in those days, to put the baby outside to get fresh air. I would have Kenneth outside even in the snow, all wrapped up and cosy in shawls, with his arms tucked in, his wee red nose showing; we really all felt this is what we had to do. I would be doing the washing and keep looking out the window to see that the pram was still there alright. In fact there were three of us mothers with baby boys the same age, and we would put the three prams together outside. Then they would be brought up for feeds and changing every few hours of course. Why we thought we had to put them outside I don't know but it was the done thing. But they were very healthy children. And for a time we were living in this second top flat in a tenement and we had to bump the pram down all these stairs.

I would go up to the clinic to have the baby weighed and looked over. You would be given cod liver oil and orange juice all free. And because I couldn't breast feed, I fed them on the free National Dried Milk and this was also free but it was excellent; it certainly produced big, fat, healthy babies. It was cream, full cream milk. It was quite delicious actually. So I religiously gave them cod liver oil and orange juice every day. The cod liver oil was a messy business, because it stained everything. Maybe they would have on a lovely wee romper suit and then they would burp and this oil would make marks that you couldn't get out. But they had to have this oil and orange juice. What surprises me now is that we never paid for anything. It was all free – this was in the late 1940s but perhaps it was because of the rationing, to ensure babies got the right food. But at that time babies did seem to grow up so well. My children hardly ever had a cold, and we used to walk everywhere; we used to walk miles, to the park, to the shops, to my mother's house. I used to like going out every day with the children in the big, cosy pram. And we were as happy as could be.

Mary Boulcott [born 1922]

I read the *Good Housekeeping* baby book when I was pregnant with my first child as I knew nothing about babies whatsoever. I found it offered good practical advice. My husband did not share in childcare responsibilities and I did feel it was my job, which was conventional for the time. When I became pregnant for the third time, I had an au pair to help me. I had twin daughters and did not have sufficient milk to breast-feed them both. I had very swollen painful breasts feeding the other two babies. After five months or so I began to give them different foods – Farley's

Rusks, cereals, brains – too many foods too soon I later realised. I was not aware that it was bad for allergies.

Joyce Macpherson [born 1923]

We had five children between 1955 and 1963. I did start to use the Truby King method with Neil, my eldest, but I did relax the strict feeding times when the others arrived because I was far too busy coping with them all. Neil was such a difficult baby and I really felt instinct was a better thing. In fact my mother-in-law was awful over this business. I was all on edge with Neil, and when he began crying I would want to pick him up and she would say, 'Oh no, he hasn't had his four hours,' and she would try and keep me to the right times. I would get really worked up over this because I wanted to hold and comfort him but the book says that you must leave the baby for four hours. My mother-in-law would only give water in between feeds. She was very kind, she was a good grandmother and only meant the best but it was a different way of looking after the children.

I used towelling nappies and muslin Harrington squares, and they literally had to be boiled. I had a machine which boiled them and it had a kind of wringer thing on top but this took ages, wringing out the nappies by hand. That was what I had for the first baby. When Elizabeth was born, I eventually got a washing machine. The nappies would be soaked in a pail with Napisan and then rinsed out and put in the washing machine. It had a spinner which was brilliant. We also got a hot dryer which made the nappies lovely, soft and fluffy, but it was very extravagant because it took a lot of electricity. In bad weather if I couldn't put the nappies outside, I used the dryer and was glad of the excuse.

I was very fortunate to have some domestic and childcare help. I had somebody to help with the rough housework when the third one came along, and then I employed a young girl as a mother's help so that was another pair of hands. In Edinburgh in those days, the grocery, fish and bakery vans came round with your orders. You could put in an order to the grocer on a Tuesday and it was delivered on the Friday. A great deal of the linen – towels, shirts, etc. – went to the laundry and they all came back clean, ironed and folded. I just had the children's clothes and smaller things to wash at home. So I was really fortunate, and it was the best time to bring up children.

My mother's help did not live in. She came every day – well she was meant to be with me from eight until five but she wasn't very reliable.

And then we had a dreadful experience. One day she decided to take Elizabeth, who was a toddler at the time, out for a walk so that I could look after the baby, while Neil was at nursery school. So she took the little girl out and stupidly took her on the bus to take her home to show her mum, without permission from me. I just thought she was going for a walk for an hour or so. She was gone for about three hours and the child was only just out of nappies and not at all reliable. I had almost been on the point of calling the police because I was fearfully worried about them. But she arrived back, stinking of cigarettes, and with Elizabeth soaking wet. So she got the boot.

Then I had my mother-in-law's daily help as a sort of mother's help. She did the rough housework, and helped out with the children. She was magic. She came to us when I was expecting our fourth child, when she would take the children out in the afternoon so that I could have a nap, and would babysit if my husband and I wanted an evening out. She was with us for thirty years and only retired two years ago when she was over seventy. She was simply marvellous.

'A baby who is fed according to a schedule may be perpetually uncomfortable, because he alternates between feeling stuffed and starving. The baby who is allowed to take exactly as much milk as he wants, as often as he wants it, has the best chance of being comfortable most of the time.'

Rosalind Coward, OUR TREACHEROUS HEARTS.

Jane Ward [born 1924]

I had three children under three years of age by 1954, and five under the age of eight by 1958, so this entailed a daily routine, careful budgeting, use of jumble sales, and happy acceptance of any cast-offs from better off relatives and friends. I graduated from a single Silver Cross high pram to a big twin pram with baby number three. Both prams were second-hand. I could get four children into the twin pram if need be and it was necessary at times.

My husband loved the children and right from the start they were seen as our children, and our responsibility, not just mine. Bathtime was normally a case of all hands into action. There would be three at a time in the bath; remove one and wrap it in a large towel and, as the bathroom like the rest of the upstairs, was so cold in winter, they would be taken down to be dried in front of the fire. It took two of us to bath them all.

I didn't follow any baby care advice books, except for the first one and I have always regretted it. Poor little scrap, he was under-fed and then left to cry because 'It was good for babies to cry', and 'you must stick to a strict feeding and bedtime routine.' I never made that mistake again and I began to adopt my own views on feeding and routine. Babies two to five were breast-fed on demand and never left to cry. With the second one, I lost my milk and had to turn to National Dried Milk, which certainly produced fat babies. There was not much choice in the way of proprietary baby food, and it was expensive. Nevertheless, Heinz baby foods were regular purchases. I had a Moulinex machine which mashed and minced food and that was used daily.

Domestic help was extremely difficult in the 1950s, and even more so in a New Town, where we lived. The few old faithfuls from before the war were guarded like the treasures they were. My husband and I were new to the town and such treasures never came our way. The Home Help office did the best it could but it was easy to find women who were willing to do domestic work. At one stage I found myself helping to train new immigrants from Ireland. I remember one who had never seen a vacuum cleaner and was afraid of it and whose knowledge of preparing vegetables ended with the potato.

In the end my doctor put me on Drinamyl (purple hearts – though not really purple, more a gentle shade of mauve as I remember) and on three of those a day, I coped. By the time number five came along, I could tuck him under one arm and get on with cooking dinner for the rest!

Davina Thorpe [born 1927]

I had four children between the late 1940s and early 1950s and I more or less expected no help with them; they were my responsibility and I just got on with it. Probably this was because of my own experiences in childhood, when my mother did everything.

When my babies were very young, neither one was out of nappies before I was expecting again. As my husband was a twin, my mother would say, 'Oh dear, what are you going to do if its twins?' Thank goodness it skipped a generation. Two of my children have twins.

As it was, it would be quite something getting ready to go out. One washed, dressed, saying 'Sit down and don't get dirty,' perhaps putting them on a seat too high for them to get down, while I got the next one ready. My husband would then call up, 'Are you ready yet? Why are you always last?' It was so unfair; they only have themselves to get ready. Most mums will know the feeling!

I don't remember any babycare books, but I would get a lot of advice from my mother who would say, 'You should put a bonnet on that baby,' and insisted a scarf was tied round the child's neck, crossed at the front and held with a safety pin at the back. Most folk have photographs of themselves as children looking like that.

I breast-fed all my children for a good long time. My second baby wouldn't touch anything else for about nine months. It is best for baby, certainly, and also a great financial saving. So much easier in the night instead of filling bottles. I needed my sleep. However I hated the un-comfortableness of my breasts when nursing, the leaking and the smelly blouses. I think that's one problem never yet solved.

I only bought packet baby foods for convenience if we were travelling. Otherwise I just gradually weaned them to fit in with family meals. I was pretty lucky as they accepted and tried new things.

We followed all the family traditions and festivals I had enjoyed as a child: on Good Friday, and not before, hot cross buns; Easter, eggs and something new to wear, even if it was only a hankie. Whitsun, Bonfire Night, Hallowe'en, and Christmas: the tree – not put up too early, a stocking at the end of the bed, with an apple, tangerine, nuts, chocolate, crayons and a puzzle book. After breakfast, the big presents from under the tree. After lunch, the King.

I was always knitting school jumpers, cardigans and sewing baby clothes from the Viyella gown stage. At weekends we went for walks, picnics, the zoo and church together. My husband was not ashamed to push the pram, and in those days, men didn't do that. It was a big pram with one baby at each end, one on a seat in the middle, and the eldest walking. I remember an old lady passing one day, saying 'That's the happiest time you'll have; take them by the hand and off you go.' I took this with a pinch of salt, thinking it was an old wives' tale, but how right she was! When they grew up and wanted to go their own way, it could be such a worry.

Pamela Wells [born 1928]

I was a Truby King baby myself and regarded his views as inhuman so I followed my own instincts. I had three children during the 1950s and I read and continue to read baby care books by Hugh Jolly, Penelope Leach and Miriam Stoppard since becoming a grandmother. I didn't follow a rigid routine but bedtimes were important and fixed according to age. Babies and toddlers were in bed by 6.30 or 7.30, following their bath and story, and as they grew older we would have a bedtime chat to see that they were alright. Later on I was fairly strict about homework, music practice and television viewing times. During the week the children had their separate meal times, but we ate together as a family at weekends. When the third baby came along, I had an au pair girl to help me which was very welcome.

Barbara Henderson [born 1931]

I had my first four children within four and a half years, followed by three more. I usually breast-fed for about three months; I wanted to feed them longer but my milk petered out as I was always exhausted, although with the third baby I carried on for six months. The first six babies had towelling nappies but for the last baby we had family allowance to buy disposable ones: Golden Babe nappies used in rubber pants.

We got tins of government dried milk, cod liver oil and orange juice. They then had Farex cereal, and I would mash the food I was preparing for us. They had soft-boiled eggs, custard puddings and bread crusts dipped in jam, then pieces with jam or syrup. I bought *Mother* magazine for advice and tips, but I usually disregarded my own mother's advice as old wives' tales.

My husband was a farm worker and meals revolved around the time when he arrived home for his midday and evening meals. He was up at five or six am and so our bedtime was often around 9 pm. His wage when the children were young was £9 a week to feed nine people. The children had to be kept under control on the farm as the farmers couldn't be angered. This might affect my husband's job there. We couldn't afford paraffin for lamps, and although I might help out with the milking, this was not paid for as it was included in the husband's wage.

Later on he was a distillery worker, a van driver, then he did tractor work but we could never really afford the basics. The children knew that they couldn't go abroad on school trips so they didn't ask. Our teenage daughter wanted to go on a five-mile hike for charity, but we couldn't afford to replace her shoes if they wore out so we couldn't allow her to go.

Margaret Cruikshank [born 1933]

I had four children between 1952 and 1963. I didn't bother to read any baby care books when I was bringing up my children because I listened to my mother who told me about feeding practices, bedtimes and discipline. She always said, 'Babies kept to a routine, clean and fed, were contented.' She was better than any book. She advised me but the bottom line was 'They're your children, so get on with it.' I would only get help in an emergency or when another baby was due.

My husband was a cattleman on a farm and would go off to work at 6.30 am, come back for breakfast at 8 am, dinner time, as we knew it, was about 11.30 am, and supper at 5.30 approximately. Baby feeding times were every four hours from 6 am through to 10 pm.

I did want to breast-feed but wasn't able to do so after about two months. I would feed the baby and put him back in the cot, while tending to the older children. While father had his breakfast I would begin to make soup, because it took about three hours to cook on the open fire. We had no cooker when we first married. All meals were good home-cooked food and the little ones would have theirs mashed down with a fork. I always made a pudding of some sort. We couldn't afford to buy any prepared meals, puddings or cakes. I would wash the nappies before the 10 o'clock feed. So much water was needed for a baby and all water had to be fetched and carried in buckets, and dirty water carried out. For hot water to wash and boil the nappies, I boiled water on an old fireplace outside, in an old jelly pan. No wonder we toilet trained them early on. Some children nowadays still have disposable nappies on at 2½ years old because mothers are too lazy to train them. I also never used a dummy teat; horrible things I feel. My mother said they were the sign of a lazy mother. Well, there are certainly a lot of lazy mothers around judging by the amount of dummies I see.

Then, later in the morning, baking and ironing could be fitted in. We only had lino on the floor when we had the first three children and this had to be washed and polished. After the third one went to school, I went to work picking tatties, brussel sprouts and carrots, and also chicken and poultry plucking, to help to buy things for the house. This is when we got a carpet for the first time.

Money was scarce. In 1952, the year our first baby was born, my husband's wages were £5.18s.9d. In 1955, £4.18s.9d, as we had moved to another farm. By 1971, £15.00, but out of this we had to pay for coal and Rayburn fuel. So things improved after I went out to work and we had electric light and carpets.

I sewed the children's clothes from anything I could lay my hands on. I made my son's first suit for starting school, sewed the girls' blouses, pyjamas, etc. Do you see present-day mothers doing this? No chance.

My children were very disciplined, with regular meal times and bedtimes, which had a lot to do with father's work, coming in at set times. Today I hear mothers asking their children what they would like to eat! My children had two choices, take it or leave it, you get nothing more. But I believe they were grateful for what they were given and they were happy and healthy.

'Some mothers felt complete failures because they could not achieve the standards expected of them by the clinics and the textbooks. For most the anxiety and disappointment was greatest when bringing up their first child.'
Steve Humphries and Pamela Gordon, A LABOUR OF LOVE.

Sheila Brown [born 1934]

When I first brought Susan back from hospital (we were staying with my husband's parents at the time), I popped her into her little cot and then I sat down on the edge of the bed and just wept. It was the enormity of looking at this little child and being solely responsible for her, – and I felt it was my responsibility, not Ian's – and I knew so little about babies. It was a fleeting feeling but it totally overwhelmed me. That I was now responsible for this little life and was expected to be a good mother. Well, I said to myself, you just have to get on with it.

I tried to do everything well, not so much by the book but it was important that she was well-fed and well cared for. It was difficult because she was a crying baby, always crying. I don't know if it was because she sensed I was a nervous new mum. The only time she was good was when she was in her pram, being wheeled about, so I had to march out with her in all weathers, in rain and snow. I didn't care as long as she was good and quiet. I spent all my days in the park until the day I met Ivy, my nursing friend, and we just fell on each other, and I was saying how much I missed her and everyone. She and I were the only ones now tripping along with our prams. The others would be doing finals now. So after that we spent every afternoon together, at Duthie Park, Aberdeen, feeding the ducks and chattering endlessly about pregnancies and babies.

It was hard work bringing up four girls. The biggest change I found having had babies between 1955 and 1963, was the different attitude to breast-feeding. I wasn't well-endowed but wanted desperately to breast-feed. I knew it was so important to give the baby the best start. I breast-fed Susan for six weeks but then put her on the bottle. With Alison the same thing happened and I tried, I really tried. I had breast pumps, breast abcesses, cracked nipples, you name it, I had it. I thought 'I want to do this so badly' as it was expected of a mother, the natural thing to do.

When I had Gillian, the midwife asked 'Breast or bottle?' I nearly fell out of bed with shock. I said, 'Pardon? What are saying to me?' I wasn't being pressurised any more to breast-feed! I said, 'Oh the relief! I really *do* want to breast-feed my children but I am one of those mothers who just can't.'

I was so envious of the mothers around me with their babies slopping and slavering in the next bed. One had twins and was coping with both of them. I felt so inadequate as a mother, but we just made do. I was very conscious of their diet; it has always been important to me a good healthy diet.

I couldn't afford to buy these packet cereals or tins of baby foods. I would make porridge for breakfast and batter it through a sieve for the little ones whose digestive systems couldn't take ordinary porridge. Lunch time, I would batter liver and mince through a sieve, mashed potatoes and gravy, mashed carrots. There was something suitable for everyone at the table, even the youngest to have with a spoon. We never had much money but we always had a good table. Cakes once a week for Sunday tea. We always had fresh fruit and vegetables, and fresh fish.

And I thought I always tried to be fair to them, whether it was counting out the Smarties when they were small. I didn't lose my cool very often; I had to work up to it and then it was momentous. 'Mum is in a rage' they would say and then they walked on tiptoes because it didn't happen very often. Seldom but memorable, I think you would say, when mum lost her temper.

Mary Anderson [born 1934]

I had very similar attitudes to my own mother, and adhered to strict feeding times and discipline. I breast-fed the first baby for thirteen months, but the second and third baby for three and six months respectively. The children more or less ate what we had as adults except it was liquidised or mashed. I was very aware of good vegetables and fruit, and little sugar. By the time I had my third baby, I used tins and packet meals alongside my own food; there was more choice available and attitudes were changing. In fact it was only then that I read any babycare books, and read Dr Spock when I was expecting my third baby.

Routine and discipline were important, with the family sitting down together for three-course meals, a half-hour television allowance [for the first one especially], and set bedtimes.

———◆———

'Almost all children have a few temper tantrums between 1 and 3 years. They've gotten a sense of their own desires and individuality. When they're thwarted they know it and feel angry. When the feeling of fury boils up in them they can't think of anything better to do than take it out on the floor and themselves. They flop down, yelling, and pound with their hands and feet. You can't dodge all temper tantrums. Parents would be unnatural if they had that much patience and tact. When the storm breaks, you try to take it casually and help to get it over. You certainly don't give in and meekly let the child have her way; otherwise she'd be throwing tantrums all the time on purpose.'

Dr Spock, BABY AND CHILD CARE.

———◆———

Liz Sanderson [born 1938]

The midwives at the Cottage Hospital were helpful and encouraging when it came to breast-feeding. I had never thought of anything other than breast-feeding. I did have problems with the other babies, because with baby number two I had flu after six weeks and she decided that the milk tasted awful and I didn't know what to do about it. But then I had to put her on the bottle as she wouldn't take my milk. I didn't know how to get rid of the milk. Looking back I should not have been so stupid, trying to cope without advice. I should have gone to the doctor and got pills, but I didn't know about such things, and so I just went through agony and eventually it went away.

But in those days, the 1960s, you just thought, 'This is what I have to get on with.' Now I think there is far more support, the antenatal and postnatal classes. Where we lived, in a small village in the Scottish Borders, I had a rather elderly general practice doctor. I remember phoning him when baby one was about a month old, saying, 'I don't know what to do but the baby's cried all morning.' He said, 'Oh, it'll be wind.' I got no sympathy, no help and that certainly put me off asking the doctor much.

So it was a big help when this young GP joined when I was having the third baby, because this baby was quite asthmatic and the doctor was absolutely wonderful. I could ring him up around the clock. He also had a child who was asthmatic, and he was very understanding. And there was a time when Georgina was a year old and I had asked the doctor to call. He was going to visit after the morning surgery. But by 10 o'clock I couldn't stay at home any longer; she was getting worse so I wrapped her in a blanket and took her in to the surgery. He took one look at her and said, 'Right, take her to Peel Hospital.'

But in those days the visiting hours for children were horrendous.' You could only visit three times a week, and one of these times was at night, when the children were asleep. I think there was a big push a few years later from the parents who thought that this was unacceptable, and then they allowed open visiting which was an enormous improvement.

But I remember taking this little one in and she was there for ten days. It did affect her for quite a time afterwards because at that age she wouldn't go to anybody but me.

There were endless books of course, but I'm afraid they made me switch off. All these people, these experts telling you to do this, that and the other. I think I decided to let instinct tell me what to do, rightly or wrongly. My mother was extremely helpful. She came to help me when I came out of the hospital, for a week or ten days, and that was invaluable.

I copied a lot of the things from my own childhood and basically followed the ruling 'No, means No'. I do think that if I've looked after them all day, then six o'clock means bathtime and bed. I had a right to my evenings, to do what I wanted, have friends for supper or whatever.

When I had babies number three and four, I did have local girl to help me, but with the first two I was on my own.

The first child went to a small, local private school, but it closed soon after. Then the others went to the village school, which was fine, with a good headmaster and staff. They all then went on to boarding school.

Jennifer Harper-Jones [born 1939]

I was given conflicting advice from my mother and my mother-in-law. My mother and I agreed on the level of discipline, and she liked children to have spirit. My mother-in-law disapproved of the way I brought the children up; thought I was too lenient and not tidy enough.

I read Dr Benjamin Spock but disregarded a lot of what he advised. I was strict about bedtimes and rests during the day and I think when they were older, we always had family meals together.

I really persevered with breast-feeding but couldn't continue beyond a few weeks. My first baby would hardly eat anything and was very difficult to wean, while the second had a normal appetite. I never used jars of baby food, and they always had liquidised home-cooked meals.

'Carol' [born 1942]

It was sheer joy to breast-feed my son. I fed him for about eight months. By about twelve months he ate more or less what we ate – and he was very fond of garlic cheese! He was a happy little boy who was usually smiling, except when we tried to persuade him to sleep more than three hours per night! We were advised by an elderly aunt to leave him to cry. His lungs outlasted my tears. Our doctor suggested a mild sedative. We didn't agree. We were warned never to put him in our bed, but this is what we did and we all slept blissfully from then on. He suffered from colic and my mother's advice was 'He'd be better if you'd have him baptised!' My aunt said, 'Wean him.' We eventually did both but his colic went away before then.

Sheila Davidson [born 1944]

With my first son, I kept to a routine. Up at 7 am, fed, changed and out in the pram, to let me get the washing and cleaning done. A sleep after lunch, then out for the afternoon in the pram, to the park, the shops or to friends. Back for tea, bath and bed. Steven never got up at night unless he was under the weather.

Steven was five when Paul was born and perhaps because it had been a difficult birth, he was quite ill as a baby. He cried a lot of the time and never slept. I tried to keep to a routine but for a while, as a baby, Paul had to sleep in our bed, where he settled, so that I could have some sleep. He needed me beside him and I accepted that and nursed him and cuddled him. Steven was of course jealous of all this attention. I tried so hard to do my best for them both.

I was very particular about their diet. I started weaning them with stewed apples, carrots and potato, custards, banana, chicken, lentils, all blended smooth to get the baby used to different tastes. By the time they were one they were eating almost anything.

Jenni Smith [born 1946]

I would have liked to have breast-fed but because the babies were premature, I was advised not to as they thought it would be too much trouble. The first one was too weak to suck, and at three weeks had to be weaned. I fed on demand and was not overly concerned about a strict routine for feeding or bedtimes.

My own upbringing had been very strict, based on the 'children should be seen and not heard' principle. I was determined that my own children should be brought up differently, and tried to involve them in all the decisions that were taken. I always tried to give them a reason for doing or not doing something, although of course there were times when my answer was 'Because I say so.' Needless to say, theory and practice are not at all the same thing and they were probably more heavily disciplined than was wise. Partly this was down to the fact that my nerves were at breaking point all the time they were small. My husband did not help very much at all, so the children were my responsibility. I was extremely unhappy in my marriage and very afraid of their father. Consequently they were probably not treated as fairly as they should have been. I finally found the courage to divorce my husband when the boys were six and seven.

Vivienne Leighton [born 1947]

I never had a child minder or mother's help. My mother would help me out quite a bit; if I needed someone to babysit or if I needed to go out for an afternoon, it was my mother who would come every time. She would often give me advice about how I should do things. Even today, if she is watching me cooking, she might even say, 'Oh you shouldn't do it that way, it is easier if you stir it like this.' She has her ways of doing things. We still fall out over things like that.

I know a friend whose mother came to stay after she had her baby and one day, when she was hanging out the baby clothes on the line, her mother told her, 'Oh, no you can't hang those like that. The nappies must all be together, and these vests or whatever must all hang together.' And she proceeded to rehang all the baby clothes, to do it her way.

I breast-fed Martin but only for a fortnight, and stopped because I couldn't give him enough. I was told I had wonderful nipples but no breasts. Once I started to supplement the feed with a bottle it was too much so I gave up breast-feeding. It was just the same with Emma and she went on to the bottle after a few weeks.

I used Harrington's nappies, a good make of nappy, nice and thick and they lasted both children. I also bought Mothercare nappies, which were less expensive, and I used those occasionally during the day. I did read books about childcare but never stuck rigidly to, say, Dr Spock's way of doing things. There were health visitors for advice and they were very good, and always available.

I did have a strict routine for them as babies and young children. I am a very routine oriented person myself and I hate change. When they were older I would expect them to be home for meals and in at a certain time, but as they went through teenage life, I would say you must be in at a set time. But again, what do you do if they don't come back? I must be a failure. I don't seem to be able to make them do what I want.

Mary Law [born 1949]

I had always wanted to breast-feed, it was an inbuilt gut feeling, and while I had all the problems possible, I succeeded and loved every minute of it. I fed the first one, Fiona, for nearly two years, Douglas for four and a half years, and Gavin for over three years. I was able to feed both the baby and toddler successfully. This was demand feeding. I started the babies on stewed fruit and vegetables at around four to six months. They had no sugar for the first year and no cows' milk while I was breast-feeding, except on cereal. They then had soup and finger foods.

My mother-in-law is very old-fashioned about childcare and believed that men should not involve themselves in looking after the babies. She did not understand my wish to keep breast-feeding and she liked a very strict routine. We don't see eye to eye. She forces her advice upon me; I don't want it and I don't take it. She makes me upset and angry.

Neither she nor my own mother believe in demand feeding or in picking up the baby each time it cries. They think it's a battle of wits and believe in strict bedtimes and in punishment even at a young age. I ask advice from my mother who is not so strict and has been a great support and very important in helping me with the children. I wished she lived nearer!

We have school day and holiday bedtimes and I expect my children to be there for meals. They do not always have to sit at the table but can eat watching television occasionally. Up to now family meals around the table have been spoiled by an overstrict father, which was a shame. We make wee rules like changing out of school clothes and not playing outside after dark. The television is off at 9 pm but there are many exceptions to these rules.

I read all the childcare books I could find, I find them so enjoyable. I like Hugh Jolly because I agree with his views. My favourites are Sheila Kitzinger, Claire Rayner and Miriam Stoppard. I like to be flexible with no set routine. I am a baby-led mother.

'To be a mother is to take on one of the most emotionally and intellectually demanding, exasperating, strenuous, anxiety-arousing and deeply satisfying tasks that any human being can undertake . . . For many women birth is an ordeal that leaves them with lowered self-esteem and feeling emotionally and physically battered, just when they need the strength to take on the new challenge of motherhood. In our technological society, mothers are often socially isolated and left to get on with mothering as best they can. But we are not alone. There is a great sisterhood out there – the diversity, ingenuity, the energy and the courage of mothers.'

Sheila Kitzinger, OURSELVES AS MOTHERS.

Janice Mackenzie [born 1950]

My mother's attitude was similar to my own with regard to caring for babies, although she had followed the very strict routine of four-hourly feeds when I was a baby in 1950. I tried to follow the advice from the NCT and Penelope Leach's book *Baby and Child*, newly published in 1977. She advised set routines for bedtime but feeding on demand; more close contact and not pushing a young baby into a room by itself at too early an age. So I breast-fed my first baby on demand for about nine months and the third one for about five months. My mother-in-law had ideas differing from mine, especially on breast-feeding. She felt it was a sign of poverty to breast-feed; it indicated that there was a lack of money to buy formula milk. She couldn't understand why I wanted to, saying it would ruin my figure and exclude my husband from the feeding routine! She did not like me breast-feeding Wendy when we visited for a holiday, and asked me to go to the bedroom to do it as it was not nice for her husband and twelve-year old son to see it.

I was careful about their diet in the first year, and they had milk, fruit juice, home-made soups, mashed bananas, boiled and scrambled eggs. I also bought tins and jars of baby food. When they were older, 2 to 5 years, no special meals were cooked and they ate with the family. As they have grown up they have always had strict bedtimes, homework times, censored television viewing. We always have an evening meal and Sunday lunch taken together as a family.

———— • ————

'Only you can decide whether to breast or bottle feed. It is your body and your baby. Nobody has the right to pressure you either way or to criticize you whatever you decide. Breast milk is physically better for babies because it is the milk that nature intended for them. It feels very right and very pleasurable too. But if you find the whole idea embarrassing you many not enjoy actually doing it. Both you and the baby may be happier using a bottle.'

Penelope Leach, BABY AND CHILD FROM BIRTH TO AGE FIVE.

———— • ————

'Penelope Leach, the British Dr Spock, was the childcare guru for the 1970s; the companion of every young mother's sleepless nights, of every helpless parent in despair as a toddler screamed himself blue, of every out of practice granny, giving young parents a rare weekend off. Her book Baby and Child has sold more than two million copies world-wide, in 27 languages.'

Angela Lambert, THE INDEPENDENT, 12 April 1994.

———— • ————

Sheila Gray [born 1951]

My husband was in the oil business and we were living in Brunei when our first baby was born in 1978. I felt totally out of my depth with no health visitor. I had a few friends there but it was a case of the blind leading the blind. I read books by Penelope Leach and Miriam Stoppard; any help was appreciated and I agreed with a lot of what Penelope Leach had to say. I breast-fed all my three children for about a year. After initial problems I loved it, and I could do it in restaurants and shops discreetly, with the judicious use of jumpers and jackets. I don't think I offended anyone – I don't think anyone knew what I was doing. My babies got fed when they needed it. I then went on to Milupa packet baby foods – I am not fond of cooking for any age – then fruit, vegetables and sausages.

My mother-in-law would say that her children were potty-trained at six months. I was training them at two years. She'd tell me to let them cry and get them into a feeding routine. I fed them on demand which was often. She felt I should discipline them more than I did when they were older. However I was strict about bedtime. The two boys were in bed by 7 pm each night.

But things were not easy and I wept with unhappiness and frustration nearly every day when my boys were little. I hated it. I used to pray to God I wouldn't become bitter. My husband hadn't wanted children and he took very little part in their upbringing. We separated in 1986 and I brought up the boys alone. I married again in 1990 and my second husband desperately wanted us to have children. I said no, I'd had my family, but Jenny arrived by accident. I enjoyed pregnancy and childbirth and I am happy now as she is growing up. When my boys were small, it was just awful because I was on my own with them; my first husband didn't take any of the responsibility, but now I have a caring husband who shares the joys and burdens of our family life.

Ailsa Gray [born 1953]

Although I now have five children under five years of age, I don't have any outside help. I gave up work when I had the first two children, who were aged two and one, and was expecting my third. My husband helps to an extent but I do feel caring for the children is mainly my responsibility. Both my mother and mother-in-law are helpful and supportive but my mother-in-law's attitudes are very different from mine and this can cause a lot of friction and tension. My own mother is brilliant. She offers advice when asked and is very tactful and we see eye to eye, but we live 400 miles apart unfortunately. I read lots of childcare books but mainly out of interest, not really for day to day advice on what to do. I tend to turn to one in the case of illness, for example, to check if the spots are chickenpox or measles! I read Penelope Leach, Sheila Kinzinger and Miriam Stoppard.

I have very firm bedtime routines and also daytime naps for the babies. I breast-fed my first baby but I felt uncomfortable and found it painful so the later babies were all bottle-fed. Then I used a mixture of home foods and jars. I am a vegetarian but give my children fish and white meat. They love pasta, bread, milk, fruit, cereals and potatoes. Sadly they are not too keen on other vegetables!

Liz Hodgson [born 1954]

As I suffered from septicaemia after the birth of my son, I stayed in hospital for two weeks on antibiotics, and certainly felt the 'three day blues'. Because of this I found breast-feeding very hard at first. Other women in the ward were offering me bottles, saying how brave I was to persevere. But I was getting individual care and we both got the hang of it by the time we left hospital. I was actually under par for about six months. I could now breast-feed forever! Well, I'm still giving him three to four feeds a day at ten and a half months because of the risk of asthma and because I'm too lazy to sterilize anything.

I read a few childcare books but was put off Penelope Leach by her television programme, when she went on about 'asking permission to wash the child's face'. Silly of me, but still. However, I have flicked through her books to get ideas in order to counter my mum's insistence on potty-training. My mother is flummoxed by *all* of it; she can't *believe* demand feeding, agitates for me to start potty-training, and expects him to sleep all the time. She is the classic stereotype of the old child-rearing approach.

I do not follow a strict routine with Toby. No chance! He only sleeps a little more than we do, so evenings have been a bit gruelling with lots of feeds. Mind you, I did try to get an idea about routines at the start but everyone said, 'Go with the flow.' Now it seems we should have let a routine develop.

———◆———

'Late in the first year most babies have learned to sit up by themselves and some have adopted quite regular times of day for passing bowel movements. Some parents decide that they might as well sit their baby on a pot at these times. They call this toilet training, but it is important to realise that there is no training in it

at all. The baby is simply being put in the right place at the right time. The baby can neither understand nor cooperate. True toilet training means helping a child to recognise his own full bowel or bladder and then to do something about it like telling his mother or going to find his pot.'

Penelope Leach, BABY AND CHILD FROM BIRTH TO AGE FIVE.

――――――●――――――

Barbara Buckley [born 1954]

I have two sets of twins, aged 7 and 4. Because my mother had died twelve years before my first child was born, I read Penelope Leach for advice with the first set of twins, which I found helpful. I had a nanny to help me with the first twins but since the birth of the second set, my husband has given up work and cares for them while I work full-time. The babies have been rather ill since birth, and they continue to be monitored by the Great Ormond Street Hospital.

I breast-fed the first set for eight months, and the second twins for five months. However I returned to work after twelve weeks with the first twins, and eleven weeks after the the second twins were born, leaving my husband in charge!

Trudi Barnet [born 1954]

When I had my second baby, I had full-time living-in help and I must say I was very lucky. The first girl, Elizabeth, had a proper nanny's routine, so that really helped me. The reason why I needed full-time help was because my husband was away so much of the time as a restaurateur, working long days and nights, six days a week.

Elizabeth stayed with us for six years, and then a year later we had another nanny who stayed for six years. It was fortunate to be able to keep staff for a continuous period, which was good for the children.

I was never successful at breast-feeding at all with any of them until I reached my fifth baby, so the moral of the story is keep trying! Perhaps it was my fault. I would get to six weeks with the first, second, third and fourth, and I just couldn't carry on. So when the fifth came along, I made a point of asking the midwives and nurses what was going wrong. I was sent to a breast-feeding clinic at the Eastern General Hospital in Edinburgh, and this sister got me through it. At six weeks your hormone level starts to change and this hormonal imbalance can make you feel exhausted; the hormones which have kept you going for a month or so leave you. This is where I was going wrong before, so this time I rode over the problems and persevered through the hormonal changes. I am still breast-feeding her and she is six months now.

'Oh I loved the baby. I know a lot of women who hate those night feeds but not me. I remember those as peaceful and happy times. On the sofa in our living room, cushions piled around both of us, a throne of warmth and comfort, a book, a box of those wonderful dark Bentick chocolates, and the pale scrambled egg coloured dawns, thickening visibly out of the grey times at the end of the darkness.'

Sarah Maitland, APPLE PICKING.

Carol Walton [born 1943, midwife and breast-feeding counsellor]

Today women often stay in hospital for just twenty-four hours, perhaps less. In the hospital where I work in Wales, the majority are out within two or three days; even women who have had Caesarean sections only stay in for a week, so they go home very quickly these days. This has its advantages and some do benefit but for others it is a disadvantage because it might be just at the point when I am establishing their breast-feeding and they go home at the wrong moment. They do not have the family network of support as they would have done in the days when they had their babies at home with other women looking after them. Also from the point of view of breast-feeding, which is my hobby horse, you often find that the girls' mothers did not breast-feed anyway, so they haven't a clue about it. Along with the change in the attitude towards childcare, there has also been a big change in their confidence in their ability as mothers.

Young mothers today don't know anything about it, have never seen it done, and they don't think they can do it, so the first time they come across a hurdle, they can't cope. You send them home on the third day, just when they might hit all their biggest problems, and they give up. In my area it is mostly a lower class population and we don't have many of the articulate, educated career women who would go to the National Childbirth Trust classes and would seek help. We try to make the antenatal classes mother-orientated and ask what they and the dads want to know, but we don't get the girls who really should be coming for advice.

Of course in the pre-NHS days there were no antenatal or postnatal classes and very little advice. But now people can expect all this care and attention during pregnancy and after the birth. Maybe we have gone over the top and probably one of the reasons why attitudes have changed is that people feel that the responsibility for childcare isn't theirs anymore, it is someone else's. Recently I remember a father saying to me, 'Well, it is all very well for you, but you don't seem to realise that we have never had to pick up a small baby before.' So it was very difficult not to reply, 'Well you have had nine months to think about that!' That was his attitude, and he was very cross with me that I should consider that they should now take the responsibility for their baby, get to grips with it and learn to look after it. It seemed beyond him. I don't think you would have got that response twenty or thirty years ago.

My mother told me that when she had her fourth baby, it was at the time when health visitors were just starting routine visits. So this health visitor came to call and my mother, with children at both feet and one in each arm, opened the door and said, 'No, you may not come in. I have had four children and brought them up myself. I don't need the state's intervention with this one, thank you very much.' And that was the end of that!

But my mother is quite horrified that you have to take your baby to the clinic and the health visitor has to call regularly on the new mother after she gets home. She thinks mothers should be able to manage on their own, as she had had to do.

'Cathy' [born 1955]

I have been married twice and have three children, and neither husband has taken a share in childcare, but I feel my husband contributes so much and supports us in other ways where I am wanting. It is intelligent equality.

I did read Penelope Leach for advice. At least it's detailed but too funky for me, I think – by which I mean, her views on 'child as tyrant, God, Pope' in the home.

I do have a nanny now, but I am not unimaginative and have for long stretches not had one. I used traditional towelling and muslin nappies and although I wanted to breast-feed, could not, and moved on to SMA and Milupa powder for travelling. They then all began on avocado; the first was an eccentric, greedy eater, the girl fussy and the baby a committed carnivore. The first two liked mashed artichoke base, a Breton baby feed I believe.

Having been raised with baby routines, the children genuinely set sensible routines for themselves. I have television rules, restricting viewing to as little as possible in the week, and then only allowed when accompanied by an adult. We eat Sunday lunch and festival meals together, but otherwise I seem to be catering, too busy to sit, or they are with nanny, or my husband is working, so we are rarely together, all five of us, for family meals.

' "It's not the getting up at night. It's the way they bring you down in the daytime." Alex had a castanet rhythm going with his fingers. "All that crying and feeding and please Mummy-ing." Click. "Oh the boredom of it all." Click. "The stroller-shopping, the avocado mashing, the bottle sterilising." Click. "Do you really want to spend your entire life worrying whether your toilet cleaner is getting right up under the rim?" Click click. "Do you really want to spend your life straining prunes?" And when they're not boring you to death, they're turning you into Nietzche. "If God made us, who made God?" "Where does wind blow from?" "Where do roads end?" "How do eyebrows know when to stop growing?" The other day Felicity actually used a word with more than two syllables in it. The word was tranquilizer 'cos that's what she needed.'

Kathy Lette, FOETAL ATTRACTION.

Winifred Fyfe [born 1955]

I had an elective Caesarean section for all three of my babies, because I am so small. It is quite unpleasant afterwards because you can't move for two days. I wanted to breast-feed but it was very difficult because you've got this wound and you have to put a pillow over it and then the baby on top. I did manage to breast-feed them, although it took eight days' determination and hard sweat and unpleasantness. My breasts got so big, enormously big, and it was painful, but I managed it.

I had trained as a nursery nurse so I didn't read Dr Spock or anything like that. I had experienced babies from about six weeks, in the nursery, but it's still not like having your own; when you need to deal with them twenty-four hours a day, it's a different story. However, I always believed that the father should share the responsibility of looking after babies. So my husband Steve would come home by about seven, and then he would often feed Sarah. Sarah never slept – she was a good baby otherwise, but she would wake in the night and I would dump the baby on Steve's chest and I'd have to go through to another room because I was so angry. I think from the time Sarah was born to when she was two years old, she never slept and I was in desperate need of sleep. They should tell mothers about babies. 'Oh you want to have a baby? Well, you might not sleep for two years. Are you prepared for that?' Stephen used to sit with her while I would slam doors, put the nappies through the wash, empty out the toy box; furious, I was always furious. You know you can deal with baby things during the day, but at night it's like you're the only person in the world sitting in the dark. I would eventually get to bed around five or six in the morning, maybe get an hour or two of sleep and then Steve would go to work. Like many women, I felt very isolated during the day, having to deal with the babies and running the home on my own; it can be very hard.

Didi Hopkins [born 1956]

After the trauma of the birth and what followed, I did notice that during the first few days after she was born, my entire boundaries and perceptions – everything in terms of how I related to myself and the world around me, changed. We immediately left London and went to Cornwall, and we lived by the sea. So we had a relaxing time to begin with, away from the city noise and bustle, getting to know each other quietly because the birth experience naturally affected our baby. When she was born Alice looked like a frightened dormouse and she remained so for the first six months of her life. She was in a panicky, stressful state a lot of the time, panting, breathing quickly, and understandably so. For the first few months she couldn't be put down to sleep normally by herself. She needed constant physical contact and so we have become closely linked. For the first nine months of her life, I would have to take her into bed and lie with her until she fell asleep and then, once she was settled, leave her quietly. She simply could not bear to be left alone, she was so nervous. But Alice is not fragile, she is a sturdy old sausage now, and she has taken well to training. It was a difficult transition when we decided it was time she left the family bed and learn to sleep by herself in her cot.

I went out one evening so that Oliver could put her to bed on her own. She screamed for an hour and a half. But each night she cried less and less. After three nights she went into her cot like a duck to water. She was fine although at the time, with all that screaming, I thought it was damaging her in some way. It was awful to hear but it had to be done to help her. We have now managed, without causing us especial grief, to get her to bed by 7.30 every night, and she wakes at seven in the morning. She also sleeps for two hours in the day.

I just find babies are so extraordinary, and to watch their ways of learning, they are so quick. It is fascinating and so exposing. I feel emotionally exposed by my daughter. I think I need to learn how to relax out of the mode of working and into the mode of mothering, of motherhood. Even now, when Alice is eighteen months, I still haven't got there. I am always dashing around, saying, 'We must do this, that, the other.' When I really concentrate and stop for a moment and play with her, which I do, it is really rewarding. I really do believe there is something valuable to be had from quality time with children.

Sue Rook [born 1960]

I deliberately and studiously avoided reading any childcare books on the grounds that they would only panic me into a lack of confidence about my own ability as a mother. My mother was very helpful on breast-feeding and produced a marvellous historical piece of advice with her babycare pamphlet from the early 1920s, which her mother had been given during her pregnancy. It makes incredible reading.

The attitude of my parents and father-in-law has been very positive and helpful, not interfering. They've never said 'You should do it like this.' I think they like the fact that Hannah has a routine which I've stuck to and, as she is such a cheerful and happy child, they accept that it must be working. My husband does share childcare jobs; the planning and thinking often lie with me, but he is capable of carrying out a task I ask him to do.

I breast-fed for the first year. I just liked the idea of 'have Mum will travel'! We were all breast-fed as babies, my mother flying in the face of the 1950s fad of bottle-feeding.

She is now at the toddler stage of eating what we eat: fresh fruit, yoghurt, chicken, ham, fresh vegetables. I have a daily routine consisting of walks in the morning and an afternoon nap. Playtime might be painting, colouring, baking or singing. Then tea, bath, story and bed. No television is allowed during the day before 5 pm, and she sits at the table for meals. So far I have not allowed sweets except on high days and holidays.

Jo Davidson [born 1960]

I returned to work four months after the birth of Rosie, our first baby, and have now just returned to work full-time, six months after the birth of Calum. I breast-fed both for the first three months and then provided a mixture of breast and bottle. I have had no problems with either baby and in fact, on returning to work, I love coming home to have a round bundle leap on me and have a long, peaceful suck. Rosie now eats more or less the same diet as us, which is generally a vegetarian one, but she likes fishfingers and beans. For a time that was all she ate, together with cheese, apple and banana, but she has improved.

Responsibility for the welfare of the children is a bone of contention. When we are both there, I feel that the ultimate responsibility rests with me. My husband does help with everything and as he is a teacher, he has sole care of both children during the school holidays while I continue working. We have an absolutely superb child minder – a nursing hero, who has a huge and close family. My two are part of that family. We also use friends for babysitting.

My parents are delighted to be involved as much as possible. They see grandchildren as a new lease of life, although they disapprove of me working full-time.

I read Penelope Leach and also Dr Christopher Green's book, *Toddler Taming* for good commonsense advice.

Lucy Owen [born 1961]

My mother is terrified of very small babies so she wasn't much help at the beginning with No 1. She's brilliant now though, and is less terrified of No 2. She gives advice when asked and has approved of most of my childcare innovations. We are homeopathic and she likes that as she disapproves of antibiotics, etc. She is ecstatic about the fact that my husband baths them and changes nappies, and is a bit jealous I think. My mother tends not to want me to feel she is interfering. She just tells me afterwards that she lets me make any mistakes rather than pass criticism at the time. My parents-in-law are very traditional and so I have had to overcome lots of opposition to late potty-training, etc. I either ignore the criticism or say, 'I am doing it this way' and dare them to disapprove.

I was determined to breast-feed even after Caesarian section problems and infections, because of the high incidence of asthma in my family. I breast-fed my son, Archie, for eight months and am still breast-feeding my daughter, who is now five months. When they have a bottle it is soya formula. Archie wouldn't take home-cooked food so I spent hundreds of pounds on organic baby food. Tabitha has home-cooked apple, pear, banana, courgette, potato, parsnip, sweet potato, avocado and carrot, and she seems to eat anything! I put it all down to my being more relaxed with no 2. and to buying a Braun hand-held liquidiser, an essential implement for any mother going over to solids.

The diet for three year old Archie is plain but wholesome – no red meat, lots of vegetables. He eats with us and has to eat properly or not at all. If he doesn't finish, fine. But he gets no more till the next mealtime. I find small portions mean he has more second helpings. I try to ban chocolate but it's impossible with grannies around and other children. So he has it, but not sweets.

I have a strict routine for Archie: bath at 6 pm, storytime, teeth cleaning, songs, kisses, lights out at 7 pm. The door is closed, with one Thomas the Tank Engine nightlight. He never comes downstairs and mostly goes straight to sleep. We have closed the nursery door since he was born. Tabitha, the baby, has a bath, massage, last feed and is put into her cot. The door is closed. I put lavender and chamomile in both their baths to make them relax!

I have read several childcare books. Penelope Leach is reassuring on development and feeding albeit a bit moralistic. Richard Ferber solved sleep problems at five months; Christopher Green is good on toddlers.

This routine is essential for my sanity, and it means that Archie and Tabitha have the same reassuring ritual, so it works!

Diane Connolly [born 1961]

I have two small boys under five and I work part-time as a midwife. My husband is marvellous with the children and I could not have coped without him. He is certainly a better mother because he is so good although I do like to have control over what they eat and wear.

I found the first six weeks with my first baby really hard work and so was feeling low at times, but I think this is quite normal in view of this drastic change in your life and lack of sleep. I did breast-feed each baby for ten months although my sore nipples were hell for a week each time. I breast-fed on demand although our parents were not impressed with this. I often heard the comment, 'Feeding again?' Also to reduce the risk of cot death, I kept the boys cool at night and my mother-in-law expressed concern that my first baby was not covered up enough.

I started them on solids with rice, carrots, occasional packets and tins. Milupa cereal for breakfast and mainly home-cooked, blended meals the rest of the day, so that there was an incongruous smell of garlic from the mouths of young babies. They both like roast dinners and fruit, but still enjoy crisps and sweets when they can. The elder child likes novelties such as dinosaur-shaped food, and I indulge this.

They have a bath at 7 pm and are in bed by 9 pm after a story. Television is limited. We are strict but loving and everybody comments on how well behaved the boys are. In honesty I dislike rough boys, and I am sure that is why I am firm.

I didn't read baby care books as I am a midwife but think they must be helpful to new mums. I truly believe that 'follow your instincts' is the best advice ever.

' "Anybody can breast-feed", said the midwife severely. "Those who say they can't are only making excuses."

"I'd just like to say," said the fat weary-faced woman seated by the window. "I'd just like to say that it's not as easy as it looks. I have been through it, you see."

She looked pointedly at the midwife, who obviously had not. "And what I think," continued the woman, "what I think is bottle-feeding is better. My first was latched on twenty four hours a day for the first two months. I still wasn't up or dressed by mid-afternoon. Also, it was excruciating. It made me bleed. He just sucked on the end like it was a straw. It felt like red-hot pincers."

"You've obviously had an unfortunate experience," interrupted the midwife frigidly. "Shall we move on?" '

Helen Simpson, FOUR BARE LEGS IN A BED.

Angela Blanchard [born 1962]

I didn't 'decide' to breast-feed; it was a gut feeling, an instinctive belief that this was what a good mother would do. With hindsight, I know that my first baby Clare had a slight tongue-tie, which made it difficult for her to suck, and the action of the tongue is crucial. I became sore and got to a stage at five weeks when I was crying before every feed, and could not face the next one. With the help of the health visitor, I eventually overcame the problem and went on to breast-feed her happily. The tongue-tie disappeared. I think that fifty years earlier, midwives would have known what to look for to help me position her correctly and save me all those weeks of agony.

Clare moved on to baby rice [awful stuff] and other packet meals but I didn't like these as it took me so long to read the list of ingredients, to check what was in them, so I made liquidised meals for her. John moved more or less from breast milk to adult food. They have a largely vegetarian diet: lots of fruit, vegetables, fish and pulses. I used Rose Elliot's book, *Mother and Baby Book*, for some recipes.

I don't really have a routine as such, but a pattern of feeding emerged: breakfast at 8, lunch at 12 and tea at 4. Bedtime crept forward from about 9 pm to 7 pm because they both seemed ready for it. I think it helps to have a framework but it can be flexible. Clare is now at playgroup in the mornings, and in the afternoon we might go out, or John has a nap and I read to Clare. Bathtime is at 6 pm, and then go to bed at 7 pm with a hot bedtime drink. They have a nightlight on all night, as I used to have. It never crosses my mind to put on the television during the day; Clare sometimes asks to watch it but rarely watches for long. We only have a black and white portable so it doesn't hold her attention. I did not have television until I was thirteen, which was an advantage, so I probably will limit their viewing.

I try not to be unnecessarily strict but my rules are absolute rules: 'If I say no, I mean no.' In principle I don't approve of smacking, but of course I sometimes do it. Ultimate punishment for Clare is to be sent to her room, which usually works. I recently started to read *Toddler Taming*, which had been recommended, but found it too depressing. I'd done many things wrong already. I was also given booklets from the midwife and health visitor which contained some useful advice, and some that was totally misleading, especially about breast-feeding. They actively contradict each other. Much more realistic and enjoyable to read is *A Parent's Survival Guide*.

Linda Macpherson [born 1962]

When I came home with Magnus I wasn't really that confident about looking after him. Bathing him scared me and in the hospital I had managed to avoid it altogether; the midwives did it for me and I watched each time but didn't bathe him myself. So he didn't have a proper bath for about four days and then I thought I better try it. We had practised changing nappies in hospital so that was alright. A midwife came in to see me every day once I was home, and the health visitor also came round. I felt anxious all the time, because I had this little person to care for. He was feeding alright but I was slightly concerned. Every time he cries you wonder what is wrong, because he has been fed, changed, everything. I didn't relax for weeks. The health visitor was a star; I would ring her and she came regularly to see him, and would say he was fine. I think she realised I was a worrier and came for weeks on a regular basis. She put my mind at rest.

He feeds when he is hungry and that can be every two or three hours so we don't really have a planned routine. Breast-feeding was awful to begin with; I had cracked nipples which were really painful. But after three weeks they healed and since then it has been fine. It is wonderful that I don't have to heat and prepare feeds. It is all there on tap and I want to continue as long as he gets what he needs. The thought of sterilising bottles and everything doesn't thrill me. I am all for breast-feeding. I think it is great and it is worth persevering through the painful times.

His father is much calmer than me and really copes well if things are difficult. I get in a state if Magnus has a sniffle and feel I should call the doctor. But my husband just takes things easily and reminds me that babies cry and have colds and that he is a strong little thing. I can't let him cry for more than a couple of minutes. I just have to pick him up.

Liz Suttie [born 1964]

I felt an awful sense of responsibility, especially the first couple of days. When she cried I didn't know what to do. It took a few weeks to get to grips with it. In the hospital it is not a realistic situation because all the nures are there to help you and do things for you. But once you get home, you have to get on with it on your own.

My problem was that I was in a ward with noisy babies but she was tiny and just slept. I thought she was ill, not wanting to feed. But I was told this was natural. I didn't feel instinctively how I should look after this baby. I challenge anyone who says that looking after a baby comes naturally – it doesn't. In the hospital I was scared to do very much. I got differing advice from the midwives, too much conflicting advice from midwives of different ages. One said I had better stay another day because

I hadn't got the feeding routine worked out. I had stayed in for four days but I thought if I went home as planned, I would be left alone with her. In the hospital, you felt you were being watched and assessed all the time. When I did get home and develop a routine, I think Emma was happier and it became easier.

I found the hospital routine was like a production line. There were regulation starched gowns for the babies, and enormous regulation size nappies which were far too big for Emma. They came up to her arm pits. All the babies were dressed the same and drinking the same milk, unless they were on the breast. I suppose hospitals have to run wards like that so the mothers and babies are cared for efficiently, but it was nice to bring her home and put her in nice baby clothes and micro-size nappies.

I am not breast-feeding. I had to give up because her mouth is so small. I had to get a nipple shield for her to suck and I persevered for three weeks but she was not putting on weight at all. She would feed for two hours, stop for half an hour and then cry and want more, so she was not getting enough from me. I was advised to put her on the bottle and it was the right thing to do, she is thriving now.

She goes to bed at seven, she lies and cries for a bit but will be asleep by eight o'clock. She might wake twice in the night. I am getting quite good sleep really and my husband is very supportive. He feeds her during the night at weekends so I get two full nights' sleep. When he is at work during the week, it is not fair he should get up for her then.

Rachel Hanks [born 1967]

Breast is best I feel, and more convenient. It kept me slim and I could eat what I like. It developed a good relationship between me and the baby, and apparently breast-fed babies are more intelligent. I breast-fed for the first year and now he has home-cooked food, with jars of baby food for journeys only.

My partner does share in most things. I'm keen to have a 50/50 relationship in terms of parenting but there are some roles that I have found myself pushed into. I arrange childcare, I wash the nappies, I take the baby down to Cornwall on my own. So he's had a lot of time off from the role of father. Now that I have stopped breast-feeding, things are getting more balanced and I'm going out more.

I don't follow a strict routine as he's only one year old. My boyfriend is much stricter than I am about a feeding routine and bedtime.

I do feel that mothers are expected just to stay at home. Unless you have a car getting out and about is a real task with a baby. Public transport is completely inadequate; British Rail have no facilities whatsoever for nappy changing. It is incredible that breast-feeding in public is still taboo in the 1990s, yet images of topless women are prolific. Things really haven't changed in the last few years because this is still a patriarchal society, designed by men for men. It doesn't help that Britain is light years behind some other western countries in terms of childcare and maternity leave.

Rachel Lockey [born 1967]

Having a baby made me think about what I wanted to do with my life. I had two years of full-time commitment looking after her, when I was nineteen until I was twenty-one. I was much less settled then, than I am now, and I kind of thought, 'Well I've got a baby, but I'd like to travel.' So I took her to Australia and stayed with my sister, and then we did quite a bit of travelling together, to Thailand and Africa. She was small and I could carry her everywhere.

I breast-fed her until she was six months. I fed her about four or five times a day, whenever she wanted it. If she woke up in the night, I'd take her into my bed and we would both fall asleep together. That was lovely as I am not very good at getting up at night and I think I'd fall asleep before she did.

It is difficult sometimes living in a different culture but I had lived in Africa before, when I was doing voluntary work after I left school. So I went back to that place and they welcomed me there with open arms, and I felt very connected with the women there. They had children and I had a baby. There were a lot of absent fathers so we got on very well, despite the cultural differences. I felt so free. Now, looking back, I sometimes wonder why I took her there, it seems such a risk, but I don't think it really was. I was just adventurous. I think it has helped Bella because she has grown up well, and she appreciates the difference between people, nationalities and races. That is important. So were very mobile for the first two years of her life.

I really thought I'd bring her up well, with non-sexist toys, but it isn't really working out that way. She was given a Barbie doll when she was three and that was my decision taken from me. So even if you have a set of ideals, you can't control them. It was a friend who gave the doll to her and I couldn't say no, you can't have that, because she loves it. And at school, the girls play together with their dolls, singing girly songs, and the boys are very boyish and play their games. You can't prevent that natural development. But I try to ensure that she has a balance of interests. I am not religious but I don't mind that she sings hymns at school, it is a lovely communal activity, but I also teach her that not everyone believes in one God, and that there are other churches and faiths. They are meant to learn that at school but they don't and I think it is important that she knows the differences between people.

Andrea Duffin [born 1970]

My partner and I are vegetarians so I have always brought up my two little girls as vegetarians. Lauren is a picture of health and she was really quite fat when she was little. When she was just newly born, the doctor said to me, 'I don't know about this vegetarian lark', and in fact he advised me not to bring her up as a vegetarian. Later, when he saw how healthy she was, he told me he took back what he said, and that he wouldn't dissuade mothers if they were vegetarians.

I was very aware about their feeding. I breast-fed Lauren until she was nine months, and Molly until she was ten and a half months. I was very health conscious when they were being weaned. I never bought jars or tins of baby food. I am really against them but I can see the benefits of having it sometimes, say if we got back late one day and she was hungry and I had nothing prepared. It would be handy if you went away from home because you could take a jar and it's clean with no mess. But they were both weaned on solid, home-made food. I'd cook lentils and vegetables and puree that for them. And they only have sweets very occasionally. Lauren will now come to me if, say, she is given a sweet or something she is unsure about, and she asks me if she can eat it. Her response if people ask her why she and the family are vegetarian is 'Because I like animals and am not going to eat them.'

I have always used terry towelling nappies but, as with the bought baby food, I do have some disposable nappies for emergencies or if we go out on a journey. However I think it must have been so much harder years ago, when you had no choice but to use towelling nappies and make your own food. We have a fairly strict routine. They are both in bed by seven thirty. I really feel I need my time, so by seven I feel I have given them twelve hours and it's time for a bath, story and bed. Then I can enjoy the evening.

Nourishing and Nurturing

Their father, Barry, loves spending time with the girls. Lauren is a real Daddy's girl, because he had to look after her so much when I was ill with a miscarriage. As I had not grown up with a father, I never really knew what his role was. But Barry is excellent. He didn't know anything about children when Lauren was born but he is so good with them. Barry is a brilliant dad – one of the best.

CHAPTER SEVEN

Commitment to Motherhood

MOTHER LOVE

'Mother love is a mighty benefaction
The prop of the world and its population
If mother love died the world would rue it
No money would bring the women to it.'

Stevie Smith.

Violet Stevenson-Hamilton [born 1902]

In my day, bringing up my three boys in the 1920s, it wasn't seen as normal for fathers to push prams or look after the children. But I do think that running a house and looking after the children is mainly the mother's job. I do feel that women should either have a career or concentrate on their children for such a time as they require you. Once they go to school that is a very different matter. Mind you, I do admit that there were moments of extreme boredom; just the daily round and common tasks that you do day after day. If you are not prepared to do it yourself, then I think it would be better not to have a child.

Janet Stewart [born 1904]

I left my job as a secretary to bring up my children. I do think motherhood is a full-time commitment and I never worked outside the home. Looking after the home, my husband and two daughters was a full-time job. I do think a mother is needed in the home and even when my daughters were older, in their teenage years, I was just as concerned about them as when they were small. I worried about them having boyfriends and was very strict. Not much leeway was allowed. Both girls had to be in by 10 pm, and this was the latest time they were allowed out up until they married. They were given ten shillings for pocket money, even when they were out working and right up until the time they left the home as brides, even though they were trying to put a new home together and have a trousseau.

Margaret Dixon [born 1905]

I gave up work when I married and did not have a job until my three children were grown up. I did have a part-time maid to help me in the house, which was very common in those days when so many girls went into domestic service. My husband did not share in the responsibilities of the children or the housework and I always felt it was my job. There was always somebody at home for the children after school; either myself, my husband or my mother was always there. I may be old-fashioned but I feel strongly that until a child is at least sixteen, they should never return to an empty house. When the children were much older I took a part-time job as a photographer at Sheffield College of Art. I think motherhood is a full-time responsible commitment to the family and only financial necessity justifies women working whilst their children are young.

Susan Curtis [born 1905]

It was certainly my responsibility to look after our two boys, especially as my husband was still away during the war. I was lucky to have a nanny/housekeeper, a lady in the parish who needed a home when I needed live-in help. I did feel I needed intellectual stimulation outside the home and, when the boys were quite young, I took up part-time teaching and coaching work. The boys were being safely looked after by Nanny. I don't actually agree that mothers necessarily have to stay at home full-time because they can get too possessive and paranoia can set in, even an Oedipus complex. It can ruin a marriage.

———•———

'For a life of her own, he had substituted his life with its interests, or the lives of her children with their potentialities. He assumed that she might sink herself in either with equal joy. It had never occurred to him that she might prefer simply to be herself.

'Shocking, unnatural thoughts had floated into her mind. "If only I had never married . . . if only I had never had any children." Yet she loved Henry to the point of agony, and she loved her children to the point of sentimentality.'

Vita Sackville-West, ALL PASSION SPENT.

———•———

Eileen Brown [born 1908]

I had no help with looking after my two children and it was not common for fathers to help in those days, so it was certainly my job. I suppose the phrase is that I was 'just a mother and housewife.' I had a very strict routine with the children, with an afternoon walk every day. I never went back to work after I married and devoted myself to my family. We had few problems as they grew up. They had little money, they were disciplined and they were very obedient. I was always there for my children.

———•———

'Her love for her children was stronger than any trouble they could cause her, and while she realised the essential loneliness of existence and found it strange that in spite of so much love she should never feel secure . . . it brings with it danger, anxiety and grief, and in that moment she saw herself honoured with the right to suffer; she was proud to do it.'

E.H. Young, WILLIAM.

———•———

Patricia Rogers [born 1909]

While I had a mother's help before the war, it was difficult to employ girls after that. Looking after the children and running the home were my jobs. I did keep in touch with the original maternity nurse who had attended some of my home births, and she even came to look after two of the children sometimes. My mother looked after the third while my husband and I went on holiday. I also had a lady who cleaned for me and she would come in for extra hours to look after them. And we babysat for each other, friends and neighbours. This gave you a chance to get out. You don't want to feel your own personal life is on hold for many years.

When I had had four children I began to help out in a primary school when they were desperate for supply staff. It was too much and I developed a spot on my lung and had a period in a nursing home to recover. It was an expensive attempt to reduce our overdraft. The girls went to boarding school at the age of eleven but were nearby and had frequent home visits. Our son went to boarding school when he was ten. I didn't work after that until the children had grown up. I think every woman should decide for herself if and when she should return to work whilst her children are young.

Mary Maclennan [born 1911]

My mother was there all the time, and all the mothers of my friends were always at home. We never thought it would be any different. It wouldn't cross a mother's mind to do anything other than be there. When you rushed home from school, you would want your piece, your tea, and mother would be at home for you. They were always doing things around the house, cooking, mending and fixing things for you.

I did go back to work as a supply teacher but only when my youngest child was at school. My husband was rector at the High School, Blairgowrie, and I would stand in during emergencies. I also went up to one or two of the country schools nearby. It's difficult to say whether motherhood is a full-time profession because a married woman cannot always just be a wife and a mother. I don't think she has to be there all the time, when they are older and at school. But I think she should be there a lot of the time – it is quite important – and not be getting rid of them a lot of the time.

May Stephen [born 1911]

A baby's first year is very important and shouldn't be spent with anyone else. The baby should be played with, taught through games and reading; they shouldn't be left in a crowded nursery of children at a young age. They need peace and quiet and personal attention. The first few years are very important as they learn so much, and I think mothers should give up their work for a little while for the sake of the child's development. My little boy used to come home every day for lunch because we lived so near the school. And then at night he was so full of stories about what had happened during his school day, all his friends, and I was at home to talk to him. He was always told to come straight home and not to dawdle. He then asked me, 'What does dawdle mean, Mummy?' and I told him.

I remember some time after that my husband was away ill with TB in a sanatorium. We were really very hard up for a long time, counting every penny, and I decided to go back to teach at a primary school. Our daughter was eleven by this time and our son, seven. Well, my son said, 'Oh no Mummy, you mustn't work. I promise to come straight home from school, I won't dawdle. If you are not here, I won't come straight home.' So I felt I had to be at home for him and I did stay home. Maybe he was spoilt, being looked after so much. I don't know. Whether children become more independent with the mother out of the home, I really don't know.

Eileen Watkins [born 1912]

I did not work after marriage but did some voluntary bits and pieces later on. I still consider that a mother should be at home if at all possible. You can't really expect to have everything in this life. You have to make choices, and interests outside the home can be managed during school hours or by reading books and doing other hobbies in the evenings. It is my opinion that there is no substitute for father going out to work and bringing home the income and mother being at home to look after the children, but I know it isn't always possible. I am sorry for mothers of young children who do not or cannot stay at home to look after them. Not for anything in the world would I have turned over the care of my young children to someone else or have deprived myself of the daily shout of 'Mummy!' when they came tearing in from school. It seems to me as I look back over a long life, that two of the essentials in bringing them up are your time and your encouragement. Proper discipline is the reverse side of the coin of love.

Emily Heggie [born 1912]

It was easier bringing up children and teenagers in the 1940s and 1950s than today. Mothers were at home more with their children and there was far more discipline generally. To do things properly, to bring up your children correctly, a mother should stay at home. When we married we were very, very poor, and I said to my husband that it was no good; 'I will have to go out to work.' And he said, 'No, you have enough to do here.' So I taught myself to do needlework, and made everything as my mother used to do, and I think we were as well off as if I had gone out to work.

My husband was a policeman and did very long hours at the House of Lords, and he often came home around two in the morning, so the boys didn't see a lot of him. But if he was home earlier when the boys came in from school, the first thing they would say was 'Where's Mum?' They would be pleased to see their dad but they still wanted their mum. They had grown up to rely on me for their meals and clean clothes, and I was the person in the home after school, always there for them.

For mothers who have been working in professional jobs, it must be very disappointing to consider wasting that education and give up a career. If they are earning good money and can afford to employ someone to look after the children properly, and have nannies, that is fine. But if you cannot afford to do that, then it is not good for the children; they become latchkey children and it is not fair on them.

Doris Melling [born 1914]

I stayed at home until my son was sixteen. In those days men didn't share in the responsibility of childcare and running the home and we women didn't expect it. There were still no jobs for married women, so I started a millinery stall in the local market in Barrow-in-Furness. As I was self-employed, and only opened my business on three days a week, I could always manage to attend school meetings and functions. Although my husband did not approve of me working, he accepted it, and as his job took him away at times, I was glad to be occupied. I liked it. I started working at the age of forty and carried on for twenty-two years, when my husband retired.

Until children are fifteen or sixteen, I do believe mothers should be at home for them. My daughter and daughter-in-law both stayed at home until their children were in the teens.

Nancy Beaty [born 1914]

Women of my generation were committed to our families and our children. We would never think about leaving our husbands however tough it might be. *Never.* We had lots of fun, dances and so on in the village. It wasn't all hard work on the farm; not all work and no play. It was a busy life being a farmer's wife, a cook, running the guest house and being a mother to our four children.

Joan Counihan [born 1915]

I do believe a mother has a full-time job, looking after her children and the home. I can understand, however, why so many women now have been rebelling against their lot as mothers and homemakers, but my sister and I have not too much sympathy for them with their constant moans about the ties and problems of coping with only one or two children, and their constant need for babysitters. We were pitchforked into having to do everything, without having been taught to cook and with no modern domestic conveniences. During the war I was bringing up three children on my own in a primitive farmhouse where we had been evacuated, with five more children born after the war, and my husband working abroad a good deal of the time.

However, I did start working full-time when my youngest child was eleven and the older ones could look after the younger children when they came home from school. The eldest children had already left home. I became a civil servant in the Education Department. I had not worked since my marriage in 1939. I decided to start for financial reasons and then found I enjoyed it very much.

———•———

'She had continually in her life only been somebody's something. She had begun by being somebody's daughter – Then, when this phase was over, for twelve years, she became exclusively somebody's mother; but how had she not, when that too ended, stretched out her arms to the sun and cried out all to herself, "Now I'm going to be me!" '

Elizabeth von Arnim, LOVE.

———•———

Mary McKerrow [born 1915]

I was a full-time mother – I never worked outside the home. I honestly couldn't have worked as well as being a proper mother to my three children. I wouldn't have been any good at all; I would have got flummoxed and cross and taken it out on them, I suppose. We didn't think of it all, although we weren't very well off. Those days of motherhood were very happy ones, knowing many other young mothers nearby. We all had similar problems and were very supportive of each other. We were always watching the pennies but we enjoyed exchanging notes with friends as we all coped together.

I remember my daughter didn't get a new coat until she was eleven, because her godmother had two daughters and she always passed on very nice clothes and no one was too proud to wear them. That was normal in our day. Children did not expect new clothes and, as long as they were neat, tidy and clean, they just had to have what could be afforded and hand-me-downs from brothers, sisters, friends, and that was it. No question of buying totally unnecessary, expensive, fashionable children's clothes.

We didn't have a car either. Sunday was always the day when we might go off on an expedition, with two walking and one in a pushchair. Then we would enjoy long walks in the countryside. Weekends were our times for outings and being together as a family.

I suppose I have always loved caring for children. Apart from having three children of our own, we also looked after two other boys for a while. Friends of ours in Coventry had fallen on hard times, and the wife had to go back to work as a Sister at the Royal Infirmary. She had to work to keep the family. We were living quite near by and I rashly said they could come to us. I don't think my husband's mother ever forgave me, because it really was a very full life and not altogether easy. They would have to be bathed in pairs, and the little one would be bathed with our daughter and objected as he had always been bathed with his older brother. Silly things like that caused problems. But he got used to it. I had to look after them but of course bring them up in the way the mother would have wanted. She preferred to keep the younger boy as the baby, while I would have encouraged him to do things for himself, potty-training and so on. When she came for weekends she would treat him like a baby, so we had different views on this but it was really only over trivial things. We cared for those boys for about a year. Looking back it was a very busy household, and a difficult family life. But the boy's mother had an equally difficult time, being forced to work, leaving her children behind.

We got through it but I often wonder how. It was quite an experience and I can't imagine how I coped, with all these children to feed.

When our family get together today, they are always reminiscing about the various things that happened, about the fun and laughter they remember from their childhood. I know they believe they had a happy family home with 'mother' always there for them. I think there is one thing that comes into it in my case, which is that having lost my parents so quickly when I was a child, and I was very fond of them both, this made me appreciate having my own family. I didn't put claws around them or try to cosset them, but I felt I wanted them to have the kind of happy, stable family life which was taken from me.

Emily Hagues [born 1916]

Family life was very different for a lot of mothers during the war. I had my first daughter, Jennifer, in 1943, and for four years we lived with my parents so she became very fond of her grandparents. She was very good to her grandparents and they loved having her in the house.

When my husband came back from the war, after three years, the first few months were like hell upon earth. Our daughter would say, 'Get that man out of the house', and 'He's not going into that bed.'

This was quite a common problem. I had a friend who had a little girl who was a bit older than Jennifer. She had become used to going to her aunt's house every Tuesday night during the war, and when her father returned she continued doing this but he told her to come home at seven o'clock, not to stay until nine as she had always done. Well she paid no heed to this and said to her mother, 'When's that mannie going away?' The girl did not understand that this strange man was her father, just as Jennifer did not accept her dad for a while. Things were much better when our second daughter was born in 1948, and my husband was a great help, looking after Jennifer, taking her out to the park. Oh aye, he was very good with the children.

We had a terrible sadness when our daughter Jennifer died. It was a very sudden illness, thrombosis; she was only twenty-three and she had a son, Richard, who was five and a half months old. So we took him in and I brought him up until he was over three, when his father remarried and took him away.

I do think mothers should stay at home with their children and not go out to work. I could never have let mine away with babysitters. There was always someone here when my children came in from school. I think that all these young kids in trouble today, it's just a lack of discipline, that's all. There is nobody there when they come home from school so they go out looking for trouble.

Elizabeth Grey [born 1917]

I had to work when the girls were wee. My husband died when I was in my early forties and the girls were ten and thirteen. I had trained as a nurse when I was young but I didn't think I could go back after so many years. My sister worked in the chicken factory and she said, 'Come down and get an evening job.' I went down there and began working. I knew quite a crowd of women there from schooldays. Anyway, after about three weeks I met my doctor, who had attended me at my births, and she asked why I was in that chicken factory. She told me that I was qualified to work at the cottage hospital, and that they needed people to relieve nurses during times of sickness and holidays. So I went up to the hospital and the doctor arranged work for me with the matron. I did the night sister's job, which fitted in with looking after the girls. I had been away for fifteen years but I went back just like that and stayed for sixteen years.

Milicent Woolner [born 1917]

I was a full-time housewife and mother and I was totally happy with my role because I had had my career before marriage, training and working as a nurse. I do not agree with mothers working outside the home. The mother is the hub of the household and life has to be accepted as it comes. The right to have children should not be claimed without taking the responsibility of caring for them.

Mary MacDonald [born 1920]

I married for love when I was very young, eighteen. In my generation our aim was to have children and stay at home to look after them. I never worked outside the home and I do feel all mothers should be there for their children, at least up to the age of five, otherwise they are missing so much of their children's growing up and development.

Catherine Begg [born 1920]

I married at the age of 26 and lived most of my married life in the glens, as my husband was a farm worker. As we could not have a family of our own we became foster parents. The first boy, John, was two years old and came for the summer months to start with, to see if he would thrive. That summer never ended and he stayed with us. Then we were asked to help by taking another two year old boy, Bill, who came to us as his parents were deaf and dumb. He couldn't speak a word at two years old as he had had no one talking to him. He did have some sign language but that was all. Having the elder child, who was five by then, helped him greatly and he soon developed normally. The 'temporary' fostering continued for many, many years. He eventually moved to another 'home' when he married!

Our boys certainly thrived, grew up quickly, and had healthy play-times, with plenty space for games around the farm where we lived. There were hills to roam at will and streams to fish in. They were fortunate that our farmer tolerated their company when they went to look at the tractors and the sheep, but they were useful for opening and shutting gates.

John was slightly unstable mentally and we had eleven very worrying years coping with his illness, but it gave me a great insight to social work and psychiatric treatment. We were not told of his history of mental illness until he was eighteen years old. Our neighbours and employer were very understanding and helpful. At least we were able to provide a home for John, but he may have been better off if there had been more special schooling.

My husband worked on a farm and, since we lived ten miles from town, the only work available to mothers was helping part-time with the potato harvest and picking soft fruit. I think mothers should be with their children in the early years, but they can have a lonely existence unless they have some outside interests. I enjoyed the church guild and Women's Rural Institute, and we lived in a friendly community. Mothers should spend most of the first five years with their children, and then perhaps do part-time work if help is available in the form of granny or a child minder.

We have had our bad times as well as good times but the bad years help you appreciate the good ones. Our older boy eventually had to go into a hospital and is now in a hostel. He visits but still blames us for depriving him of his parents, but this is due to his mental condition. The younger boy soon spoke and could hear, having his brother as a companion. He joined the army at sixteen, and is now happily married with two children, and we have a very close, friendly relationship. I have had a happy family life.

Joan Hill [born 1920]

My daughter was born during the war when my husband was away in the army, so I was a single mother from her birth. I lived with my parents and my mother looked after her when I had a part-time job, from 1943 to 1945. My brother was killed in action in 1942. I was then widowed during the war and continued to live at home with my parents. As a single parent, I followed my own maternal instincts about bringing my daughter up, and didn't worry about spoiling her. I had a code of discipline regarding homework and helping in the house which has stood us both in good stead.

———•———

'During the war, her husband gone, Melody would stand in the doorway of her daughters' room and listen in this way, her face forward, her nose and eyes listening too, all recording the soft soughing of their infant breaths and the innocent, infrequent rustlings when they rolled or shifted. Then despite Melody Simpson's early knowledge of loss – her husband of the future she had wanted – hers was a defiant listening, as though simply absorbing the sounds of her children's sleep could protect them forever, as though she alone, by doing so, kept them alive.'

Clare Messud, WHEN THE WORLD WAS STEADY.

———•———

Mary Sparrow [born 1921]

I never worked but had lots of other interests. I feel it is good for a mother to be home when children come in from school. I always got them to wash their face and hands and brush their hair when they came home. I personally found that being there when the teenage children came home, calling out 'Mum!', was as important as when they were much younger. So few women seem to want to stay at home and be Mums now. Working mums get so exhausted there is no time for proper food or talks with the children. The extra money seems to be used up on convenience foods and luxuries for themselves and unnecessary clothes for the children, who would surely be better off with the mother's time and a listening ear.

Jean Charleson [born 1922]

Looking back at those early days of motherhood, it's strange to think how well I must have managed. I had never cooked a meal when I lived at home with my parents; my mum always did the cooking. But here was I straight after the war, I was a housewife and a mother without a blink of an eye.

I don't know how I managed but I did. I had my mum to ask a question or two. In fact you just emulated what your mother did. My mother always had big pots of broth on the stove and stews boiling away, so I just continued the way I had been brought up. I did a bit of baking; I wasn't a great baker, perhaps because my mother hadn't been a great cook, but I'm much better now, with all these years of experience. I remember when we were first married, I decided to make pancakes because I knew Jack liked them. Well, I produced these misshapen things that were alright but didn't go down a treat, and Jack said [he knew afterwards that it was the first wrong thing he said to me in our marriage] that I should get his mother to show me how to make pancakes! I had tried to do things properly for him and he put his foot in it by saying that. It was the first row we had. But being a housewife and mother really came naturally to me. I had been away for four years in the WAAF so it was not as if I had been at home, preparing for marriage and family life. I just cooked plain food, of course, nothing adventurous like we have nowadays.

I stayed at home to bring up my three children; that is what we wanted to do in my day. It is difficult to make comparisons with what women feel they want to do today, and say one way is better than the other. But we lived through a *war*; the war disciplined us for a whole lot of things. It disciplined us in terms of the value of money and possessions, so it taught us economy. We also valued our husbands and family life because we had been separated for so long. We were so glad to have our husbands, our children and our own homes.

Joyce MacPherson [born 1923]

I think it is very stressful for women to try and combine motherhood with a paid job and not feel guilty about one thing or the other. I mean either the work has got to slide or the children don't get attention. That is obvious. Children grow up so fast and mothers miss out on a lot if they go out to work. I wouldn't have liked it. Playing with children, just sitting watching them, talking to them, you learn so much about them, their characters and personalities. You hear them trying to speak for the first time.

The father's role was very much in terms of discipline. I used to say, 'Wait till your father gets home,' and he would be the one to chastise them when they were naughty. Actually my husband was excellent at helping with the children and wanted to be very involved. He used to take them out and play with them. We had a very strict bedtime routine. There was an unbroken rule of bed by 7 pm (8 pm when they were older). Then my husband and I had our evenings to ourselves.

Unlike many women today, I did not feel I needed work or stimulation outside the home. My own interests were things like cooking and knitting which involved the family. I had a sewing machine and used it constantly, knitting the children woollies. This was relaxation for me, my hobby time, and I didn't see it as a chore. And baking too, that was another relaxation. I liked doing it. I saw myself as a mum and a wife. I accepted that as my role. I was not a person in my own right in those days.

———•———

'What made the home appear so attractive was the development of a mass of labour saving devices. The inter-war years were the era of the vacuum cleaner, the washing machine, and the gas cooker, gadgets which promised to take the drudgery out of housework. The ideology of modern housewifery and suburban motherhood was promoted in a rash of new mass-circulation women's magazines which replaced those which earlier catered for the Victorian lady administering a household staff. The leader in the field was Good Housekeeping [1922] followed by Woman and Home [1926], Wife and Home [1929], Woman's Own [1932] and Woman [1937].
Steve Humphries and Pamela Gordon, A LABOUR OF LOVE.

———•———

Pamela Worthington [born 1923]

I had married in 1942 and had three children, between 1944 and 1950. I never wanted to go out to work and never even considered it. Making a home and looking after a family was my full-time job. I thoroughly enjoyed it, making buns and scones for when the children came home from school, making jam and bottling fruit, plus all the usual chores:

washing, ironing, decorating, mending, gardening. I am amazed that women manage to go out to work when they have a young family. The big advantage is that you are your own boss and can do a household job when you like.

I had a strict routine and could plan my day, cooking times and jobs, much more easily. The children were usually in bed before dad came home, but he always had a chat with them before they settled down.

Life was so very different in those days, particularly with regard to shopping and food. There were no supermarkets and no out of season fruit or vegetables, and very little choice because of rationing. Shopping took some time as you joined queues if you saw one in case there might be fish or fresh fruit or something with which you could vary the diet. I do wonder what would be the reaction if the young mums of today were able to put all their shopping in a small basket to carry home. The variety of food today compared to the little grocer of the old days, is incredible.

Discipline was reasonably strict which I am sure is essential for everyone, and I am sure children are happier when they know exactly how far they can go. I think a stable, caring and loving family background is very important for children if they are to become caring responsible adults. A sense of security is vital.

Jane Ward [born 1924]

There was no question of going out to work. It was not essential financially since we could manage, and in any event I do not remember a crèche or nursery being available. Moreover we were one and a half miles from the town centre for office jobs. In those days, after the war, cars were relatively scarce. I do not think it would have been possible for me to take small children on a bus to get to work even if there had been suitable nursery provision. I do not remember when crèches first appeared, but I am certain nurseries were not common until the 1970s. So we managed on a careful budget. I had a sewing machine and was perfectly competent to alter or remake clothes. I could knit and crochet. Jumble sales were regular events. My husband had to be well-dressed and I always managed to look it – although I did not have any new surface clothes for many years. My husband was made redundant when the eldest was fifteen and the youngest seven, and initially he could find no other employment. After six months, I got a part-time job lecturing in economics, which became full-time eighteen months later.

Commitment to Motherhood

I much preferred a regular monthly income. By then my husband had decided to become self-employed and to work from home. Most days I was able to see the children off to school, and he was always there if I wasn't.

I had anticipated working at some point, because I knew it would be soul-destroying to be home all day, once they were all at school, when I would have no one to talk to. The youngest was at school before I started working and we had got through the usual childhood illnesses. I was a graduate in economics but needed some sort of revision before teaching. I took two A levels in geography and economics and found myself teaching geography when a staff member was taken ill. I then took an evening class in economics and soon found that economists were thin on the ground at that time and I quickly secured a job.

I did not and do not approve of latchkey children until the child is well into the teens, and then only from time to time. We seldom encountered problems here. If I was not there my husband was, and my type of work gave me a lot of leeway. I was lucky in the sense that my husband accepted my need to work, and not only for financial reasons. I gather I was much easier to live with after I started working!

I do not think full-time mothering is always necessary. It all depends on individual financial circumstances and the women concerned. For some women being a mother is the only thing they want to do.

'It is possible to carry on working, when families arrive. In this way gifts and talents that would otherwise be wasted are developed to the benefit of the whole community. The idea that the family suffers is, I believe, quite mistaken.'
Margaret Thatcher, 'Wake Up Women', THE SUNDAY GRAPHIC 1952.

'It is possible, in my view, for a woman to run a home and continue with her career, provided two conditions are fulfilled. First her husband must be in sympathy with her wish to do another job. Secondly where there is a young family, the joint income of husband and wife must be sufficient to employ a first class nanny-housekeeper, to look after things in the wife's absence. The second is the key to the whole plan.'
Margaret Thatcher, THE LONDON EVENING NEWS 1960.

Pauline Grisbrook [born 1924]

I married at the age of 27, after training as a sick children's nurse, but sadly after five years, medical investigations showed that we couldn't have children of our own. We then adopted twin baby girls in 1957. I think the most wonderful moment was when we went to collect our babies, at the age of three months; they were still tiny, just eight pounds in weight. The administrator of the orphanage, a priest, said 'Are you going to take them into your arms?' We were paralysed with wonder. Since then we have counted our blessings many times over.

My mother had trained as a sick children's nurse, like me, and had worked in child welfare during the first world war. Her professional advice when I was bringing them up was excellent and exemplary. My parents had brought up four children between the wars, with an attitude of total physical and emotional commitment to childcare, and unselfishness. Their experience guided my own views towards motherhood and basic childcare. I do believe mothers should be at home while their children are young, but due to financial necessity, I returned to work when the twins were three and a half. However I had a job in the casualty department in our local hospital and I worked an evening shift from 7 pm to 11 pm, three days a week. The girls were in bed and my husband was at home when I went out to work.

I have enjoyed every aspect of motherhood. The girls have been a constant source of joy. There was never any need for us to work at parenthood, any more than our children needed to work at being themselves.

Pamela Wells [born 1928]

I do believe a mother should be at home with her children until they are about ten years old but only as long as her need for outside interests and personal development can be met. I went back to work twenty years after my marriage, when my three were 18, 16 and 13, because I needed an outside interest and extra money for university education for the children. I worked as a medical librarian and then trained as a reflexologist. I did feel guilty at times, although my children were teenagers, and the youngest didn't have the attention the others had had. Certainly mothers today are much more 'part of the world' than the middle class mothers of my and my mother's generation, and infinitely more independent. They are definitely not totally committed to motherhood and the home.

Joan Longmuir [born 1930]

I did go back to work when the youngest of our six children was five. This was my husband's wish, not entirely mine! I was a department store assistant and later on was promoted to a buyer. I think it is ideal if women can stay at home when the children are younger but I do feel it is better for them if the mother does work outside the home when they are older, so that they learn to be independent. They were all taught to help in the house and undertake chores. They all had pets which they looked after themselves – at one time we had twenty-six!

I will always remember the advice of the wonderful Irish midwife who delivered my first baby. She said, 'Make sure you absorb this baby into your life – don't try to remake your life around her.' One has to bring up one's family within the limitations of your life.

———•———

'I knew that . . . a man . . . secretly wanted . . . (his bride) to flatten out underneath his feet. I also remembered Buddy Willard saying in a sinister, knowing way that after I had children I would feel differently. I wouldn't want to write poems any more. So I began to think maybe it was true that when you were married and had children it was like being brainwashed, and afterwards you went about numb as a slave in some private, totalitarian state.'

Sylvia Plath, THE BELL JAR.

———•———

Barbara Henderson [born 1931]

I felt trapped being a mother at home with six children. In my mother's and my own generation, women don't realise they have made slaves of themselves. In an ideal world the father would work for four days, and the mother for three days, sharing the home and childcare responsibilities.

When my eldest was sixteen and the youngest three, I went to work in a factory. I had to find work because of financial problems. My husband's farm working wage of £9 was far from sufficient to feed nine people. I worked an evening shift from 5 pm to 10 pm. Then I had seasonal work in a hotel and, later, an office. I returned to the factory after five years, and stayed there until I retired. I worked for twenty-five years altogether, from the time my youngest was three.

— 245 —

We couldn't afford holidays but took the children to the seaside or museums, and once took them on a ten mile journey by train to give them the experience of a train ride. As a family we would go berry picking so that we could afford new school uniforms. It was a continual struggle to feed and clothe them but we have been married now for forty-five years and have thirteen grandchildren. I am proud to see my second daughter working hard to give her three children a better start in life; the youngest son graduated last year, and has just begun a scientific research career at Aberdeen University, which is wonderful.

Mary Anderson [born 1934]

I left my job when I was expecting my first baby. I did not take maternity leave; I left my job to start bringing up my family. I believe that motherhood is a full-time commitment. I did return to work when the youngest was five years old. I decided to go back to work to do 'something for me'. My husband was not very happy about it, but part-time work was 'allowed', providing the children did not suffer. I was there to see them off to school and there when they returned, until they all went off to university at age 18.

Sheila Brown [born 1934]

It was certainly a full-time job looking after four girls. Being sensible about it, it is best if circumstances allow for the mother to be at home. It is the ideal situation, certainly in the formative years. Playing with them, talking to them, teaching them to feed and speak properly, is all so much easier if the mother is there with nothing to worry or stress her except the family. But with the best will in the world it is not possible for every mother to do that. It really is pie in the sky to say, 'Every mother should be at home, looking after her children.' I always got such a thrill as I saw them growing up; the first tinkle in the pot was just magical! You felt you had achieved something. I couldn't wait to see Susan sit up, talk, walk, and then the day she went to school, I couldn't wait until she came home, I was beside myself. I don't think I did a thing all day – I am sure I remember just sitting there, nervously waiting until it was time to collect her and hear all about her first day. It was the same with each one. The excitement and thrill at everything they do.

I do think it's a shame that the women who choose to work, the mothers who can afford a nanny and can swan about socially, are missing out on quite a chunk of their child's life.

Daphne Laing [born 1935]

I enjoyed motherhood and have no regrets at all, although I wish my husband had been more supportive. He was fine when they were small; we went for long walks, had picnics and they were happy days. As they grew up, they were entirely my responsibility but I was totally committed to encouraging them, stimulating interests in clubs and out of school activities. I was involved in the playschool, the Parent Teacher Association and Sunday school: I helped at them all which also had a knock-on effect on the children and got them involved. For various reasons, financial and personal interest, I took a part-time job in a hotel, when the youngest was five.

For the past ten years I have virtually brought the family up by myself; my husband and I have been separated for six years. Divorce proceedings are underway due to my husband's addictions to gambling and alcohol. I had to deal with teenage tantrums with the eldest. I really don't know an answer to them, you just try and deal with them as best you can without laying down the law too much, and you have to be ready to listen and to give advice if required. It proved to me that during teenage years a mother is needed at home almost as much as when they are small – to be there to talk things over. The three younger children have grown up into sensible well-adjusted adults. We have always discussed things together, as they have always been involved with all family decisions. They have always known that there is a limit to what they can have and they've kept to that limit. I have never promised them something and then not kept to it. We have no car and we get about by bus, bicycle and on foot. We have never tried to keep up with the Joneses and it has done none of us any harm. We were short of money but made the best of things and I believe I have brought up my family to appreciate what we do have even more.

Liz Sanderson [born 1938]

Because we lived in the heart of the country, in the Scottish Borders, we felt we should send the children to boarding school. The boys went first to prep school and then boarding school, and the girls went off to St. Leonard's at the age of ten. I suppose I looked upon the term time as my and my husband's time. Russell was travelling quite a bit as a textile agent, and so I used to go with him, and he'd also got more and more involved in the voluntary side of politics. I didn't want my own career: I was very happy just to back Russell up in whatever he did. I didn't want my own job in politics, but I would go anywhere with him if it was a help to him. I just stuck to that as an interest outside the family and home.

But the holidays with four children, we had an active time. It was very much a case of do-it-yourself events, such as parties when we didn't bring in a caterer. It was how I was brought up and it was fun and they all learnt to help. I made the mistake of not teaching the boys to cook; the girls loved it from an early age but it was as much as I could bear just having the two of them frittering around the kitchen. So when David went to university he had to learn to feed himself and he had no idea how to deal with his washing, so I had to tell him to find a launderette. The younger boy, Andy, thought he could live off baguettes, cheese and spaghetti for three months until he became interested in cooking. He had never ironed a shirt until he went to work in London. I realised I had made a mistake there, spoiling the boys and allowing them to be dependent on their mother at home!

When the children were younger and I was looking after them full-time, we thought it was a good thing to have a holiday occasionally without the children. So I used to drop them off with my parents in Yorkshire and we would get a fortnight off, without them, and to me that was bliss. You could get up when you liked, go to bed when you liked, and you didn't have to worry about a babysitter. But the rest of the year I totally accepted my job of looking after them and I was quite happy doing it. I also think that I was lucky in the person I married.

Jennifer Harper-Jones [born 1939]

I do believe motherhood should be a full-time committed 'profession'. Caring for and bringing up children is a responsible job. I took a part-time secretarial job when my youngest was ten years old, as I needed an interest outside the family, but the few hours I worked enabled me to be at home for the children.

I still feel my own generation falls between two stools. We are educated and can do a successful job, but we still feel we ought to run the home. I worked full-time for two years recently, when my husband was out of work but I still did *all* the shopping, cooking, washing, ironing, housework and gardening.

'Carol' [born 1942]

My mother's reaction on being told I was pregnant was, 'Well I don't know how you think you're going to manage!'

I was working full-time as head of department teaching English. My husband, a mature student, was at college. Having had an insecure and rather unhappy childhood myself [I was adopted by a middle-aged couple], I did not want my child to go to a child minder. As a result we took what was then an unusual decision. When my husband finished his college course, he would take a two and a half year break to look after our baby. This was regarded with dismay by our families. It is not so strange now, but eighteen years ago we were pioneers! We did get tremendous support from our health visitor and she often had my husband and son down to the local clinic to demonstrate how well a caring father could cope and what a healthy, happy, intelligent baby we had. Our local newspaper and radio station were also keen to interview him, especially at the time when he was gaining an OU degree. Our home was spotless, he was a terrific cook and we had a very happy little boy. Many of my husband's male friends were envious of the time he had with our son, but admitted that they could not cope with such a situation. Only on one occasion did a man, rather the worse for drink, suggest that my husband was less of a man for childcaring and being 'kept' by a woman, but then my husband was defended by several hefty friends who admired what he was doing. Quite often, female friends needing a babysitter during the day, would leave their children with him and the kids were always keen to come back. Our son bonded very strongly with his father. Because I breast-fed for eight months, despite returning to work when he was seven weeks, I also maintained my bond with him. I think the arrangement worked well, although I still feel I missed out a little. The pay-off, apart from the most important one of a secure and happy child, is that because of unbroken service teaching, I have been able to retire early and have therefore been on hand for the difficult teenage years. Until then, we both had jobs where we either had long holidays or worked flexi-time, so this fitted in well with school activities, holidays and illness. We always took turns to have time off when necessary as we considered both careers equally important once they were established. However, my mother never accepted the situation!

On the subject of adoption I have very strong views, being an adopted child myself. During the last twenty years, the majority of children appear to have been told about their adoption when they are old enough to understand. There is much helpful literature produced for parents and more important still for children, to explain the problems and pleasures of adoption. From what I observe today, there is a much healthier attitude to adoption because there is less secrecy. Since I was not told of my adoption until I was thirty-four years old, this atmosphere of secrecy and dishonesty must have been at the root of my unhappiness as a child. I did not feel secure or loved, although as a 'chosen' baby I must have been wanted.

And love is the most important thing to give a child. I adored every bit of motherhood as a shared role with my husband, both of us ensuring that the needs of our son came first. As in my case, this might mean a mother who is more cheerful and loving because she goes out to work!

———— • ————

'I had love to spare. That happens when you have a child. There must always be more. Not more of everything, but more of love. You never know when it might be needed.'

Candia McWilliam, A LITTLE STRANGER.

———— • ————

Jennifer Manning [born 1944]

As a single mother with my first baby, I had to go back to work when he was eight weeks old and my mum cared for him. I had to work. After I married and had a second child, I ran a playgroup after training but did not have paid employment until he was fourteen. I have mixed feelings about a mother's place being in the home. It is fine if things are shared between husband and wife. Childhood is very precious.

Jenni Smith [born 1946]

I was brought up just after the Second World War, and in those days mothers simply did not work. My own mother felt it was a total disgrace when she had to take a part-time job to help to make ends meet, and she left it as soon as she was able. My own generation expected to work until we had our first babies, and after that it was acceptable to work part-time once the children were at school. It was not seen as acceptable to work when the children were small, or to take a full-time job until they were teenagers. Nowadays it seems that young mothers can work or not as they choose, and many seem to manage quite happily to work either a few hours each day or else a couple of days full-time each week. This balance is probably good for both, since full-time childcare can be very stultifying unless one is one of the 'earth mother' types. I am not!

I do feel that mothers should be the primary carers for children at least until they start school. After that the mother should be able to work part-time if she wishes or needs to.

When my two boys were quite small I had wanted to go to college to gain some qualifications that might form the basis for a career when they were older, but this was not allowed by my husband. I soon realised that my marriage was a dire mistake, I was bitterly unhappy and I know my children suffered. Their father was violent and a philanderer. I finally found the courage to divorce my husband when the boys were six and seven. I started as a temp and then found a permanent job, and while it was not ideal to have to work full-time, it was necessary.

I felt the boys did not have the time and commitment from me that they deserved while they were growing up. It was frowned upon to have time off at all, and certainly there was no sympathy for me having time off with the boys. Consequently they more than once had to go to school when they were not completely well, with many feelings of guilt on my part. I never had anyone with whom I could leave them. Once they were older, say over ten years old, I allowed them to stay at home on their own if they were not well, and we kept in contact by telephone. This was better but far from ideal.

As a single-parent family, life was much better and we all felt the benefit. I knew I had made the right decision when my six year old said to me, 'Isn't it nice at our house now that Dad doesn't live here any more!' It would have been nicer not to have to work full-time when they were so small, but we adapted.

Vivienne Leighton [born 1947]

Martin would have been about seven and Emma was five, starting school, when I began to go back to work. I had a chance to return to the same laboratory where I had worked before, and I decided I would like to return. We hadn't discussed the possibility at all; it wasn't necessary for financial reasons. Emma was going to school so I felt it would be ideal if I could go back to my old job.

Motherhood, I believe on reflection, should be a full-time commitment for years on end. I feel a bit of a failure at the moment, because I have been thinking back on what has happened in their teenage years – staying out late, being rude, and both of them giving up college courses and jobs. Neither of them knows what they want to do with their life. And so recently I started examining and questioning things. Did I do something wrong? Have we spoilt them? Should I have been at home all the time that they were growing up? Maybe I didn't do it right. Ideally a mother should be at home with her babies and young children. I certainly wanted to be and it was the done thing. Even when I had my children in the 1970s, it still wasn't usual for mothers to go out to work. I felt that I would like to influence my children in the sense of teaching them to feed, playing games, hearing their first words, and being the one they come to, rather than relying on nanny or a childminder. I wanted to be their main carer.

Once I went back to work, I always tried to attend special events like sports day, and I was a member of the Parent Teacher Association. My son was in the Boys' Brigade and I was on the committee there. I took part in as many school activities as I could. I enjoyed that. My parents were also very helpful when the children were young, and because they lived nearby my mother was always there for them, when they came home from school. They have grown up with their grandparents as very much a part of family life. So although I worked they were always well cared for.

———◆●◆———

'Five years off work while the children were small; back to work with seniority lost. What, did you think something was for nothing? If you have children, mother, that is your reward. It lies not in the world.'

Fay Weldon, THE WEEKEND.

———◆●◆———

Mary Law [born 1949]

I stayed at home as a full-time mother for eleven years, bringing up our three children with very little help from my husband. By the time my youngest child was seven my husband nagged me to go back to work, and there was pressure from friends and my mother-in-law. I was also bored of being in the house all day and I was sick of housework which was monotonous, like painting the Forth Bridge. I was nearly driven up the wall as I wasn't being stretched mentally. I felt worthless being 'just a housewife and mother', so I went back to teaching, as a supply primary teacher. I found it very difficult, however, as it was an hour and a half of travelling each way and our eldest child, my daughter Fiona, made a great fuss about me going out to work.

After six years teaching I decided to have a change of career and try something new. After waiting nearly two years for a place, I began a three-year midwifery diploma course in 1994. I still have to travel an hour each way to college, and even at the ages they are now, 12, 14 and 16, I do feel guilty about it. I would still like to be the mum at home, to be there when they are ill, to have their tea ready and the house warm when they come in from school. My mum was always at home for us, with the laundry, shopping and cooking done, but she felt trapped and tied to the house and wasn't always happy.

As the children grow up, things have become easier, because I am happier having an interest outside the home and finding enormous fulfilment from studying again. My teenage children are a joy to be with; we talk through things and as a family we all get along OK.

Janice Mackenzie [born 1950]

I believe children need their mothers to be with them all the time until they are at least five years old. I planned my children and wanted to be actively involved in their upbringing as I believe they need security and stability that a series of nannies, au pairs and child minders cannot give. I resumed my teaching career when my youngest was four because my husband was made redundant. I also wanted to go back to work as I am a career woman and personally need to have an interest outside the home. But in our circumstances I had to return to work earlier than I intended because of financial necessity. My mother-in-law looked after Richard. As a teacher, I had the same holidays as my children so that was not a problem.

Sheila Gray [born 1951]

In my first marriage my husband and mother-in-law did not approve of working mothers so it didn't enter my head to look for a job when my first son was small. But a few years later, I decided to take a part-time secretarial job – about twenty hours a week – when my youngest son was three. My husband still disapproved but mother-in-law was now 400 miles away. This led to me regaining confidence in myself. I loved the freedom of dropping the kids, one at school, the other at a child minder, and was 100 per cent happier with life. Two years later I went to university, when the youngest was starting school, and I chose subjects which allowed me to be at home in time for their return from school, and I had all the university holidays too. I loved this even more than my part-time job – along with all the freedom I now had the intellectual stimulation I'd been denied for years. My husband was highly critical of this arrangement and we separated during my first year at university.

I was then a single parent for around four years which was difficult, if not a nightmare, at times. I then married again and we had a daughter. Interestingly, even my second husband leaves most of the mothering jobs to me, as though women can cope better with the noise and mess; I suppose we naturally just get on with it.

I returned to work when my daughter was one as I needed the mental stimulation. This was minimal part-time work, around four hours per week. Although I adore her dearly, I dislike the dependency of small children and prefer children when they are older and independent. You can talk on the same level with them. However, occasionally there are problems when children are off ill from school, so I now work as a self-employed reflexologist from home.

Barbara Buckley [born 1954]

When my first set of twins were twelve weeks old I returned to work for two reasons: financial necessity and because I had a good career as a marketing controller in the publishing business. My husband worked as a museum curator and so we employed a nanny at this time. Three years later when I had my second set of twins, my husband decided to give up his job in order to look after the children. I returned to work eleven weeks after their birth. I never feel guilty about working away from home full-time; I sometimes feel frustrated, disappointed, resentful, but not guilty. My mother remained at home after marriage but she longed for a wider scope to her life. I think her discontent was limiting for us all. She loved us but wanted more. I do not see that motherhood has to be a full-time commitment if women are happier going out to work.

Trudi Barnet [born 1954]

I quite understand women who feel they cannot cope once the baby comes along. Suddenly after years of a contented lifestyle, doing what you want to do, you cannot have a meal without a baby at your breast or dangling a child on your lap. You are not used to the noise they make.

Friends, who are still childless, suddenly desert you. They might come round for coffee to begin with and then, when you can't have a normal adult conversation without the baby interrupting and they think 'This is ghastly!' they are out the door, saying, 'See you sometime', hoping, perhaps, to do so without the baby. They think of you as the same person, but believe me, you are not. You are a different person the day the baby is born. And you cannot hand it back and try and revert to your previous existence.

The first six weeks are the worst when you really do feel low. It can be a killing shock to the system, when you have been used to years of getting up in the morning, putting on your make-up, looking glamorous, working, enjoying meals on your own – even going out in the evenings! That all changes dramatically and after some years of this, women begin to think there must be another life out there.

———•———

'When a child enters the world through you, it alters everything on a psychic, psychological and purely practical level. You're just not free anymore to do what you want to do. And it's not the same again. Ever.'
> Jane Fonda, LOS ANGELES WEEKLY, 28 November 1980.

———•———

Jano Rochefort [born 1955]

My expectations on leaving school were very high-minded: I was going to university to have a good education and then a good career. I was not going to marry or have children. I studied for a history degree and then trained as a nurse and midwife. However, at the age of twenty-two I married and I now have three boys, aged 9, 6, and 4.

My husband has a busy job as a manager in a plastics factory, which takes him abroad a good deal. In 1989 his job moved to the USA, which was when my youngest son was born. We returned to Britain in 1993 and I now find that my nursing and midwifery qualifications are out of date. There are no jobs nearby anyway and part-time midwifery work is very difficult to find; the midwifery shiftwork in the National Health Service is incompatible with families that have no extended family to help. Even if there were jobs, childcare would be a nightmare because of my husband's working schedule.

So here I am at home, on call twenty-four hours a day, trying to stop my brain atrophying, doing a lot of thinking about the role of mothers. While my husband shares the childcare responsibilities at times, it is mainly my job and the buck stops with me.

Being a full-time mother is not a state I am happy about. It seems to me now that it was in a previous existance – another life entirely – that I was a history graduate, a registered nurse and a midwife!

———●———

'Housework and motherhood are political issues. They challenge us to political action, both at the national and international level, to eradicate discriminatory practices which ensure that women's work is either lower paid than men's, or has to be done voluntarily, and that it must be concentrated in caring for the needs of the young and the elderly.'

Sheila Kitzinger, OURSELVES AS MOTHERS.

———●———

Winifred Fyfe [born 1955]

My mother worked full-time even before I started school, and in the late 1950s that was quite unusual. But I suppose having my grandmother and extended family living in the same stair and same street, allowed her a certain licence to do that. She worked very hard in a shop in Aberdeen and she eventually went on to become a buyer with the House of Fraser. She worked Saturdays too and until eight o'clock on Thursday evenings. I think she may feel guilty now and regret it because when I had my children she said, 'Oh, Win, don't go out to work, not unless you have to.' Of course that's somebody older looking back but I do think there's something to be said for staying at home with children, especially when they are young. When I look back, my sister and I did suffer for her working. I dare say maybe we had more material things than the children next door, and we went on holidays and had things other families never had, but I think we suffered because there was never any time for her to attend school choir concerts or parents' nights. She was always in such a hurry and fluster, you tended to get slapped out of the house; by the age of ten we were getting ourselves up and organised in the mornings.

My father worked shifts as a train driver, going out at all times during the night. Often it was my dad who gave us our dinner. He was never very happy about it and would never bother cooking anything, but would open tins and heat up packet meals. We were looked after, clean and we had the things we wanted. But for the marriage and the family as a whole, it did cause a lot of strife. I think my father would have preferred her not to be out working. They were divorced when I was in my teens – I don't know if it was a factor but he was never happy about it.

I think as a child I looked at my friends; their mothers were always in the house and I wanted my mum to be like that. My grandmother had a similar attitude to my mother. I remember her telling me, 'Never be a housewife. It's the most thankless, God-awful job you could ever have.' I remember her saying she would have loved to be an accountant or something but she was taken out of school at fourteen and put to a sink, and I dare say that's where she stayed. So I think I come from a long line of the most disgruntled women, who were never happy with being at the sink. But my grandmother took over the role of my mum, because she lived so close by and cared for us after school when mum was working.

I had trained as a nursery nurse but didn't go back to work until the youngest of my three girls was at school. I then went to work at a local playgroup which fitted in with school hours. Perhaps because of my own family background and experience of my mother working when I was young, I wanted to stay at home as I feel small children need the stability of knowing their mother is there for them.

My husband was a manager of travel agents and things were fine. He was part of the rat race and had a company car. His pay wasn't enormous but we managed. But then with the recession, the trade went through a bad time and he was made redundant. When the oil came to Aberdeen, all the big travel agencies came to the city but the boom didn't last. He lost one job and then when he joined another firm, he was made redundant from that as well. I decided to earn as much as I could under DHSS regulations. I work as many hours as I can do in a crèche but it varies from week to week. My husband has a voluntary job in the Citizens Advice Bureau. I think there is very little compassion for unemployed people. I mean everybody sympathises at the beginning but then they get fed up and forget about it and ignore you.

I am glad I am always at home for the girls, now that they are growing up. The eldest, Sarah, is beginning to go out at weekends with her friends, taking the train to Aberdeen, but she is very responsible. She's never let me down so far and I always say, 'If you are not going to be home by five, let me know', and she always does. I want them to enjoy their adolescence and I encourage them to have lots of friends.

I think as a family we get on because we are honest. The girls know their dad's unemployed and that we don't have much money and they accept that. He's been unemployed since Amy was born in 1986. I think that what was was wrong with my childhood was that I was never told anything. Nobody said anything about the arguments in the middle of the night and you take a lot of the guilt for it as a child. I never wanted my own children to experience that.

Communication is very important for a family and being a full-time mother is part of that.

I find now that as the girls are getting older they need me more than when they were babies, and in a different way. They don't need that physical attention of keeping them clean or fed, but they need so much more. It's their conversation. They are constantly talking and I can talk to them and discuss things, which is lovely.

'Cathy' [born 1955]

I think motherhood is a full-time committed state, not a profession or job. Whatever other work a mother does she is never actually away from her children. I am lucky that being a writer, I work mostly at home, so my working schedule is flexible and I'm beholden to no boss, except my conscience really. In my case it wasn't a question of returning to work. Writing is *what I do*, for financial need and satisfaction. My own mother was, I think, frustrated by motherhood [I do not mean to deprecate her love for and treatment of me] in a way I am not. Conventions have relaxed. I love to see women who genuinely enjoy being mothers, who enjoy being with and caring for their children, seeing them not as commodities or a tiresome duty, but as new life.

———————◆•◆———————

'It seems to me that since I've had children, I've grown richer and deeper . . . who else in the world do you have to love, no matter what? Who else can you absolutely not give up on? My life seems more intricate. Also more dangerous.

Anne Tyler, STILL JUST WRITING.

———————◆•◆———————

Roma Young [born 1956]

I definitely wanted to be a full-time mother. I personally feel that you can't devote yourself to your children and the home and hold down a full-time job. If you have got two or three children you are just spreading yourself too thin. I have worked off and on whilst the older ones were at school, if Allan's shift allowed for it. But I often found it very difficult to switch off and on. When the children were ill, they came before any job. With the four of them at school, there was many a time when one was not well and you can't keep taking time off.

After all if you are running a home you are a cook, a cleaner, a nurse, a chauffeur, a gardener, and twenty other people; it is a full-time job. That is the way I look at it. I'd rather stay at home. It is hard work to juggle everything to keep them happy, to bring them up properly and keep everything in order.

There are so many unemployed anyway, so I don't think it is fair to take a job. If the Government would pay the mother a sufficient amount in child benefit to enable her to stay at home, it would be a far better thing. Other countries manage it. It would solve a lot of problems. It would stop the latchkey kid syndrome. Children would feel more secure knowing mummy was at home for them and it would give jobs to those who really need them. I am well aware that some mums do need to work financially but some just do if for the sake of getting out of the house. My youngest, Oliver, has started at nursery, and he is happy knowing that I will come back for him. As they get older I feel they do need you to be at home for them, whether they are four or fourteen.

Didi Hopkins [born 1956]

I think it is such a great leveller, childbirth, and especially having a daughter first; it puts you in touch with your mother, your grandmother, and all the females down your family line, – and it levels you in the respect that ego and ambition just disappear. They may come back but you just stop for a moment and think 'This is life: Birth and Life'. This is what life is really about.

However, I certainly suffered a serious trauma during the long labour. And so my body reacted. Exactly six months to the day after Alice's birth, my hair started falling out. I would say until then my health had been fantastic and no doubt heavily improved by breast-feeding and hormonal changes. But after six months my skin started to disintegrate and my hair started falling out. This went on for three months and then it stopped. Sixty per cent of my hair had gone. Whether it was stress related or because my body had had to deal with so much in the past eighteen months, my immune system just completely collapsed.

Perhaps I didn't recover from the birth, and the first six months I was running on good hormones, and after that I was paying for the fact that I hadn't taken proper time to recover from spending fifty hours in labour.

My whole life has revolved around her more than I could anticipate. I think the best thing that has happened to me in my entire life is having a baby, and she is the apple of my eye. I hope I am not going to be one of those dreadful mothers who dote and brag about their children – 'My darling daughter' kind of thing! My life has changed entirely and I can sit and watch her for hours. I learn so much but I learn as much about myself, caring and being responsible for her. I see so much of my mother in her and a bit of me. Since my mother died a few years ago, she is so much in my mind just now and it saddens me to feel how much my mother would have loved seeing her.

I had thought that I would definitely go back to work quite soon after Alice was born, but because she needs such close contact and motherly care, I have put that on hold because the best present I can give her is my time and everything she needs from me, until she is, say, three or four.

However I find full-time motherhood, after eighteen months, is something I wasn't prepared for and something I'd like a break from just occasionally. Alice will now go happily to a friend who is her child minder on those days when I need to have time to myself, whether it is to go out, phone people or just sort things out around the house, so I don't have her around me all the time. It doesn't mean I love her any less.

Deborah Holder [born 1959]

Before having children I was a full-time journalist in a staff post. I took six months off when I had the second baby, and then returned to work on a part-time basis, two to three days a week. This was partly because I needed to earn some money and also to fulfil my needs as an individual. I wanted to work. I have not felt guilty but sometimes it was emotionally difficult while getting to know and trust a carer for the children.

Sue Rook [born 1960]

I think it is right for women to choose what they want to do in terms of staying at home with their children or going out to work. I am very lucky as I have been able to have that choice because my husband has a full-time job and I don't have to work. I feel it is my responsibility to look after my own child and I have decided to work on a very ad hoc basis about a couple of days per month. Before I had Hannah I worked full-time as a personnel and training manager and now I work from home, writing and delivering management training courses.

My decision not to return to work full-time was based on the fact that I feel I chose to have my child; I planned and wanted her so it's my responsibility to care for her in the best way I can. For me that was by staying at home. I couldn't leave her with someone else or in a nursery all day.

What I find interesting is people's amazement that I did not return to work! I've also amazed myself with how much I have enjoyed these first two years and how much it has enriched our lives.

June Williams [born 1960]

It is so important to have a break from the home because then you appreciate your children more, not having to deal with them twenty-four hours a day, and they appreciate you more as well. After about three months I went back to work as a practice nurse, running an immunisation clinic, meeting mothers with young babies, and they always ask lots of questions so they treat me like a health visitor. I also do other nursing duties so I meet all ages. It is very satisfying work and not too demanding. And of course I do get paid which gives me some freedom, some money of my own. Being a mother myself helps me with the job I do. My elder son, Alexander, has always been independent and I have never had trouble leaving him with a child minder whom he has known since he was a few days old. She now looks after Jonathan while Alexander is at school.

However, mothers are not encouraged to work. I'd say the mother's place is still very much in the home. It is very difficult to find good part-time work where the hours are suitable. With nursing jobs, you are still expected to be on the ward at half past seven in the morning, which is not easy when you have children to care for. I start at half past eight which is easier.

Jo Davidson [born 1960]

I don't believe that motherhood always has to be seen as a full-time job when the children are young and under school age, as long as there is reliable, alternative childcare. I returned to work four months after the birth of my daughter and six months after our son was born last year. The problem of childcare is not so difficult for us as we have an excellent child minder. My husband is a teacher and is at home during the school holidays. However, I often do feel dreadful if we both go off to work when one of the children is slightly off colour, but on the other hand I think children can benefit from not relying on having their mother always around, as long as the childcare is nurturing and of high quality.

I enjoy being with my children more as I am not so bound up in the daily minutiae of feeding, cooking and playing all the time. I am an education officer, involved in special educational needs, hence my concerns about the health and welfare of my own two children. Motherhood has given me more confidence. In my job I work closely with head-teachers, politicians and members of the public. Being able simultaneously to calm a fretful baby, disentangle a toddler from a violent ambush by another child about a doll's pram, organise tea and pack to go away means that I now have a healthy disrespect for the pomposities of other people. I also very rarely get upset by anyone because it's the children who matter, not anyone else. I don't see a lack of commitment towards motherhood today, I see a better sharing of the childcare and responsibilities between partners.

Lucy Owen [born 1961]

I believe motherhood is a full-time job which is I why I am very lucky because as a writer and children's author, I work from home. I began writing again immediately after the births of my two children, sporadically at first, even if it was just for an hour at a time, but if I don't write it drives me crazy! I also have a mother's help and my mother enjoys looking after them and babysitting from time to time. I couldn't go out to work, I'd feel I was missing out on their growing up. So I am with the children or available most of the time, if not all day.

The first smile, the first word, the first step, day at school, or picture are all earth shattering marvels. Tabitha laughs and says 'Da-da,' and I rush to the telephone and proclaim her achievement to the world [which is less interested that it might be!]. I find endless stores of patience in me that I never knew existed and my mother remarks on this all the time! I have rediscovered playing. I think motherhood is about learning to be a child again – but better. It is a gift, a chance to teach a child to develop and learn about the world, preparing him or her for life, and to give the child within you a second chance. It is giving and receiving unconditional love, such unconditional love that it makes your stomach hurt to think of it. All mothers make mistakes with their children but however many

I make, if my children say of me at 70, as I say of my mother, that I am their best friend, then I will have done a good job.

Diane Connelly [born 1961]

As a nursing sister and trained midwife I wanted to return to work after the birth of each of my sons. However the NHS does not make it easy for us. The hospital where I work does not allow sisters to return part-time and so I dropped from Grade G to E and was demoted to staff midwife. We needed my salary, so I returned to work six months after the birth of my first son and worked around twenty hours a week on night duty. Now with a second baby, I have reduced this to ten hours a week, working a Saturday night shift. Essentially the children are not aware that I am at work.

I have found motherhood wonderful. I thought I would want to return to work full-time, but all ideas of a career have vanished. My few hours are done just to earn a little extra at no cost to my children. I have more patience and tolerance. My husband is wonderful with the children and I know I could not cope if I had the level of help some friends have from their husbands. Having lost my parents – my father died when I was very young, and my mother died recently – my family is very important to me. I miss my mother terribly and am saddened that she did not live to see our second child, but I have treasured memories of her with her first precious grandchild.

Angela Blanchard [born 1962]

I think it depends on the mother, whether she wishes to stay at home to care for her children full-time. She should be able to choose. However I find that friends who go back to work, though they rationalise it, feel guilty deep down and overcompensate with their children, and this often leads to discipline problems. I thought about going back to work outside the home, as I had worked full-time until our first baby was born, as an administrator and researcher for employment head-hunters. I decided on balance that I could bring them up better than anyone else. I now write occasional articles for the local paper and am involved in the National Childbirth Trust, helping them to edit the newsletter. I am also training to be a breast-feeding counsellor.

When I had Clare I had little contact with other new mothers, and actually quite enjoyed the feeling of being the only mother in the world with the only baby in the world. However I would have benefitted from some contact with other new parents, just to compare notes about what was normal and what wasn't. I resisted the health visitor's gentle encouragement to join a 'mums and toddlers' group to meet other women. I think I was just having trouble getting used to the idea that I was a mother. Looking back I got a lot of moral support – long distance over the telephone – from one of my sisters, who has always been very interested in and fond of Clare, and gave me a lot of encouragement, telling me how worthwhile motherhood is and what a good job I was doing. She has no children!

From personal experience, it is not easy for an honours graduate to cope with being treated like a nobody – just because I am a full-time mother.

Linda Macpherson [born 1962]

I feel my job is too look after the baby when Jamie, my husband, is at work. When he comes home I feel it should be split fifty-fifty. Why should I have a twenty-four hour job when he has a ten hour job? But there again the battle for shared parental responsibility for childcare in this country is more difficult than it would be at home in my native Norway, where equality in the home is conventional. If I am breast-feeding, fine, that is my job. But nappy changing, and trying to stop the baby crying in the evening, at night, or over the weekend, that is equally the father's role as mine. I hope he shares my view.

It is difficult because his family have old-fashioned views and they are perhaps under the impression that it should be mainly my job, and that I should always be the one to sort out the baby, but I don't agree with that.

Magnus is just a few months old, so it will be interesting to see how it works out.

Liz Suttie [born 1964]

I don't feel the care of a baby or child is solely the responsibility of the mother. I think it is a shared role between the parents where that is possible. And if, God forbid, something happened to me, he would have to take over. I mean the mother has done her bit, giving birth, so I am a strong believer that a man can do everything a woman does, except breast-feeding. There is no reason why they can't swop roles so it is not just strictly a motherhood concern. I think it is a fifty-fifty responsibility between mother and father.

I am planning to go back to work part-time, five days a week, but mornings only. Really this is because I don't want to get into the usual situation of full-time mothers. I know many women who have given up work completely; they have had a couple of children and then they decide they want to go back to work and they can't find suitable jobs. I have never been one to say I want to get married, have children and do nothing else with my life. I think I need it for my own sanity. I don't think it does the baby any harm because if I am there fifty per cent of the time, she will be off at nursery, mixing with other children the rest of the time. I think that can only do them good. I just do not want to sit at home every day, not all day. I think I would go off my head.

We have got a nursery place booked, a day nursery recommended by friends. We had to book the place six months before Emma was born, would you believe, as it is so difficult to find good nursery care.

Carol Walton [born 1943, trained as a midwife in the 1960s, and now a counsellor in pregnancy, antenatal and postnatal care]

I do think the basic commitment to mothering and childcare has changed radically over the years. It is difficult to define but it is something to do with women's attitude to their role as well as men's attitude to their role. Women don't seem to have the same feeling that bringing up babies and children is their responsibility. When I had my children my mother made absolutely certain that I knew it was my responsibility – not hers and not my husband's. It was mine. I was the mother and therefore the main role was mine. That is certainly not the case these days. Girls rely heavily on other people taking their share. In a way it is a bit of a worry really. I don't know whether I am being old-fashioned or condemnatory but it worries me hearing them, even before the baby is born, saying that they want to start going out again straight away. When they get home they want *him* to take his share; this is a common expression round where I work.

Sometimes this changes once they have had the baby; instinct takes over and they wouldn't dream of leaving their baby with someone else, but for a lot of them, they become quite resentful that they are expected to look after this little thing all the time. They get quite cross when they are tired but they don't seem to appreciate that a baby needs twenty-four hour care. They get resentful that the baby won't sleep through the night and ask how they can be expected to look after it all day if they have had little sleep. It is strange, and I can't put my finger on it, but there has been a definite change in some women's response to 'mothering'.

Rachel Hanks [born 1967]

When Jack was nine months old, I began to find some part-time work, doing bits and pieces for friends. My partner Rory is a political researcher but has no regular work at the moment and is looking. He does some voluntary work and so if one of his jobs clashes with my work, then I have to find a child minder. Luckily I have a casual arrangement with a very good one, but as soon as her books are full I will no longer be able to leave Jack for a few days here and there at short notice, as I do at the moment. When that happens I don't know what I'll do.

I need to work out of financial necessity, as Rory doesn't have a job at the moment. I also need to work outside the home for my own sanity. If I had to look after a child full-time until they were twelve or thirteen, I think I would go mad, unless I had lots of money to travel the world, things like that. Looking after a brood of children is a full-time job, but not obligatory. I'm all in favour of introducing crèches in the workplace. I've been shocked at the prejudices that exist against parents; their needs are not accounted for at all. Childcare is so expensive, unless you have an au pair. But I'm not sure if I could collude in paying such low wages. In many households they do a lot more than childcare so they are the modern equivalent of maidservants.

I do feel guilty leaving Jack sometimes, but I'm trying to train him not to be one hundred per cent dependent on me. I would not be happy working full-time at the moment but take on part-time and irregular freelance work. I am determined to enjoy the experience of motherhood as much as possible. I know that I am lucky and only too soon he'll be off down the pub every night! I do regret not being able to give him any brothers or sisters right now, but my lifestyle and finances are just too unstable. We couldn't cope with more than one on our own at all.

Rachel Lockey [born 1967]

Having a baby was something I wanted to do on my own. It has its benefits because a lot of my friends who've had on-going relationships from which they have had children, have had problems. It has given me complete autonomy and I am able to make all the decisions, about discipline, how to bring my daughter up, and choice of schooling. There is no one to argue with about that.

I devoted myself to Bella during her first two years, when we travelled abroad. Then when I went to university, Bella was fine when she was at the crèche and nursery, but discipline became an issue when she began to go to school. She really began to grow up, to the point that she would come home and simply ignore me or be rude to me. School can be very harsh, mixing with a lot of much older children, so it has changed her. She was bullied to begin with by a boy in the top year, which I thought was awful but the school couldn't do much about it. So she had a difficult time settling in and has been influenced by bad behaviour at school.

So I have to instil in her certain manners, about how you address people, and say please and thank you – to such an extent that I keep telling her, 'Say "Thank you",' 'Say "Please" ', and it makes you think, and question why we do and say certain things in our society. But I still need to do it. I don't want a rude child who doesn't say please or thank you.

But she is not bad. She would never draw on walls, hit other kids or run away. It is more a case of a verbal problem with rudeness and attitude. I just need to nurture some respect in her, and she is eight years old so she is old enough to understand that she must give me time now.

Andrea Duffin [born 1970]

Lauren is now five and Molly two and a half, and I have been very happy to be at home with them during these early precious years, as they are growing up. I think I still want to study and work for a career. As I missed my opportunity of going to university when I left school, I think I would like to go to art college. And as I am only twenty-five, there is plenty of time for me to have a career later on when the girls are older.

It is a very different attitude in the small rural community around Leven, Fife, where I was brought up. It is still very traditional there, with all the mothers at home. Here in Edinburgh, in the city, I feel more pressure to work. People expect you to have a job outside the home. I mean we do need more money, we are always skint. At the moment though we agree that we'd rather scrimp and save rather than have me doing a job just for the sake of the money. My responsibility as their mother is to be with the children and I am quite happy about that.

CHAPTER EIGHT

Social Change and Family Life in the Modern State

In 1901 the percentage of illegitimate births across the UK was around four per cent. Towards the end of the first world war there was a short, sharp rise to around 6 per cent before it dropped back once more. During the second world war there was another steep increase between 1941 and 1944 to around 9 per cent but this dropped just as dramatically by 1946, returning once more to the turn of the century level. From 1964 there began a steady rise, reaching 10 per cent by 1975, and from then until 1992, the increase has been threefold such that today one in every three babies is born outside marriage. [32 per cent]. Merseyside at 42 per cent boasts the highest rate of illegitimate births while Surrey, with 20 per cent, has the lowest.

To give another comparison, in Scotland in 1964 there were around 5,000 illegitimate births, and in 1993 there were just under 20,000.

The younger the mother, the more likely that she will be unmarried. In Scotland and the North of England, nine out of ten mothers under the age of twenty were unmarried in 1992.

The UK is not the only country where the number of births outside marriage is rising. All the countries in the European Community have seen at least a doubling in the proportion of births outside marriage over the last thirty years. In 1991 almost half the births in Denmark were outside marriage. The largest proportionate increase was a tenfold rise in the Irish Republic, from 1 per cent to 16 per cent between 1960 and 1990. Greece has remained the country with the lowest proportion, now at around 2 per cent.

The birth rate in the UK has slowly decreased in the past twenty years, from

2.43 to the current 1.80 children per family. The European rates have dropped too, the lowest being in Italy and Spain, now down to around 1.25.

The percentage of women marrying in 1964 was 92.9, and in 1993 this had dropped to 75.2. Women are also marrying later. Up to thirty years ago the average age of a bride was 24 and the groom 26. Today both men and women are often in their late twenties or early thirties. The average age for women to have their first baby is now 29.

In recent decades there has been considerable social change, reflected in such indicators as marriage, divorce and cohabitation. Since the 1970s, the number of marriages has fallen by almost sixteen per cent whilst divorce has more than doubled over the same period. In 1991 the number of divorces (in Britain) was over 171,000, the highest on record; for every two marriages in 1991, there was one divorce, the highest figure in the European Community and twice the average.

In 1993 forty per cent of the population in Britain lived in a household made up of a couple and dependent children. Current surveys indicate that people are more likely to cohabit before second marriages than first marriages, and that couples who cohabit before marriage have higher rates of divorce than those who do not. Overall, in 1992 18 per cent of unmarried men and women aged between 16 and 59 were living together. The majority of cohabiting couples are aged between 25 and 40.

SOCIAL TRENDS, Office of Population Censuses and Surveys 1994.

Violet Stevenson Hamilton [born 1902]

After having had our three boys, one after the other, I realised regrettably that my husband and I had absolutely nothing in common, except the children. Unhappily in the eighth year of our marriage my husband and I decided to divorce each other. We eventually decided, when the boys were at prep school, that we would go our own ways, which we did. I had been leading a very isolated life devoid of companionship of my own kind, and I missed adult conversation and relaxation in my exceptionally busy daily life tending three sons under five. My husband was sympathetic and understanding and admitted he had woefully neglected his duties as a husband and father in favour of furthering his career. He said he was unable to 'do the decent thing' in providing me with evidence as he would have forfeited his position and have to seek other employment, which would not help the situation. We had discussed our problems with a close male friend who offered to provide me and the boys with a home.

The financial situation was satisfactorily dealt with, and made legal in the Divorce Court where I was given custody of the boys. Although divorce in those days was regarded along with illegitimacy as being the ultimate disgrace to sully family life, it did not affect my social life, except when I was put up to stand for Parliament, where it ended any prospect of that career.

We both remarried, but we always put the boys first and they spent the holidays equally with each of us, and we always provided a home background for them. I knew some years of great happiness until tragedy struck and I lost my much loved younger son and my second husband. I had a wartime marriage to a Wing Commander, who was later killed. After some years of civil service work, I married for a fourth time. I am now a widow but continue to be on loving terms with my sons.

Therefore, rather contrary to the way that I was brought up, I do feel that living together for some years is ideal. I had had the normal short courtship before my first marriage and didn't know my husband at all well. Some of the happiest marriages I know have been those of couples who have lived together. They have had an opportunity to get to know each other, to decide if they have a lot in common, and they are very good friends. They can then marry, have children and have very happy marriages based on a much more solid understanding. However, I do not believe in the promiscuity which is carried out these days, from far too early an age.

Margaret Dixon [born 1905]

I look upon the present rise in the divorce rate with dismay. I think there is much to be said for the idea of 'Keep your eyes wide open before marriage and half shut afterwards.'

Susan Curtis [born 1905]

I am not a feminist though I approve of contraception. I have a horror of abortion unless it is medically necessary. Gym-frock pregnancies are a direct result of forcing knowledge upon impressionable schoolchildren before they are ready for it. It seems that now children of eight are to be taught about AIDS. What next? A little learning is a dangerous thing. Ignorance and innocence can be protective as well as hazardous. My view of single women choosing to have babies is that selfishness predominates. What they gain personally they lose socially. I have had sixty years of a happy family life, all pros and cons considered.

Patricia Rogers [born 1909]

Of course there is very little thought of marriage these days. Young men just live with their girlfriends and I feel very sad about this. I think they are on the wrong track but they have to work it out for themselves. But once they get to university these days, they immediately start close relationships and don't question it, as if they have to get so involved so young.

I think it wrong to start a serious relationship virtually the day after meeting each other. They should try keeping it as a friendship instead of jumping into bed so quickly, because the thing is, where are they going from there? How are they going to learn slowly and carefully about the other person, to find out if they will really be suitable for each other for a long marriage ahead? If sexual attraction comes into it too soon with young men and women today, that blurs your judgement. It's your heart ruling your head then. It really is a changed world today but they will just have to deal with it.

I also think all this divorce today is very sad, all these separated families. I was happily married for fifty years. The cynics of course say it is because women are relieved of the dread of pregnancy, so therefore they have complete freedom. They become accustomed to a different kind of life: education, work, a career, and planning when or if to have children. Many women don't seem to want to be 'just a wife and mother', and if there is friction in the home, divorce seems to be the next step, rather than trying to sort it out together.

But I have two divorces in my own family. It seems to be the way things go in contemporary marriage. I think in both family cases both partners were to blame. It affects the children. It affects their education. I really don't know what the answer is. You can't generalise as it is a different reason in each case, but it is an avalanche now, the rise in divorce.

Unfortunate Coincidence

By the time you swear you're his,
Shivering and sighing,
And he vows his passion is
Infinite, undying –
Lady, make a note of this:
One of you is lying.

Dorothy Parker.

Mary Maclennan [born 1911]

We didn't think there was anything wrong in our generation with marrying when we decided we wanted to live together. We loved each other and wanted to be married. It is not a good idea just to live together and to experiment all round, you know what I mean. I believe it is better to make your mind up about someone and to commit yourself to that person and then get on with your life. If you just live with each other, the rules are all different. It is too complicated to set standards.

I can't say much about the current rise in divorce. You don't know if people have happy marriages or not, and you don't know what they are putting up with. It wasn't really a shock when my daughter got divorced as she had been thinking about it for a wee while. She left her husband, or her husband left her, I don't know which. She got married when she was very young, despite advice to the contrary, and it wasn't surprising that it didn't last. But my two other daughters and my son are happily married. I think we just let them understand it was their own responsibility, what they did. You can only show them by example that we believed in the conventions, and it has worked out more or less happily.

I am in no position to dictate about it all. I have lived a sheltered life with a husband for fifty years and very happily so. I don't know much about the changing family ways today. Every case is different and everyone just has to sort it out for themselves. If things don't work out, then it is better to separate and find some other way of living. You cannot make rules. Every family is different.

———•———

'I find it very odd that women who are otherwise perfectly sensible say that the "sexual revolution" of the sixties only succeeded in putting more women on the sexual market for the pleasure of men. What an odd way of looking at it. This seems to deny the possibility of sexual pleasure to women except in situations where it's so hedged around with qualifications that you might as well say, like my mother used to say, "Don't do it until you've got the ring on your finger." '

Angela Carter, TRULY IT FELT LIKE YEAR ONE.

———•———

May Stephen [born 1911]

I don't approve at all these single women having babies. A child needs a father. I really do think so. Our children didn't see much of their father because of the war, but he was always there when they were a little older, and I do think God has meant us to be male and female, father and mother.

I think women were oppressed far too much but now it has gone the other way. I personally believe that men have become more violent because women are taking their virility away from them. I am as old-fashioned as that. Men are no longer the boss around the house. They are no longer the main breadwinner, providing for the family, and can't decide things. I really do feel that it is wrong to have children without being married – you need the stability of the family unit.

I am amazed at the attitude of my young hairdresser. She is a young girl who comes to me to do my hair. She is living with her boyfriend but has no children – yet. She says you don't need to get married now. And I told her that women need some kind of security. 'You are silly, Debbie,' I keep telling her, 'to let it go like that. There was a case of a soldier killed in Bosnia, and he has a girlfriend and a child. Now the soldier is dead. She could have been getting a pension from the Army, but she will get nothing because they were not legally married. Surely it doesn't take much to go to a registrar office, even if you don't believe in a church wedding. But get a piece of paper to say you are married, that this is your husband; then he is responsible for you as well for any children you have.'

There is no commitment any more.

Emily Heggie [born 1912]

I think it is just plain immoral, all these cohabiting couples and single women choosing to have babies without marrying or, sometimes, even having a partner.

I know a young girl near here who has a baby. She doesn't see the father; she is not getting any help from the father, but she is living with another chappie. He is taking over the baby as if it is his own and apparently she is very lucky there. She was given a flat – furnished – and in fact I wouldn't like to say how much else she was given, and that is all coming out of the country's local government or the state. I think that is totally wrong. No country is going to be well off if they have to keep paying out all that money to these stupid, irresponsible young girls.

In my day, people waited to save up until they could afford to marry and support a family.

Eileen Watkins [born 1912]

I was married for fifty-four years, until my husband died of cancer two years ago. I miss him more than I can say. However my three children are happily married and I have six wonderful grandchildren. It therefore appalls me to hear about the number of single mothers in society today and, as a Christian, I believe cohabiting and casual sex are absolutely immoral. But basic morals have drastically changed. In my day an abortion was a criminal offence, and in middle class homes, if an unmarried girl became pregnant, this was a terrible disgrace.

I view the rise in divorce with horror, but I see the reasons for it; the girls, especially if they are out working, now have total freedom to consider someone else.

———————

'The less social status women have in public in terms of work, the more likely they are to feel that pregnancy confers status. This is often taken to be one of the reasons why teenage girls go ahead with unplanned pregnancies or even plan them in full knowledge of the likely financial and social problems that might follow.'

Rosalind Coward, OUR TREACHEROUS HEARTS.

———————

Alice Wands [born 1912]

I personally believe that some of these single mothers have got pregnant to jump the housing queue. They are teenagers unhappy perhaps at home with their parents and they want a home of their own, so they get pregnant, and most honest people will say that. My two children agree with me on this. It is unfair that this should happen, because there is a housing list and the priority should be for those on the list, not just for girls who decide selfishly that is what they're going to do and get money handed out. I see them on television saying, 'I'm not going to bring my baby up in second-hand clothes.' They get the clothes, the pram, a flat, they get everything. I don't think that's fair at all, it can't right. In one paper I read of one single mother being given driving lessons at great cost, hundreds of pounds' worth. Her boyfriend was willing to support her and the baby but the social services said, 'No, you must be independent of your boyfriend and, as you're living with your mother, you'll get £80 a week. Your boyfriend doesn't need to contribute because that's taking your independence away.' And they gave her all these expensive driving lessons. Of course I read this in the *Express*, so it may not be true.

Doris Melling [born 1914]

My father died when I was two years old, during the first world war, so my mother brought me up in a single-parent family and we survived. However I do think two parents are definitely needed for a stable family background. I think single women having babies is wrong, but it seems to be the trend today. Many very young mothers seem to cope well and love their babies which is the main thing.

I was married for forty-five years and my husband died ten years ago. I live near my daughter and her family. I do think the relationship between parents and children has altered. I always thought my mother was old to me. I think she was thirty or thirty-two when I was born. So was my daughter but her children are friends with their parents and they do everything together.

Mary McKerrow [born 1915]

I think divorce has become too easy now; it is, so to speak, the thing to do. If divorce happened at the time when we were young and getting married, it was a shocking thing. No one got divorced.

I feel it is difficult to judge today's rise in divorce. Possibly it is due to the pace of life, which rules out the time for affection and being together as a family. The home atmosphere is essential, making children feel they are being cared for, that there is someone there, a shoulder to cry on or whatever. They don't have to be spoilt but to have two parents with time to be with them is more valuable than anything else. I think it is very sad because you can't blame children who are disrespectful to adults and have a rough, casual attitude to everything, if they come home and there is no one there, and they are expected to fend for themselves. It makes them grow up too old too soon. I am probably very old-fashioned – I am, I know. But what's the answer to it?

I think tolerance has gone out of the window in human relationships; I think tolerance in married life is a very important feature. We have been very fortunate. We had our golden wedding anniversary last year and it hasn't really been a struggle. We have had some very happy times.

Joan Counihan [born 1915]

The radical change seems to be that mothers give up too quickly now and find they can't cope with husbands, running the home, and caring for the children. But most of my observations come from television programmes which may not reflect modern mothers properly. I believe men's attitudes towards the women's role as mothers hasn't changed very much, though some younger men do help their wives a great deal more than in the 1920s. Although in some ways the parent/child relationship has improved since my childhood, I think that things like morality, respect for one's elders and discipline have swung too far the other way.

Emily Hagues [born 1916]

We're going to a wedding this week and oh, the fuss about it! I just said, 'I hope to goodness they stay together'. Couples don't try hard enough now. I think that some of them just up and away. Now if we'd done that in our time my mother would have said, 'You've made your bed, now just go back.' No, I don't think people work at marriages somehow, and the least thing wrong, they're up and away and upset and that's it.

Milicent Woolner [born 1917]

Balanced family life is preferable but a marriage does need working on as a partnership. Marriage should be the axis from which we live stable and secure lives. The breakdown of that lynchpin has caused more misery and problems than needed to arise. In many cases the attitude of men and women is very self-centred, and there seems to be a lack of caring and therefore a certain lack of sensitivity towards each other. The home seems not to give the developing adult the support he or she needs. They mistakenly leave home and hope the state will find them houses and benefits to allow them to be an independent adult before adolescence is over!

Lucy Firth [born 1917]

When we married it was a serious thing and it really meant for life. I think it is dreadful to hear of single women having babies. When I see how young mums dress and behave I don't think they look very motherly. We need to return to Christian principles. I have been happily married for fifty-four years and we have two lovely grandchildren.

Elizabeth Grey [born 1917]

My view of single mothers is that it's the Social that brought that in. It was the money. If they didn't get all this extra money and things, they wouldn't be so keen. I think it is ridiculous the amount of money that some of them get. I don't think they should be living on money that other people have worked for all their days. We were all workers, but that doesn't mean a thing now. Half the folk who are getting the Social, they want a bairn, so they become one-parent families. Then they get houses and everything. Now I know a lot of girls who are not married, and they have one or two bairns. Then their bidie-in, the man they have, he goes away oot of the road, and the girl gets a council house and everything. They get settled in and they get carpets and cookers and fridges, and then he slowly comes back. That's Dundee, day in, day out. And that's what I think is all wrong. They should go out and find work of any kind. If they took the money away from them they wouldn't have bairns.

When our Alice was born, you got nothing, there was no family allowance. But when you had a second bairn, then you got it. I think it was five shillings a week for Janice. The first bairn got nothing.

A traditional family is important but it will come the time soon where there will be no such things as weddings; och aye, the days of weddings and marriages will be finished – it will be just bidie-ins, and bidie-oots, that's what it will be. And the government will give them money to have all these bairns.

Barbara Littlewood [Sociologist at Glasgow University]

In Britain today we probably have the highest proportion of single mothers in the whole of Europe – I think it is around 15–20 per cent. There are a few countries outside Europe which match that rate but certainly, within Europe, we have by far the highest number of single mothers.

I think in part this is something to do with legislation, social security laws and divorce laws in Britain, rather than supposing that the British are more lax sexually than any other European nation. Most of the single mothers in fact have once been married. The children are not necessarily illegitimate; they were possibly brought up in a 'normal household', and this is obviously a reflection of rising divorce rates.

Most divorces are initiated by women, but quite why this might be is less clear. I don't think we can automatically assume that this is because women are less satisfied with their marriages than men. Every case will have different reasons. One significant feature of divorce is that a man is most likely to remarry after divorce than a woman. I think partly this is because he has a wider range of possible wives to choose from, not only the women round his own age, but also five, ten years younger, whereas it is still relatively socially unacceptable for a woman to marry a younger man, or even have a relationship with a younger man. So women are more likely to remain living alone after divorce, with custody of the children. This is associated with what sociologists call a 'feminisation of poverty' in this country: single parents are particularly likely to depend on various forms of assistance, Income Support and so on. Most of these are women, and many of the children who are living in poverty are doing so because they live with their mothers alone.

I think it's possibly significant that the women least likely to marry at all, statistically, are the wealthiest and the very poorest. I think this suggests that, whether women are conscious of it or not, that there is some kind of economic calculation going on when women are deciding whether to marry or not, as compared with cohabiting. Marriage makes very little difference to women who are fairly well off, professionals in their own right, and they see no particular economic advantage in marrying, so they remain single or cohabit. For the poorest women, where marriage would most likely be to a man of more or less the same class, perhaps unemployed, again as an economic arrangement this is not going to have much affect on her life. So these are the women who are least likely to marry.

Marriage has traditionally been the way a woman consolidated her status and ensured her survival, because women's wages have typically been too low for her to support herself let alone any dependents she might have. She has needed to marry a man, to have her standard of living improved through access to his salary or higher wages. Now this no longer seems to be affecting women who are in the extremes of society. The independent career woman can afford to support herself independently, and for the very poorest women, their potential husbands aren't earning a wage anyway, or a very low wage. They can see in a sense that they don't need an economic relationship with a man.

There have been studies done and there doesn't seem to have been much change in people's behaviour over this period, when numbers of single mothers have been on the rise. A survey looking at the category of single mothers who have never been married does indicate that significant numbers are not living alone, but cohabiting. Most children in fact are registered with a father's name as well as a mother's name. So you might assume that there is some kind of relationship between the couple, although they are not married.

Of the young – especially lower class – mothers who have never been married, it seems that their behaviour has not necessarily changed a lot from their mothers and grandmothers. In other words, in certain parts of the country it has been quite normal for young people, once they begin courting, to start having sexual relations. The expectation would be that quite soon after that they would get married, possibly when the girl was pregnant, possibly before that. But it's the marriage which has now been omitted. There can be very little doubt about this. It can be seen as a kind of series of steps and stages in a relationship which young girls have been following in the same way as their mothers did: the progression from courtship to sex to marriage. Now this progress has been interrupted after courtship and sex. Young working-class people in communities where male jobs have virtually disappeared over the course of a generation, now see no particular benefit in getting married. This doesn't mean that the couple are not cohabiting and bringing up their children together.

Mary Boulcott [1922]

I don't understand all this divorce business nowadays. With so many couples living together before marriage, they should know each other so well, yet the breakdown of marriage is much greater than in my day, when we never had the opportunity of getting to know our future husbands very well at all. Marriage used to be seen as a serious thing – and we've been married for forty-seven happy years; now it is all so casual.

Joyce Petchey [born 1922]

Mothers nowadays seem to have children as prestige items and play-things, not realising they can be quite a challenge to bring up correctly. Some parents worry all the time about the right thing to do and their children become unsure of themselves. Some parents turn them out by the age of sixteen and couldn't care less about them. I don't understand about the rise in divorce. I am still trying to work out why it has happened. There must always be two sides to the question. Do couples talk to one another enough? I do believe too much emphasis is put on sexual enjoyment by the media and books; couples follow these fictional examples as being the correct or successful way to live. There is more to life than sex!

Pamela Worthington [born 1923]

I think a stable family background is very important for children to grow up in if they are to become caring, responsible adults, and a sense of security is vital. One of the sad things today is the very high divorce rate with the children probably the main sufferers, when their world is suddenly destroyed.

As for the changing role of motherhood, I dread to think of the future of the family. I am appalled at the selfish and irresponsible behaviour where single girls are having babies by various boyfriends. There are also the thousands of divorced mothers and fathers starting new families with their new partners and their children. There will eventually be so many half-brothers and half-sisters around they will be marrying each other, with all the problems that can create.

Joyce MacPherson [born 1923]

I think the increase in single unmarried mothers is terribly wrong. In the Quakers we have one or two families which are so very mixed up. The mother will have one surname and the living-in partner has another. The children live some time with one parent and then with the real father. It must be so confusing for the children. Some families made up of second marriages or relationships have a mixture of children from the two sets of parents. Maybe I'm just old-fashioned but I think it is dreadful. Parents should work at staying together. If I was in the same situation now as I was when I was first married with young children, I might have given up and goodness knows what would have happened to the children. My husband has a frightful temper and he flares up at the slightest thing. He blows his top. Once or twice he used physical force on me, because he was so angry. But I understood that this was part of his nature. I was more docile if things went wrong. It's nice when we make up and it's never very serious. Even if we rage and fume, it is alright in the end. Nowadays if that happens one partner or the other would walk out. They don't stand for it anymore. There is no commitment to the marriage.

———◆•◆———

'She would have a baby with her husband, to make up for the absence of love, to locate love, to fix herself in a certain place, but she would not really love him.'
Joyce Carol Oates, THEM.

———◆•◆———

Jane Ward [born 1924]

I think the biggest change in family life and the approach to motherhood lies in what seems today to be an accepted attitude that 'I must have a baby to fulfil myself'; the father is almost incidental. If the couple are not actually married and the partnership breaks down, at least you are free to take off. With so many divorces today, *to some extent* that suggests that there must have been a lot of very unhappy married women in the past, but very few of them could ever have managed to live on their own because they had no training to enable them to do so. In any case divorce, up until recent years, was expensive and very difficult to obtain, and women normally had no money of their own. Today divorce is easier, cheaper and, in theory, women are as educated as men and can find work to support themselves on their own. To that extent there is more equality and women are not dependent on their husbands. But there is also a feeling that the institution of marriage has been weakened; increased independence for women, plus their own separate career, brings more self-interest and less concern for the problems of their husbands and families. Marriage becomes something we look to to bring personal benefit, rather than a joint venture. And that is when the relationship can break down. But should those of us who pay income tax be expected to provide, through the welfare state, for women who cannot cope with marriage, who cannot, apparently, cope with contraception either, and who happily continue to produce children as single parents?

I do not think I was a romantic type. When it came to thoughts of a husband, and I was twenty-five before I married so I had plenty of time to think about it, I was looking for someone I liked, someone whom I felt I could face across the breakfast table for the next thirty or forty years or so. Physical attraction had to be there too, but I recognised that it would not be enough on its own. I had already seen several unhappy marriages [the war had a lot to do with this] so I suppose I was wary. My husband and I had a lot in common and, hackneyed though it sounds today, we stayed in love and continued to enjoy each other's company – not the same thing at all. We both wanted children; I had every intention of having four children from the age of 15, and so our fifth baby was a bonus. My younger daughter and her husband chose to have two children. My two elder boys married divorcées, thereby acquiring ready-made families, and have had daughters of their own. I don't think my elder daughter, a childcare officer, will marry and have children.

I think if I were young now I would not want to have children at all. It is a very different world. But then, I am an economist and I have grave reservations on future conditions both on a UK and world basis.

Pauline Grisbrook [born 1924]

Men and women do not give enough thought to entering into marriage or a partnership today. They then blame everyone else when things go wrong. I believe there is a much more selfish attitude in both husbands and wives. How many times do we hear 'I need space', 'I need to do my own thing', an attitude possibly bred of a higher standard of living, the welfare state and easy divorce laws. Every single day of my marriage was happy. Perhaps not ideal but for forty-one years, although we had cross words and different opinions at times, we were together and of one mind, with never a question of parting and breaking up the family we cherished.

Is Feminism Destroying the Family?
'I don't think the decline of the nuclear family is due to a feminist conspiracy. I think the family is in flux and changing rapidly. I think notions of femaleness and maleness are also changing and I see those changes as very positive. I don't think

the male is marginalised. I think the male is being humanised. The kind of traditional qualities of maleness – of assertiveness, of dominance, of strength, of being the breadwinner, also involve a lot of bad qualities of aggressiveness, of a denial of intimacy, and a denial of a lot of those characteristics which have traditionally been seen as female. I see these notions as being under flux but I see it is a painful revolution, a very painful revolution, and I think young men do need help in coming to terms with those changes. I don't think the feminist campaign is directly responsible for anything very much, unfortunately. Feminists and single parents are the scapegoats of these massive social changes which are occurring not only in Britain but throughout Europe. They are very positive changes.

Women want to be equal and meet men on equal terms. They want an equal place in the work force and in the home and they also want men to take equal responsibility in the home. What they want is for masculinity to change. They want men to be more compassionate and to be more capable of having more intimate relationships.

Sue Lees, THE MORAL MAZE, BBC Radio 4, 29th December 1994.

Davina Thorpe [born 1927]

There has been such a great change in family life that most people, even young ones, think it will go full circle and we will get back to Victorian virtues. Of course in those days, while life was very strict and moral, a lot was hidden under the mat so it might not have been all good. I do think it is regrettable that married couples do not have any patience or faith in their vows to stay together. It is simply dreadful that men and women can simply walk out after perhaps a few months or weeks of being together. However, we should remember that after the two world wars there were many one-parent families, where mothers had no choice but to bring up their children alone and they managed very well. A father is not always essential for a happy, stable family life.

Pamela Wells [born 1928]

I cannot see a thing to recommend single motherhood and cohabitation in place of marriage. The lack of discipline in children and, in certain districts, the rise in crime and violence even in primary school children, is frightening. Where are their mothers? People now expect to be always happy, and are not prepared to work through problems in a relationship. But it can only be good that truly awful marriages, where women were badly treated or abused, can now be easily dissolved.

I have been married for forty-two years and we remain good friends. I always had my own interests outside the home, and have developed these as well as maintaining personal friendships which has been very important.

While people may generalise and we read reports in the press about the decline in moral standards and family life, I find it interesting that one of my daughters, who teaches in a rural comprehensive school, says that what most of the teenage girls think of and aspire to is marriage and babies, just as in previous generations!

Joan Longmuir [born 1930]

I think it is very sad that many women today are being conditioned into thinking a baby is a 'right', even if they cannot afford to give it a home. It frightens me to see such a change in family values. I don't see how so many of the present teenagers and young mothers are going to be able to construct the stable framework of a family when they have so little valid personal experience of it themselves, to fall back on. Discipline and moral standards have to be learned from within the family and some of these young girls have had little family stability or moral guidance themselves.

I also deplore the increase in divorced parents. My son, number five, is divorced with three daughters, but at least they all see him regularly. So many children have a succession of 'fathers'.

Barbara Henderson [born 1931]

Around me, where I live in the Highlands, I see a generation of young, unmarried and divorced mothers with young children, often to different fathers. They are dependent on state aid, and their men come back and forth. They have parties lasting all night with music blaring and the children running wild around the house. These people have not worked in their lives and the government is to blame for this. My husband and I had to work all our days to support our family. I really do believe in a stable two-parent family, with an extended family close by, to establish identity and respect for your elders.

For some it is good that divorce is easier today, whereas before women couldn't get out of situations where they suffered cruelty or unhappiness.

At one time I would have advocated a five-year renewable marriage licence.

There has been so much change in the last fifty years. Possibly this is a phase which will pass like so much else has done. You have heard the expression that even the worm will turn. Women were held down so long that they are determined to do their own thing, but society may very well change and adapt again when women realise they have made slaves of themselves.

'Auntie Emm pulled her stockings up over her veiny legs. "My mother had ten children in two rooms – my father was a drunkard, most men were then. There was nothing to do at home so they went to the pubs.

"I was kicked around as a kid – and I vowed no matter what happened I'd take care my kids never got badly treated – I used to kneel down and pray at night, 'Dear God, don't let me die before my kids are old enough to fend for themselves'. Now they're all grown up into fine kids and I don't care now what happens to me." '

Nell Dunn, POOR COW.

Margaret Cruikshank [born 1933]

Everything seems to be back to front these days. Women have a baby, then they get engaged and married. They have children even if they don't have a job and can't afford to, and so many families then live off the state and have the best of everything while pensioners haven't enough to live on.

Mary Anderson [born 1934]

It appears to me that families are losing out with working mothers. My daughter-in-law did very little as a home-maker – little housework and expected my son to do most of the cooking and cleaning, and bringing up the babies, which he did for five years. She has just left my son, causing great upset to him and ourselves. She does not appear to want to bring up her two baby girls and expects my son to bring them up. I am appalled at the number of divorces these days. We all must have gone wrong somewhere; this cannot be right. I see it as morally wrong to cohabit rather than be married, and I can only see this as a slippery slope as the children may follow their parent's example that marriage is unnecessary. It is not the right atmosphere to bring a child up in; they are missing out on so much of a normal family life, and there are so many children experiencing broken homes and all the sadness that brings.

Sheila Brown [born 1934]

I was a school nurse for some years and I have seen so many things which make me very sad. The separated families, the live-in boyfriends. The teenagers would come to me to open their hearts. They felt they could talk to me as someone they knew and trusted who was not too close. Young girls who had been molested by their mother's new boyfriend; the problems caused by mothers out working, where girls and boys feel neglected and unloved; the worries children have these days when they are in their young teens – growing up, school work, bullying, friendships, first boyfriends, changing emotions, as well as worrying about their mothers, their problems and relationships. I couldn't believe some of the stories I heard. There were also many occasions when children would be sent off to school when they weren't well, because there would be no one at home to look after them. One boy came to me on a Friday with a bad stomach pain and I told him to tell his mother to take him to their doctor. On the Monday morning he was back at school, still in agony. His mother – he had no father – had done nothing to help him, unconvinced he was really ill, and he was whisked off to the hospital· with appendicitis.

I do see a decline in moral standards and the start of the decline is the element of selfishness. In my day, a lot of people, when marriages went wrong, admitted it wasn't ideal but you just worked through it. We have had our ups and downs but you don't give in. You just try and make it better. But this element of giving up at the first hurdle, it's a shame.

But that is only one side of the way family life has changed. In many families the 'New Man' has arrived. My daughters' husbands have been so good with their children; they will change nappies, do the washing, iron clothes. These young lads are wonderful and a great help to the mums today. My husband would read the children stories or take them for walks but in my day they didn't help so much, because we mothers were at home all day looking after the home. But today, mothers are working too and the parents simply have to share the daily responsibility, the chores; they need all the help they can get.

———◆·◆———

'Now that she is at home – and sometimes irons baby things – does he assume that she will iron his? It may be entirely reasonable that she should do so; divisions of labour often are. But any assumption that today's mothering throws their partnership all the way back to the marriage roles of yesteryear demeans her new role, and any implication that she would take care of the man who is supposed to be her adult partner, as she takes care of the baby, is unfortunate.'

Penelope Leach, CHILDREN FIRST.

———◆·◆———

Jennifer Harper-Jones [born 1939]

There has been such a tremendous change in women's attitudes towards work and marriage. We have been to five weddings this year of friends' daughters and the youngest bride was 28. Girls – especially from middle-class families – have such high expectations these days, and certainly want a good education, a good job, or a fulfilling career before they even think about marriage, if they think of it at all.

With regard to single mothers I think they are selfish and don't put the interests of the child first. Boys need a father. And in marriages where children are involved, parents should strive hard to make the relationship work and make sacrifices for the children, rather than take the easier option of divorce.

Patricia Turner [born 1941]

I was nineteen when I had my first child; I was married to Robert at the time, but he was in and out of jail. I fell pregnant again and had twin boys. They weren't planned – I just fell pregnant. I wasn't using anything, put it that way. I wasn't bothered, I was quite happy. So I had five children by my first husband but I looked after them myself. We just had a room and kitchen. I wasnae working and I got help from the social security. It was hard because one of my daughters was retarded, and she was eventually taken away. I've seen her since, mind, but she had to go into a home. But the main problem was my husband being in jail because he would be in for maybe eight years at a time. In fact it was ten years the last time, and I thought, 'No, that's it', and I ended up getting a divorce. At times I just couldn't cope, and I did take to drink. I wouldn't say I was an alcoholic, but I did take to drink.

Motherhood

Then I met another chap, which was not a very good relationship. I had two kids by him but he beat me up most of the time, and the kids. So I finished with him and ended up at the women's refuge. I met someone else, married him, but that only lasted a few months – he went away. Then I lived with another man. He beat me up as well and gave me a lot of hassle, physical and mental abuse, and my son ended up fighting him, and was charged with hitting him with a baseball bat. But his dad is a registered alcoholic and a liar. My son had to go to court with no one to speak for him, and they believed his dad; they took his word and my son was found guilty, which was so wrong. He has no offences and had only just turned sixteen.

It never bothered me being a mum with so many kids. I have had nine bairns. I never hurt them never. It was just I was in and out of hospital, and they were taken into care a lot. The twins were fourteen at the time and they got into trouble, truancy, and they were going to have to be taken into a home or go with their father. So they went to their dad's. I've been to see them. And my eldest daughter went to stay with her dad but she came back again.

I feel bad about it. I wish we could have stayed together but they wouldn't house us. And I would rather they went with their father than go into care. I suppose if I could go back, I wouldn't have had so many kids, put it that way. But I always seemed to meet the wrong man and I think I kept looking for someone who would take care of me. But they never did. I think it is because I'm awfy soft-hearted, and I tend to run after them.

I did try to use contraception but none was any good. And they refused to sterilise me. I did ask to be sterilised, but I was divorced and they wouldn't do it, in case I met someone else who wanted a family. I used a lot of contraceptive things but they weren't any use at all.

I just live with my son now. He is an awfy aggressive laddie, but he is settling down now that we've moved away from his dad.

I've got sixteen grandchildren. My eldest daughter has three. Of the two laddies, one has two children, the other has three. My two other sons seven – no eight – between them. So my children have wanted to have big families and I haven't advised them otherwise. I mean I've been surprised if I've heard one of them is pregnant again, but they turn round and say 'Who's talking? You had nine!' I think it's good to have your kids young, so that you can go back to work later on. But I think if a woman just goes on working and has a career and she is thirty or forty, they get their home really immaculate, they wouldn't want children after that and change their lives.

I've had my problems, but I'm always cheery. I'm always laughing.

Sheila Davidson [born 1944]

In my teenage years there was no way I could have stayed with Ian before we married, but I think it's a great idea. Sandra and my son Paul lived together, as do Steve and Dawn. Paul and Sandra got married when their son Jordan was one year old. I found it quite difficult to tell everybody that they were having a baby and not getting married, but as time went on I got used to it. Sandra knew more about Paul in a few months together than I knew about Ian in five years of courtship. They share the household chores and childcare and I think that is good.

In our day marriage was for better or worse, and if it was worse you made the best of it and accepted your lot because there was nowhere to go, no money and the children would suffer. So you soldiered on until the children were away from home. Nowadays everybody's expectations of marriage are higher and they don't believe in sticking at it if they are unhappy. The children come second. I've never experienced a divorce so I cannot comment personally.

Jenni Smith [born 1946]

As a divorced mother myself, who had a very unhappy first marriage in which I and my boys were afraid of their father, I see the rise of the divorce rate as inevitable. Men do not wish to change and women are rightly no longer prepared to be badly treated.

When I started to go out with my present husband, the boys were always included and learned that a father is not the man who passed on his genes, but the man who looks after you, who is always there for you. We courted for four years, and for the latter two the boys ran a constant campaign of pushing us into marriage. My husband finally gave in and from the day we were engaged, they insisted on calling him Dad, and I have never changed that. When we married I was 38, with two children. He was 31 and still living at home so you can imagine the gap we had to cross there.

We had many, many problems to contend with, not least from the boys' father who was still seeing them for a few hours each week. He often treated them badly, beating the elder boy at times. I was not able to stop this, much as I wanted to. He had a court order giving him access, and my solicitor insisted that 'There is not a judge in the land who will prevent a father from chastising his own child.' When the boys were 13 and 14, their father said they did not need to see him any more and they have rarely seen him since, and a lot of strain went out of our lives.

Ten years on the experiment is a huge success and from being a totally dysfunctional family, I feel that we are close and as happy as we could possibly be. My elder boy left home at 16, drifted and got into trouble but he has settled down now and is planning to go to university this year to read law.

I think there has been a dramatic rise in divorce because the gap in the expectations between men and women is currently getting wider. Men have not changed; their expectations still seem to be that they will have their lives and careers, unfettered by childcare. Women, on the other hand, are now wanting the same right to a career. The ethos in the workplace will have to change quite dramatically before men are free to take up their share of the burden of childcare. Currently when they are approaching managerial level they are expected to work longer and longer hours so that they cannot be at home. Since any woman wanting to progress is expected to do the same, the family has to suffer.

I feel women are less prepared to put up with the idea that men get to do as they please and the woman has to stay at home. Many of us have had to cope with violence and cannot see why we should continue to accept that. The stigma of divorce has pretty well gone, and that has made it easier to face the decision. I found it quite agonising having to shoulder that burden on top of everything else, and it was a hard decision to make. Woman today are prepared to take that step.

As time goes on, I think the divorce rate will start to fall again. People are marrying later, and are therefore more aware of what they want from life. Or else they are not marrying at all, and cohabitees do not show up in the divorce figures when they separate. I do feel that we are undergoing a vast social upheaval and it may take another ten or twenty years before things settle down again. I am not against cohabiting women deliberately having children, so long as they are in a good and committed relationship. Similarly if a single woman chooses to have a baby, she should at least be self-supporting and have a partner who will provide moral support, whether that partner is male or female. What I do not agree with is women deciding to have a baby instead of a job, and at the taxpayers' expense.

I don't think that marriage is strictly necessary, since there is no guarantee that a marriage is any more secure than any other form of relationship – after all divorce is pretty easy these days from what I can see. I do however feel that children do better if they are in a happy home, whatever the configuration of people within that home. We are in a state of fluidity at the moment and no doubt before too long, a new norm will be established. In the meanwhile, people are trying to sort out all sorts of new ways of living and I don't think that that is wrong. What is wrong is for the state to tell people how they must live. So long as children are well nourished, physically, mentally and emotionally, I do not see why they cannot live in any set up that works for their family unit.

Vivienne Leighton [born 1947]

It does sadden me to hear of all these single mothers; it must be so very hard to bring up a child on your own with all the attendant financial problems and lack of support. I admire people who can cope. It must be a struggle. I am sure it is best to have two parents, to share the responsibility with a husband or partner. You do need that. The rise in divorce figures is alarming. People get married, live together for a year and then pack it in. They can't seem to tolerate anything they don't like. They have no stamina to put up with it. Speaking of my own daughter, in the way she has not been able to stick at her job, I would be very reluctant to pay for a big wedding when the time comes. It would be a waste of money. I don't trust today's youngsters committing themselves to anything.

There have been difficult patches with my own husband. Well, that's not really fair. There has never been a time when I would have thought of leaving or divorcing him. Never. Maybe an argument or something but it never ended with me saying, 'Right, I'm leaving.' I have never left him, and he has never left me, even for a night. We've always managed to sort things out. Perhaps because we are well-suited. He's very even-tempered and easy-going. He always helped out with the children and it was never a case of saying, 'It's your turn.' It was all part of sharing the work to be done. Every generation is different. In my father's time, men often had nothing to do with babies. It wasn't expected of them. The woman's place was in the home.

Mary Law [born 1949]

Family life is in a state of change and the government must get their act together and go with the times. Trying to keep the nuclear family would be ideal, but only a few will stay together for life. They can't dictate it for everyone. I think all this divorce is a worrying trend and children feel very insecure. Marriage itself has a thin foundation if both partners feel they could move on at any time if they do not feel happy. In my generation there will be few diamond wedding anniversaries.

The 'men as breadwinners' attitude must change to 'men as fathers', wholly at times. Men must learn how to be fully responsible for their children in a flexible role reversal, depending on the work situation and health of both parents. I do think a two-parent family is best as boys need a role model. Women appear to be good at mothering, but fathers have not adapted well to a more involved paternal role.

Wendy Walker [born 1949]

I have been extremely active within the Pro-Life movement for twenty-five years. During that time I have witnessed some heartrending events and it really does make you realise how much pressure girls and women are under to have abortions. Once the deed is done, not many people really care how and when the pieces are picked up. Because my own children are mixed-race, I am particularly aware of how much pressure is put on mothers-to-be of mixed babies and also black women to have abortions, often late into pregnancy. Some girls carrying white babies tell the doctor the father was black because this seems to guarantee an abortion immediately.

I myself married a West Indian man who was very family orientated and good with our eight children. However he was brutally cruel and I divorced him after seven years of marriage.

Sheila Gray [born 1951]

I was married the first time round for twelve years, but only the first eight years were happy. I believe that divorce is easier and quicker to achieve nowadays so that people are not trapped in an unhappy situation. However it is bad that so many children suffer from it. I have now been married to my second husband for four years.

Liz Hodgson [born 1954]

There is certainly a media image of the changing role of mothers and family life, but the reality doesn't seem that different. There are lots of women who seem to be at home full-time, men working full-time as before. It's just that there are other expectations of the family unit which make it look like we are reinventing the wheel.

I am not so impressed by the so-called nuclear family because of personal circumstances. My maternal grandparents were deeply unhappy; my grandmother was frustrated and they separated for a while. She was wooed back with a new house but she couldn't divorce him because they were Catholics.

My own parents were blissfully happy but my father died in a car crash after four years of marriage. His brother, a respectable farmer, had four children with a woman other than his wife. This is not an inspiring model for the success of the traditional family. Because I am so aware of the lack of a father myself, for me both parents make sense but it's not the whole story.

Lyn Mungall [born 1954]

The first time I married more or less straight from school, I was seventeen. I hadn't wanted to get married but I just wanted to leave home. I had a dreadful home life, and when this guy came along and was really nice to me; I began to live with him and then we got married. I was pregnant when I got married. The wedding was arranged for the August, but I was already pregnant so we got married straightaway but not in a church. My mum said I couldn't get married in a church.

It wasn't a planned pregnancy. I wasn't taking the pill because I was too feared to ask my family doctor for the pill as he had been our doctor since I was knee high. I went in loads of times to ask him but never got round to it. In the end he put me on the pill, but my boyfriend and I had an argument and I threw them away.

I was a bit frightened and apprehensive when I was pregnant because I was on my own. Well, I had Stewart, but I wasn't close to my mum and dad. But I wanted the baby. I thought this was something for me, it was my baby and nobody could take that away from me. I was convinced I would have a girl, and I would dress her up in nice little clothes. Naive, I think I was! I had a girl and we moved to London when she was two weeks old so that we would be near my husband's family. I got on OK with his mum. Things started going wrong in the marriage and I left him and went home. But my mum said I had to go back because I was now married and I had made my bed and must lie in it. So I went back and I was soon pregnant with Dawn. She wasn't planned either. Then four years later I was pregnant again although I tried to hide it for a bit. I knew that Stewart didn't want any more kids, and all through the pregnancy he abused me, kicked me and beat me up. I had Hayley, my third girl, and then two years later we split up. I was in such a state though that I couldn't look after the girls and they went to stay with his mum, and I didn't see them for about three months. I was on anti-depressants and I had dropped to about six and a half stone in weight. I could only live from one day to the next.

When I left Stewart, there were a lot of personal problems to sort out. He had physically abused me and in my own family I had been abused as a child as well. So looking back now, I can see that I had just married into a worse situation, because living with Stewart was not a normal family life. I thought it was the norm though. For instance he was into wife swapping and he made me go to bed with other men, actively encouraging me to go out with men so that I could tell him what it was like. In the end I just felt humiliated and hated myself for what I had done. I ended up drinking and left him. I had been married to him for eight years.

I lived in a bedsitter in London and I eventually got a job as a barmaid, and then as a receptionist. I met this guy who I thought was wonderful and he would take me out for drinks. He would come shopping with me and did everything I thought a man ought to do in a relationship, you know, sharing things. One night I went to a friend's twenty-first party and he came up to me there and just beat me up. I had two black eyes, a broken nose and cracked ribs. I had bruises all over my body and he nearly killed me. He was put away for six months. After that I went home to my mum but she still didn't want me back. I was told to get on with it myself. The kids were still living with Stewart's mum so I didn't have them to look after. I went to live with my gran, my mum's mother.

I then met Bill, who was my second husband and I think I married him on the rebound. He was in the Marines so we had to move down to Portsmouth. That was in 1981, during the Falklands. I got pregnant with Katie and I felt so ill. I think it was because I didn't have my three girls and I felt I had no right to be pregnant again, if I couldn't look after my children. I had my fourth daughter but I had dreadful postnatal depression after that. I was not well after the birth and a friend looked after Katie for the first six weeks. But then Bill brought her back and said she was my daughter and I should look after her. Shortly after that Nicki and Dawn, my two eldest girls, came to live with me because they wanted to. I explained to them that I hadn't really left them, but that I had married too young and that we had separated when I had been too ill to look after them. They accepted that and it was great to have them again.

I had another daughter, Clare, my fifth girl. There was no way I wanted a boy anyway. I began working nights as a care assistant and Bill could look after them when I was out. He had had a vasectomy when Clare was born because we did not want any more. But I became pregnant again and I remember sitting in the doctor's waiting room thinking he was going to believe the worst of me. However they found out that his tubes had rejoined and so I was pregnant again. They offered me an abortion but I couldn't cope with that. So I had another baby, a sixth girl. Things began to go wrong. Bill was more interested in playing basketball for the Marines, he was in the national team and played for Scotland. He always put the Marines first, before his family. After that things went downhill. I wanted to move nearer to my brother and sister, but he wanted to move to Scotland to be near his mum and dad. So we moved to Wester Hailes in Edinburgh. His parents didn't really accept me, especially his father because I hadn't given him a grandson. I stopped going to see them and then Bill and I split up and I was on my own again. Nicki was fine, doing alright at school, but Dawn was causing problems and I put her into care because I couldn't handle her any more. She was running away from home, pinching things and into drugs.

Then I met Henry and he was really nice. He came from a very different upper-class background but we had a fantastic time together. We were worlds apart but we got on so well. He was mad, totally crazy. But I knew I had to end the relationship because he would feel in time that I was after his money.

I then had my first wee boy, Christopher. He was born on my thirty-sixth birthday. After that I decided I wanted to get on with my life, to go to college. Then I met Al and he was really nice. Eleven years younger than me. He is Mr Wonderful. I can talk to him about everything. He is so understanding and kind. I have known him for four years now and we have a five month old baby boy, Jonathan. Al likes being a househusband. He loves being at home with the kids. I go to college and to work. I now feel that I've got to the stage in my life when I can do my own thing. I know I have all these kids but that doesn't mean to say I want to stay at home all day with them. I want to catch up with what I missed years ago.

Nicola is 23, Dawn 21, Hayley 17, Katie 12, Clare 10, Amy 9, Christopher 4 and Jonathan four months. And I am a granny at 40! Dawn has a baby girl, Rebecca Violet, and she lives with her partner in London. She came up here to have the baby because she said I was the most important person in her life. We have a very close relationship now. I am sad that she is down south and I can't be with them.

We survive on income support at the moment. We get in our hand £143 a week and that is basically for food and bills. But by the time we pay bills, put money away for insurance, the catalogue, school money, there is nothing left. At Christmas there won't be much for them.

Childcare is so difficult. There is some provision for nursery care and after-school care at primary level, but once they go to secondary school they have to become latchkey kids. Even if I did manage to get work I'd have to earn over £250 a week to look after us. Then they would take away school dinner money and uniforms and we'd have to start paying rent. You get caught in a trap of financial problems. So you can't win. They don't make it easy for mothers to go to work in order to support their families.

'Some women, and a handful of men, choose to stay out of employment because they believe that their children need more of their time than they could otherwise give, but most are kept out by lack of available work and above all by lack of work that can be combined with parenting.'

Penelope Leach, CHILDREN FIRST.

Barbara Buckley [born 1954]

I believe a two-parent nuclear family is ideal, because it is the parents themselves who need each other for a healthy, stable emotional life while bringing up the children. I am ambivalent about divorce: perhaps people don't work hard enough at relationships, but it is better to part than to exist in a destructive environment. As regards single motherhood, it's fine to have a family on your own if that is what you want, but not just a way of escaping other decisions. I think single parenthood would be very tough.

Jano Rochefort [born 1955]

The traditional family hasn't been that wonderful for women so I'm not surprised that many are now refusing to go down that path. But having children is hard work and if you don't have a husband or partner, you do need other support. I very much miss having an extended family living near by. My mother died several years before my children were born. Children need a whole community of grandparents, aunts and uncles, cousins, friends, and neighbours let alone two parents.

Women are saying 'What about me for a change? Why should I be the one who always sacrifices? Whose idea was this marriage institution anyway?'

Some men are slowly changing their views with regard to child-care responsibilities but it depends on how much parenting they are expected to do. Many still feel that women have a natural instinct for mothering so it can all be left to them.

Trudi Barnett [born 1954]

My marriage was going wrong before I had my third baby and we separated by the time he was three years old. We didn't get divorced for about seven years, my husband always hoped that we would get together again. But I knew it wouldn't happen. I knew I wanted to marry again and start a new life. I actually got divorced on Christmas Eve and I married my second husband on the 15th March. I don't think my first husband even knew I was seeing someone. I am sure no one knew he had been there in the background for about five years!

I was thirty-six when I divorced and married again. My husband was nine years younger than me so it was quite a strain on him taking me and my three boys on. The main problem was that I had had a sterilisation after my third baby was born. Before we married, of course, I knew that we would want our own family. So off I went to the doctor and he got me an appointment to see if I could have a reversal of sterilisation. Then I had a medical investigation, and they agreed that this would be possible. It took about eight weeks to recover fully and it was very sore indeed but all worth it in the end. They said they would give me until the January to see if I became pregnant. If not, they would be be able to give me a little help to conceive as I was getting older. I was very lucky indeed that it worked. I became pregnant within six months and I have now had two children by my second husband.

I think the reason for the high divorce rate is that many women nowadays are either marrying at a later age or at least having children much later; they have had their independence, had a good job or career, and when they stop that kind of life and have children, it is such an incredible change. Any woman who has a baby would say it is a complete shock to the system, emotionally and physically. The books do not tell the whole story. Babies do not sleep and eat every four hours. So mothers may feel they cannot cope as easily as they thought they would, and they might resent their partner who is probably still living an ordinary life, being part of the working and social life they both used to enjoy. The expectations of both the husband and wife for a happy family life together often don't work out and that is when the marriage begins to break down.

———— • ————

'She watches herself, the young matron, efficiently removing a wet and stinking nappy which her nose and fingers deny, wiping, powdering, rebinding the child's legs with a fresh square of white towelling. She hugs the baby, poor little thing, what a start in life, I will love you. I will make it up to you, I swear, you shall be happy as I am not, I will do my best to be a perfect mother to you.'

Michele Roberts, A PIECE OF THE NIGHT.

———— • ————

Winifred Fyfe [born 1955]

I often wonder how our marriage has lasted as long as it has. So many things have happened: my husband has gone through two redundancies and we've had times when we've had no money. One reason for not leaving him is that I have no family near here. I think if I had a family home near here I would have gone but there was nowhere for me to go with three children. I mean, we've stuck together because we've had no alternative. And I do care deeply for him. But there are times in a marriage when you question things; I've got to the point sometimes when I asked myself, 'Do I even *like* him?' – as bad as that! It has been difficult. Steven has had long terms of unemployment and it really has been a struggle but the girls haven't suffered. He has found it easier once the girls have got older, but he never really wanted children.

I often think that we women put men through terrible things; we expect them to work, support their wives and families, be good fathers, and they don't always get much thanks for it!

I find it hard to believe that people now, in the 1990s, still go into marriage with all the great white frocks, and the mothers swept along with the whole thing. I find that very hard, the romanticising of marriage.

I'm perhaps just too cynical – it's a really nice, happy day for the family but do they actually think that this is going to last?

It was the opposite for me with my mother warning me off getting married. I'll probably be like that with my daughter Sarah in a few years. I do think young girls go into marriage with this false idea of everlasting happiness. I don't know what they think it is going to be like; with all the reality of separation and divorce all around, they actually think that their relationship is going to be different.

So as I say, there was a point when I could have left the marriage and brought up my girls alone, but I'm glad I didn't. I think people should work at the marriage if there is still something there. You should question things carefully. Sit down in the dead of night and think, 'What do I feel for him; could I walk out?' And you may think, 'No, I couldn't', so obviously you still feel something. When you can sit down in the dead of night and rationally think 'I don't care for this person', then I think you have to do something about it. I've never had that feeling. I've always felt, 'Well, yes I do care about him.'

But I think people get caught up in the idea of marriage. It seems to be the only ambition for some people and I just think how sad, there has to be something else. I think marriage is unnecessary, but that if you choose it, you should do your best to make it work.

Once my children leave home I'd like to think I had a life after them, that my husband and I will still have a good relationship together. It does scare me, the thought that I'll get to the end of our family life and I'll see this person and think 'What is there left?' I'd like to think I had another life that didn't revolve around my children, sitting waiting for grandchildren. I wouldn't like that.

My sister had her baby at 21 and now her daughter, much to her horror, has become engaged at 21. I'd advise my girls to enjoy their lives and wait until they're over 25 or even 30 before having children. Family life take so much from you: it's like being sucked dry sometimes. But I don't want to put my prejudices on to my children and if one of the girls came and said 'I'm pregnant and I want to have the baby', I would accept it and do my best to help, but I'd be disappointed.

'Cathy' [born 1955]

I suppose it is true that some women are marrying, or at least 'settling down', at a later age, having enjoyed an opportunity to study, work and develop a career. Then the *Cosmo* idea of baby-as-accessory begins to hit them when they reach thirty-something, and family life takes over.

I also view the rise in the divorce rate as being accompanied by a 'tinselled' stress on marriage, aimed especially at the female section of the population. I think women who count on the 'New Man' believe in fairy tales!

Roma Young [born 1956]

Each one of my children's best friends comes from a broken home. They are either living with a father or mother. I find that very odd and very sad, that this now seems to be the normal family set up – the broken home.

With regard to single mothers, I don't know whether this will happen to my two daughters. They know the facts of life, they know to be careful. Lindsay keeps telling me it is not for her, it is not what she wants, and I trust her enough. Lindsay was fifteen when her little brother was born and she saw the birth, here at home. She was very emotional afterwards and couldn't go to school for three days she was so upset. It wasn't that she was unhappy, but because for the first time she understood the reality of childbirth and what having a baby really means. She knows from experience that a baby needs to be cared for twenty-four hours a day. She and Kerry have both had to babysit for their brother and I have come back to find the baby and both girls crying because they have not been able to cope, so they know it is not just a fun thing, having a baby. As a result I don't think they'll jump into motherhood very quickly.

I don't know if it is because girls just want to get away from home, so falling pregnant appears to be the only option. I do know young girls who have had an absolute life of hell at home, with parents and step-parents not understanding them, and under those circumstances a baby seems to be the only way out. They need help, and the parent or guardian needs advice. Perhaps if the social services offered more help to young girls then there would be fewer teenage mothers.

Jo Davidson [born 1960]

Family roles have certainly changed with a better sharing of childcare and household responsibilities. In fact I think men have changed their views more than many women have.

I don't see a problem if people aren't married and decide to have children, although I don't really understand how women cope on their own unless they have a strong network of support. I also don't believe children always need two parents. They benefit from being with people who respect each other and the child and many traditional parental relationships do not provide this.

I think the current divorce rate merely provides statistical evidence of marital breakdown which has been happening for decades anyway. It is just that people were not able to divorce so easily, because of the social stigma, financial circumstances or complex laws.

Sue Rook [born 1960]

I think it must be very hard to bring up a child on your own. I also think the child misses out. In this day and age, pregnancy is avoidable. It annoys and upsets me that people have 'accidents'. I find the lack of accountability and responsibility alarming and frightening.

Often these are very young girls, *children having children,* who are just perpetuating a cycle of deprivation. I fear that society will increasingly degenerate into the haves and have nots. With the stable framework of a family often absent, I worry that ultimately the idea of obligation and duty to others will just get lost in a sea of selfishness. As a mother I worry about my child growing up in that sort of world.

My husband and I, married now for four years, are lucky that we are a traditional nuclear family. We also have an extended family living very close by; my parents are an hour away and my father-in-law visits regularly. A very stable family unit; perhaps it is unusual in the 1990s to have such wonderful family support.

I am saddened by the rise in divorce. Everyone is looking for *personal* fulfillment, at the expense of each other's happiness.

I do see that parental roles are changing and fathers do help a great deal more, but ultimately the responsibility for thinking about childcare and domestic things often lies with the mother.

Julie Smith [born 1961, daughter of Patricia Turner]

I was homeless when I first fell pregnant. I was staying in different houses up at Wester Hailes. I was seventeen and I wasn't using any contraception. I think I was five months when I went to the doctor for the first time. I was sick and everything and friends said, 'You're pregnant!' and I said I was definitely not pregnant, because I didn't want to believe it.

I had actually wanted a family when I was young, thirteen or fourteen. I thought, 'When I grow up, I'm going to get married and have a proper house and have a nice family'. But when I did get pregnant, I got married to this guy but I didn't really want to marry him. He was in the army and I saw it was a way to get a house and get oot of the homeless situation I was in.

We went to stay with his mum and dad in Kilmarnock for a wee while. Then he was sent across to Germany and I was meant to go there to live in the married quarters with him, but I didnae go. I went to stay with my dad. I didnae know him as he'd been in prison a lot when I was a kid and my mum had left him. I just felt it would be a bad idea to go abroad at that age, pregnant. I just wanted to stay here and see what happened.

I went to stay with my dad, my step-mother, her son, and my two brothers who live with him. There were quite a few of us. I had the baby and they gave me a flat but it was in a bad area, really awful flats, and there was a lot of prostitution going on in the district. I lasted there for nine months and then I came back to Edinburgh.

I was very badly off. To begin with, I got some money from my husband's army pay, £25 a week. Then when I came back here, my husband left the army and came to live with me but we didn't get on too well. He got a job in the Post Office. Then he killed my dog. I came home and the police were there, and I heard he had beaten my dog to death with a shovel. Crazy. So that made me realise there was something wrong with him. At times he was a really, really nice person and then he would behave really different. I mean you would have to put the chest of drawers against the bedroom door to stop him coming in. He would be making noises and banging on the wall.

So I left him and went to stay with my mum and her boyfriend. But that didn't last long. She put me out so I had to go to a hostel. Then I got a house at Muirhouse.

I was really in despair. I had no one to help me cope. I went to the doctor to see if I could get some valium. He did give me valium and I was meant to take two at night to help me sleep. But the bairn was screaming all night, so me taking the valium was no good. I took it once, and I was all drowsy and sleepy but the bairn was greeting, so what was the point of that? Then I got up the next again day, and I couldn't move. I thought this was worse than before and I knew I couldn't go on like that for the rest of my life, so I gave up the valium.

I then started going out with Lennie, a guy I knew before I got married. So we got back together, and we're still together and we had two kids.

I had the first one right away. I think the reason was because I wanted to settle down. It was always in my head to settle down and my idea of a happy family life was the husband, the wife and the bairns. I have never had that and I thought that was what normal life was all about. I wanted a proper family. I didn't marry Lennie though. At first I did want to get married again but my ideas changed. So we just live together. Although I thought that marriage and kids was what I wanted, I realise now at thirty-three that it is not what it is all about.

If I could do it all again, I would wait before having kids. My first was really hard to cope with because I was so young. I had helped my mum with all my brothers and sisters and stuff like that but he was far worse than them. The second one was easier, and the third one was fine as I was older. I don't say it was easy, but easier. But with the first bairn, I was too young and didnae ken what to do and had nowhere to stay.

I'll make sure my kids learn from this. I want them to be educated. I never went to school much and yet my kids have never had a day off school. I have had to go back to learn, so I tell them, 'Look at me! I'm thirty and I have to do this school work now because I missed out earlier.' My son, who is fifteen, understands and settles down to his work. It helps them I think. I've been studying English and maths and one day I'll get a job; I'd like to do something with youth work. I get on well with teenagers.

People say Lennie is laid-back but he's not really. He is just calm. He is amazing. But I think where I live, how I have lived, with a lot of difficulties since childhood, makes a difference to how I have coped.

My house is OK now. We've got three rooms. I'm on the Social as Lennie hasn't got a job, just bits and pieces – some garage work here and there. It's very hard. He doesn't give me very much to help. Even if he had it, he wouldn't give me enough to pay the bills. I'm definitely not happy but there is nothing I can do about it. Well, there is, but as I say, having the bairns, it would be worse to leave and be on my own.

I keep thinking that if I keep going with my studies, when I am forty my youngest will be sixteen, so I could leave then and get a job. I wouldn't need to worry about money and looking after them. But leaving now, and just surviving on the social, that's not the way. It would be difficult to support them on my own.

'My life seemed to be a vacuum of desperate nothingness. Surely there must be some reason why I was married to a man who was my enemy most of the time

and the mother of children I merely tolerated. I must break free, I thought, panicking . . .

. . . If only I could pack up and leave it all I thought, but I had no suitcase, no clothes and worst of all, no money. . . . Meantime I must wash the dishes and tidy up a bit, before I could do anything.'

Agnes Owens, A WORKING MOTHER.

———◆———

Diane Connelly [born 1961]

My husband's parents separated just before we married, so it made us think very seriously about what we were doing when we saw the heartbreak it caused.

As a midwife I often see children viewed as a commodity: couples have nice homes, a good job and so on, and now want a nice child to fit in. No leeway is left for damaged children or loss or problems of any kind. Society fails these couples. It also puts terrible stress on midwives and fear of litigation is an increasing problem. In my opinion couples have an unreal expectation of childbirth – they've read the book, seen the film and now want a wonderful experience to 'bind them eternally'. In reality it is often messy, painful and frightening. Then come the stressful, demanding years of caring and nurturing which change your life for ever. Many couples are · not prepared for what family life is really like at all. Many men still have a very traditional view of a mother's role because they have been conditioned into it from their childhood and social expectations.

Lucy Owen [born 1961]

I feel very lucky in that I have known my husband for fourteen years, we've been together for eight and married for five. We are best friends. In so many cases extended family ties are looser because of children living much further away to find work or whatever, so advice and more importantly support from mothers and grandmothers is lacking. With so much divorce these days, a happy family life is sadly not very common. I also see divorce as inevitable given the traditional British lack of male and female communication. In my experience, men are certainly changing their attitude towards their role and responsibilities as fathers; they are more loving, and will change nappies, bathe and feed babies, but I think women are still dominant in the home and in the maternal role of bringing up the children.

I think children do need both parents, whether married or not. I feel worried for the children of young single mothers with no influential male role model in the home.

Angela Blanchard [born 1962]

I think the traditional nuclear family is a figment of some planner's imagination. Traditionally we lived in extended families, where women shared the work and childcare. I do not think it is natural or healthy for one woman to be left in sole charge of her children. Children thrive in the company of several children of a range of ages and adults too. I think nuclear family life is hard on parents because of the strain on their relationship; young women used to have mothers and grandmothers in the home or nearby to offer advice and a helping hand. The friends who have coped with the early years of parenthood best are those with immediate family within five miles, who can help share the burden of responsibility.

I think enough has been said about single women – what about all the single men and married men who duck their responsibilities? I know at least two women who have left physically violent husbands for the sake of their children's safety, and a number of others who have left or thought of leaving husbands who, while outwardly kind and reasonable, have been so repressive and intolerant in their private lives that they have allowed their wives no individual life of any meaning.

Many couples find, as I did, that during cohabitation or the early years of marriage, both husband and wife perhaps are out at work, so it is easy to maintain equality. Once children arrive mother starts – perhaps subconsciously – to follow the model her own mother set, or she might try to resist it and do what she wants to do, but her husband will almost invariably expect her to fall into the lifestyle of his own mother, which might be completely different, and this is where conflict arises. This is often the crux of the problem, that men and women have such vastly different expectations of family life.

I do believe married couples are often under tremendous strain once children arrive, which is never predicted, so that marriage is sometimes undertaken too lightly; many couples expect marriages to provide constant happiness rather than a working partnership for life.

I have however witnessed not so much a change in the role of mothers but definitely one in the role and image of fathers. To my knowledge, my father never cooked, washed, cleaned, tidied, vacuumed or shopped for the family; my husband does these things, frequently.

Lorna Reid [born 1962]

I think there should be freedom of choice for all women, and if a baby is born to loving parents, lack of marriage should not hurt. Love and a caring, responsible parent is more important than a stereotypical family.

I see the rise in divorce as a result of women finding financial independence through work and successful careers. Marriages may have been just as unhappy in previous generations, except that women had no opportunity to leave the security of the marital home.

Carol Ziyat [born 1962]

I think there are more serious mothers these days, as often they are generally older before having their children and have taken a conscious decision to have them, say in their thirties, when they are more mature and intelligent about the whole business.

If single women are confident about giving their children a happy, stable upbringing, then why not? I believe it is not essential to have two parents – two happy parents yes, if not one happy parent.

There has been a lot of change in society and family life. People, mainly women, are no longer prepared to stay in unhappy marriages that are going nowhere, because they are more independent and have the means to leave.

In general, I believe men have not altered their views about the women's role as mother and homemaker very much, but I am lucky in having a very helpful husband who is not just willing but insists on participating in the upbringing of our daughter. I think promoting happiness in the household, especially towards the children, is the best method, even at times of fatigue and stress. A little smile in return can make a world of difference.

Moyra Heggie [born 1950, head of department and tutor in midwifery]

Many schoolgirl mothers conceal their pregnancies until it is too late to terminate. You quite often get girls coming in *in labour*, not knowing what is wrong. How their mothers don't know their daughters are pregnant, I just don't know.

The youngest mother I delivered was twelve years old. She came in with her mother who herself did not look as if she was old enough to have a twelve year old. I was in charge of the labour ward at the time, and I remember the houseman was quite young and he really looked ill. He said, 'My God, she is younger than my kid sister!' And it really hit him, how awfully sad it was. She looked so immature. Of course some twelve year olds look extremely mature, more like fifteen or sixteen, but she looked like a little girl.

Certainly amongst the teenagers in this area, there are many pregnancies. There is a very good family planning service but they don't choose to use it. The clinics are allowed to prescribe to the under 16s, without the parents' consent if it is thought to be in the best interest of the girl, but they do try to persuade them to talk to their parents. There are Brook Advisory Centres and teenage clinics on a Saturday morning.

In this area, Camberwell, South London, they are very liberal with their abortions. Different health authorities have very contrasting views on this. Camberwell has very good counselling services, and they won't allow a girl to have a termination unless she has been to a counsellor, which I think is good. The abortion counsellors are superb, wonderfully understanding. But you still get these young girls, fourteen or fifteen, having babies. It is not uncommon.

It is one of the 'Health of the Nation' targets to reduce teenage pregnancies. It was increasing for a time as I think it is associated with lack of job opportunities, so it is a way of proving you are an adult. You know, 'I am a parent.'

A lot of people believe single motherhood is associated with girls wanting a home of their own and getting on the council housing list. I don't think it is really. But we have had and still have a teenage clinic. It is run by midwives, and is more a drop in centre, providing education then and there, and there is a doctor in Bromley who does a lot of work with teenagers. There are different social class areas and ethnic groups who need their own advice. Camberwell is around fifty per cent white Caucasian, whereas Bromley is about 90 per cent. But there are still many teenagers who are delivered over there. And not many are legally married. A lot are in stable relationships, cohabiting, but some are not – just girls on their own, perhaps choosing to have a baby.

There is very little adoption now for these single mothers. I remember one girl when I worked in Dulwich, who was from a traditional Irish Catholic background and whose family did not know she was pregnant.

She was admitted antenatally and had a Caesarean section. She looked after the baby for a few days and then it went into a foster home. She ended up in the psychiatric unit, and was in contact with us for quite a while afterwards as there was no one else with whom she could share her feelings. The baby's father was in Ireland and was not providing any support. She felt the best thing was if the baby was adopted.

Sometimes the younger teenage mothers sail through childbirth with no problems, unlike those who feel they have planned the pregnancy and are well-prepared. They often have a tough time.

The older ones, those in their forties and having their first babies, are amazing as well. There was one woman, whom I believe was unsure how she got pregnant, and she just sailed through the whole thing and didn't let it bother her. There are others who know it is their one and only chance and they get quite twitchy about it.

There are far more women nowadays having first babies in their early forties. We had one of our own midwives having a baby when she was 43 or 44. She desperately wanted a natural, normal birth, if she could have it. Typical of course, nurses, midwives and doctors all do the wrong things. Anyway she had been in labour all day and the midwife suggested giving her morphine, not usually done, and it knocked her for six. She had a good sleep over night, and they got things moving the next day. The senior registrar was providing care and he was wonderful in letting her try for a normal delivery. And she did, but it was tough going.

You don't get many having the big families these days. You get women who go through hell to have one. The motivation to have a child is so strong, and then you get the others who have had terminations who then lose the baby they did want, some years later. There are some very sad cases.

Rachel Hanks [born 1967]

In many ways motherhood and family life have not changed at all. The majority of women that I meet in parks and playgroups are very stereotypical, and probably have lives similar to their own mothers. I have found the whole experience much more difficult than I could ever imagine, largely due to the British attitude to children in public places and public transport. Housework and childcare are still very difficult to divide equally between partners and I suspect the rise in divorce is very much a result of women deciding to put their foot down at last.

Rachel Lockey [born 1967]

I decided to have Bella on my own as I didn't think the relationship with her father would work out. We split up when I was six months pregnant. He just told me he wouldn't be around for me anymore. Just before Bella was born, I phoned him for a chat, to talk about financial arrangements and visiting. And he said, 'Oh I'm sorry, my girlfriend says I am not allowed to have anything to do with you or the baby.' And I said, 'Is that what you want too?' I was rather shocked at this. But then they started sending her birthday cards and Christmas cards but nothing to me. He never contacted me about how I was or anything. Then they wrote to me when Bella was three, a ridiculous letter saying that they – he and his new girlfriend – would like to see Bella. I hadn't seen him for four years by this time, so I ignored it. I thought if he really wants to see me and our child he can approach us properly. I felt it was an appeasement of guilt. You know he could say to his friends, 'Well I asked to see Bella, but she wouldn't let me.' And he hasn't contacted me since then so I think this is right. I don't know how he really feels but I feel very distanced from him. It hasn't been painful for me, because we weren't involved for very long.

I don't think a two-parent family is essential. For some, marriage or a relationship really works well, but of course for a lot of people it doesn't and they split up. It is nice not to have to be dependent on it. It is all about choices, to be able to say 'I want to do this', 'I want to have a baby on my own, and there is nothing to stop me.'

I think the criticism about single mothers is not so much wrong as just not based on the truth. A lot of those women do not want to be on their own, they certainly have not all just decided to have a baby. Many of them have had, say, three children and then after that their husband has left them. I have never had a council property or even expected to ask for a council flat. I think it is a myth – the image of the single mother. I am in a minority in that I did choose to have a baby on my own. I wanted to be a single parent. Most women do not choose to be single mothers. It is hard work having a child; most women do want a partner around, whether that is a man or a good friend. They are not having babies just to get a flat and more money. And it is not a lot of money, it is about £70 to live on if you are on income support.

The reality is that people are conditioned by society into having a partner and to marry. Then when they have a baby and the relationship goes wrong, and the woman, or the man sometimes, becomes a single parent, it is still stigmatised. The government has recently been scapegoating them. It is a lot of playing around with words and ideas, but there is not a lot of truth in it. It is playing around with long standing ideas and morals which, if you look behind them, they are not real anyway.

———◆———

'The mythology of ungovernable female appetite permeates the furious response, for instance, to the increasing numbers of single mothers. Instead of inquiring into the causes of marriage breakdown, into the background to so many fatherless families, into the reasons why women have become heads of households, instead of attending to the needs of women who are raising children on their own, instead of acknowledging the responsibility most of them are showing towards the task of mothering, and recognising the way the work of care still stitches together the torn fabric of society, lone mothers have come under prolonged and continuing attack.'
Marina Warner, MONSTROUS MOTHERS.

———◆———

Andrea Duffin [born 1970]

It's interesting how people are so conditioned by social conventions, with fixed notions of what's morally right and wrong. When I was pregnant a lot of things were difficult for us. Not only our families but some of my friends didn't understand me at all, because most were going on to university or something. My best friend and close friends were fine and are still great about it all. But some didn't try to understand: 'Silly girl, getting pregnant', they seemed to say. They obviously thought I'd become a non-being, having fallen pregnant without planning to, without being married, twenty-five and living in a suburban house, – that kind of thing.

Barry and I got engaged, I think because I felt rather vulnerable. Barry wasn't bothered but it was quite a small community, in Fife, and I felt that people were talking about me as if I wasn't respectable. So I got this notion in my head that if I got a ring on my finger that would help. So we got engaged but it was a bit of a sham because we haven't wanted to get married, and I think if I had been in a saner frame of mind, not my pregnant mind, I would never have done it.

Now we have two girls, and I don't know why I am still not keen to get married. My dad now has a third wife and I went to this third wedding and heard him say, 'Till death do us part' and I thought, 'Rot!' It's not just that. On the religious side I don't know what I believe in or don't believe in. I don't want to be a hypocrite. I think we are contented *not* being married as others are who are married. I used to say, 'I don't believe in marriage', but I do now if that is what people want and think is best. A lot of friends are now getting married. A close friend married last year but Molly had just been born so I missed the wedding. I saw her photographs afterwards and they both seem so very happy. They are so settled as if something has miraculously changed in them. I am happy for her. My not-being-married gives me the same feeling. I think I would feel very tied down if I was married. Not that I feel there is any less commitment between Barry and I. I think it will be just as hard for us to split up as any married couple with two children. I don't think it makes any difference. I think the commitment is there because we *want* it it be there, not because we had a wedding day.

I just feel very settled not being married. I don't like getting dolled up – I could never be a fairy on a Christmas Tree! As people say to me, I'd never get a wedding dress to go with my Doc Martins, which is all I ever wear. It is just not me. I want to be independent, I don't want to be Mrs Nobody, I don't want to feel attached to him, but that we are two equal partners who have come together. I would never want to change my name.

Gillian Watson [born 1977]

I was going out with my boyfriend for six months and I fell pregnant when I was fourteen. Mark was seventeen. I told one of my friends and I asked her if she would help me have an abortion because I was scared to tell my mum. When it came to the day to go to the clinic for the abortion, she said no, she wouldn't help me. She decided that she was totally against abortion now, having thought about it. I was really angry with her, because she had said yes and then said no. I told another friend and she went with me to the Brook Advisory Clinic, but by this time I was three months pregnant and so they advised me about what I should do. They said they would tell my mum for me. I said 'No. I'll tell her.'

I went up to my boyfriend's house the next again day, and my mum phoned his house to tell me to come home because she wanted to see me. I knew then that she knew and she must have found out from somebody. I was petrified. When I got home she showed me this bit of paper, and it had the clinic address on it. She said 'What's this for?' And I said, 'Well I tried to tell you.'

'Are you pregnant?'

'Aye.'

'What do you want to do about it?' She was brilliant, she really was. She was understanding and not really angry with me. She started knitting that night!

I knew right away I was pregnant. I don't know how but I knew. I went to the doctor and had a test done and I was right. We hadn't ever used contraception, I don't know why.

So once my mum knew and was fine about it, that was one less problem to worry about. During the pregnancy she came to every doctor's appointment with me. I had a horrible pregnancy because I was in and out of hospital quite a lot with kidney infections and things. I was very nervous and scared the whole time. I didn't feel well and would take it out on my boyfriend. He was very good really; he said he would stick by me and be happy with whatever decision I took. His mum thought we were too young and that I should have an abortion.

Then when the time came, they started the labour off because I was two days late and I didnae have any water left. My waters had broken. They told me that there might be something wrong with the baby as he was too wee. I was in labour for twenty-three hours and when he arrived he was actually 8lb 3 oz. He was massive!

He was born at 4.15 in the afternoon and they took him away to check him over. A nurse came back at 3 in the morning and woke me to tell me that he was up in the special care unit because he had a blood infection; He had a heart murmur and everything was wrong with him. I stayed in hospital for an extra week and then I got out and was alright by then. I don't know if his illness was because I was so young. I've never thought about it.

I'm now seventeen and I live with my mum, my step-dad, my little sister, and little Jamie who is one and a half. My big sister used to live with us. She wasn't happy about the baby and kept saying how could I have been so stupid. My wee sister was ten when Jamie was born and she is very excited about it, but my mum gives my baby more attention than her so she does get annoyed.

I've got my name down for a house and I hope to get one quite soon hopefully. My boyfriend lives with his mum but has always come to see Jamie and he gives me money every week for the baby. So that's good.

My mum is fine with the baby but she tells me quite a lot of the time that I am not a good mother. She wants me to do things her way and I want to go out with my friends. She doesn't want me to go out and feels I should stay at home and look after Jamie. We argue quite a lot. I don't want to go out all the time, but just once in a wee while. She doesn't think that's right, unless it's with my big sister.

My friends were fine when I told them I was pregnant. They weren't really shocked at the news because they have had pregnancy scares too. They were very supportive, apart from the friend who said she wouldn't help me have an abortion. I'm glad I didn't have the abortion now, but at the time I couldn't have told my mum and I didn't know what to do.

It hasn't been easy looking after Jamie. Sometimes it's OK but I do get depressed because I don't have the normal life of a seventeen year old. I do want to go out with my friends who are having a good time. But if I don't think how old I am, it's alright.

I worried about what I was doing to begin with, caring for this little baby, but it came quite naturally so it was alright really.

I go every day to the Wester Hailes Education Centre, which has a crèche for babies. It is a normal school, but it is a centre for young mums who come from all over the Edinburgh area to continue their education while they are pregnant and after the baby is born. I heard about it from my guidance teacher at my old school who advised me it would be best for me to go there because if I'd stayed at school I would have been a bad influence on the other girls! I refused to go first of all because I hated school, but then I was brought to see it. They give you a taxi to get there and home again, there are free dinners and the crèche for the babies. I was nervous the first day but after a few weeks I thought it was really great. And it's good to mix with all the other young mums; some are younger than me, fourteen or fifteen, and we have a moan about our mums telling us what to do. We talk about how our babies are developing and problems we have with their feeding and sleeping. Kate Hart runs the school; she is really good and helps and advises us, and she treats us like adults not like silly schoolgirls. It is really good here.

I can't imagine life without him now. I sometimes have regrets when I hear of my friends getting jobs and enjoying themselves. I am happy most of the time, but I do get depressed thinking what did I do this for, why was I so stupid, but I wouldn't be at this school now if I hadn't had Jamie. I would have left school as I hated it. But I am so glad I've continued my education and I love school now and they canny get rid of me!

So things haven't been too bad. I've never known anyone to be unkind or say anything bad about me having a baby. Maybe some of the girls at school, maybe they do behind my back. But now I do realise I was far too young to have a child. I am not having any more. I was far too young and immature to have a baby.

I think it has made me grow up very quickly. I do think so. It makes you responsible. And just think, when I am thirty Jamie will be almost grown up and then I can go out and enjoy myself while my friends are having babies. That will be good!

The worst thing about having a baby at my age is thinking about my friends doing what they want to do, and I am stuck at home with a child who won't go to bed until half ten at night. The best thing is coming to this school and continuing my education because that is going to be good for me and Jamie, because then I'll be able to get a good job.

Most of the time though, I do like being a mother.

CHAPTER NINE

Having it all: Fighting for Equality

'Women can Have-It-All: men, family and a career if they really want.'
Helen Gurley-Brown, Editor, COSMOPOLITAN.

'I have yet to hear a man ask for advice on how to combine marriage and a career.'
Gloria Steinem, American writer and feminist.

Barbara Littlewood [Sociologist at Glasgow University]

The rise in employment of married women and mothers has been particularly noticeable since the 1960s and 1970s. More recently it has become the era of women returners; this is quite a novel and dramatic phenomenon. The women who have worked until they married or had their first child, and then go back to work immediately afterwards. What we are now seeing is that women are going back to work in between having children. They are not waiting until their family is complete or at school. The period in which women stay off work caring for children, is dropping significantly. Britain has a very high percentage of women in employment, especially in part-time work, compared with other European countries. Employers have been able to increase their labour force in a very flexible way by taking on part-time and short-contract staff who can be laid off in times of slump. They have inferior rights in terms of holiday, sick pay, maternity pay and National Insurance contributions.

I think we've seen some kind of revolution in the expectations of young women, about what they can expect out of life. It is not that they have to choose between marriage and motherhood or a career. More and more women feel they can combine both, and they want to combine both. I think this has had a great impact on their relations with other family members, especially on their husbands or partners. This change in women's employment has had a dramatic effect on family life, childcare, and also, I believe, on the divorce rate. Women's attitude towards marriage, motherhood and their right to work has radically changed in the last decade or so.

Another of the changes that is affecting women is an extension of the fertile years by starting to have children later. Women feel they must give a full-time commitment to their profession or career as they cannot afford to take time out, so they daren't risk taking maternity leave. They postpone having children so that having a first baby at 35 or over 40 is not uncommon and also not such a medical risk as it would have been for their grandmothers.

'Women are choosing to start their families later than ever before. By the year 2000, 40 per cent of all babies will be born to women over thirty. The trend is most marked in the professional middle classes, where the executive mother is becoming the norm, choosing to have children after ten or fifteen years in a career. The birthrate among women in their twenties is lower than at any time since 1945. And after having the baby, nearly half of all working women return to work within nine months, twice as many as ten years ago. In the professional managerial class that figure is 60 per cent, double again. It's a sudden and marked social change. Many women would argue we still don't have real choice and won't have it until there's better state provision for childcare, but the possibility of being more than just a mother, more than just a childless worker, became real, even though it meant sacrifices as well as increased personal satisfaction. The Pill had brought another form of choice with it too; it gave women the power to choose when to have their children, to control their fertility.

The babies they have are wanted and planned babies, whose mothers have had years of independence and fulfilment and find that now is the time for children. Instead of feeling trapped by motherhood, they walk into it through choice and find it isn't a trap after all. They're less likely to feel resentful because they've had a fair crack of the whip already.'

Jill Parkin, EXECUTIVE MOTHER.

<hr>

Margaret Dixon [born 1905]

I would be too lazy to have-it-all! I can't think how they do it. But I remember asking my second daughter if she really needed to work and she said she couldn't bear being at home with the children all the time.

Patricia Rogers [born 1909]

I suppose human nature is not meant to change but there will always be people like me that want a shoulder to lean on, to have a husband who is the stronger personality. I had a better education than my husband and he liked that. Today so many women have important jobs, and if both husband and wife are supportive and admire each other's achievements then that is fine. But if the wife is very successful in her own right, and the husband is not doing so well and is jealous, I can understand that it can be hurtful and it won't work. Men aren't used to women being the dominant more successful partner. Quite frankly I didn't want to go back to teaching and for many years there was a marriage bar; married women would not be employed as teachers. Classes of forty children were hard work and I had five children and a husband to look after.

In a way women are more successful at bringing up children these days. They teach them to help around the house and to be much more independent, because these mothers are now out working. My daughter Carol, her husband is very good around the house, and it seems that he takes over the cooking. She gets cross because everyone says, 'Isn't Michael wonderful', as if this was so extraordinary in this day and age, and that he shouldn't really help in the house as that is really her job. But her husband does like cooking and their sons like cooking too.

My other daughter, a zoology graduate, was a university lecturer who left her children at home with a mature mother's help. Now their daughter is an engineer and has just had a baby at the age of 33. She is soon returning to work leaving her baby in the care of her sister-in-law.

———◆———

'You know I've been reading so many articles in the papers lately about how wrong it is that women teachers have to leave their work when they're married. There was one in the Daily Telegraph only this morning pointing out what an advantage a real experience of life is to a woman in charge of growing girls.'

'I think it's all nonsense about married women making better teachers' I said quickly. 'Nine times out of ten they're so occupied with the housekeeping and their own brats that their attention isn't on their work.'

Ruth Adam, I'M NOT COMPLAINING.

———◆———

May Stephen [born 1911]

I think it is very important for mothers to give up work for a little while for the sake of the child's development. The first year is so important as they learn so much. My son works in the north of England and he sent his son to the local school, but after one year he hadn't learnt anything so they went to see the headmaster. This is a mining area and and the school is full of miners' children. The mothers all go out to work full-time and nobody has spoken properly to these children. They weren't read to as babies or stimulated to play and learn to talk. So in this school the first year in the infants class is not spent teaching them the alphabet; the first year is spent teaching them to speak, to string two words together.

But it seems so many women go out to work so they can afford nice clothes and holidays and things they don't really need. Children need personal attention and to be nurtured by their mothers.

Mary Maclennan [born 1911]

I think it is very common these days for women to have-it-all, a career and children. One of my daughters has a very successful career in medicine but she couldn't have done it without leaving the children with a very good nanny from the start. If you have a career which takes years of training to develop, as in medicine – which you can't leave and come back two years later, it's not the way it works – you must stick to the job. So my daughter was very lucky and found a good full-time nanny when the children were very wee. That is ideal. A very good, reliable, live-in nanny to replace the mother in a way, when she is on night duty and working long days.

Doris Melling [born 1914]

I do know some women who do all three successfully but it must be difficult. They do need an understanding and helpful husband and then I think that they can add to family life, but they must find time for their children.

Joan Counihan [born 1915]

I do believe women are capable of running a home and working full-time, but it is not necessarily a right. I have done it myself for some years after I joined the civil service, when my youngest child was eleven, but the older children were able to help in the house and watch the younger ones.

Emily Hagues [born 1916]

My daughter Vivienne went back to her career in a laboratory when Emma was five. But it worked out fine because the children had their granny to see to them after school and they were very happy. I can understand women needing to work to pay for everything. I don't think they're selfish – they're doing it for the family.

There's one lady I know whose grandchild goes to a minder in Kintore who is paid £85 a week. I have a relative in Edinburgh who is a banker, and his wife works in the bank and they have a son who was two last August. He goes into a nursery two days a week and it costs her £70 just for those two days. And she provides all his food for the day. So it must cost a bit and take away from the extra money that she is making. I do think women should think twice about it. It's different when granny lives near by as she can always be there and the children feel at home and secure being with family.

Elizabeth Grey [born 1917]

There are too many mothers nowadays who seem to prefer to go out to work. I think if mothers want to work full-time, they're not going to have much enjoyment of their bairns. They'll be worrying and thinking about their work, they'll no have time to think of what their bairns are doing or needing. You see, with the likes of us, mothers of our generation, we couldna suit ourselves all the time. We'd always be saying, 'I hope the bairns are alright.' We'd worry about them all the time. They don't nowadays. There are far too many mothers that get other folk to look after their bairns. Usually that type of person, when they are with the bairns, they're full of the 'Oh, how lovely darling; hello darling', and they're awa oot, saying 'Mrs So-and-so will look after you'! They don't want to be with their bairns all day.

My daughters laugh at me when I say it won't be long until the time comes when it will be the men who'll look after the children. Because the women are taking over factory work and a lot of big jobs too . . . and I'm sure there's not many jobs left for these men now.

Lucy Firth [born 1917]

It shocked me when my daughter returned to teaching full-time after maternity leave as she had no financial necessity. Personally my daughter makes me feel tired. She has two small children and works full-time as a deputy headmistress. She says she doesn't want to waste her education and training. Did I do wrong to ensure that she had the education and training for a career which I missed? My grandchildren went to a private nursery at a few months old. I must admit they are very happy and self-possessed and, knowing nothing else, they accepted it. A lot would depend on the carer if we are to judge whether women should work full-time. My daughter's carer is very good.

Milicent Woolner [born 1917]

Not all mothers need to work. Their commitment to their children is very much second place. Others must work to make ends meet. They must be given the childcare help that is needed to enable them to help themselves.

Olive Banbury [born 1920]

It is impossible to do all this and enjoy life; a lot of outside help is needed to avoid frustrations. I do feel mothers should be at home with their children. A house sometimes isn't a home these days. For those women who choose a career instead of having children, I worry about the effect in some forty years' time, when there will be many very lonely retired career women with plenty of money and no family.

Joan Hill [born 1920]

Mothers should only continue with their careers if it can be done successfully and if the temperament of the individuals is such that no one suffers. I must confess to a niggling doubt; I wait to see how those children develop. I think there is still a hard core of male chauvinism – even amongst those who think they are supportive of women's role, so many women must find it difficult to juggle several jobs. Also in years to come, will the parents feel they have missed something?

Joyce Petchey [born 1922]

Women are quite capable of doing all three things but if they choose to do so they should not moan about having a lot to do. If one cannot cope, then do one thing at a time and be happy.

Joyce MacPherson [born 1923]

I don't think mothers can really have it all without something sliding. My eldest daughter was sensible, she didn't go back to work until her youngest was at school, but my middle daughter, who has three young children, went back to work because they are hard up. She is a teacher and she had no outside help and was stressed out coping with it all. We visited her last October. She couldn't find enough hours in the day to do everything. She was screeching at the children, rushing around like a maniac, and with no time to herself at all. I thought this was awful. This is no life. There are some days she couldn't cope.

But my daughter-in-law has an MA and hasn't worked since she had her two children; they are now eight and ten. She is still a full-time mother. She makes out she is a terrible mother but it's all put on. She takes them swimming and to the library. She helps them out at school, with baking, and is involved in running the house, decorating and painting, so they save because they don't have to pay someone to look after the children or decorate the house or do the gardening.

The children are being brought up in a happy, secure environment. They play musical instruments and go to Beavers and Brownies, and all of this needs Linda to chauffeur them around. This couldn't be done if she was working full-time because all these activities take place just after school. I think of them all and those two grandchildren have the best home life. But Elizabeth is working herself into the ground, trying to be the perfect mother and trying to do a full-time job as well. At least she has the school holidays with the children.

I do help out with the grandchildren if need be. If one of them is sick, I am phoned up and I have to go and look after them, because she is working.

Jane Ward [born 1924]

I do not think it is possible to generalise. That only leads to sweeping statements and they can be dangerous but when I see how women's attitude towards motherhood has altered since my day, I am not happy about the idea that having a job and having a child is a right. I have reservations about the numbers of rights we demand these days anyway. There are women who can have a career, children and run a home and do it all successfully. I did not work until my children were no longer babies, but then I had five children which very few do today, and there were very few if any crèches or even nursery schools when I started my family. By the time I retired colleagues at work were managing as career mothers perfectly well. We had a good crèche at work and they seem to manage to juggle it all. I do feel that working mothers are missing out a lot if someone else has the upbringing of their children. Why go through all the bother of having a baby if you don't want to enjoy it? And despite all we hear today about the trials and tribulations of motherhood, most of it is enjoyable. Where it is necessary to work in order to earn a crust and live, then sacrifices have to be made – like missing the chance to know your baby as a child, but if it is not essential to earn money, then it seems a pity to miss out on childhood.

Pauline Grisbrook [born 1924]

The main and radical change is that mothers feel encouraged to continue in their careers. There is no such thing as combining both. There are plenty of options now *not* to have children, not to have a career, not to be a single parent. Running a home is so much easier and quicker today, so give the time to the children. A second income is unnecessary if there are no playgroups, childminders or convenience foods to buy. Expensive holidays are not needed. Spend time with each other. What's the use of an expensive mortgage on a luxurious house if no one is ever there? This brings me to think of the sheer selfishness of some parents today, possibly bred of the higher standard of living, the welfare state, and easy divorce. I was fortunate in my career as nurses were very much needed, and I chose my working hours to suit my husband being at home. My husband and I didn't need to go out to socialise – we entertained at home, so never needed babysitters.

Davina Thorpe [born 1927]

If mothers can do it all from choice, good luck, but many make it harder for themselves and others by doing too much. They then feel it is expected of them but certainly not appreciated. You cannot do two or three jobs without help. If women only realised it is downright slavery for them – 'Having It All' is rubbish.

I did work part time when the youngest was at school but I was lucky my children had good health – all the mumps, measles, etc, were mostly taken by all of them when the eldest caught the infection! I always tried to fit work hours to their school hours as much as possible. My memories of my mother were work, work, work: washing, baking, gardening, and so on. She had no choice because of the expectations of her day. I never once remember her playing with us as children. As a mother, I wanted to be with my children as they grew up.

Grace Rae [born 1928]

I don't believe in having it all. If a mother wants a career, she needs a househusband or housepartner at home. Someone who can manage all three jobs successfully must be marvellous or a robot!

Joan Longmuir [born 1930]

Wonder Woman might manage it! It would certainly need a lot of cooperation from the partner. The way in which women have altered their attitude towards their role as wives and mothers, I think men are suffering by not really knowing what their place in the family is.

Barbara Henderson [born 1931]

It is too exhausting. You land in a trap that you can't get out of. The Government should pay mothers an allowance to stay at home so that there would be more jobs for men. They should reduce the pension to sixty and take men off the dole.

Margaret Henderson [born 1933]

I definitely do not agree with working mothers. Some people want everything. It is too much a notion of 'Keeping up with the Joneses'. The younger generation want granny to look after the baby while mum goes back to work.

Motherhood

Liz Sanderson [born 1938]

My daughter is a GP and she worked almost up to the time she had the baby, and she went back through choice almost three months later. The only suggestion I made when she went back to work was, 'Try and find somebody who will come to your home and look after the baby rather than use a nursery.' I do believe that a mother would rather know their child is warm and secure in their own home rather than unhappy at being in a nursery.

I remember when she got married she said, 'Don't expect to be a granny soon, because I must get through my training before I have a family.' She then did six months medicine, six months surgery and three-year GP training. I think having slogged for ten years in all, and she does love medicine, she feels she can't drop out of it because everything moves on so fast, drugs and treatment, so I was supportive of her carrying on her career despite having children.

I know when I hear young mothers today saying 'Oh, I couldn't bear to be stuck at home', I'm sad that they feel that way but I think some mothers who have had careers, suddenly panic at the thought of the end of the career they have worked so hard for. They find it difficult to adjust. I think if they would only meet other mothers in a similar situation that might be an enormous support for them. I do admire the way mothers can manage to combine children, husbands and jobs, but I think that when it goes wrong, there are a lot of pressures and that is perhaps the reason for the high divorce rate.

———◆———

'Women who are following a career with clear stages of promotion invariably experience a conflict of priorities once children are born. They see that their own new priorities of nurturing and protecting a young baby, which feel so immediate and real, will be deeply antagonistic to the career ethos of many professional departments.

Women leaving careers or downgrading them have no other language to explain their decisions than the pull of biology, the triumph of maternal bonding over the shallowness of careerism. And at a very deep level women are programmed to expect breaks in their career.'

Rosalind Coward, OUR TREACHEROUS HEARTS.

———◆———

Sheila Davidson [born 1944]

I trained as a nanny in the early 1960s. The residential and day nurseries were for the babies of single mothers and those in financial difficulties. I then worked in a nursery school for pre-school children from two-parent families.

Since 1982 I have run a child minder business in my own home and I employ an assistant. This service is highly sought-after because so many mothers work full-time. The mothers of the children I look after all have careers: computing, nursing, medicine, physiotherapy, and various businesses. Each will say that they have worked hard at their career and don't want to give it up to look after children. I expect before crèches and child minders were popular, these women would have had a nanny living in. Ordinary working-class mothers work for the money and can't afford to pay a child minder. They usually have a member of the family looking after their children.

The mothers who work for financial reasons alone are very guilty about leaving their children, but they have no option and I feel sorry for them. But there are many other mothers who do have the choice whether to work or not. They don't find childcare stimulating enough and they don't go into motherhood thinking that they will stay at home all day. They decide during pregnancy that they will continue working. These women often have cleaning ladies, an ironing service and gardeners so that their free time is spent with the children. I still think a happy mum makes a happy child because they do have quality time together, and a working mother who enjoys her work appreciates her children more when she is not with them all day. But children do need a secure person to replace their mother and then it balances out and works well.

The children I mind have come to me since they were about three months old and they know nothing different, so we get to know each other very well. Career women often breast-feed their babies, but tend to use tins and packets when they are being weaned. I give the children home-cooked meals, sieved carrots and potato, stewed apple, banana, custards, lentils and chicken dishes blended smooth for them.

I look after babies and children of all ages. When older children are off ill from school, they can come to me and rest quietly and join in depending how they feel. I also pick a child up from school if they are taken ill and their mum can't leave work. My assistant and I also go to the sports days to represent the mums who cannot go, and the children accept this.

The children I look after know that when I say no, I mean NO. My crèche has a strict routine and the children love it. They respond to knowing exactly what comes next. If I do something different and miss out story time, for example, they'll say, 'We never had a story today, Sheila.' They know I'm consistent and mean what I say. They love my cooking and I teach them table manners. They say 'Please may I leave the table?' when they have finished. They love meeting each other every day and become good friends, because I usually have each child for a few years at a time. I find that most mothers do not have a mealtime routine at home which I find too relaxed, but I teach the children manners and good behaviour at all times. However most of the children do have a bedtime routine when they are with their mothers.

Discipline is so important in bringing up children. When they are difficult, the ultimate punishment is to be put out of the playroom, into the hall. This happens a few times until they learn to behave and quietly get on playing.

A mother will sometimes tell me that their three year old child has a tantrum and won't get dressed in the morning to come to me. I just say bring them in their pyjamas, and they only need to do it once as the threat is enough, which proves they were just playing up. When they are little they don't want mum to leave them and they begin to scream, but as soon as the mother goes off to work it always amazes me how quickly they calm down, no matter how heartbroken they have been.

It is accepted today that mothers will often work full-time. I try to provide a happy, homely place for the children, which gives me a wonderful job in my own home while their mothers get on with their careers.

Jenni Smith [born 1946]

We do not live in an ideal world and there are times when women, like myself when I left my husband, have to go back and work full-time too soon, when perhaps part-time work would be better for the children. For other women, in order to keep on the career ladder, it may be necessary to have a full-time nanny for the children from a very young age, and if this works that is to the good, but I feel it may not always benefit the children. To be honest, I cannot see any point in having children if you do not intend to stay at home and look after them, at least for a year or two. I realise that to have a career this is how it has to be, and I don't see that the workplace is going to change, to accommodate more flexible working patterns. If anything, at the moment it seems that the ethos is more and more to work longer hours, and if women want a career then they have to fall into line. This is not good for women, children or families.

It is not possible to have everything – home, family, full-time career, without something suffering. If the women feels she has to be Super-woman then in the long run she will suffer; either her health will give out or she will find that she is not happy because there are too many calls on her time, and she is being pulled in all directions. Choices have to be made and at the end of the day, to be a woman is to have to do without. Whether one does without children, a job or a husband is her choice, but to keep everything on track requires vast amounts of energy and cash, most of which we simply do not have.

Barbara Bryan [born 1946]

I am very surprised at the change in attitude of mothers today who so often feel that personal fulfilment and a full-time career are more important than bringing up their children. I don't agree with the rather selfish 'Having-it-all' approach. I do think it is very sad that they do not appreciate or realise the importance of being with children when they are young. It is such a vitally important and, most of the time, creative and fulfilling job to encourage and watch little children develop and grow up. I do think that many women have a great sense of guilt when they show any independence from the family. Dividing yourself down the middle into a mother and career woman is not easy! Women should, if they wish, have space in their lives to pursue their career or interests on a part-time basis when the children are older.

I enjoyed a career in broadcasting until I was pregnant with my first daughter. I distinctly remember suffering with appalling morning sickness as I sat in front of the microphone, broadcasting to the whole of Scotland at six in the morning! I never envisaged continuing a full-time career but it has not prevented me from keeping up an interest in the arts, music and reading. And my husband's involvement in the music business has always been part of my interest too. Since my youngest child is six and at school, and the other two are growing up, I have more time to involve myself in writing and recording work, and I can work from home. I have designed my own little study at the top of the house where I can hide away and write! We do not have a television in our house and the children have always been encouraged to play the piano, read and amuse themselves.

It has been a joy and a pleasure to bring up my children, and as they get older, I know that I can enjoy my own interests and work for many years to come.

'Mother never left me, Angela thought, not when I was tiny. Mother was always there . . . She promised herself that when Sadie could talk and understand, she would leave her without a qualm. But leaving her now, at two years old, was a betrayal. She had no right to want freedom from Sadie. Mother had never wanted it.'

Margaret Forster, MOTHER CAN YOU HEAR ME?

Vivienne Leighton [born 1947]

With the shortage of jobs, women seem to take their restricted maternity leave and then feel that they have to go back to work or they will lose that job. It means they keep up their standard of living. Also professional women are obviously keen to keep working despite having children so they don't lose out on the career ladder. I don't know if they are selfish or not. But it hasn't been proved that it does any damage if the mother goes out to work and the baby is looked after properly by someone else. In the hospital where I work they have just opened a crèche and that is the first time there has been a nursery available for all the employees. It is shocking to think it has taken so long to provide childcare for working parents. There is a girl who works beside me and I know for a fact she pays £700 a month for her childcare. That is a lot of money.

Mary Law [born 1949]

It is all very well for women to want to have it all, but do they manage all three successfully? Some women shouldn't try. I am sorry if it is the children who suffer, or the woman's health. Who cares about the job? I put that third. Many women now feel that it is their right to have children, a job and childcare. They feel it is the Government's job to supply suitable childcare at little cost to themselves. They want the money and fun of working more than the need to mother. I believe this more and more as I see them go home and then spend time doing housework and chores, instead of spending time with their children at night and at weekends. They are not committed to making a relationship with their children.

Janice Mackenzie [born 1950]

Most mothers now work and society has yet to come to terms with this. As a working mother and teacher myself, very often at school we have children sent back too soon after illness because their mother feels that she cannot have more time off work, especially if she is a single parent. Or children are taken ill at school and it takes ages to contact the mother at work, and she is reluctant to come and take the child home. These are still minority cases but they are on the increase. As parents we must balance children's needs carefully, especially in their early years. They are not children for long and grow up so quickly.

Sheila Gray [born 1951]

I believe balancing full-time work and family life is impossible. In our little village it's still very traditional. Most women give up work to have their families and some do part-time work later. I know very few who have full-time jobs. People seem to want more material goods and holidays nowadays, and feel they have to work to keep up the standard of living they had before the children came along. I don't believe that has to be the case. I think being there for the child most of the time is more important than an affluent life-style.

Ailsa Gray [born 1953]

I think 'something has to give': you can't do two or three jobs without compromising somehow. I do think women today are under so much pressure to have-it-all, even if they don't want to. Running a home and being a mother is often no longer seen as a proper job! Sometimes I feel it was easier in my mother's day because there were fewer choices and you were expected to be a full-time mother at home. I have an old-fash-ioned attitude to childcare and think a mother should be at home when the children are small if at all possible. Career and working women have a very difficult time as there is still a very male attitude towards the mother's responsibilities, despite the 'New Man'!

However I do feel it is important for mothers to have a little time to themselves if they can possibly manage it. I try to get away for about an hour a day and I am lucky in having a very supportive mother-in-law who comes round to look after my three youngest children, when the eldest is at school and another is at nursery. I sometimes just go out to sit in a cafe and do some writing. I keep a journal and I really do need this short time away from the family. I call it my sanity time.

I do find family life a bit easier to cope with now that they are growing up. I believe once they are past the age of three, they become little people rather than babies. You can have little conversations with them and they help me round the house. Even my eighteen month old toddler gets the nappies for the baby. He's well-trained at that age to help his mother!

'Why was it so hard to be the woman she wanted to be? Once women had no choices, now they could be anything they wanted to be. Yet somehow choices made it harder to be happy. If you chased success you lost out on those small, domestic pleasures which have given women satisfaction for centuries. Creating a home that's warm and welcoming, watching your children grow, entertaining friends. Yet if you stayed at home and brought up your babies and baked your pies you were left with the niggling sense that somehow you were missing out.'

Maeve Haran, 'HAVING IT ALL'.

'Morag' [born 1953, counsellor on women's employment courses]

I recognise the notion of women wanting it all, the mentality of equal roles in the home and at work, but that doesn't work out in practice. The women I work with and also personal friends are all in the position that they have to work. There is not any kind of decision. The cost of living today, with wages being so low and many men out of work, means that women really do have to work. I live in Corstorphine, in west Edinburgh, where the women are either child minders or they go out to work. You can't afford not to have another income.

The women in my workshops don't think in terms of a career; their main ambition when they left school was to marry and have children. After they have had two or three children, and very often a great number of them have been let down by their men, they are now in a position to try to better themselves. They want an education to try and get a better job, one that isn't cleaning or childcare work.

It isn't easy for mothers these days. There is something about the isolation that has come about to a certain extent, and at a very basic level, with us having our own washing machines, for example, so women don't all gather at the local wash house, and that kind of thing. Women just don't gather together in the neighbourhood as much now. You ask any woman at a mother and toddler group or at community centres, and they talk about the relief they find in sharing their feelings with other women in a similarly isolated situation. There isn't the support around so many women want to go out to work.

When I was pregnant with my first child, my husband was seconded as a social worker to a rural district in Galloway, so I gave up my job in community education to move there with him and start our family life. I had been a career woman so it was a complete change of lifestyle. When I was left by myself, alone with this baby in the house all day, I found it very hard. I had been educated at a very academic school. My mother and grandmother were career women before me and I had been brought up to understand that motherhood and housework weren't meant to be full-time jobs. I thought I was failing all the time and always felt I had to have something else to do.

I was unable to continue my career when I brought up the children because there was little work for men or women in the area. I became interested in the anti-nuclear campaign because they wanted to bury nuclear waste in the hills nearby and we lived across the water from Sellafield. So I was involved in various environmental groups, mixing with many other strong women, and we gave each other a lot of support, which helped as many of us were incomers to the district and had no extended family nearby.

After my third baby was born, I became very ill myself through a build up of exhaustion, resentment and stress. The marriage was breaking down as my husband had become extremely critical of me all the time. We separated, I moved back to the city, and although I was ill for some months, once I felt able to cope and found suitable childcare, I began working again.

I would never recommend that a woman give up her job when she has a baby because so many women give up their jobs and then regret it six months later, having lost that out-of-the-home stimulation. A lot of women echo my own experience because they hadn't realised what it was going to be like at home looking after children all day.

Of course there are women who genuinely love it. There are women who are very glad to give up the pressures of a job. Every individual woman will have different opinions on this, and maybe I am painting a very jaundiced picture according to my own experience.

Liz Hodgson [born 1954]

I'm going for bits and pieces of everything rather than having it all or nothing. My partner and I are able to share it all and that feels good, especially as Toby's dad will be so involved with him. It feels important to have a balanced approach and as the parental roles are now so fluid, we're having to make up our own version. We both happen to be keen on part-time work and also have separate opportunities to earn from our music making, barn dances and voice workshops. We got together in our mid-thirties so we combine two households, skills, experience and tin openers, and Toby can work out what suits him! I don't expect to take on all the housework just because I'm currently here a lot!

I see people caught up in having high material expectations and therefore needing high double incomes. Trying to become a working mum is not as easy as it seems. My new boss rings to offer me the job. I put the phone down, look up and see Toby with two hands on the dining room table, one foot on the adjacent chair and one in mid-air, about to take off. Life's full!

'To suggest that a woman choose between her relationship with her child and her individual adult identity, largely vested in her salary – or wage-earning role, is as idiotic as asking her to choose between food and drink. It is not only that both are essential to her, it is also that they are inseparable because they are both part of her. But to suggest that she cannot fulfil the role of mother, or worker, unless she is with her child, or at her desk, seven, or five, days a week, is equally idiotic. Only flexible integration and sequencing of people's various roles can defuse the conflict between parenthood and paid work.'

Penelope Leach, CHILDREN FIRST.

Barbara Buckley [born 1954]

As a full-time career woman with four children, I suppose I have to say yes, I believe in the right to have it all. But it should be more to do with happiness, rather than women demanding equality. I work too hard at my job and in the home, and don't feel I do 'Have it all'. Even taking a few months off is not easy. During my maternity leave I had to work incredibly hard to ensure everything was covered for my absence, which in fact resulted in promotion while on leave having my second set of twins!

I think that there is still too much guilt involved, trying to be perfect and not succeeding. Most women who are trying to do both jobs and have it all, are perhaps thinking more about roles and values. Not enough men have altered their views on women's responsibilities for children, nor is there much acceptance of a father taking a more caring role.

Jano Rochefort [born 1955]

I think if women can combine a full-time career and a family life it is great, if they can manage it in a happily balanced way. But can they? When it comes to the crunch, whose career takes precedence, theirs or their partner's? When the children are ill, who gets the call at work? Who cooks the evening meal? Who cleans the loo?

I feel many young women are going to continue to fall into the same trap. You think you can have it all – career, children, husband and home, and then find out that you are doing the bulk of the housework and childcare *and* trying to juggle a responsible job as well.

My own mother worked while I was a child as she had a professional full-time career as a nursing officer. At that time she was unusual. Now I am a full-time mother and I'm unusual!

Trudi Barnet [born 1954]

All the magazines today are telling us to be career women and have a family, to 'Do It All'. And so mothers may go back to work and think they can do it all but it puts such a strain on them. I really do believe the crisis comes during the bringing up of the children, and many women quickly realise that it is not going to be a 'happy ever after' story. At the time, both parents may have dearly wanted and loved to have a family but at the end of the day it is the woman, the mother, who is left most of the time to care for them. And for women trying to fulfil themselves personally and intellectually by continuing in their jobs and careers, this causes serious problems in trying to manage everything.

Winifred Fyfe [born 1955]

Mothers today have a very different approach to motherhood and childcare. They always seem to want to do their own thing, and have a life outside the home. They go out to work all day, leaving their children to the care of other women as they find it very difficult dealing with small children, even though they may still love their children. There is a lot of self-interest these days.

However I don't think this is necessarily due to a lack of responsibility or commitment, because with the change in social attitudes, women today are seen as doing something wrong whether they stay at home all day, ['just a housewife'] or go back to work ['a career woman neglecting her children']. They are criticised whatever they decide is best for themselves and their family circumstances.

'Cathy' [born 1955]

I think that temperamentally women are good at thinking of and doing several things at once an ability perjoratively known as being scatty, but they can lose this ability and become obsessed with work and this can – I stress can – cause children to suffer, just as an obsession with children can, paradoxically, isolate the children.

———◆———

'The unspoken rule is never to mix the two, or evoke one in aid of the other. The image of the capable woman must never be tainted by the smell of baby powder; efficient women have that side of their lives well under control. Motherhood is like some skeleton kept in the cupboard and most of us collaborate in keeping our children invisible. In the legal profession, it is certainly more acceptable for a male counsel to explain his late arrival because of a car breakdown than it is for a woman counsel to evoke the illness of her children's nanny.'

Helena Kennedy, Q.C., from BALANCING ACTS. ON BEING A MOTHER.

———◆———

Sue Rook [born 1960]

I did feel slightly discriminated against when I took maternity leave although they behaved in a very subtle way. I felt the goal posts kept being moved and although I decided in the end not to return to work after having Hannah, I feel that had I wished to go back, I would have had to fight my corner to keep my job.

I think the executive mother is an ideal; if you do all three something won't be done properly. Guilt and fear probably hold most women together and I'm just so grateful I could choose to have my child and stay with her, and continue doing some work from home. So often it is a financial decision as most people have to rely on two incomes to pay the mortgage.

Jo Davidson [born 1960]

My parents disapprove of me working full-time although strangely they disapprove of this less than they do of the fact that I have retained my maiden name!

Although I am a career woman and returned to work when my children were just a few months old, I do have mixed feelings about the whole business of working mothers. In my case my children have given me a different perspective on life; work no longer has the importance which it did and I no longer work such long hours. Most of the time I wonder why we need to work, why women feel pressurised into pushing themselves to the limit in and out of the home, although having said that I personally could not cope with being a full-time mother, and while I need to work for financial reasons, I also desperately need the intellectual stimulation of work.

I did feel discriminated against when taking maternity leave for both children. I was left out of important projects both because people were trying to be kind in one sense but also they thought I couldn't cope. Each time, especially recently, reorganisations have been made while I have been away, although I've always returned to my original job. I've been anxious and had worrying phone calls about my job going elsewhere.

During my childhood mothers who worked were in the minority. Mothers stayed at home, looked after the children and house, and seemed to be in contact with family rather than friends. In my experience most mothers work now and rely on friends for support as families perhaps live too far away. There is also a vast expansion of playgroups where mothers can meet and make friends rather than being in the house so much of the time. Motherhood used to be a career. Now it is more of a short career break.

Lucy Owen [born 1961]

If a woman can manage a career and a family, fine. If not, she shouldn't feel guilty or pressurised. I'm lucky that as a writer I can continue my career from home. I couldn't go out to work – I'd feel I was missing out. So, no, I personally don't live by that approach. I notice that women who do work often do so at a cost to their children's emotional welfare or overcompensate for their lack of mothering.

Angela Blanchard [born 1962]

If any women do manage to have it all, I envy them, admire that and am very happy for them. I think most of us end up making compromises in some areas of our lives and some women manage it by denying their femininity, which is a loss to society.

One friend who seems to have achieved this is a farmer's wife, who grew up with farming and appears to want nothing else. She and her husband are equal partners both in marriage, farm work and family life. She is very hard-working, I know, and ambitious for a bigger farm and bigger herd, but she and her husband seem to work very harmoniously and see the children as their joint responsibility. She seems very happy with her life; I don't know many women who combine all three so well. But I think we all have a right to try if we want to. The so-called *traditional* wife/mother role, doing all housework and childcare, only goes as far back as the late 1800s.

I know some women are forced to go back to work full-time because of financial hardship but many feel they must continue their careers because society defines women by their jobs.

Carol Ziyat [born 1962]

I certainly believe in working mothers but I am not sure that I want to be responsible for three jobs – career, children and housework – full-time for ever. There is also the help of the father to consider in this age of equal partnership and parenting and the real possibility of having domestic help. Life is for living and we need time to live.

———•———

'Of all the rationales offered for woman's presence in the home, the myth of motherhood seems the most persuasive, for even if the housewife role and the wife role are capable of change, the maternal role is not. Women's position in the family is founded in their maternity, now and for all time . . . since woman's maternal role is unalterable, their oppression as housewives might just as well continue. As with other myths the function of the myth of motherhood is a validation of the status quo.'

Ann Oakley, HOUSEWIFE.

———•———

Lorna Reid [born 1962]

Men have had it all for years. I believe many women manage very well, especially the likes of two 'housewife' friends of mine, who were in my university class and who juggled home, husband, children and studying.

There have been great changes, I think, even in the short time since I left home, fourteen years ago. My mother stayed at home to look after us all and I would love to do the same, but I have worked since university and would feel a pressure to return to work, after having a baby, rather than waste my degree. And the increased demand for childcare has created employment for many women, often in their own home.

Rachel Lockey [born 1967]

I didn't feel I had blown my chances of going to university and getting a degree just because I was having a baby at 18. I knew I could maybe catch up later, and I did go to university when Bella was 2½ years old. I went to the University of Sussex in Brighton and took a degree in anthropology. There was a crèche at the university, which was perfect for Bella. When I started out five or six years ago, the grants were still reasonable and I got a dependent grant because I had Bella. There were still places in the nursery, whereas now I know it is far more difficult for mothers – the nursery and crèche are completely full. I was very fortunate because it was quite manageable for me over those four years, both financially and with excellent childcare. I had three and a half days full-time childcare and it really worked out well. I enjoyed it and it was very empowering to be a single parent and be a full-time student at university.

I learnt ever such a lot and I felt so much more mature and confident from the experience.

I am studying to be a midwife. Now that Bella is eight she can be very demanding and want constant attention but she has learnt to give me time. She's recently started sitting in her room, drawing or looking at her books, between say, five and seven. She has to understand that I can't always be there and I have my work to do on my own.

'I'm beginning to think that we've all been conned; these days you're supposed to be able to have a great career at the same time as being a good mother and cheerfully beaming wife. Maybe there are a few superwomen out there who can manage the juggling act but I can't. I was 27 when I was pregnant with my first child and I had no idea how my life would change.

'I went back to work when he was fourteen weeks old because my maternity leave had run out and we needed the money to pay the mortgage. Anyway, would I be a real person if I didn't work.? But I hated leaving him, and he hated being left.

After my second child was born earlier this year I thought I'd be able to carry on in this way. But for the time being I'm only working two mornings a week and that's at home.

What I do know is that I'd be miserable if I never had a job again. Still, I keep reminding myself that babies become children very fast; and I'm seeing this one grow up, for a little while at least. Sometimes you just can't have it all.

Justine Picardie, THE INDEPENDENT ON SUNDAY, 11 December 1994.

'She was tired of pretending [that] being a working mother was easy, sick of glossing over the pain and the panic and the guilt. Maybe it was time to tell the truth. That women had been sold a pup. Having It All was a myth, a con, a dangerous lie. Of course you could have a career and a family. But there was one little detail the gurus of feminism forgot to mention: the cost to you if you did.'

Maeve Haran, HAVING IT ALL.

'The myth that feminism had nothing to say about motherhood has become commonplace. Yet as any woman who was involved in feminism will tell, this could hardly be further from the truth. What about all our campaigns for

*community crèches, what about emphasis on shared parenting, what about all
the support we gave mothers as a routine part of feminism? Suddenly women find
it's difficult to combine motherhood and career, and they blame feminism, which
has actually been saying that for twenty years'.*

Rosalind Coward, OUR TREACHEROUS HEARTS.

———◆———

'*I decided to write Having It All when I had gone back to work after having my
second child and I realised I just wanted to change my life. I was working in a
very highly paid, successful job but I never saw my kids, and so I became a writer
for very odd reasons – really to be at home. Having decided that I wanted to be at
home, I then set out to write a sex and shopping novel because this was the vogue
at the time, about five years ago, and I was absolutely terrible at it. Here I was
with two small children, I couldn't remember the sex and I am hopeless at
shopping, so I actually spent six months writing this book before my agent said to
me it was hopeless! I had to throw it away. That was a very "dark night of the
soul" moment, and she said to me there was no passion in it and why didn't I
write about something I really cared about. So I thought "Well, what do I really
care about?" and then it struck me that there was one thing every woman I knew
talked about all the time, and that was how to balance the demands of work, home
and family and stay sane. So there was my subject.*

*It was a very heartfelt novel because I had lived through that dilemma. What
happened to my heroine didn't happen to me in precisely that way but the
dilemma was definitely autobiographical. What I wanted was to write an
enjoyable and entertaining novel which would touch people's lives. It was
accidentally feminist because I think feminism has filtered down into real life
now, it is not a theory anymore; I think we live it now and that is why my book
was about it.*

*I think what has astounded me more than anything about the success of Having
It All, is that it has been translated into twenty-two languages. When I began to
write it, my worry was that it wouldn't be a wide enough interest. OK, this was
something I was living through and I had the feeling many other women felt like
I did too, but the fact that it should be a dilemma worldwide from North Korea to
Taiwan and Mexico absolutely gobsmacked me.*

*I think it is distressing that there is still no real equality for women who have
to juggle a full-time career and childcare. I think things are moving forward and
women are living in a better time than ever before, but the downside is it is still
very slow. At least it is talked about, the employment side of it, how to make work
more flexible and family-friendly.*

Motherhood

I suppose it was rather tragic that I felt I had to give up my career in television, but I did so partly for my children and partly for me. What I wanted to get out of life was a more balanced life where I could have family and work and something else. You can just about survive with children and jobs but life is very narrow, there is no time for friends, there is nothing else and it is all just exhaustion. That is the saddest thing. In a way our generation are losing a lot of the fun out of life. We need the structures of society and employment to change. It is a great challenge.'

Maeve Haran in conversation about HAVING IT ALL.

CHAPTER TEN

Women's Destiny: The Changing Experience of Motherhood

My children have determined my life; since the day they were born I have never thought of myself as an individual but as part of an inseparable trio. It never occurred to me that motherhood was optional, I thought it was as inevitable as the seasons.'

Isabel Allende, PAULA.

Violet Stevenson-Hamilton [born 1902]

Summing up, I consider it essential to the proper upbringing of children that there is a joint male and female influence in their lives. The conventional and religious side of marriage is being taken over by people living together although there are deeply committed couples who eventually marry and have children and prove to be very good parents. Divorce is on the increase and young teenage pregnancies are commonplace. Children's state allowances have certainly contributed to the increase of single-parent families, and the school girl who has two or three children before she is twenty through careless copulation, adds to an unhappy, turbulent generation, and the problems of an overcrowded world. Single women who long for a child can now have one without the responsibility of marriage but the child lacks the shared parenthood of a father and a mother.

Janet Stewart [born 1904]

I was a mother of young children during the war when my army husband was posted to France and Germany. It was a very difficult time to bring up our two little girls on my own. We did not have much money and no holidays together as a family but times were happy. Later on, my husband enjoyed playing golf and tennis with his daughters until shortly before he died aged only sixty-four; I never saw him age. It made me realise how precious family life is and I feel very sad to see young mothers today who seem to think about themselves more than their husbands and children. Why have children unless one wants to be at home with them? We were were married happily for forty years but I have been a widow now for twenty-four years.

Family life has of course changed dramatically since my day, as I see with my own grandchildren – three of them unmarried but living with their partners. Women may have changed their attitude towards how they approach motherhood, but I think it will take men a long time to alter their views on the traditional role of women in the family, and this is how I think it should be – a mother's place is in the home.

Margaret Dixon [born 1905]

Unusually I have lived in the same house for sixty years, since I came to it when I was first married! I think it has been a stabilising fact, and made it easier to cope with any problems. This is the family home. I think many people have too much money these days. Mothers don't have to make toys and things for their children to play with but the ready-made, expensive toy is soon boring. I made a tent during the war from unrationed sackcloth, which was a great success with my three. We were great walkers and keen flower hunters which children don't seem to be anymore; country walks and nature rambles are free. As parents we did not have to pay to entertain our children. Today they are driven to school and taken everywhere in cars so they get little exercise by bicycle or on foot.

Bringing up a family today must be so very much more expensive because of all the expectations and demands of modern childhood, which in turn creates the financial necessity of mothers having to go out to work. Changed days indeed! All I ever wanted was to be married and have a family.

Woman's Destiny: The Changing Experience of Motherhood

Susan Curtis [born 1905]

Motherhood is not a role, but a *fact*. To have produced and have responsibility for a life, a child entirely dependent on you, should, all things being equal, be sufficient to guarantee dedication and commitment to motherhood. Too much has been left to the state, and discipline and responsibility have become short-term. Nowadays a child seems to be a by-product or even a risk of marriage or living together. I am not religious and do not wish to sound sentimental, but a newly born baby seems a most 'holy' thing, just by having happened in all its vulnerability and beauty.

Patricia Rogers [born 1909]

The whole approach to marriage, family life and motherhood has so radically changed. All I can see is that the fact of the Pill and early sexual experiences have altered women's values. I don't say it's made girls promiscuous, but I had moral scruples, so if they have no moral scruples and if they don't think it's wrong, then the only wrong is if it is causing harm to themselves and other people. I think it does harm other people. Couples seem to become sated with each other; they are no longer satisfied by the one partner and give up so easily on the relationship or marriage and then separate. When they come to the hard parts of marriage or if they feel there is an injustice, perhaps the wife doesn't want to be be left to look after the children, or whatever, then they take the easy way and jump. They just do it without much thought to everyone else. Then people are hurt; the children of divorced parents are confused and hurt. People don't seem satisfied with an ordinary family life any more.

When I was bringing up my six children people were sorry for me, wondering how I could cope with such a large family. Now that I am a widow, all my children visit me, or take me on holidays and confide in me, and people say how lucky I am!

———•———

'For the women of the pre-war generation the new changes often seem destructive. First there was the fear that sexual freedom would devalue women. To some extent their fears were justified. Inequalities in power relations meant that sexual freedom had different implications for men and women. Now they fear that in overthrowing traditional rules of discipline and routine, women are making

themselves slaves to their children. The older generation may be right in realizing that some of the old ways, although not ideal, might have had some benefits for women. At least old attitudes to marriage ensured support for your children; at least not working allowed them some rest.'

Rosalind Coward, OUR TREACHEROUS HEARTS.

Eileen Brown [born 1908]

It was such a happy time when my children were little and before they left home. We had no money to spare, no luxuries, but I loved it. I always felt in control and kept to a routine. I never got into a mess with the running of the home. I had far less trouble with my children because they had no money and few opportunities; they did well at school and got good jobs. I think our generation regarded marriage as our career – we've been married for over sixty years now – and I feel that young women today would be much more fulfilled personally if they regarded motherhood as a very important job.

Mary Maclennan [born 1911]

If I were to sum up my life, I think we are just an ordinary family. We managed to bring up the children successfully, and happily, between the two of us. I have ten grandchildren who nearly all live quite far away but I have one near me. It is very nice having grandchildren, very nice. I do think it was easier to bring up a family in previous generations. When I think of my husband's family, he was the youngest of ten children. The oldest ones were working by the time he was born. His mother must have had a hard time but she lived until she was 98, a perfectly healthy woman, and she had brought them all up. It was a full-time profession then, being a mother and running the home. From Victorian times and for many generations up until well after the second world war, the mother was just there all the time, looking after the children, feeding them, teaching them how to behave; it was the same for all women. In a way I think they were marvellous, dedicating their lives to their children and husbands, looking after their families and homes.

Nowadays women are expected to do all sorts of other things apart from looking after the children. It is a changed role now so many mothers work. I am not against working because if you get a good education at university, it is important to use that training so that women can play their part in society. Then perhaps they can employ someone else, – a nanny, or a good father can take on the mother's role. I think men are getting better at taking more responsibility at sharing the job and can fulfil the role of the mother by simply being there. I don't think you can make rules about it any more. Women want to work and have an equal chance in life.

May Stephen [born 1911]

We've had a very long, happy family life despite wartime separation, my husband's illness, and the great difficulties we had to encounter when we knew Ruth was deaf. But the children both did extremely well at school, in their careers and are happily married with children of their own. My husband and I, now in our early eighties, still recklessly drive off around the M25 to see them as often as we can!

A few weeks ago my daughter wrote to me saying, 'John and I think we are failing as parents'. I had to smile, and I wrote back to say, 'I have made many mistakes as a mother, I am sure of that; all parents make mistakes or feel they have made the wrong decision or whatever – there are no perfect parents, but as long as the children are loved and cared for they will survive and make their way independently in the world.'

Eileen Watkins [born 1912]

I would say we were a very, very happy family, and, as far as we can be without Father, our Head, we still are. I don't remember any problems, even in teenage years, and it isn't that I have forgotten them – the pleasures were manifold. My three children are very well-balanced adults, the girls married now for 28 years and the boy for 23. I have six grandchildren who are wonderful company for me. Family life has changed so much that I sometimes worry about how much childhood children really have these days. They are given so much freedom to do what they want and expect so much to be bought for them that their sense of values is so wrong. Television is a menace and thank goodness we didn't have it when my children were growing up – we sang round the piano instead! If people's expectations and 'needs' – the car, television, video, computer and all kinds of machines – were lower, perhaps more mothers could stay at home?

———————————

'What was left of her time was spent in the dread of having children. Yes that was her real grudge against life; that was what she could not understand. She was broken, made weak, her courage was gone, through child-bearing. And what made it doubly hard to bear was, she did not love her children. It was useless pretending.'

Katherine Mansfield, AT THE BAY.

———————————

Alice Wands [born 1912]

I am glad that a certain aspect of motherhood has changed; annual childbirth. In my mother's case she was pregnant every one to two years. My sister was two years three months older than me and my brother was two years before her, so that my eldest sister was quite a bit older than I was. However there had been miscarriages and other babies in between who had died. My mother had three children who died before I was born. She didn't want all these children but it just happened. I was the youngest of six children and on top of all of us, my nephew and his brother then came to live at home with my parents when their father died when they were very young. Their mother, my elder sister, was very poor so they weren't very well off. In those days there was little support for widows and there weren't any jobs for women without training. She did work a bit during the war but it was a dreadful struggle. But perhaps because of this hardship, her two boys had great ambition to do well, and both ended up very comfortably off indeed through sheer determination. My own family was very, very poor, but it was happy and very secure.

Emily Heggie [born 1912]

I often say I would like to live my time over again, with the knowledge I have now. As you go along, you learn an awful lot as a mother. I think we made mistakes and I would like to do it all again, both for the children and for my husband. We had a successful family life, mind you, there was no trouble at all and they've all done very well. Stuart was never a bad boy; he was a bit of a monkey but he was a very kind person. He actually married a woman who had four children!

I suppose it was easier in my day. The boys used to play in the street, you never bothered about them getting into trouble or hurt. The front door used to be open during the day. It isn't safe these days, mothers should realise these dangers. It is awful to hear of little girls and boys being allowed out to the shops to get sweets or ice-cream and then you hear of all these attacks and murders. It is not wise to let young teenagers out alone, even fifteen or sixteen year olds, and I wouldn't allow the freedom some parents give their children.

Nancy Beaty [born 1914]

It seems that girls today want and expect everything in the home when they start out in married life. We had to build up slowly as life went on, saving up for even essential bits and pieces and only eventually being able to afford a fridge or a washing machine. Our children, too, did not expect to be given luxuries, unnecessary clothes or things. Today the young ones are of course lucky to have so many nice things at the start but they do get a bit dissatisfied with nothing to look forward to. They haven't got the urge to work for things.

It is lovely to see your family grow up and they have all married – three lovely daughters-in-law and my daughter lives three miles from here. Her husband has just retired this year which makes me feel very old! I have ten grandchildren and five great-grandchildren. One of my sons runs the farm my husband and I had; farming life is very traditional. There is a closeness which keeps people together.

I don't like to think too much of what happened. I like to look ahead. If you just sit and think of what you might have done with your life, you get despondent. We had a happy family life, a very busy life on the farm, but in the main very happy.

Mary Mckerrow [born 1915]

Now that our children are all into middle age, they tell us that they look back on their childhood as an extremely happy time, and if I don't seem to be boasting, they have all grown up into thoughtful, caring, hardworking people, each with a strong sense of humour, and an ability to tackle hard times without self-pity.

I don't envy today's mothers who have to take jobs to be able to buy today's 'vital' luxuries and gadgets, and then hand their little children over to others while they work to help keep the family budget going. The role of motherhood has changed and it's not an easy life for them, and the cost of living today can't be compared between then and now, anymore than the style of living can be compared. I just wish that today's pace of life could calm down to allow mothers time to enjoy their children, and children to enjoy their mothers fully within the home, without all this desperate shuttling to and fro, and no one being there when the children come home.

I think things have changed so very much, that it is difficult to say what advice I would give my children or grandchildren. My daughter says she sometimes wants to know more from her own children, to find out what they are feeling or getting up to. Children are so often away from home, with all their activities and friends. Their evenings are spent away from the family which I think is sad. Our children spent their evenings at home, playing card games as a family in front of the fire, or we played table tennis. Today they always have to be taken out to be entertained, to the cinema or theme parks as if these were vital in their lives. I am not saying they don't give an enormous amount of pleasure, but in our day the children played together at home as a family.

I have felt it a great privilege to be a mother and be blessed with the love of my children, despite going into motherhood completely untrained, finding I could rise to the challenge and enjoy it after many mistakes along the way. The war years taught us useful economy and a sense of value; life in the services in wartime gave us an appreciation of someone to love rather than someone to help to kill.

'This isn't a war for mothers with children . . . it's all right for young girls – they can go into the WAAF, or make munitions – do something – but the married women get the rough end of it.'

Betty Miller, ON THE SIDE OF THE ANGELS.

Joan Counihan [born 1915]

The effects of the 1939–45 war on mothers and children were devastating. I would say that era formed a watershed between the life we had known growing up in the 1920s and 1930s, and what it gradually became from the 1950s. The war years were quite different from the family life we had been expecting to enjoy. Having been brought up in a comfortable middle class household, with domestic staff, a governess, and boarding school education, my sister and I were pitched into marriage and children in the early years of the war. With my husband away I had to do everything, and this without having learned how to cook or run a home, and there were no modern conveniences either. But we coped, and having a large family in the circumstances was very rewarding in the long run, and now that my husband and I have been married for fifty-five stormy years, we can truthfully say we wouldn't be without the children for anything now. Our six children are fine and loving, and we have six wonderful grandsons.

Elizabeth Grey [born 1917]

Before the last war, we never saw mothers in pubs. There wasnae such a thing. I mind long ago the pub up the town and a woman would be standing outside the pub, and she would have a tartain plaid over her shoulders, holding a wee, wee infant; the husband would come out with a flagon, and gie the mother a drink, and even give the wee bairn a drink of beer. But there would be no women inside. Until the war. That's what started it. But after the war that's when women got into pubs and demanded their night out and the husband had to bide in. They were getting their own way.

I do think mothers have changed their ways a lot. They tend to spoil their children, giving them things to keep the peace, to keep them quiet instead of old-fashioned discipline and saying, 'No, we can't have that. We can't afford that. We don't have money for that.'

Like everything else there's good mothers and bad ones. There's ones that just love their bairns, and others that just shout at them. It's a mixed lot and they've a lot to learn.

As a mother myself, oh, well, there were good bits and there were bad bits. And if you didnae have good bits and bad bits, it wouldn't be worth living. So it's best with a little of each.

Lucy Firth [born 1917]

I didn't always enjoy motherhood when my children were growing up because I worried a lot at all stages. I think I strove for perfection and I still have very high standards. I think it is easier today with washing machines, disposable nappies, convenience foods and, above all, less ironing. And men do far more in the home than they used to, but they have to if the wife goes out to work too. My husband earned it, and I spent it. Lovely! We were unusual in that as a family we moved sixteen times because of my husband's job. I guess that either makes or breaks a marriage and I am happy to say that after fifty-four years, my husband has been an absolute rock to me.

Milicent Woolner [born 1917]

Our peers, like their parents, adopted the values of that generation. As mothers we stayed at home. Our fulfilment was in the rearing of the family. As young mothers in my community, we were a cross section of professional and working class people. Our aspirations were much the same and we helped each other gladly and willingly.

Today I see a marked inclination of many young mothers to wish to throw out all perceived ideas as to how babies can be successfully reared – common sense, tender loving care and example, hence the unmarried mother is disadvantaged. In feeding, the almost universal use of home-cooking has given way to convenience foods as far as babies are concerned. Discipline is slackening in relation to such things as giving sweets between meals, and the choice of meals is often now dictated by the child, as opposed to what is available and mother decides to cook. Careless speech, bad language and poor manners are seldom checked.

The divorced have abrogated their responsibilities to family life. There seems to be an 'I must have' attitude to life. If it means going to work to achieve this intangible but material desire, it is so. The children seem to take second place. In turn the children's 'want' and 'must have' are accepted. Instant gratification is the norm. I see a lack of femininity too. Where have all the pretty dresses gone?

I do however see a much more positive role in what young parents do that we could not. They travel much more, taking their children on interesting outings and holidays, and are generally more adventurous.

I have been married for forty-four years and undoubtedly it has been very happy. Our retirement was overshadowed by cashflow problems for both sons-in-law. Both businesses have suffered. Marriages have been strained and both girls work hard and are good mothers. I do not think they know the happiness we knew.

Mary Macdonald [born 1920]

My husband and I have been happily married for fifty-five years and we've had a busy family life. After having had three girls I did wish for a boy. After a gap of four years I produced another girl, then after a gap of seven years another girl. While my husband doted on these girls, I would have liked a son to carry on the name.

Mothers expect their partners to take turns in bringing up their children. My age group expected the fathers to work hard and provide for the family. I was lucky my husband did help with domestic chores like washing dishes and stoking the fires. There have been great changes in family life: the need for money to keep up with the Joneses; the introduction of the Pill has given mothers more freedom and the means to limit their family; mothers want to be financially independent which can cause problems. Meanwhile couples continue to have babies as it is expected of them, but mums and dads do not seem to be willing to spend time with their children.

Joan Hill [born 1920]

I think it was only after 1945 that attitudes changed between the generations. I was influenced by my mother's experience, to bring up your own babies by following the example and strict routine of your mother and grandmother. Of course in my case, I had a part-time job during the war while my husband was away in the army, and my mother looked after my daughter, and after I was widowed, we lived with my parents until my father died when my daughter was eight, so in the circumstances, there was obviously a great deal of influence on how to care for my child.

Now seeing my granddaughter's methods, I realise that the role of 'mother' has not changed fundamentally, just the approach is more relaxed. I do think most of my generation didn't really enjoy motherhood in the same way that mothers of today do. We were so much more structured and, in some ways, hidebound. In that sense, motherhood has progressed over the generations, as long as the more free and easy approach still maintains the respect between mother and child. As more women combine careers with family life, I feel the modern child will adapt well, because this is the only life he knows.

It has been difficult as a widow, but I have had a very happy life and have been lucky to have a family relative for whom I have kept house since my retirement, and I visit my daughter, granddaughter and her three children fairly frequently, and they all keep me young at heart.

Catherine Begg [born 1920]

The role of mothers since I was a child has gone from one extreme to the other. When I was a child working class mothers were little more than household drudges, often taking in washing to eke out the budget.

Now I think mothers have gone too far the other way: working while children are small; children going between grannies and parents who are trying to cope with a job and the family. Most mothers today have been brought up in a land of plenty, with family allowances and help with their rent. Some young mums do a wonderful job, combining work with childcare, working during school hours, but if partners are on shift work they leave themselves so little time to be together as a family. In our day we had to wait until we could afford to set up a home and save for anything we wanted. Thrift was something we were taught from an early age.

My married life has been a happy one. We have had our bad times as well as good times. The bad years help you appreciate the good ones. We had eleven worrying years with John and his illness and had I not had such good neighbours, I don't know how I could have coped. Glen life was a very friendly close-knit happy way of life. But everyone gets something as they journey through life.

Olive Banbury [born 1920]

Motherhood is for life but is ever changing. In my 75 years, only 12 were taken up full-time with motherhood and the rest has left me to lead my life as I wanted. The hardest career is bringing up a family; I wish education didn't push girls into other jobs and careers. Men should be the breadwinners, and I feel sorry for them today because their identity as providers has been taken from them. Our children are our future and mothers play a big part in this. It's a great responsibility.

Mary Sparrow [born 1921]

We have had a very happy marriage and fifty wonderful years of family life. If we hadn't I probably wouldn't have volunteered telling my story! Nobody is perfect and there have been times when we've said, 'Children – who'd have 'em'. Our relationship with our adult children is good now. When they were first married we felt cut off, but they were feeling their way with their husbands and their own families.

Joyce Petchey [born 1922]

I have been married very happily for over 45 years and I feel I learnt how to be a good, caring mother. I am saddened today by the decline in standards and the lack of discipline in children. I feel children should always say please and thank you but if adults don't why should they? If you shout at a child he will learn to shout back. If you don't carry out what you say, he will never believe you again and you have lost his trust. Parents must always be fair and seen to be fair. Never argue in front of your children. If they have a secure feeling, they won't have so many problems. Children should always be able to confide in parents even if they don't take the advice given.

Mary Boulcott [born 1922]

Mothers today are much more laid-back than we used to be. They do not discipline their children, who are allowed to cause mayhem in supermarkets. Bedtime is seldom a fixed time and children are kept up much too late. I enjoyed evenings without the children interrupting and tearing about. Family life is all so much more casual and there is no longer the stigma attached to having a child out of wedlock. In fact it is often the norm and supported by social security payments. It is all very worrying.

On the bright side, I think the young husbands of today generally help more in the home and with the children, far more than forty years ago.

'While I would never advocate a return to practices of forty years ago – at least women at that time could fall back on the old routines and customs around children. Children were expected to sleep and eat at set times. These routines ensured the mother had some separation from her children. Now many women no longer accept such routines, nor will they accept external sources of authority. The fact is, contemporary mothers pretty well have to reinvent the wheel when their children are born in terms of routine, authority and boundaries. Their journey is thus far more intense and perilous than when these things were more clear cut.'

Rosalind Coward, OUR TREACHEROUS HEARTS.

Joyce Macpherson [born 1923]

When our children come to see us with our grandchildren, I see a big difference in how children behave today. They are quite cheeky to their parents for instance. They please themselves far more with regard to what they will eat and won't eat, and how they spend the day, and the hours they keep. It is discussed with them if they would like to go swimming, or whatever, whereas I told my children what we were going to do and the children did it. There is a great difference in attitudes and the level of respect towards parents. And routine doesn't seem to matter any more in some families. We had breakfast at 8 am, lunch at 1 pm, children's tea at 5 and my husband and I had our evening meal at 8 pm when the children had gone to bed. When we go to my daughter's home, lunch might be anytime between noon and two o'clock, and nobody seems to mind.

I also find it very strange how much the mother's role has changed now, so much freer. My son-in-law thinks nothing of collecting the children from school, after work, giving them their supper and putting them to bed, while our daughter goes off to an aerobics class or something. Now my husband would never have been happy to do that. He helped with the children, certainly, but he would not have expected me to go out for the evening, to do my own thing. Women are very independent these days. They want their own life outside the family.

Having said that, I am very pleased at how they have all turned out. They are all responsible parents now, very fond of their children and they spend a lot of time with them, on the whole, but it is so different nowadays, with women working.

———— •◆• ————

'Mother was right. She was clever and gifted and ought not to have spent her life cleaning out grates and lugging vast baskets of washing about. She had wasted her considerable energies scrubbing floors and mending clothes. She had got herself into a trap she ought to have seen and escaped.'

Margaret Forster, MOTHER CAN YOU HEAR ME?

———— •◆• ————

Pamela Worthington [born 1923]

I have had fifty-three years of very happy married life. We have an excellent relationship with our adult children and with our two grandchildren. Motherhood has changed so much but what I notice as well is that men's attitudes have changed and they seem to enjoy being fathers and getting more involved with their families and babies.

Jane Ward [born 1924]

Looking at mothers and their children today, I do not like some of what I see. Today's little 'baby movers' – you cannot really call these things prams – terrify me because of the obvious risk to the baby. I accept that they are ideal for car use, but to me, the baby is so exposed – to sniffing dogs and, even worse, to car exhausts. Many mothers pay little attention too, for example, the sun may be shining straight into the baby's face, not, I would have thought, desirable. Many pay little attention to what Junior is doing. Far too many children seem to have the words 'I want' at the top of their list. I do sometimes wonder what we are doing to babies today. Thirty or forty years ago the baby sat up on high in its baby carriage and was well-protected from the elements.

I have no doubt at all that the vast majority of children are every bit as well looked after and cared for and loved and as well-behaved as I and my children were.

Davina Thorpe [born 1927]

We have many photo albums tracing our family life and it looks as if it was fun, although it was hard work bringing them all up. Sometimes I feel I missed out somewhere when I see today's mums but I couldn't put a finger on it. Life revolved around family and I took very badly when each one left home when they got married. I can't say that I feel old even now, except on days when it is difficult to get going. I got the first feeling of getting old when my eldest went to school at five. What a responsibility.

All the hard work has been worth it and if I could choose I don't suppose I'd change anything, which I always feel is the test of whether it has all been successful or not.

Motherhood is changing but I think most men still look to their mothers as the role model for motherhood. Maybe the children of tomorrow might be more equal in outlook and understanding of the mother's role. Everything has completely changed, from sex education in school to a far different view of childbirth. Mothers usually have a job outside the home now, but there are so many for and against the idea I don't suppose the children will suffer, and they will have a different attitude towards motherhood. The wheel will probably turn full circle in a few years.

I have been married for forty-seven years and on the whole my family life has been very successful. I always tried to do what was best for them. Hindsight is not much good and one can rarely apply it to be useful for the grandchildren. We have twelve grandchildren and the ones we see are great fun. Those abroad we keep in touch with – phones are a blessing in some ways. I often think of the Queen. She is my age, she has been married the same number of years and has the same number of children. But I had a rather different life than she has had!

Pamela Wells [born 1928]

I've survived forty years of motherhood and am deeply grateful for all it has brought me and taught me. There has been deep pain, the worse for the inevitable suffering life brings to my children at times, and great joy, the greatest perhaps at holding my own newborn and latterly my daughter's newborn baby, and every possible emotion in between. Learning to 'let go' is the hardest lesson of all and it applies from the moment they're born. But the rewards are infinite.

'Oh, but she never wanted James to grow a day older, or Cam either. These two she would have liked to keep for ever just as they were, demons of wickedness, angels of delight, never to see them grow up into long-legged monsters. She would have liked always to have had a baby. She was happiest carrying one in her arms.'

Virginia Woolf, TO THE LIGHTHOUSE.

Grace Rae [born 1928]

I would have enjoyed motherhood more a second time around had I been given the chance. I worried far too much about the one child I had.

Rosemary Walker [born 1929]

I enjoyed motherhood very much but we always think of our son who died with much sadness. My husband is seventy and I feel he has missed out a great deal as naturally our daughter is more company for me. I see a big change in everything, especially from my mother's time. I have had a good house nearly all my married life, with hot water and electricity, but my own mother never had the same. Most mothers today have a better lifestyle except single mothers perhaps.

Joan Longmuir [born 1930]

Motherhood now seems to be regarded as not a very rewarding occupation, while children are becoming ever more demanding and respect is becoming an unknown word.

I think mothers are afraid to trust their own instincts and to exert any form of discipline. Women are keen to carry on with their careers and spend less time with their children; I sometimes wonder if this has anything to do with our greatly increased life expectancy, that they are all too aware of all the years to be filled, post-motherhood.

I have been married for forty-three years – it hasn't been easy. My husband is a depressive but I have a very good relationship with my adult children and six grandchildren and we all get on well together.

Barbara Henderson [born 1931]

The mothers today can't wait to get the children into playschool and nursery schools; anything to get them off their hands. Children watch far too much television. Mothers think that a packet of crisps is a meal. There is still a very male attitude towards the women's role as mothers but men will shop and push prams whereas this was not the done thing in my day.

———————

'Fatherhood is not yet fashionable. Men are not present at the births of their children; if they can possibly help it. They do not shop, push prams, design the home. Marriage to the unmarried male is a trap, and sex the bait. Poor passive outnumbering middle class girls do indeed manouevre, lure, plot and entice in order to bring men to the altar . . .

'Getting married and not pregnant? There's posh for you!'

Fay Weldon, DOWN AMONG THE WOMEN.

———————

Margaret Cruikshank [born 1933]

Bringing up children is so very different these days. Children, not more than a year old, being pushed around in push chairs, drinking a bottle with Coca Cola or tea in my part of the world. Children are not disciplined, they swear and are very cheeky. If visiting friends they don't behave and mothers don't check them. In doctors' waiting rooms they are little horrors. Don't get me wrong, I like children. Mothers seem to have a lot of time for themselves, going to bingo and the pub. In nineteen years I attended three weddings and two concerts with my husband. Often only one of us could go to a concert as there was no baby sitter.

There seems to be so much money around, with families buying microwaves, tumble driers, washing machines, televisions, computers and toys. Dress must be in fashion and I cannot understand how women have the time to be so nicely dressed first thing in the morning; no aprons. In spite of all this children seem to be very discontented. They are completely spoilt.

Looking back people say 'those were the days', and mind you, in spite of all the hardships, I wouldn't change my place with present day young wives. Some, not all, have a very uncaring attitude to their families and life in general and are not well-mannered. I did enjoy motherhood and would have enjoyed it more if I had had more time to devote to them.

Mary Anderson [born 1934]

The days of bringing up three children bring back happy memories – it was easier then than when they are grown up. I continually worry about them now at the ages of 33, 31 and 25. There seem to be so many pitfalls awaiting young people now. I despair when I see what is going on with people living together with no marriage. They are missing so much. Also with so many children having broken homes and all that brings. It makes me so sad.

Sheila Brown [born 1934]

In comparing how motherhood has changed, one thing I have noticed is the element of selfishness now in women which worries me. They are so keen to have a life of their own. Now I always felt there would come a time when my children were independent and I would be able to lead my own life, and this has been so now they are grown up. But that doesn't mean to say I am not there for my children, and for my children's children.

In this respect I do think one of the most helpful things for a mother is if families live nearby. It doesn't happen so often these days, when men and women move away from their home town, but it is ideal if granny or auntie lives down the road.

This is how it was in fishing communities like Peterhead, where I grew up. There was always someone in the family to help out, say if the mother had to work. My father was an only child – this is going back to 1914 – and his father was at sea, his grandfather had been drowned at sea, so his mother and his grandmother, who was widowed very young in life, looked after him. His father was away at the whaling and fishing. They put up a barrier round him, and protected him and cared for him. So that was a one-parent family, virtually the norm because the fishermen were away for long, long periods at a time.

————•————

ANNIE: What use is all this weeping and wailing, eh? Atween the five of us here and poor Maggie Sinclair that's at home in her bed – we've twenty six bairns to clothe and feed and bring up decent!

We'll no do that by weeping oceans, Chrissie. We've a hard and bitter struggle ahead of us all and if we're to make a job of it, we better learn to leave our tears behind.

Donald Campbell, THE WIDOWS OF CLYTH.

————•————

So it is helpful if you can be in a community with lots of relatives but now there is so much total isolation. You can have a young mum in a city where she has nobody, which must be very difficult. Young people move around so much these days trying to find work so they move away from their families.

I have had a very hectic but happy family life. Lots of fun, some tears, but happy. When we get together at Christmas, we are very noisy; we sing and dance and enjoy each other's company.

Daphne Laing [born 1935]

To me motherhood should be a pleasure, to be with your children, to see them develop, help them, advise them and encourage them. To be the hundred and one things a mother needs to be, to put aside your wants until they are at least old enough to do most of the things themselves. Children above all need love and to know they are loved. They do not need lots of material possessions to prove that. While family life has changed over the years, with more women working outside the home, I do feel that men on the whole still look on the woman as the homemaker and mother. Even those who appear to be more liberated, deep down they do expect women to fulfil the traditional roles just as they expect to continue the role of husband and father.

Jennifer Harper-Jones [born 1939]

There is definitely a generation gap with regard to how women now approach motherhood and family life. My daughter has a degree and works for the BBC. She will undoubtedly want to continue there as she loves it but she adores children too and I am sure she will get married fairly soon. I feel sorry for her in that she will have a hard time coping, unless her husband can support her at home. Women all have such high expectations these days. I know that none of my daughter's friends would even consider staying at home to look after children, but equally hate the thought of leaving their children with a nanny.

I always regarded myself as a miserable failure as a mother because I had two very strong-willed children; they have both turned out fine but I would have a completely different attitude and approach if I had my time over again. I would be more relaxed and worry less. I think nature is much stronger than nurture.

———◆———

'Mother had never seemed to resent anything. She had just got on with it, seeing it as her lot in life to slave away after them all. Mother must possess some secret, Angela decided, to which she herself did not have access. Either that, or she was an unnatural mother.'

Margaret Forster, MOTHER CAN YOU HEAR ME?

———◆———

Jennifer Manning [born 1944]

Looking at today's families, I feel that children aren't children long enough any more. They are dressed as fashion dictates so they become miniature adults. I think mothers have a much more lax attitude in general, going out more in the evening, so that babies and children don't have a regular bedtime and meal times.

I don't know how I coped in those early years but I did. There is no booklet to tell you what to do and you don't realise how fast they grow up. I feel my boys have grown up well-balanced and happy. The elder is married with two children, and does everything in the home that his wife does. She works at night. The younger is engaged to be married.

I have been married over twenty-seven years. You do have to work at a marriage but I would say a woman has to be prepared to sacrifice things for the sake of the children, the home and family life. The grass is not always greener on the other side.

Sheila Davidson [born 1944]

I feel the father's role has changed as much as the mother's in the last thirty years. When my daughter-in-law was pregnant my son, Paul, would feel her stomach, and they amazed me by talking and singing to their unborn baby in the womb. As soon as Jordan was born, Paul held him and spoke to him; he immediately turned his head to the voice so we are convinced he heard the voices. When I was pregnant, my husband would never have thought of feeling or speaking to the baby, and he was not present at the births. Paul was at every antenatal appointment with Sandra and they saw the consultant and the scans together. He was there for every minute of Sandra's labour and stayed with her most of the day while she was in hospital. My husband, Ian, saw our baby when he visited but never held Steven until he was at home. Paul and Sandra nursed Jordan every waking minute, and he slept in their bed. Everything else, cooking, cleaning, washing, was left to the evening so that Jordan got all their attention. In our day, the washing, cleaning and cooking had to be done first thing in the morning so that you could spend the day with the baby.

Watching my son help his wife so much in the home, I know that many fathers do share childcare and other jobs, but I feel women are still the homemakers and without the mother's influence, the home wouldn't be properly run. If my husband helps me, he'll say, 'I've done *your* dishes', or 'I'll get *your* shopping'. It's never his dishes or his food shopping!

I wish I could do it all over and be like Sandra and Paul, and spend more time with the baby. We were too worried that the Health Visitor or even a relative would call in and find me not up to date with the household jobs.

Jenni Smith [born 1946]

It is a human need to love and be loved and people will always want to enter into relationships and have children. I am glad that I had my children. There have been many times when I thought that it had been the wrong thing to do, many sleepless nights when I have wished that I had had a career instead. Even now I am resentful that it is a woman's lot to be the one to adapt to the domestic circumstances, rather than having the right to make the domestic circumstances fit to her needs. I accept however that a lot of that is caused by our conditioning, the way we have been brought up to nurture and consider other people's needs before our own. It does not need to be so, but for all that it is the way things are. I would like to think that today's little girls would be brought up differently, but I rather doubt that they will. We carry our psychological baggage with us all our lives, and no amount of conscious effort can eradicate all our programming. We have to learn to be adaptable, and to settle for what we can have, rather than what we would like. It is never easy, but I tell myself it is character-forming.

Vivienne Leighton [born 1947]

I think I coped – and I did enjoy motherhood – until the teenage years. I have found it very hard going latterly. My husband was ill last year, and even then I don't think the kids made enough allowances for that, knowing he was ill and we were upset and worried. My daughter still packed in her job for no reason and they carried on as before, staying out late and so on. If it had been me in that position, I would have tried to please my mum and dad, knowing they were going through a bad time, but that wasn't the way they behaved.

I don't think I would give any advice to a young mother. Everyone is different and you just have to find out for yourself. Mothers nowadays seem to cope very well with their babies and they can get plenty help if they need it. The only thing is that when the children get older, the child minding problem is difficult if the mother wants to work. For a young mother starting out, they seem to know what they are doing and manage OK today.

Mary Law [born 1949]

I've a rosy picture of my years with babies. The bad parts fade. The days when I was too tired to get dressed. Days when the children just climbed all over me. The loneliness plagued me and I craved adult company and the ability to keep a house clean and tidy.

I would like to see a wage for mothers who stay at home to mind their children. I would like to see the role of motherhood valued in society and the worth of their job applauded, and for Motherhood and Fatherhood to be taught properly as a subject in school.

Moyra Heggie [born 1950, tutor midwife]

Being a midwife, I have become so emotional. I can vividly remember the first delivery I ever saw. It was a forceps delivery; they are not the best but I thought it was marvellous. There are times, even now, when

I go in to see a birth and it still has the same impact; it doesn't alter. The fact that you can really help the mother in that moment is wonderful. There are times when it is so emotional for them, it gets emotional for you. That was something, years ago, midwives would not do. It wouldn't have been professional. There are good things, bad things, sad moments and wonderful moments.

Sheila Gray [born 1951]

Motherhood has been difficult at times, being a single parent for over four years, coping with two boys on my own, and managing without my first husband as he was offshore half the time. My present husband feels they've been let off with too much, but he also understands why; the father figure wasn't there to discipline them when needed. I think they've turned into nice people all the same and believe the good example of parents, being honest, polite and pleasant, is more important than what you say to them.

They now have a good relationship with their father, whom they see often. The last time I disciplined my eldest was a couple of years ago. I screeched at him to go to bed *now*. I can't remember what he'd done wrong but it was something. He said, 'No' and stood his ground. I stood my ground and said it again. He went eventually but I realised I was looking up at him and he was looking down at me. I knew I wouldn't get away with it again!

'Morag' [born 1953, counsellor with women's employment groups]

I really do feel that women have huge burdens, and I think as well that the burden is worse now than in days gone by. I think there is a myth that women have better opportunities, and that myth is absolutely wrong. I think men feel *less* responsible about looking after their wives or partners and their children, perhaps because of feminism or because of the way society has altered. It is a theme I hear from so many women, over and over again, that men do not take on the responsibility.

I arranged a very interesting assertive training group a few years ago in Pilton, Edinburgh. There were a number of older women in their seventies there as well as a few younger women. The older women had had horrendous lives, bringing up many children while living in cramped conditions, and the younger women had very different problems, simply coping with one or two children with little support. What happened was that the older women could not believe how the younger mothers' partners treated them. They could not understand why the younger ones had difficulty expressing their anger towards their husbands. They were flabberghasted that 'we' women now let our men get away with selfish behaviour. For example, on the money side of things these women used to have total control of the weekly wage and the family finances. The men had very defined roles within the family and took on a great deal of responsibility in terms of providing the money to support the family. Another issue is that the women married for life and their husbands thought that way as well. They might argue about things but would sort it out in a way that women are perhaps too frightened to do now; if they give their husband too much grief, he will leave them. Women today don't have the same kind of control over the family finances. There may be more money coming into the home, but they don't see it.

My personal experience has helped me understand how women's self-esteem and confidence go way down once they have children. Every individual woman has different problems and different ways of coping. There will be certain women who feel their marriage is coming to an end and will say, 'I knew when he did that, when it reached that stage, that was enough.' And other women won't admit it. One thing I feel quite strongly about – maybe this is a romantic idea – but I believe there used to be a culture of women supporting each other. When roles were clearly defined women did support each other. There were relatives and friends and neighbours around, the proverbial maiden aunt and a whole community of mothers, who of course didn't go out to work, who helped the younger women. But because of geographical and social mobility, and sprawling urban developments, that family network has, in many cases, completely vanished.

Barbara Buckley [born 1954]

I have changed in many ways since becoming a mother, having learnt to be more patient and tolerant. My responses to others have been heightened by my feelings for my children, which can be painful. Life was much easier without children but easier should not be read as better.

Liz Hodgson [born 1954]

My partner and I are trying to create our own network because we feel keenly the lack of a warm, stable, low-key, extended family such as my partner knew. All our relatives are scattered long distances away and visiting is like a performance, not an everyday occurrence. So being parents involves a kind of isolation we hadn't noticed before, although it is also a very sociable activity.

I'm also rather appalled at how much mothers, gathering together, talk about the really boring aspects of children and not about the kind of things that made us want to have them. My mum does this too! It's maybe because we have very little sense that what we're doing is OK, because so much of motherhood is private and learnt from professionals and books.

'Control over fertility has arguably been the most important change for women this century. It has brought a degree of choice and freedom women never had when motherhood absorbed their best years. On the other hand, with outside jobs and higher standards of housekeeping and childcare, women strive to be Superwomen.'

Angela Holdsworth, OUT OF THE DOLLS HOUSE.

Trudi Barnet [born 1954]

I believe women's approach to motherhood through the century has gone from one extreme to the other and I do think it will go back again. Women are trying to achieve everything they can in life. They feel they have to work so they put babies into full-time nurseries from eight in the morning to six at night, but I think women will soon realise the children are missing out. No one can be Superwoman. I do think it will go full circle and women will appreciate that their status as a mother is so very important. Friends have said to me that they felt they had to get some kind of little job, just to get out of the house and use their brain. They feel their brain has gone on vacation; they want to talk to adults, so that at a dinner party they have something intelligent to talk about. They want to get away from watching the weather forecast to see if they can put the washing out, and to do something other than mince baby food. It is society's attitude to being a mother and housewife, as if it is not fulfilling or important, that you are 'just a mum, just a housewife' and have an unpaid role, that is very wrong.

It really is a curious and saddening predicament sometimes. Women seem to think, 'I have a baby but I want to go back to work now. Sorry, I'd rather be at work, I don't want you.' I know a friend who waited six years to have a family and then, when she did have a baby, it was such a change to her life that she even said to me that she could easily have left it outside a shop and run away. I think you will find this is a very normal attitude nowadays. Very normal. Even for women who have gone through years of fertility treatment, when the baby comes, motherhood is not quite what they anticipated. It takes such a lot out of you and if only someone would write a truthful book telling women what to expect, not the old story that a baby will soon follow a routine of feeding at ten, two, six, ten, and so on. It is not like that.

Childbirth itself has changed during the period when I have had my five children. In the 1970s they used to shave all your pubic hair off when you were in labour. They don't do that now. They would automatically cut your perineum, for an easier birth. It didn't hurt because it is like stretching gum, and it is a clean cut, better than letting you rip. The stitches were a bit nippy, mind you! With the first two babies I wasn't allowed to get out of bed, and I had a bed bath. With the third one I wasn't allowed to go in the bath by myself. But with my last baby, born in 1994, twelve years on at the grand old age of almost forty, I was lying there looking forward to my tea and toast. Oh no! 'Up you get, there is the shower.' It is so different now. For the first baby I stayed in for a week, which was fine and I had a good rest. But with this little one, I went home the next day.

Pregnancy advice has changed too. For the first one, eighteen years ago, our diet included liver, eggs, lots of milk. Now you are not allowed to touch liver, soft cheeses or soft eggs, so that has changed.

The actual moment of giving birth, even though women talk of the agony, is the most special experience you could ever have. I can't think of anything else to compare it with. It is so fascinating, a miracle, and they are such a part of you. You don't know what it might be, or what it will look like, so all that excitement compensates for the pain. I don't think many women say they will never go through that again. Well, they might, but the memory of the pain goes so quickly. And you are in this state of euphoria for weeks on end. It is the start of a new life, and friends and families visit with presents, and it is such a lovely time. And as babies grow into children and little adults, all the treasured memories and moments make motherhood so enjoyable for years to come.

Dr Bernard Lunan [Clinical director, Obstetrics, Glasgow Maternity Hospital]

In obstetrics what strikes me so much is the general condition of women has improved following childbirth. As a student and as a young doctor, I would go round the postnatal wards seeing women who were very sick after their deliveries. Often they would have had long, hard labours, general anaesthetics, and often their underlying level of nutrition was poor, so that they were less fit to cope with pregnancy and labour.

Women recover from childbirth much more quickly even compared to twenty years ago. The general health of the community has improved and women are physically better able to cope with the stress of labour. In addition the management of labour has changed. A willingness to intervene has meant that women have shorter labours, and the supervision of them is better. They get fluids intravenously, they get antibiotics, the whole medical care is excellent. If the baby is not doing too well, it is assessed and recognised. If the baby is in distress and not coping with labour, then the baby is delivered by Caesarean. We are delivering healthier babies, and quite definitely healthier mothers. The plus side of that is that the mothers recover from the deliveries and are able to look after their babies.

The form of anaesthesia which is used has changed significantly. In prewar days conventional analgesia such as pethidine and morphine often had a debilitating effect on women. Nowadays we have epidural anaesthetics so that the woman can labour in relative comfort, and we use forceps and even Caesarean sections under epidural so that the woman is conscious during the delivery. And it means that her husband or partner can be present at the birth, and that is good for the involvement of the father in the procedure. I can remember when I was a junior doctor, in the fifties, it was felt that any man who wanted to be present at the birth must be a bit kinky, a bit off the beam. Whereas now the pendulum has swung completely the other way, and if a woman doesn't have anyone with her, be it a sister, mother, husband or friend, then you are raising an eyebrow, because it is seen as odd not to have someone with you.

In the past, pregnancy was regarded as a risky business, and mothers were glad if they survived, never mind the babies. Nowadays most women are much more in control of their lives and their fertility, and they plan their pregnancies, but then if something goes wrong, they are very upset.

To that extent we in the medical profession have become victims of our success. We have become so successful that for the vast majority of women everything goes according to plan. The number of mothers dying in pregnancy is so small that most people will not have had a direct experience of that. A lot of women have not had contact with anyone who has suffered the loss of a child, and their expectations are based on the fact that so many of their friends and family have had babies perfectly easily, so they expect the same for them.

Of course at the back of every woman's mind is the worry that something will be wrong with the baby or something will go wrong during pregnancy, but the overall expectation is that they will get pregnant when they want to, and it will all go swimmingly. Unfortunately that doesn't always happen. Part of our job is to try to make sure that expectations are realistic. Women these days have read so many books on the subject that they will have a preconceived notion of what labour is about and what to expect, and we have to make sure they know the realistic side of the whole business.

For example sometimes a woman will come saying that she doesn't want to have any pain relief in labour. It is true that some women can manage with good breath control and have normal deliveries with no stitches. Unfortunately, it doesn't always work out like that; sometimes the position of the baby is such that the labour is longer and harder, or the baby is bigger than can safely be accommodated and the labour proves to be more difficult and painful than the woman expected. So it is better to discuss these things in advance, to prepare the woman before she becomes distressed in labour, maybe at a point when she is not coping. If the woman understands beforehand what might happen, then she can accept that pain relief or medical intervention has proved to be necessary.

In our experience in the west of Scotland, there is not a huge demand for home births. It is less than 0.3 of 1%, a very small number of women requesting to have their babies at home. Our belief is that if we can make the hospital more amenable, less threatening, they will be willing to come in and they only need to be here for as long as it takes to deliver the baby safely and to ensure mother and baby are well. It is possible for women to go home within six hours. For women who believe the alternative is a home confinement, we certainly believe a six-hour discharge is a much safer option.

Woman's Destiny: The Changing Experience of Motherhood

A great many factors have clearly changed. We are seeing a greater number of teenage mothers and also a significant increase in the number of women who are over the age of thirty or thirty-five when having their first baby. I think the greatest change in the pattern of childbirth has been the fact that families have become smaller. Most women have two or three children and it is unusual to see more than that. And that is across the social spectrum.

The health and survival of babies has improved enormously in forty years. I can remember as a student when we were talking about trying to achieve a reduced perinatal mortality rate of around twenty to twenty-three per thousand, that is, twenty-three babies out of a thousand would be stillborn, or die within a week of birth. In Glasgow we are today down to around nine deaths per thousand. I think you could still argue that there is room for improvement. There are still babies who die who in other circumstances might be saved. There are babies who will die because they have abnormalities, but if there is more advanced testing during pregnancy and more abnormalities are aborted, then the perinatal rate will be reduced further.

There is a social aspect to it. If we were to improve nutrition, to reduce the habits of smoking and drinking, these sorts of issues, they would have a very important impact on the outcome of pregnancy and would not be dependent on expensive sonic equipment or sophisticated interventions. I think perhaps more emphasis should be given to improving the general health of the population, and the benefit we will see will not just be in mothers and babies but in all other aspects of people's health.

Infertility can cause deep heartache as the desire to reproduce is a very strong biological urge. The treatment of infertility has risen as a sub-discipline of obstetrics remarkably rapidly in the last decade or two. The work of men like Patrick Spence and Robert Edwards in the field of in vitro fertilisation, where the egg is fertilised outside the female body – literally 'in glass' has become legendary.

Jenny Carter, WITH CHILD.

'The new reproductive technologies seem to offer women more choice. But they make it very hard for any woman to say, "I don't want a baby" or "I've decided I've had enough of the treatment". In contemporary Western culture, as in traditional societies, women are under pressure to marry and produce babies. Reproductive technology serves to sustain that old order.

Sheila Kitzinger, OURSELVES AS MOTHERS.

Jano Rochefort [born 1955]

Women will only gain true equality in the home and workplace, if men can learn to alter their traditional attitude towards women as housewives and mothers, with the implication that they care for the children full-time and run the home.

I've been married for eighteen years and we have three small boys. Because of employment and childcare problems, I am now committed to being a full-time mother and housewife in the traditional manner, but I wish I wasn't!

'Cathy' [born 1955]

All I would like to add about my role as a mother – and I know I am very lucky that I have help to look after my children, which allows me to write and work – is that, wherever I am, my children are with me always, in my heart and my head. I wish only for their blossoming and happiness.

Winifred Fyfe [born 1955]

I loved my girls when they were babies but I often felt lonely and isolated. I am glad they are growing up and our lives are moving on. I encourage their education in everything, not just school. We have had many problems as a family and will have many more but we communicate as best we can and always find something to laugh about. I hope they know how much they are loved.

My grandmother and mother have been my support through life and, though I have no physical contact with my mother now as she lives abroad, I know my mother is there for me. I can never remember her being critical or negative about me, although I know I gave her cause for concern. My grandmother is now dead but I think of her often and tell my children about her. If I can give my children the love and understanding they passed on to me, that will be fine.

Roma Young [born 1956]

I have no regrets about having my babies at nineteen and twenty – I had four babies by the time I was twenty-three. I have grown up with them and am much closer to my eighteen and sixteen year olds than I ever was with my own mother. I told her nothing. My daughters come to me with any worries at all – emotions, boys, sex. If I had told my mother that I had gone to bed with a boy at the age of sixteen, she would have gone up the wall, but I talk openly with Lindsay.

Now that our own children are growing up and Lindsay has recently left home, we have begun to foster children. As motherhood seems to suit me rather well, it is lovely to be able to offer a warm, happy family home to children in need.

Sue Rook [born 1960]

Unless and until you have a child you cannot possibly imagine the depth of emotion and the level of responsibility involved. Women's and men's approaches to family life have altered so much in my generation. I am now very concerned about the future as a lot of my friends have decided not to have children; they think about society today, and all the ramifications of the world, and feel that they would rather not bring up a child in the modern environment. Meanwhile others, especially very young single girls, are having babies without thinking of the consequences at all.

━━━●━━━

Prayer Before Birth

I am not yet born, console me.
I fear that the human race may with tall walls wall me,
with strong drugs dope me, with wise lies lure me,
on black racks rack me in blood baths roll me.

I am not yet born; forgive me
for the sins that in me the world shall commit . . .

I am not yet born; rehearse me
In the parts I must play and the cues I must take when
old men lecture me, bureaucrats hector me,
lovers laugh at me, and my children curse me.

Louis MacNeice.

—————•◦•—————

June Williams [born 1960, mother and midwife]

I think it is just so comforting now that the medical staff these days are willing to listen to women, and in fact in my case it was the midwife who suggested I stand up for the birth, to see how it feels. I hadn't known what position I would prefer because you can't predict the strength of the pain, but I thought standing up might be easier. I think younger midwives, if they have been trained properly, would be keen to help women deliver in whatever position they felt comfortable, but the older midwives, trained in traditional methods, might be a bit uncertain if a women said she wanted to stand up and might not encourage it. Likewise the birthing pool is far more common now but staff must be trained to use it safely. I think the water might be very soothing even just for the first stage.

In the old days it was a case of 'doctor knows best'. Now it is a case of women wanting to be informed of the choices available, so they can discuss the options with their midwives. You can read plenty of information for pregnant women, about every aspect of pregnancy, medical tests, stages of labour, pain relief and delivery procedures. There is definitely a move towards home births now. Women are given the choice. In this area in south London anyway, if you requested a home birth, you could have one. If you have had a normal first delivery, you are encouraged to have a domino birth where the midwife advises you through your pregnancy, up until labour, at home. They want to keep the hospital beds for complications which was always the case until the 1960s.

Up until ten years ago, they would induce you if you were a week late or so. Now a lot of consultants would let nature take its course, even if the woman is three weeks late. If you go into labour naturally, you are more likely to have a normal delivery than if you are induced, because it can speed things up too much. Attitudes towards childbirth do take time to change because the tutor midwives and those in charge of medical training have to change their attitudes first, before they pass on modern views and ideas to the students.

———— • ————

'It is not ultimately a matter of High-Tech versus natural childbirth. The doctor does not necessarily always know best. A woman having a baby is doing what she was designed for and that equips her with a kind of knowing. Surely humility and respect on both sides is what is needed.'

Mary Ellis, BRITISH MEDICAL JOURNAL, 25 January 1986.

———— • ————

Carol Walton [born 1943, midwife, antenatal and postnatal counsellor]

What I don't think anyone can prepare you for is the emotional and physical changes you go through both being pregnant and as you give birth; the emotions you feel in relation to this little baby and the responsibility you now have for this child. There is often an overwhelming fear of doing anything wrong and learning how to care for it. You cannot explain this very well and it is difficult to define. I don't think you need to have had a baby to be a good midwife, but being a mother myself, it does give an extra dimension because you have been through it and you understand what the woman is feeling. They may feel inadequate and totally at sea. I find that the older mothers, the professional career women, often go totally to pieces. Perhaps it is because they have had years of being in charge or in control of their lives and jobs, and they suddenly find they are not, so it affects their confidence. It is a huge emotional and physical upheaval having a first baby and the body needs time to calm down and resume its natural order of things.

In comparing motherhood through the years, I find it significant to add that many girls nowadays have never seen a baby until they come in to have their own. They know nothing about bringing up small children or childcare because they come from much smaller families and were not accustomed to helping with their siblings. They are also not encouraged to play with dollies anymore. This is sexist and I do think this is another reason why they don't have a natural feeling for mothering. It is one of my private theories. You do not see many little girls, by and large, playing with dolls, tucking them into bed, pushing a doll's pram. They have teenage Cindy dolls which are very different. In the old days, when there were large families, the elder daughters knew a lot more about mothering and looking after children. That's one of the biggest changes in the past thirty years.

Lucy Owen [born 1961]

Finally, being a mother is amazing. I look at my two children and can't believe the wonder of them. You hear about the phenomenon of mother love but never believe it till it happens to you. For instance, just now I have seen Archie, clad in red waterproofs and Paddington Bear sou'wester, wheeling his own little barrow of manure in the rain, together with a friend who is helping to turn our garden into a paradise. He looked so gorgeous I had a big lump in my throat. No one, except a mother, would think I was even sane for considering the combination of a small three year old boy and a barrow load of manure remotely tear-jerking. But he was so happy!

———◆•◆———

'I picked him and up and pressed him close. I felt his body throb and pound with excitement. He stiffened his arms and pushed himself away to see my face. He kissed me and then started crying. He took a fistful of my hair and twisted and pulled, crying all the time. I had loved him and never considered that he was an entire person. Separate from my boundaries, I had not known before that he had and would have a life beyond being my son, my pretty baby, my cute doll, my charge. In the plowed farmyard near Bakersfield, I began to understand that uniqueness of the person. He was three and I was nineteen, and never again would I think of him as a beautiful appendage of myself.'

Maya Angelou, GATHER TOGETHER IN MY NAME.

———◆•◆———

Diane Connelly [born 1961]

Raising the next generation in a loving family where they feel secure is a vital job. I think it is appalling to see babies as young as three months being put in nurseries full-time. But it seems that the only women who get applause are those who work and run a home. My thoughts are that something has to give and that women are spoiling their lives and their children's lives by trying to prove something. Being at home can be boring and frustrating but it's what you make of it. I also think people in general want it all: the car, house, holidays, toys, computers, everything and society emphasises this. Not having material things is seen as a sign of failure.

For me, I have found motherhood wonderful!

Angela Blanchard [born 1962]

The best support I got locally, apart from family advice, was from a secretary in a previous job, a lady who was in her fifties and had two children. She kept in contact with me, enquired regularly about Clare's progress and was, I think, the only person who remarked how well I was doing when I said I was still breast-feeding Clare at six weeks. She also made two remarks which stuck in my mind. One was 'Don't look down your nose on a dummy.'; the other was 'I can remember throwing Michael [her youngest] into the cot, in anger.' She was about the only person I knew at the time who was honest about what motherhood was like. Clare did have a dummy until she was over eighteen months. John refused to have one.

I haven't yet thrown either of them into the cot, but I have felt great anger. Or perhaps anger isn't the right word: more like frustration. Sometimes I want to bang my own head against the brick wall and I have been known to throw things around a bit, including the furniture, which used to alarm me, but having compared notes with mothers whom I know through the NCT I know I am not alone in this. Nor do I believe it's the 'middle class mother' syndrome, agonising over every little minor detail of motherhood, because parents who do not come into that category do batter their children, so presumably they are subject to the same emotions but lack the resources to cope with them. I coped better with John's arrival, being more aware of women's place in the world, and having the support of the NCT. As one of the breast-feeding coun-sellors said, 'Our support network provides a sisterhood, a network of friends and neighbours of the sort that women would once have enjoyed from their immediate family'. The telephone might have replaced the chat at the village pump but the effect is the same!

Carol Ziyat [born 1962]

I think we can analyse at length the role of motherhood, changing or otherwise, but I feel that an essential point must not be forgotten, that the mother-child bond is permanent, that maternal instinct and feeling are as strong today as they were two hundred years ago, and that every mother wants the best for her child on every level – health, happiness, material comfort, academic success, etc., and she will do everything in her power to help achieve these goals.

'I would like to see not having children becoming much more acceptable. Too many people are waiting to be given a grandchild and all that nonsense. History never runs backwards and nostalgia for the old days of the stay at home mother is one of the things preventing it moving forwards. Women are not going to change back to where they were thirty or forty years ago, and don't want to, so what are we going to do about it?

I find it disgusting that women have to pretend to have a migraine in order to persuade an employer that they need to stay at home to nurse a child. We can't honestly believe that going into an office or factory is more important than the well-being of a child. The fundamental trouble is that people just don't think children are important.

Penelope Leach, THE INDEPENDENT 12 April 1994.

'The best thing that could happen to motherhood already has. Fewer women are going into it.'

Victoria Billings, WOMANSBOOK: MEETING YOUR PERSONAL NEEDS.

Linda Macpherson [born 1962]

I have surprised myself by seeing how maternal I have become. I never used to be interested in babies and never felt the urge to have children. I find now I am much better with Magnus, I am a lot more interested in him. I can't let him cry for more than a couple of minutes. I have to pick him up. I can't imagine life without him now, but at the same time I cannot believe he's there as if he's come from nothing. All of a sudden he's here and life will never be the same again.

Lorna Reid [born 1962]

Since the death of our little Martin, Geoff and I have had the most wonderful help and support to enable us to cope with our grief. The hospital was excellent in the care and attention I was given immediately after the birth. I was taken to another ward, which is especially set aside for women like me, whose babies have died, women who have had a miscarriage or a termination for abnormality. The staff are trained to deal with grieving parents. To get to the new ward, I had to pass the main hall of the maternity hospital on this Friday evening. The place was full of visitors, happy people with balloons, flowers and pregnant women. I just felt devastated, so empty I couldn't really believe what had happened. I stayed in this ward for three nights and they put another bed in my room so that Geoff was allowed to stay with me, which was great. We really appreciated the fact that he could stay so we were able to make a lot of decisions together. The chaplain visited us to explain what we had to do as there were so many tasks we couldn't get away from. Because Martin had lived, even for such a short time, we would have to register his birth and his death. And because he had lived, he had to have a funeral. I think a lot of our friends thought we were making a fuss by planning a funeral, but it is something which has to be done. Staying in this quiet ward together, away from the world, was so good. You just can't believe the world is still turning out there. It gave us time to think and make plans.

I now know how fortunate I was to have the support at the hospital. There are only three special wards in Scotland. In some hospitals women who have lost their babies go back into the ordinary ward where there are women having healthy babies. Or they might be sent home immediately. So I received excellent care from my doctor, the midwife and health visitor who looked after me for some weeks afterwards. I started having extreme pains again on the night of the funeral, a week after the baby was born. I thought they were imagined pains, but it was because some part of the placenta had not come away.

The funeral was planned for the Thursday and we didn't make it private because we felt it was important that our friends were part of our sadness so they would understand more.

Our families first and foremost have been so supportive. Geoff's parents lost their first baby, thirty-five years ago. They had a girl who was stillborn at full term; she was called Margaret. In a way they have been able to help us and I think we have helped them because our grief has brought back a lot of their sorrow. I think for them it was the one thing they would not have wanted to happen to their children. And it has. They just hoped we would be helped and counselled in ways they were not. They were given no support, and it was suggested they had another baby as soon as possible. We have been helped by the hospital, and by the local Stillbirth and Neonatal Death society, which I contacted as soon as I came out of hospital. They send me information and keep in touch about local meetings. I attended my first meeting three weeks after Martin died. The girl in charge was surprised I was in touch so soon because she said, she felt people tend to grieve with their family and friends for the first two months and then, when they feel they cannot burden their friends any more, they turn to SANDS. The society then plays a big part because there are people there who will listen and sympathise and support you for years. At the first meeting there were women who had lost their babies as long as nine years ago, but most had lost their babies about two years ago. The group is mainly for mothers. One of the nice things was that the conversation initially was just the same normal chat amongst any dozen women who would gather together over coffee. I think the greatest help this group can give me is to help me through the anxieties of a future pregnancy, because most women have already had other children after their bereavements. I cannot imagine being able to cope with a pregnancy although part of my body is desperate to become pregnant again. I just want my body to get back to normal again.

One of the hardest things to cope with, and something I never thought would happen, was that my milk came in the same as if I had had a live baby. I know a friend who lost a baby at eighteen weeks, and her milk came in too, so your hormones act as they would do and nothing tells your body that your baby has died. It does go away and is reabsorbed if there is no stimulation for it. But it was like a slap on the face. The baby died on the Friday, but by the Sunday, I had big, full breasts. I couldn't let my mum hug me because my breasts were so sore. I lay in bed at night with tears rolling down my face, and there were milk droplets rolling down my breasts. That must be one of the saddest sights that there is.

I didn't take the drugs I could have had to try and stop the milk, because it might have made me feel sick and I felt bad enough. One of the greatest problems is coping with the feeling of anger, when there is nothing or no one to be angry at. The hospital didn't do anything wrong. I know I didn't do anything wrong and Geoff didn't do anything wrong. The feelings of anger are strong, but I know they will pass.

I do look ahead to having another child but that won't be until I know not to panic at every single thing which might be different, or not happening; when I have the feeling that I can approach this new baby, who will not be a replacement for Martin. I really miss being pregnant because I enjoyed it so much, and at the moment I'd like to be pregnant again.

I will have to be able to cope with unexpected things which still throw me. I can push my supermarket trolley past the shelves of Pampers and not let it bother me. But I can turn a corner and come face to face with a young mother and her new-born baby and want to run away. I'll be ready only when I can put it behind me, and when I stop feeling as if I want to shout out to the world, 'My baby died.'

Liz Suttie [born 1964]

I can't imagine life without Emma now. She is the centre of attention and I can't think of doing anything else. She comes first. I did find I was given conflicting advice, with the younger midwives saying I should feed on demand, and the older ones telling me to wait three and a half hours. If you are a new mother you don't know who to listen to. There should be some consistent training or teaching that they advocate because we young mums don't have a clue. I am fortunate that I have a lot of friends who have had children so I had an inkling of what to do. Now that she is three months old, I have established a routine and I am coping quite well!

Rachel Hanks [born 1967]

I think that I, like many women today, am not very keen to have the same family life as my mother. She had eight children, was wonderful, caring and kindly, devoting the best part of her life to us, and says she experienced joy and fulfilment through being a mother. I want to have a life of my own apart from motherhood. I am very keen to work and enjoy a good social life.

'She glanced over at her own mother. Liz's generation had all felt faintly sorry for their mothers. Condemned to a dull life without achievement, sipping tea on the lawn while men had all the excitement out in the big wide world. It had seemed such an outrage to Liz that women lived like this – such a waste! She was never going to make the same mistake!

And yet who had more quality of life? Her mother who could choose what to do with her time? Or herself, high powered, and hard pressed, always earning a fortune with never any time to spend it?'

Maeve Haran, HAVING IT ALL.

Rachel Lockey [born 1967]

I don't know whether I am a good mother. I do what I can and I do worry about it. But what I have come to realise is that all children will look back at their childhood and say to their parents, 'Why did you make me do that? Why did you do that?' Whatever I do, there may be some come-back, but I acknowledge that. So I just carry on and bring Bella up as I feel is right. I have no regrets at all. It was just the right way round for me to have a child and then get my degree. I am not advocating teenage pregnancy for everyone. For some it might be a disaster, but for me it was wonderful. I feel defensive when I hear women say they are going to warn their daughters not to have their children until they are thirty or so, and to live their life first. I say that is fair enough, but there are cases when it doesn't have to be like that, and I am one of them. I have really enjoyed being a young mum.

The feeling when I think, 'Yes, this is motherhood', has come in odd moments. Perhaps I am out with Bella in a park, and she is looking lovely and happy; then a complete stranger comes up to say hello to her and this person turns to me and says, 'You must be a wonderful mother'. That is lovely, and I have been fortunate to have that happen to me more than once. It makes me feel I must be doing something right. I feel united then and I want to hold her. I feel that we are together, just the two of us, and that's when I have this strong sense of motherhood.

'The restraint [or the masochism] of my generation sometimes amazes me. Critisized by our parents, attacked by our children, we hold our fire, seldom fight back as we could do. Our parents were disciplined into believing that you did what you had to, not what you wanted, that the future was worth waiting for, that you respected your parents, and worked hard for your children. We have some of that discipline, though the strain is watered down, weaker and in most of our children it has disappeared altogether. Trying to provide a frail bridge between the old and the young, protect the one from the other, we accept absurd handicaps in the family game.'

Nina Bawden, WALKING NAKED.

Andrea Duffin [born 1970]

I love talking to my gran and she is so good with her great-grandchildren. When we get together, we chat away about motherhood and babies as if we were two mums the same age. It seems that in some ways, nothing has changed in the way babies are brought up. And I suppose if you just think of the basic things, and ignore modern conveniences, a child develops in the same way: learns to eat, play, talk and walk. And I find that when I am sitting talking to my gran, she remembers bringing up my dad and my uncles, 'my sons' as she proudly recalls. And when I was pregnant I would tell her how I was feeling and she would say, 'That's how I used to feel too.' I thought there would be such a wide gap between how she felt and looked after her children fifty years ago, and how I am today. I hear stories about how my uncle's teddy, which he loved so much, was lost on the bus and he caused a rumpus, and it would be just the same with me, because I know if I lost Molly's teddy it would be dreadful.

It always strikes me how alike it all is, how alike we are as mothers. We just feel the same responsibility and love for our children, that natural, caring maternal instinct doesn't change across the generations. It all seems so mystic and distant to me, all those years ago when she was bringing up her boys, but the role of motherhood then was really just the same as it is today.

———•———

'Motherhood . . . a ground which seemed to me the most painful, incomprehensible, and ambiguous I had ever travelled, a ground hedged by taboos, mined with false-namings. I only knew that I had lived through something which was considered central to the lives of women, fulfilling even in its sorrows, a key to the meaning of life; and that I could remember little except anxiety, physical weariness, anger, self-blame, boredom, and division within myself; a division made more acute by the moments of passionate love, delight in my children's spirited bodies and minds, amazement at how they went on loving me in spite of my failures to love them wholly and selflessly.

The mother's battle for her child – with sickness, with poverty, with war, with all the forces of exploitation and callousness that cheapen human life – needs to become a common human battle, waged in love and in the passion for survival.'

Adrienne Rich, OF WOMAN BORN.

———•———

Contributors of oral histories

Mary ANDERSON: born 9.9.34, brought up in Alloa, Clackmannanshire. One sister. Father's occupation: Sales Department, Patons and Baldwins, Alloa. Mother's occupation: secretary, Patons and Baldwins; left to marry. Education: Alloa Academy; Miss Simpson's Secretarial College, Stirling. Career: Medical Secretary. Married at 22; first child at 26; three children. Lives in Whitley Bay. (Daughter of contributor, Janet Stewart.)

Olive BANBURY: born 7.5.20, brought up in Aberystwyth, then Hove, Sussex. One brother, two sisters. Father's occupation: motor mechanic. Mother's occupation: housewife. Education: state school to 14. Career: bookkeeper. Married at 22; first child at 23; two children. Lives in Shrewsbury.

Trudi BARNET: born 2.6.54, brought up in Edinburgh. One brother. Education: private girls' school. First married at 21; first child at 21; three boys. Second marriage at 36; two children, one boy, one girl. Lives in Edinburgh.

Nancy BEATY: born 10.7.14, brought up on a farm near Alston, Cumbria. Three brothers. Father's occupation: farmer. Mother's occupation: housekeeper, farm helper. Education: local elementary school to 14. Married at 21; first child at 22; four children. Career: farmer's wife. Lives in Keswick, Cumbria.

Catherine BEGG: born 20.4.20, brought up in Kingsbridge, near Kirriemuir, Angus. One sister, two brothers. Father's occupation: gardener and forester. Mother's occupation: housewife. Education: local school to 14. Career: domestic service, then NAAFI. Married at 26; two foster sons. Lives in Kirriemuir.

Angela BLANCHARD: born 17.1.62, brought up in Cheshire. Two older sisters. Father's occupation: vicar. Mother's occupation: school teacher. Education: Girls' Church of England Boarding School to 18; Aberdeen University; Graduate Secretarial Course. Married at 22; first child at 28; two children. Career:

administrator/researcher, journalist, trainee breast-feeding counsellor. Lives in Stafford.

Mary BOULCOTT: born 25.9.22, brought up in St Albans, Herts, London, then Surrey. No brothers or sisters. Father's occupation: bank manager. Mother's occupation: teacher and governess; left to marry. Education: private school to 16; secretarial training. Career: radio mechanic, ATS (1942–44), shorthand typist; left to marry. Married at 24; first child at 28; four children. Lives in Fleet, Hampshire.

Eileen BROWN: born 29.1.08, brought up in St Helens, Lancs. Two brothers. Father's occupation: builder. Mother's occupation: housewife. Education: grammar school to 16; confectioner by training. Married at 25. Two children. Mother of contributor, Jennifer Harper-Jones. Lives in Helsby, Cheshire.

Sheila BROWN, born 1934, brought up in Peterhead. Only child. Father's occupation: fisherman. Mother's occupation: nanny, left to marry. Education: local school to 15; nursing training. Married at 20; first child at 21; four daughters. Lives in Westhill, Aberdeenshire.

Barbara BRYAN: born 12.10.46, brought up in Glasgow. One brother. Father's occupation: director. Mother's occupation: chiropodist. Education: private school to 18. Career: radio broadcaster, writer. Married at 30; first child at 33; three daughters. Lives in Edinburgh.

Mary LEWIS BRYDON: born 13.10.13, brought up in Galashiels, Roxburghshire. Two brothers. Father's occupation: owner, carpentry business. Mother's occupation: nurse and midwife; left to marry. Education: Galashiels Academy, trained as nurse, midwife. (Career: Queen Alexandra Corps during WWII); Matron. Travelled extensively. Married. Returned to Scotland. Later career: lady's companion; retired late 1980s. Now lives near Kelso.

Barbara BUCKLEY: born 24.9.54, brought up in Manchester. Two sisters. Father's occupation: fireman/college porter. Mother's occupation: housewife, later, factory worker. Education: (direct grant) school; university; postgraduate arts administration. Married at 26; first child at 32; four children [two sets of twin boys]. Career: marketing controller. Lives in Mow Cop, Staffordshire.

'CAROL': born 1942, brought up in Stoke-on-Trent. Adopted. Father's occupation: motor mechanic. Mother's occupation: housewife. Education: Roman Catholic high school to 16; teachers' training college. Married at 31; first child at 34; one child. Career: English teacher.

'CATHY': born 1955, brought up in Edinburgh. One half-brother and one half-sister. Father's occupation: architect. Mother's occupation: textile designer. Education: private schools, university degree. Married at 26; first child at 27; three children.

Jean CHARLESON: born 27.2.22, brought up in Edinburgh. One brother. Father's occupation: printer and bookbinder. Mother's occupation: housewife. Education: local schools to 14. Career: apprentice printer. Joined WAAF in 1941 for four years. Married at 23; first child at 24; three children. Lives in Edinburgh.

Diane CONNELLY: born 13.3.61, brought up in Leeds, Yorkshire. No brothers or sisters. Father died at 32, when Diane was 9. Mother's occupation: auxiliary nurse, dental nurse. Education: state school; nursing training. Married at 26; first child at 29; two sons. Career: midwife. Lives in Reading, Berkshire.

Joan COUNIHAN: born 8.9.15, brought up in Sussex, London and France. One brother, four sisters. Father's occupation: author, journalist. Mother's occupation: housewife. Education: private boarding school to 16. Career: teacher; Civil Servant. Married at 24; first child at 25; 8 children [two died]. Lives in St Leonards-on-Sea, Sussex.

Margaret CRUIKSHANK: born 11.5.33, brought up in Nairnshire. Four brothers and two sisters. Father's occupation: farm labourer. Mother's occupation: housewife. Education: state school to 15 – *dux* medal. Tailoring training. Married at 18; first child at 19; four children. Lives in Elgin, Morayshire.

Susan CURTIS: born 23.8.05, brought up in Gwent. One sister. Father's occupation: metal broker. Mother's occupation: housewife. Education: Roman Catholic convent; Malvern Abbey boarding school; Bristol University. Career: journalism, teaching. Married at 31; first child at 32; two children. Later career: examining English education. Lives in Towcester, Northants.

Sheila DAVIDSON: born 26.7.44, brought up in Bucksburn, Aberdeen. One brother and one sister. Father's occupation: radio and television engineer. Mother's occupation: assisted husband in business. Education: state school to 15; nanny training. Married at 20; first child at 21; two sons. Career: nursery school worker, private childminder. Lives in Newport-on-Tay, Fife.

Jo DAVIDSON: born 3.6.60, brought up in Southampton. One brother. Father's occupation: Merchant Seaman. Mother's occupation: nursing sister. Education: state school; sixth form college; teacher training college. Married at 27; first child at 31; two children. Career: education officer. Lives in Penarth, South Glamorgan.

Margaret DIXON: born 17.12.05, brought up in Bristol, Salisbury, Hereford, Nottingham and Penzance. Only child. Father's occupation: railway official. Mother's occupation: housewife. Education: private school; grammar school to 16: shorthand typist training. Married at 28; first child at 32; three children. Lives in Sheffield.

Andrea DUFFIN: born 1970, brought up in Fife by her mother (parents separated when she was eighteen months old). One brother. Education: state school to 17; plans to go to university or art college. Lives with partner; first child at 18; two daughters. Lives in Edinburgh.

Alice FINIGAN: born 3.12.19, One brother and one sister. Father's occupation: wholesale newsagent. Mother's occupation: housewife. Education: school; engineering tracer training. Married aged 21; First baby at 24; second baby died three years later. Lives in Guildford, Surrey.

Lucy FIRTH: born 25.11.17, brought up in Skegness, Lincolnshire. One sister. Father's occupation: soldier (wounded in World War I, 100% disability pension). Education: grammar school to 18; chemist's assistant training. Career: Air Ministry work, World War II. Married at 23; first child at 31; two children. Lives in Leicestershire.

Winifred FYFE: born 23.4.55, brought up in Aberdeen. One sister. Father's occupation: train driver. Mother's occupation: shop assistant, then manager. Education: state school to 15; nursery nurse training. Married at 23; first child at 25; three children. Career: nursery nurse in crèche. Lives in Stonehaven, Aberdeenshire.

Sue GAMMERMAN: Three children; the eldest age 7, is handicapped with Cerebral Palsy. Family used to live in Edinburgh and moved to the South of England.

Ailsa GRAY: born 10.10.53, brought up in Swansea, South Wales. One sister. Father's occupation: local government officer. Mother's occupation: full-time housewife and mother. Education: state schools to 18; University; secretarial training. Career: personnel work, BBC. Married at 34; first child at 35; five children. Lives in Glasgow.

Sheila GRAY: born 26.10.51, brought up in Edinburgh, Yorkshire and London. One sister. Father's occupation: civil servant. Mother's occupation: secretary. Education: state primary schools; boarding school to 17; secretarial college. Married at 22; first child at 26; three children. Later education: Aberdeen University; Scottish School of Reflexology. Lives in Ellon, Aberdeenshire.

Elizabeth GREY: born 1917, brought up in Blairgowrie, Perthshire. Four sisters. Father's occupation: plumber; fruit farmer. Mother's occupation: housewife. Education/Career: local school to 14; domestic service; later, nursing training. Married at 30; first child at 32; two girls. Widowed. Resumed nursing. Lives in Blairgowrie, Perthshire.

Pauline GRISBROOK: born 13.10.24, brought up in Leigh, Lancashire. Three natural sisters, one adopted sister. Father's occupation: municipal clerk. Mother's occupation: part-time nurse. Education: Roman Catholic primary school; convent school to 16; Sick Children's nurse training. Career: State Registered Nurse. Married at 27; adopted two girls at 27. Lives in South Brent, Devon.

Emily HAGUES: born 14.8.16, brought up in Port Elphinstone, Aberdeenshire. One brother and twin sisters. Father's occupation: joiner in the locomotive works. Mother's occupation: housewife. Education: village school; Academy to 16. Career: domestic service. Married at 25; first child at 27; two daughters. Lives in Port Elphinstone, Inverurie, Aberdeenshire. (Mother of contributor, Vivienne Leighton.)

Rachel HANKS: born 26.12.67, brought up in London, Scotland, Devon, Cornwall. Four sisters, three brothers. Father's occupation: bus driver/writer/unemployed. Mother's occupation: housewife, then teacher. Education: state schools to 18; one year of degree course; film editing training. Lives with her partner; first child at 25; one son. Lives in London.

Motherhood

Jennifer HARPER-JONES: born 3.4.39, brought up in Helsby, Cheshire. One brother. Father's occupation: manager. Mother's occupation: housewife. Education: state schools; Convent Grammar to 18; University, Sorbonne-Paris; secretarial training. Married at 29; first child at 30; two children. Career: part-time secretary. Lives in Buckinghamshire. (Daughter of contributor, Eileen Lucy Brown.)

Ethel HAY: born 4.9.14, brought up in Dundee. Three sisters. Mother left young family; they lived with father and a housekeeper. Father's occupation: fish merchant. Education: local school to 15. Left home to try and find her mother in London; returned to Dundee. Career: worker in restaurant kitchens. Married at 30, separated soon after; daughter, born a few years later. Lives in Dundee.

Emily HEGGIE: born 19.3.12, brought up in Leicestershire. One sister. Father's occupation: policeman. Mother's occupation: housewife. Education: village school to 15; nursery nurse training. Career: nursery maid; joined police force, 1940. Married aged 31; first child at 32; three children. Lives in Streatham, South London. (Mother of contributor, Moyra Heggie.)

Moyra HEGGIE: born 26.8.50, brought up in London. Two brothers. Father's occupation: policeman. Mother's occupation: housewife. Education: private girls' school to 18; general nursing training, specialised in midwifery; degree course in midwifery, King's College, London. Career: nursing tutor in midwifery; head of department; Senior Lecturer in Midwifery. Lives in Streatham, South London. (Daughter of contributor, Emily Heggie.)

Barbara HENDERSON: born 21.1.31, brought up in Morayshire. Six brothers and sisters. Father's occupation: farm worker. Mother's occupation: domestic servant; housewife. Education: state schools to 14; nursing training for one year. Married at 17; first child at 17; seven children. Later education: O Level Accountancy. Lives in Fochabers, Morayshire.

Joan HILL: born 14.3.20, brought up in Huddersfield, Yorkshire. One brother, killed in action, 1942. Father's occupation: yarn agent. Mother's occupation: teacher; housewife. Education: girls' high school, to 16; hairdresser and beautician training. Married at 20; first child at 21; one child. Lives in Wells, Somerset.

Liz HODGSON: born 17.5.54, brought up in Northumberland and Newcastle-on-Tyne. One brother. Father's occupation: farmer (died in 1955). Mother's occupation: a nurse during the war; secretary; librarian. Education: state and private schools to 18; studied gardening and horticulture. Career: bookseller. Lives with partner; first child at 39. Later career: Oxford Council for Voluntary Action. Lives in Oxford.

Deborah HOLDER: born 19.4.59, brought up all over Britain. Two sisters. Father's occupation: Ministry of Defence. Mother's occupation: market research (career begun at the age of 40). Education: state schools to 17; university degree (mature student); Masters degree; journalist training. Lives with partner; First child at 31; two children. Career: journalist; Lives in North London.

Contributors of Oral Histories

Didi HOPKINS: born 1.11.56, brought up in London. Parents divorced when she was eighteen months old. One half-sister and two half-brothers. Mother's occupation: artist; art teacher; writer; researcher. Education: schooling to 18; trained as a classical musician Guildhall College of Music. Married at 34; first child at 36; one daughter. Lives in London.

Dr Constance KÜENSSBERG [nee Hardy]: born 1911, brought up in Edinburgh. Father's occupation: schoolmaster. Mother's occupation: housewife. Education: nursing training, medical training qualified as doctor. Career: doctor Children's hospital rural practice. Married in 1941; first child at 32; Later career: part-time university tutor in medicine, while bringing up children; counsellor. Lives in Haddington.

Dr Ekke KÜENSSBERG: born 1913, Education: medical training, qualified as doctor. Career: GP. Married Dr Constance Hardy in 1941; four children. Lives in Haddington.

Daphne LAING: born 24.9.35, brought up in Gloucestershire. One brother, one sister. (Also, twin brothers: one stillborn, one died at three days old.) Father's occupation: bank clerk. Mother's occupation: housewife. Education: private prep. school; state grammar school to 17. Career: banking. Married at 35; first child at 36; four children. Later career: part-time hotel work (limited choice). Lives in Aboyne, Aberdeenshire.

Vivienne LEIGHTON: born 19.10.47, brought up in Aberdeen. One sister. Father's occupation: driver for the Civil Aviation Authority. Mother's occupation: housewife, full-time mother. Education: state school to 18; medical laboratory training (scientific officer). Married aged 23; First child at 24; two children. Later career: laboratory officer. Lives in Aberdeenshire. (Daughter of contributor, Emily Hagues.)

Mary LAW: born 9.9.49, brought up in England, Malaya and Dundee. One brother and two sisters. Father's occupation: army captain. Mother's occupation: secretary; full-time mother. Education: thirteen primary schools (due to father's job); Dundee High School to 16; College of Chiropody; College of Commerce; College of Education. Married at 24; first child at 28; three children. Later Education: three-year Midwifery diploma course. Lives in Arbroath, Tayside. (Daughter of contributor, Davina Thorpe)

Rachel LOCKEY: born 1967, brought up in New Zealand and Italy. Five siblings. Father's occupation: manager. Mother's occupation: housewife. Education: interrupted at A level stage; Sussex University. Single mother; first child aged 18. Later education: midwifery training planned. Lives in Brighton.

Joan LONGMUIR: born 23.8.30, brought up in Surrey and Oxon. One half-brother. Father died when Joan was three. Mother's occupation: secretary. Education: private primary school; Grammar school to 17; commercial school training. Married at 22; first child at 23; six children. Lives in Esher, Surrey.

Mary MACDONALD: born 6.7.20, brought up Locharron, Wester Ross, Highlands. Six brothers and sisters. Father's occupation: crofter. Mother's occupation: housewife. Education: state schools to 14. Career: domestic service. Married at 18; first child at 19; Five daughters. Lives in Pitlochry, Perthshire.

Janice MACKENZIE: born 31.8.50, brought up in Essex and Kent. One brother. Father's occupation: business administrator. Mother's occupation: telephonist (part-time when children were young, then full-time). Education: state schools to 18; teacher training college. Married at 21; first child at 27; three children but second child died aged 18 months. Career: Full-time teacher. Lives in Burghead, Morayshire.

Mary MACLENNAN: born 1911, brought up in Birsay, Orkney Islands. Two sisters. Father's occupation: farmer, landowner. Mother's occupation: housewife. Education: village school; Stromness High School (weekly boarder); Aberdeen University. Married at 21; first child at 23; four children. Career: Part-time teacher, when children were older. Lives in Blairgowrie, Perthshire.

Joyce MACPHERSON: born September 1923, brought up in St Albans. One brother. Education: left school at 16, when the war broke out; nursery nurse training; nursery teacher training. Married at 29; first child at 30; five children. Lives in Edinburgh.

Linda MACPHERSON: born 12.11.62, Norwegian by birth, brought up in Norway. Education: University. Career: worked for nine years before marriage. Married at 30 (moved to Scotland); first child at 31. Lives in Edinburgh.

Jennifer MANNING: born 25.8.44, brought up in Leyland, and Ashton-under-Lyme, Manchester. One brother and two sisters. Father's occupation: police sergeant. Mother's occupation: housewife. Education: state school; grammar school to 16; Career: social work training. Single parent; first child at 19; married at 23; two children. Career: playgroup leader; residential social work. Lives in Morecambe, Lancs.

Mary MCKERROW: born 6.8.15, brought up in Sutton Coldfield, Warwickshire, Derby and Liverpool. One sister. Father's occupation: bank manager. Mother's occupation: housewife. Parents both died during her childhood. Education: private day and boarding schools; Liverpool University; secretarial training. Married at 28; first child at 30; three children. Lives in Edinburgh.

Doris MELLING: born 16.9.14, brought up in Blackpool. Only child. Father died when Doris was two (WWI). Mother's occupation: part-time confectioner. Education: state grammar school to 16. Career: Civil Service; Post Office telephonist. Married at 22; first child at 24; two children. Lives in Swansea.

'MORAG': born 1953. Education: private school; community education training. Married; three children. Career: women's group leader, community education. Lives in Edinburgh.

Lyn MUNGALL: born 17.1.54, brought up in Kent. Three brothers and one sister. Education: school to 17 (left to marry). First child at 17; divorced; remarried, later separated. Six daughters and two sons. Career: part-time work at an old people's home. Later education: social community work training planned. Lives with her partner in Edinburgh.

Contributors of Oral Histories

Lucy OWEN: born 29.4.61, brought up in Hampshire. Two half-sisters, one half-brother. Father's occupation: professional pigeon shooter, game dealer; author. Mother's occupation: strawberry grower; game dealer; author. Education: private day school to 13; boarding school to 17; University of Edinburgh; editing training. Career: bookselling; author of children's books. Married at 28; first child at 30; two children. Lives near Towcester, Northamptonshire.

Joyce PETCHEY: born 18.7.22, brought up in Barking, Essex. Only child. Father's occupation: Port of London official. Mother's occupation: teacher. Education: primary and grammar state schools; teacher training college. Career: teacher, latterly in Special Needs education. Married at 26; first child at 27; two children. Lives in Barking, Essex.

Grace RAE: born 24.6.28, brought up in Closeburn, Dumfriesshire. Four brothers and sisters. Father's occupation: woodcarter. Mother's occupation: housewife, mother. Education: state school to 14; trained as a shop assistant, then as a milk recorder. Married at 20; first child at 39; one daughter. Career: farmer's wife. Lives in Kirkcudbright, Dumfries and Galloway.

Lorna REID: born 20.11.62, brought up in Ayr, Scotland. One brother, one sister. Father's occupation: General Practitioner. Mother's occupation: nurse; housewife. Education: local primary and comprehensive schools; University of Aberdeen; University of Glasgow. Career: reports coordinator for hydrographic survey company. Married at 31; first child at 31, a son, Martin, who died a few hours after birth. Lives in Old Meldrum, Aberdeenshire.

Jano ROCHEFORT: born 15.1.55, brought up in Cornwall. One sister. Father's occupation: oil engineer; postman. Mother's occupation: nursing officer. Education: state school; university; nursing and midwifery training. Married at 22; first child at 31; three boys. Lives in Darwen, Lancashire.

Patricia ROGERS: born 17.3.09, brought up in Seaforth, Lancashire. Two sisters, one brother. Father's occupation: grocer. Mother's occupation: housewife. Education: church school; convent to 18; University of Liverpool; Diploma of Education. Career: teacher of English. Married at 27; first child at 28; six children (five daughters, one son). Lives in Keswick, Cumbria.

Sue ROOK: born 22.1.60, brought up near Doncaster, South Yorkshire. One brother, one sister. Father's occupation: Civil Servant. Mother's occupation: school secretary. Education: co-ed state school to Upper Sixth; university; personnel management training. Married at 30; first child at 32; One daughter. Career: part-time management training courses. Lives in Lincoln.

Jill ROWE: born 1920, brought up in Hascombe, Surrey. Two brothers, one killed in action, WWII; twin brother, who died of cancer, aged two. Father's occupation: village store, Post Office and telephone exchange manager. Education: grammar school to 16. Career: worked at the telephone exchange (a reserved occupation) during the war. Married at 26; first child at 28; two children. Lives in Godalming, Surrey.

Liz SANDERSON: born 1938, brought up in Yorkshire. One brother. Father's occupation: manager of textile spinning mill. Mother's occupation: housewife. Education: home schooling to 9; village school; boarding school to 18; occupational therapist training. Married at 20; first child at 21; four children. Lives in Bowden, Melrose, Roxburghshire.

Jenni SMITH: born 27.8.46, brought up in Nottinghamshire. Father's occupation: storekeeper. Mother's occupation: seamstress, caretaker of chapel. Education: state grammar school to 17; teacher training. Married at 21; first child at 24; two boys; divorced and remarried. Later education: university. Lives in Harrogate, Yorkshire.

Julie SMITH: born 7.7.61, brought up in Edinburgh and Leith; eldest of nine children. Education: school to 17. First child at 17; married, now divorced; three children; Second Chance Education classes. Career: full-time mother; lives with her partner. (Daughter of contributor, Pat Turner.) Lives in Edinburgh.

Mary SPARROW: born 7.11.21, brought up in London. Only child. Father's occupation: Civil Servant. Mother's occupation: housewife. Education: elementary school to 11; scholarship; Blackheath High School to 17; Civil Service exam. Career: clerical officer, Ministry of Transport; executive officer (left to marry). Married at 24; first child at 26; three daughters. Lives in Brecon, Powys.

May STEPHEN: born 14.10.11, brought up in Aberdeen. Two sisters. Father's occupation: owner/manager printing press. Education: girls' high school; University of Aberdeen. Career: chemistry and physics teacher. Married at 26; first child at 28; two children [first daughter, born deaf]. Lives in Tunbridge Wells, Kent.

Violet STEVENSON-HAMILTON: born 16.12.02, Private education; nursing training. Married aged 22; first child within first year; three boys. Lives in Appin, Argyll.

Janet STEWART: born 8.2.04, brought up in Alloa, Clackmannanshire. Three siblings. Father's occupation: mill-worker. Mother's occupation: housewife. (Family emigrated to Canada, but returned to Alloa.) Education: school to 14; technical school. Career: secretary. Married at 29; First child at 30; two children. Lives in Alloa. (Mother of contributor, Mary Anderson.)

Liz SUTTIE: born 2.7.64, brought up in Edinburgh. Two brothers. Education: school to 18. Career: insurance work. Married at 26; First child at 30; one daughter. Lives in Edinburgh.

Davina THORPE: born 1.3.27, in Canada; brought up in southern England and Scotland. Father's occupation: gardener. Mother's occupation: table maid; hotel work. Education: local primary school; comprehensive to 14; secretarial training. Career: shorthand typist, Civil Service. Married at 21; first baby at 22; four children. Lives in Broughty Ferry, Dundee. (Mother of contributor, Mary Law.)

Patricia TURNER: born 29.9.41, brought up in Edinburgh. Married at 18; first child 19; Divorced; Nine children; Lives in Leith, near Edinburgh. (Mother of contributor, Julie Smith.)

Contributors of Oral Histories

Rosemary WALKER: born 17.4.29, Brought up in Longside, Aberdeenshire. Six brothers and sisters. Father's occupation: farm labourer. Mother's occupation: housewife. Education: state schools to 14; Post Office Counter Clerk training. Married at 20; Two children, a son and daughter; their son died aged 3½ years old. Lives in Montrose, Angus.

Wendy WALKER: 7.10.49, Brought up in Luton. One brother. Father's occupation: electrical maintenance engineer. Mother's occupation: housewife. Education: private primary school; state secondary school to 15½. Married at 18½; first child at 19; eight children; divorced. Career: Pro-Life Movement worker. Lives in Luton.

Carol WALTON: born 31.12.43, brought up in Lancashire and Surrey. Education: nursing training; midwifery training. Married at 25; first child at 26; three children. Career: midwife; breast-feeding counsellor. Lives in Cardiff.

Alice WANDS: born 24.2.12, brought up in Derbyshire. Six brothers and sisters. Education: village school; nursing and midwifery training. Career: war service, Queen Alexandra Nurses, abroad. Married at 30; Returned to UK; first child at 34; two children. Lives in Perth, Scotland.

Jane WARD: born 11.5.24, Brought up in Enfield, Middlesex. Only child. Father's occupation: elementary school teacher. Mother's occupation: elementary school teacher. Education: state grammar school; university. Career: lecturer in applied economics. Married at 25; first child at 26; five children. Lives in Somerset.

Eileen WATKINS: born 13.9.12, brought up in North London. Education: private kindergarten and junior schools; boarding school to 18; London University; secretarial training. Married at 26; first child at 27; three children. Lives in Brentwood, Essex.

Gillian WATSON: born 21.11.77, brought up in Edinburgh. Two sisters. First child at 15, one son. Education: Wester Hailes community school. Lives at home with her son, mother, step-father and younger sister.

Pamela WELLS: born 25.3.28, brought up in Coventry, evacuated to Leominister during the war. One sister. Father's occupation: commercial artist. Mother's occupation: teacher. Education: grammar schools to 17; secretarial training until marriage. Married at 24; first child at 26; three children. Later education: trained as a medical librarian, and a reflexologist. Lives in Somerset.

June WILLIAMS: born 1.6.60, brought up in Edinburgh. Two brothers, one sister. Father's occupation: paper merchant firm/property business. Mother's occupation: full-time mother. Education: private girls' school to 17; nursing and midwifery training. Married at 21; first child at 29; two boys. Career: practice nurse. Lives in South London.

Peggy WILSON: born 16.3.11, Education: trained as an actress. Married to an actor; first child at 23; two children. Lives in Channel Islands and Malta.

Milicent WOOLNER: born 7.10.17, brought up in Chiswick, West London. Six brothers and sisters. Father's occupation: self-employed taxi cab driver.

Mother's occupation: housewife. Father died when she was five and her mother was pregnant with youngest child. Education: state schools to 17½; children's nursing training; state registered nursing and midwifery training; children's surgical training; public health training. Married at 32; first child at 37; two children. Lives in Stroud, Gloucestershire.

Pamela WORTHINGTON: born 9.3.23, brought up in Lancashire. Father's occupation: insurance broker. Mother's occupation: housewife. Education: private school to 15; art college. Married at 19; first child at 21; three children. Lives in Romford Essex.

Roma YOUNG: born 1956, brought up in Fife, Scotland. Married at 18; First child at 19; five children, and one stillborn baby. Career: full-time mother; foster mother. Lives in Edinburgh.

Carol ZIYAT: born 18.2.62, brought up in Portsoy, Banffshire. One sister. Education: Banff Academy to 17; Aberdeen College of Commerce; accountancy training. Career: worker for BP, Married at 29; first child at 32. Later career: full-time mother. Lives in the Netherlands/France.

Permissions

I am most grateful to the following authors and their publishers for permission to quote extracts from copyright material.

Ruth Adam, 'I'm Not Complaining', David Higham Assoc. Isabel Allende, 'Paula', Harper Collins; Maya Angelou, 'Gather Together in My Name', Virago; Margaret Atwood, 'Significant Moments in the Life of My Mother', Jonathan Cape, and 'Surfacing', Virago; Enid Bagnold, 'The Squire', Virago; Lynne Reid Banks, 'The L Shaped Room', Chatto and Windus; Pat Barker, 'Union Street', Virago; Nina Bawden, 'Walking Naked', Virago; Donald Campbell, 'The Widows of Clyth'; Angela Carter, 'Truly It Felt Like Year One', Virago; Jenny Carter, 'With Child', Mainstream Publishing; Willa Cather, 'Lucy Gayheart', Virago; Rosalind Coward, 'Our Treacherous Hearts', Faber & Faber; Margaret Drabble: 'A Summer Bird Cage' and 'The Millstone', Weidenfeld and Nicolson; Nell Dunn, 'Poor Cow', Virago; Cassandra Eason, 'A Mother's Instincts', Harper Collins; Eva Figes, 'A Certain Age; Reflecting the Menopause', Virago. Margaret Forster: 'Mother, Can you hear Me?', Secker and Warburg Ltd, and 'Daphne du Maurier', Chatto and Windus; Katherine Gieve, ed. Balancing Acts, Virago; Germaine Greer, 'The Female Eunuch', Harper Collins, and 'Sex and Destiny', Secker and Warburg; Ruth Hall, ed. 'Dear Dr. Stopes', Andre Deutsch; Maeve Haran, 'Having It All', Michael Joseph; Kate Haste, 'Rules of Desire', Chatto and Windus; Tessa Hilton, 'The Great Ormond Street Book of Baby and Child care', Bodley Head; Angela Holdsworth, 'Out of the Doll's House', BBC Worldwide Ltd; Steve Humphries and Pamela Gordon, 'A Labour of Love', Sidgwick and Jackson; Erica Jong, 'Fear of Fifty', Chatto and Windus; Molly Keane, 'Taking Chances', Virago; Sheila Kitzinger, 'Ourselves as Mothers', Transworld; Penelope Leach, 'Baby and Child', and 'Children First', Michael Joseph; Rosamond Lehmann, 'The Weather in the Streets', William Collins; Anne Lemott, 'Operating Instructions', Bloomsbury; Kathy Lette 'Foetal Attraction', Sheil Land Associates; Mary McCarthy, 'The Group', Weidenfeld & Nicolson; Louis MacNeice, 'Prayer Before Birth', Faber & Faber; Candia McWilliam, 'A Little Stranger', Bloomsbury; Sarah Maitland, 'Apple Picking', Virago; Daphne du Maurier, 'Rebecca', Victor Gollancz Ltd; Clare Messud, 'When the World was Steady', Granta; Betty Miller, 'On the Side of the Angels', Virago; Naomi Mitchison, 'You May Well Ask', Victor Gollancz Ltd; Ann Oakley, 'Housewife', Allen Lane; Joyce Carol Oates, 'Them', Victor Gollancz Ltd.; Agnes Owens, A Working Mother, Bloomsbury; Dorothy Parker, 'Experience', Gerald Duckworth and Co. Ltd; Jill Parkin, 'Executive Mothers', Hodder and Stoughton, Ltd; Justine Picardie, 'Home Thoughts', The Independent on Sunday; Sylvia Plath, 'The Bell Jar' and 'Morning Song', Faber and Faber; Adrienne Rich, 'Of Woman Born', Virago; Michelle Roberts, 'A Piece of the Night', The Women's Press Ltd; Vita Sackville West, 'All Passion Spent', The Hogarth Press; Helen Simpson, 'Four Bare Legs in a Bed', William Heinemann; Stevie Smith, 'Mother Love', Virago; Muriel Spark, 'The Prime of Miss Jean Brodie', Virago; Dr Spock, Baby and Child Care, Simon and Schuster; Dr Miriam Stoppard, 'Baby Care Book', Dorling Kindersley; Elizabeth Taylor, 'The Wedding Group', Virago; Tatyana Tolstaya, 'On the Golden Porch', Virago; Anne Tyler, 'Dinner at the Homesick Restaurant', Chatto and Windus, and 'Still Just Writing', Virago; Marina Warner: 'Monstrous Mothers', Vintage; Fay Weldon, 'Down Among the Women', William Heinemann, and 'Weekend: Watching Me, Watching You', Hodder and Stoughton, Ltd.

Every effort has been made to contact copyright holders of extracts used in this book. Where this has not been possible, the author apologizes to those concerned.